WOMEN'S STUDIES IN RELIGION

WOMEN'S STUDIES IN RELIGION

A Multicultural Reader

Kate Bagley and
Kathleen McIntosh, *editors*

PEARSON
Prentice
Hall

Upper Saddle River, New Jersey 07458

Library of Congress Cataloging-in-Publication Data

Women's studies in religion: a multicultural reader / Kate Bagley and Kathleen McIntosh, editors.
  p. cm.
  Includes bibliographical references and index.
  1. Women and religion—Textbooks   2. Feminism—Religious aspects—Textbooks.
  I. Bagley, Kate.   II. McIntosh, Kathleen.

BL458.W66 2007
00'.82—dc22   2005054536

Editorial Director: Sarah Touborg
Senior Acquisitions Editor: Mical Moser
Editorial Assistant: Maureen Diana
Assistant Marketing Manager: Andrea Messineo
Marketing Assistant: Vicki DeVita
Production Liasion: Marianne Peters-Riordan
Manufacturing Buyer: Christina Amato
Art Director: Jayne Conte
Cover Design: Bruce Kenselaar
Manager, Cover Visual Research & Permissions: Karen Sanatar
Full-Service Project Management: Dennis Troutman / Stratford Publishing Services, Inc.
Composition: Integra Software Services Pvt. Ltd.
Printer/Binder: R.R. Donnelley and Sons—Harrisonburg

Credits and acknowledgments borrowed from other sources and reproduced, with permission, in this textbook appear on appropriate page within text.

Pearson Education LTD.
Pearson Education Singapore, Pte. Ltd
Pearson Education, Canada, Ltd
Pearson Education–Japan
Pearson Education Australia PTY, Limited

Pearson Education North Asia Ltd
Pearson Educación de Mexico, S.A. de C.V
Pearson Education Malaysia, Pte. Ltd
Pearson Education, Upper Saddle River, New Jersey

10 9 8 7 6 5 4 3 2 1
ISBN 0-13-110831-X

CONTENTS

PART III ❖ Embodying Our Hope 189

Index 239

CONTRIBUTORS

Leila Ahmed is Victor S. Thomas Professor of Divinity at Harvard Divinity School. She has written extensively on women and Islam, including *Women and Gender in Islam: The Historical Roots of a Modern Debate* (New Haven: Yale University Press, 1992).

Jennifer Bleyer is the founder and editor-in-chief of *Heeb—The New Jewish Review*. She has written on political matters for Working Assets' *Newsforchange* and the independent news service *Alternet*.

Fran Leeper Buss is an oral historian and writer, ordained minister, and community organizer. She is also the author of *Dignity: Lower Income Women Tell of Their Lives and Struggles* (Ann Arbor: University of Michigan Press, 1985); *La Partera: Story of a Midwife* (Ann Arbor: University of Michigan Press, 1980); and a novel, *Journey of the Sparrows* (New York: Lodestar Books, 1991).

Chung Hyun Kyung is Associate Professor of Ecumenical Theology at Union Theological Seminary, New York City, and a lay theologian of the Presbyterian Church of Korea. Her publications include *The Struggle to Be the Sun Again: Introducing Asian Women's Theology*, "Han-puri: Doing Theology from Asian Women's Perspective" (in *We Dare to Dream: Doing Theology as Asian Women*, edited by Virginia Fabella and Sun Ai Park), and "Seeking the Religious Roots of Pluralism," *Journal of Ecumenical Studies* 34 (1997).

Carol P. Christ (Ph.D., Yale, 1974) is a pioneer in feminist studies in religion and in the Goddess movement. Her influential books include *Diving Deep and Surfacing, Laughter of Aphrodite, Rebirth of the Goddess*, and *She Who Changes*, and the widely used anthologies *Womanspirit Rising* and *Weaving the Visions*, coedited with Judith Plaskow. She has taught at Columbia University, San Jose State, Pomona College, and the Claremont Graduate School. She is Director of Ariadne Institute (www.goddessariadne.org), which offers Goddess pilgrimages in Greece.

Sandra Cisneros is the author of several works of fiction, including *The House on Mango Street, Woman Hollering Creek and Other Stories*, and *Hairs/Pelitos*, a children's book. Her books of poetry include *Bad Boys, My Wicked, Wicked Ways*, and *Loose Woman*. She is the recipient of the Before Columbus Foundation's American Book Award, a Lannan Foundation Literary Award, the PEN Center West Award for the best fiction of 1991, and the Quality Paperback Book Club New Voices Award, in addition to a MacArthur Foundation Fellowship.

Gary David Comstock, the Protestant Chaplain at Wesleyan University, is an ordained minister in the United Church of Christ. He is the author of several books, including *Gay Theology Without Apology, Queer Religion, Violence Against Lesbians and Gay Men*, and *Becoming Ourselves in the Company of Others*.

Mary Daly is the author of *Beyond God the Father, Gyn/Ecology, Pure Lust*, and numerous other works. She taught for many years at Boston College.

Jacquelyn Grant is the Fuller E. Callaway Professor of Systematic Theology and Director of the Black Women in Church and Society Center at the Interdenominational Theological Center, Atlanta, Georgia. She has published a number of works on womanist theology.

Riffat Hassan is Professor of Religious Studies at the University of Louisville in Louisville, Kentucky. Hassan, a committed Muslim, is the author of numerous articles on women and Islam, and of two books on the Muslim poet and thinker Allama Muhammad Iqbal.

Inés Hernández-Ávila is Professor of Native American Studies at the University of California, Davis. Among her publications are "Saturday, September 21, 2001—Before Traveling to Harvard," *Frontiers: A Journal of Women's Studies* 23(1) (2002), and "Indigenous Intellectual Sovereignties," *Wicazo Sa Review* (Fall 1999, with Stefano Verase).

Darice Jones is a queer artist of African descent who grew up and currently resides in Oakland, California. Her many projects include a mystery novel, screenplays, spoken-word performances, painting, and photography.

Kwok Pui-lan is William F. Cole of Christian Theology and Spirituality at the Episcopal Divinity School, Cambridge, Massachusetts. She is a leading figure in feminist postcolonial theology and is the author or editor of numerous works, including *Postcolonialism, Feminism, and Religious Discourse* (edited with Laura E. Donaldson).

Ryiah Lilith, a Jewish Dianic Witch, has published articles on lesbian and gay parents' access to parental benefits and the legal analysis of same-gender domestic violence. She has also written for *Matrifocus, a Cross-Quarterly eZine for Goddess Women Near and Far*.

Margaret R. Miles is Emeritus Professor of Historical Theology at the Graduate Theological Union, Berkeley, California, where she formerly served as Dean and Vice President for Academic Affairs. She is a past president of the American Academy of Religion. She is the author of *Carnal Knowing* and *Seeing and Believing*.

Pat Mora has written five books of poetry, numerous children's books and two books of nonfiction, *Nepantla: Essays from the Land in the Middle* and *House of Houses*.

Nelle Morton was the first theologian to teach a university course on women and religion and was a mentor to many of the current generation of feminists in religion. She is profiled in the film *The Journey Is Home*, which is the title of her major work.

Judith Plaskow is Professor of Religious Studies at Manhattan College, Riverdale, New York, and a past president of the American Academy of Religion. She edited, with Carol P. Christ, *Womanspirit Rising* and *Weaving the Visions*, and is the author of *Standing Again at Sinai*.

Ellen Cronan Rose is Chair of the Women's Studies Department at the University of Nevada, Las Vegas.

Rosemary Radford Ruether is Carpenter Professor of Feminist Theology at Pacific School of Religion in Berkeley, California. She is the author of many books, including *Woman-Church* and *New Woman/New Earth*. She is also coeditor of the highly acclaimed three-volume documentary history *Women and Religion in America*.

Frances E. Wood is cofounder, with Marie Fortune, and former Program Director of the Center for the Prevention of Sexual and Domestic Violence (now known as Faith/Trust Institute) in Seattle, Washington.

PREFACE

This is a book for teachers and students that grew out of our experience in teaching a course on women and religion at a public liberal arts college. Its contents are contemporary, multifaceted, and multicultural. Of the twenty-three selections included here, three are by Muslim writers, four by African Americans, four by Jewish feminists, three by Latinas, and two by Asian Americans. Issues of identity, authority, and sexuality are central to these critiques and receive different treatment by writers of Jewish, Christian, Muslim, and African American heritage, and those who write from a lesbian perspective. While this is an academic book, many of the selections are personal in tone and compelling in their effect. They invite response. The accompanying questions grow out of our experiences in using these writings in the classroom and are designed to foster comparison, analysis, and critical engagement.

Included in this volume are "primary texts" by Mary Daly, Carol P. Christ, Judith Plaskow, and Jacqueline Grant, which were important early influences on the development of feminist and womanist studies in religion and feminist theology. Also included are writings by creative writers, younger feminists, and other nontheologians—voices that suggest the wider reach of a field whose origins are in the late 1960s and 1970s, at a moment of great social and cultural ferment. Taken together, these writings suggest the transforming impact of feminism on the religious lives of American women over the past thirty-five years. They also illustrate, sometimes in dramatic ways, how women from different backgrounds have struggled to reconcile loyalties to their ethnic and religious communities with criticism of the status and treatment of women within those communities' religious traditions.

The intersection of feminist work in religion with the world of public affairs is thrown into sharp relief by the greatly increased attention given to Islamic fundamentalism in the wake of the events of September 11, 2001. Women's studies in religion, as it has developed since the 1970s, has brought to light a more nuanced view of world religions, challenging monolithic patriarchal models as the single historical embodiment of each of the world's major religions. An important feature of the work of feminist scholars of religion, as this volume illustrates, has been to uncover the tolerant and multifaceted countercurrents present within Judaism, Christianity, and most recently Islam—currents that have been submerged and often buried within the authoritative male discourse that has usually represented the public face and voice of these traditions. The notion that sacred texts and historic events tell a single story or yield only one meaning with regard to the status and roles of women, as well as the assertion that Western feminism denies the value of conservative or traditional religious practices as sources of spiritual strength and meaning for women, are strongly challenged by the work of feminist scholars of religion, as the writings here reveal.

Many of the selections in this collection are personal stories of struggle and reflection and, as such, highlight the feminist insight that "the personal is political." Our purpose is to help students to see the intersection of contemporary feminism and feminist scholarship with women's thinking about, and practice of, religion, rather than to "cover" the field of feminist theology or the numerous subfields generated by women's studies in religion. In keeping with this goal, we have intentionally excluded highly theoretical pieces or those that require the reader to have an extensive background in religious studies or women's studies. Instead, we have chosen pieces that offer students opportunities to think about the similarities and differences beween their own experiences and the authors', and to examine the broader implications of feminist critiques of religion and spirituality.

INTRODUCTION

A Movement's Beginnings

In 1971 Mary Daly, a recently tenured professor of theology at Boston College and sometime member of the National Organization for Women's (NOW) task force on women and religion, gave the first sermon by a woman at the Harvard Memorial Church. Daly's sermon, "The Women's Movement: An Exodus Community," began with a litany of the demeaning images of women offered by early fathers of Christianity as well as contemporary theologians. It ended with a call to the congregation to "leave behind the centuries of silence and darkness" and join an "exodus" by walking out of the church (Daly 1996a, 318). As she would later write, Daly hoped that she would be accompanied by five or six "staunch comrades"; in fact, hundreds of members of the congregation "began stampeding out of the church" (Daly 1996b, 82).

Throughout American history, women have had a significant, though largely unacknowledged, impact in their capacity as members of religious communities; yet when Daly gave her sermon, they were for the most part absent from professional and leadership positions in those communities. But the actions of Daly and her followers augured the opposite of what one might have imagined; rather than a stampede out of the church such as Daly advocated, there has been a virtual stampede in the opposite direction, as the leadership ranks of U.S. denominations opened to women.[1]

In the years since Daly's "Exodus" sermon, the implications of her dramatic gesture have been explored by many actors in both the academic and ecclesiastical worlds, with transformative effects, in many cases, for both individuals and institutions. Mary Daly was one of the first thinkers within the context of the women's movement to focus a feminist analysis on religion. Judith Plaskow, a leading feminist theologian who subsequently served as president of the American Academy of Religion, reports that in 1972, at the first meeting of the Academy's Working Group on Women and Religion, "[t]he many women and men who crowded into a small room to hear Mary Daly read 'Theology After the Demise of God the Father' shared a profound sense of excitement, a conviction that we would end up revolutionizing the study of religion and religion itself" (Plaskow 1993, 11).[2] Four years earlier, in 1968, Daly, who was still then a Roman Catholic, had published *The Church and the Second Sex*, which is excerpted in Part II of this volume. Notwithstanding the author's later repudiation of Christianity, *The Church and the Second Sex* remains a benchmark in the process that led to the subsequent social and structural changes in American churches and synagogues and to the field of women's studies in religion.

In her exhaustive 1999 annotated bibliography, *Feminism and Christian Tradition*, a volume of some one thousand entries, Mary-Paula Walsh designates *The Church and the Second Sex* as the initial defining moment for feminist theological literature as it developed in the United States (15). As Walsh writes,

> The rationale for this beginning point stems from the literature on social movements which argues consistently that the presence of a galvanizing text, leader or event is an early and necessary component in the successful launching of a social movement, in that without such an event, text or leader, the population frustrated by a given problem remains unmobilized as a movement resource. (Ibid.)

Thus, Walsh concludes, while it is possible to make a case for a number of different starting points, including Elizabeth Cady Stanton's *The Woman's Bible* (1993, first published in 1895), "it is Daly's text . . . which meets the criterion of a galvanizing event" (Ibid.).

The transition in Daly's personal and professional stance with regard to the Judeo-Christian tradition, from measured critique to outright repudiation, coincided with the challenges to and changes in many aspects of American society wrought by the women's movement and other liberation movements of the 1960s. In retrospect, these challenges can be seen to have intersected with religion in three significant ways. First, the rights-based language of liberal feminism supplied arguments for women's full and formal participation within religious organizations including their rapid movement (see endnote 1), into seminaries and the ranks of the clergy in mainline Protestant denominations as well as Reform and Conservative Judaism. Second, the widespread use of consciousness-raising as an organizing tool fostered a reliance on experience, rather than traditional sources of authority, as the foundation for theorizing—a development that fueled reform movements within churches, as well as the growth of feminist theology as a discipline. And third, among its multifaceted effects, the Second Wave generated a cultural feminism that eventually helped to create spaces in which religious sensibilities in search of alternative modes of expression could find a home. Moreover, in all three dimensions this wave of change was soon enlarged, enriched, and complicated, as we will see, by the addition to the conversation of the voices of women of color; these contributors often stressed the distinctive nature of their own traditions and the specificity of the problems they faced, and they criticized the white, Christian standpoint as hegemonic in its perspectives and assumptions.

Reform or Revolution?

Judith Plaskow has noted that "connections between feminist critique and social change have been evident in all areas of women's studies in religion from its beginnings" (Plaskow 1993, 10). As the field fostered women's movement into leadership roles in American denominations, its theorists critiqued many aspects of institutional and community practice as well as theologies that had supplied traditional arguments for women's subordination. In this volume, examples of their work can be seen in Frances Wood's condemnation of the continuing patriarchal character of many Black churches and their treatment of women; in Kwok Pui-lan's critique of the ethnocentric biases of Western Christianity; and, within Islam, of Riffat Hassan's argument that the Qur'an has been wrongly interpreted as justifying a doctrine of female inferiority. All three represent the stance of reformers who, while criticizing their respective religious communities, nevertheless locate themselves unequivocally within the traditions that they critique.

Not all critiques, however, were aimed at reform. In the context of the thousands of personal awakenings and the "click" of feminist consciousness occurring in the wake of the women's movement, a wealth of first-person accounts was generated, recounting the paths traveled by individuals in pursuit of the "new and more genuine religious consciousness" that Daly had evoked in her sermon. For many, the confrontation between institutional loyalties and developing feminist awareness proved painful. Indeed, during these early years, testimonies to the anger and pain that accompanied and, in some cases, fueled the feminist analysis of religion's treatment of women can be found in both Jewish and Christian accounts, from individuals across a spectrum of religious backgrounds and denominations. Carol Christ's "Expressing Anger at God" (1987), although more analytical than most, is representative of the experiences of many in the power of its first-person account of a painful experience within a religious setting. In "Toward a Paradigm Shift in the Academy and in Religious Studies" (1987), Christ described the choice feminists faced: either to reform traditional religious institutions or to walk away from them. Writers represented here who did the latter include (along with Daly) Christ herself, who explains in her second essay in Part II "why women need the goddess," and Nelle Morton, a founder of feminist theology, who in an early piece (excerpted in Part III) writes that the God of patriarchal religions "has become a dead metaphor."

The sense of the necessity of choosing between divergent and mutually exclusive paths that Christ identified reflects the experience of a generation of writers and activists who laid the groundwork for the body of scholarship that became the field of women's studies in religion, and forged the way for ensuing changes within American churches and synagogues. The hurt and angry tone of some pieces from this time reflect a moment at which the choices, for many, seemed stark and clear-cut—rejection of a tradition whose view of women, in light of a feminist analysis, seemed demeaning, or acceptance within a traditional framework of second-class status. As institutional change took hold in various settings within the American religious landscape, it became possible to hear corresponding reports of joy and relief that accompanied a new and powerful feeling of inclusion. In her study of the modern women's movement, Ruth Rosen reports, "The first time one feminist heard a woman cantor's voice soar through a Jewish synagogue, she wept. 'Why haven't women been singing Hebrew for the last five thousand years?' she asked" (Rosen 2000, 264).

Members of the next generation might experience this dilemma differently or not at all, as reforms within denominations and proliferating spiritualities created a world more accommodating to feminist spiritual seekers. By way of generational contrast, Ryiah Lilith's "Challah for the Queen of Heaven" in Part I and Jennifer Bleyer's

"From Riot Grrl to Yeshiva Girl" in Part II each illustrate a younger generation's sense of empowerment with regard to finding or fashioning a spiritual home.

Religious History as Herstory

In one sense, the study of religion from a feminist perspective was anything but new. As Gerda Lerner, who helped to found women's studies in the United States, has shown, women in the West had argued and struggled for centuries against a misogynist interpretation of sacred texts. "Women's striving for emancipation was acted out in the arena of religion long before women could conceive of political solutions for their situations," she writes (Lerner 1993, 11). Yet their exclusion from the institutions and canons of higher learning meant that the labors of myriad talented individuals did not coalesce into a transmittable female intellectual tradition:

> Over and over again, individual women criticized and reinterpreted the core biblical texts not knowing that other women before them had already done so. . . . Just as Elizabeth Cady Stanton and Matilda Joslyn Gage undertook the monumental task of writing *The Woman's Bible* in total ignorance of the similar work done by generations of predecessors, so do some current feminist critics consider them their earliest antecedents, when in fact the tradition of feminist Bible criticism goes back to the 3rd century A.D. . . . [Because] [w]omen were denied knowledge of their history . . . each woman had to argue as though no woman before her had ever thought or written. Women had to use their energy to reinvent the wheel, over and over again, generation after generation. . . . Since they could not ground their argument in the work of women before them, thinking women of each generation had to waste their time, energy and talent on constructing their argument anew. (Ibid., 165–166)

The line of foremothers traced in Lerner's exhaustive study stretches from the mystics and abbesses of medieval Christendom to the American abolitionist Sarah Grimké— with whom, she says, "Feminist Bible criticism had reached the point where it led directly to a feminist world-view" (Ibid., 163). "For over a thousand years," Lerner concludes, "women reinterpreted the biblical texts in a massive feminist critique, yet their marginalization . . . prevented this critique from ever engaging the minds of the men who had appointed themselves as the definers of divine truth and revelation" (Ibid., 275). Judith Plaskow has described three stages in the feminist study of religion: first, analyzing and critiquing texts, institutions, and traditions; second, recovering women's history; and third, reforming existing traditions and creating new ones (Plaskow 1993, 11–12). Analyzing and critiquing texts corresponds in its modern version to the task carried out by learned women over the centuries, as Lerner documents. Recovering women's history is a central component in the search for a usable past that has informed feminist scholarship, which in the case of religious studies has been complicated by the multiple versions of the past that research soon brought into view. The creation of new traditions is an ongoing labor that has borne fruit in the areas of goddess spirituality, Wicca, ecofeminism, and the many varieties of New Age practice with roots in the insights, explorations, and rituals of feminist spirituality. Since the 1970s, theory and practice have proceeded in tandem both inside and outside the walls of the academy and of established traditions. As women's studies in religion was established as a discipline, its practitioners—in stark contrast to historical women of the past—gained access to knowledge of each other's work within an ongoing collective endeavor. With respect to religion, herstory became a permanent part of the historical record and a key element in a project that was both recuperative and transformational.

Which Past?

In the introduction to *Womanspirit Rising*, their influential 1979 anthology, Plaskow and Christ asked, "Do feminists need the past—and if so, what past do they need?" (Christ and Plaskow 1979, 9). Buddhism scholar Rita Gross, in her 1996 book *Feminism and Religion*, argues that "questions about a usable past are especially critical in religious studies. . . . The religious significance of its remembered past to a religious community cannot be overestimated, especially for Western religions" (Gross 1996, 73). And, she continues, "It makes a great deal of difference whether a religious community remembers and celebrates its patriarchal past or its androgynous past" (Ibid., 74).

This notion of multiple and even competing pasts within a single tradition is itself a product of a feminist scholarship determined to tease out and bring to light forgotten or suppressed currents within the major world religions—currents more congenial to recognition of women's full equality and humanity. Several contributors to *Womanspirit Rising* explored this theme: Elaine Pagels wrote of the Gnostics, a suppressed sect of early Christianity who imaged the divine as female as well as male and afforded leadership roles to women, and she speculated about the role that this played in their suppression (Pagels 1979a).[3] Rosemary Ruether insisted that Christianity did not originate the anti-body, antifeminine ethos that dominates the spirituality of the Church Fathers, but rather absorbed it from "the alienated world view of late classical civilization" (Ruether 1979, 49). And Eleanor McLaughlin, in a piece entitled "The Christian Past: Does It Hold a Future for Women?" argued that "it is unlikely that the Christian tradition has been unrelievedly destructive of only one-half of humanity" (McLaughlin 1979, 95). Gross concurs: "Misogyny is not the whole story of any religion" (Gross 1996, 74). Thus, as scholars unearthed the hidden, and reformers explored the boundaries of the possible within congregations and institutional governing bodies, for individuals the question of religious choice grew increasingly problematic in response to the question: Which aspect of a tradition should be regarded as important or normative?[4]

Unspoken Worlds

If extraordinary women across the centuries had struggled for equality through the critique of sacred texts, what of the lives of ordinary, even illiterate women? Beginning in the 1970s, feminist scholarship, in its commitment to illuminate ordinary lives and the sources of meaning that inform them, generated a large body of life histories and personal narratives, along with the theoretical underpinnings that gave intellectual legitimacy to personal narrative and experiential knowledge. If the approach to religion in its formal and institutional manifestations seemed to warrant, in the words of theologian Elisabeth Schüssler Fiorenza (1984), a "hermeneutic of suspicion," the richness of women's lived experience unleashed the energy of scholars to rescue that experience from the invisibility to which it had been consigned. The range of sources for theological speculation expanded to include imaginative literature as many in the field stressed the importance of looking beyond the parameters of institutional history and sacred texts.[5]

Many of those engaged in retrieving a sense of women's lived experience from across the spectrum of historical time and cultures concluded that, as Margaret Miles states, "the interface of religious symbols and social situations [was] decisive for understanding both the oppression and the creativity of women" (Miles 1985, 1). Rita Gross urged the view that religion is not just a set of ideas, but also of practices, and that half of its practitioners are women (Gross 1996, 65). She notes "the often nonverbal and almost always nontextual context of women's spirituality" (Ibid., 81). Her 1980 book, *Unspoken Worlds: Women's Religious Lives*, edited with Nancy Falk, presents case studies from both Western and non-Western societies of worlds of female experience that, although richly textured, deeply felt, and socially significant within their respective contexts, are all but unarticulated, "unspoken." In this volume, Leila Ahmed's description in Part I of the "women's Islam" of her childhood provides a vivid example of such a world. Ahmed distinguishes between official Islam, "the Islam of the texts," and "the Islam not only of women but of ordinary folk generally"; the latter she describes as "essentially an aural and oral heritage and a way of living and being—and not a textual, written heritage" (Ahmed 1999, 125). Messages about how to be in the world, communicated to a new generation through touch, gesture, and word, are nonetheless powerful, as she writes:

> [A]ll of these ways of passing on attitudes, morals, beliefs, knowledge . . . profoundly shape the next generation, but they do not leave a record in the way that someone writing a text about how to live or what to believe leaves a record. . . . Beliefs, morals, attitudes passed on to and impressed on us through these fleeting words and gestures are written into our very lives, our bodies, our selves, even into our physical cells and into how we live out the script of our lives. (Ibid., 120–121)

As Gross and Falk note and the literature of life stories demonstrates, the experience of those who are silent and invisible can be brought to light only through the agency of another. Moreover, within text-based traditions, literacy—in the present as in the past—remains a prerequisite for achieving equality. Riffat Hassan, who is Pakistani by birth, notes in her essay, "The Issue of Woman–Man Equality in the Islamic Tradition" (excerpted in Part II), the disadvantageous position of the many women in the Muslim world who are excluded by virtue of illiteracy from the possibility of critiquing the texts that their societies hold to be authoritative in terms of defining their status. In the West, as Lerner notes, there runs through the historical record the testimony of women for whom spirituality unlocked the key to the written word, like the nineteenth-century African American preacher Rebecca Jackson, who "prayed to God to teach her to read" and "miraculously received the gift of reading" (Lerner 1993, 108).

For those deprived through illiteracy or marginalization of access to written texts, imagery also serves as a tool of critique. In this volume, the narrative from the oral history of Mexican American farm worker Maria Elena Lucas affords an example, not from the developing world nor a previous century but from a marginalized population within the contemporary United States, of an individual hampered by poverty, obscurity, and semiliteracy who nevertheless addresses and critiques her religious tradition, reenvisioning its core symbols in the quest for affirmation of her own humanity. In Lucas's reimagined Virgin of Guadalupe as migrant farm worker, pregnant, dressed in jeans, balancing a basket of tomatoes on her head, we see the line of foremothers stretching back to medieval mystics who reenvisioned central aspects of the Christian story of redemption, making room within it for their own imagined participation.[6] Moreover, feminist scholarship has consistently sought to emphasize such continuities. Margaret Miles argues, for example, that "[a]ll explorations of women's lives are historical studies, in a sense; the cultural matrix and life situation of the women we study—whether these women are historical or contemporary—are integrally related, and form the ground of their ideas and symbols" (Miles 1985, 1).

Experience as Authority

When Mary Daly in her Exodus sermon invoked a "new religious consciousness," she signaled the direction of a journey that reflected the search by many feminists for a new, woman-centered religion. A foundational feature of this religion would be a reliance on women's experience as the basis for theological reflection. Christ and Plaskow identified the centrality of this concept in *Womanspirit Rising*, stating in their introduction, "The word *experience* becomes a . . . significant norm for feminists reconstructing tradition and creating new religious forms" (Christ and Plaskow 1979, 6, emphasis in original). The title of the volume's first section proclaims "The Essential Challenge: Does Theology Speak to Women's Experience?" Additionally, an essay by Christ addressed the topic "Spiritual Quest and Women's Experience" and a 1960 essay by Valerie Saiving, which was republished in *Womanspirit Rising*, becoming a touchstone for subsequent theory in the field, claimed that "[theology] has defined the human condition on the basis of masculine experience" (Saiving 1979, 39). In the essay that accompanied her tale "The Coming of Lilith," which appears in Part II, Plaskow wrote, "It is not self-evident that theology must remain close to the experiences that generate it . . . [but] in the case of feminist theology, the close relation between content and process seems imperative" (Plaskow 1979, 198–199). The act of naming the world, with its appropriation of agency and authority for the self, was seen as having been a historically male prerogative. Mary Daly had suggested that, within the Western tradition, women's inability to name their own experience was culturally rooted in Adam's naming of the animals and woman in the creation story from the Book of Genesis, which Daly called "the paradigm of false naming in Western culture" (Daly 1973, 8).

At a certain moment, many, like the editors and contributors to Womanspirit Rising, felt that under the spell of consciousness-raising, women would learn to name their own experience. Then, in the words of poet Muriel Rukeyser, "The world would split open," ushering in a new order (1978, cited in Christ and Plaskow 1979, 7).

As the literature on women's studies in religion developed, the foundational nature of feminist claims about the category of experience became clear.[7] In this volume, two voices from minority communities echo feminist theology's early and continuing identi- fication of the primacy of experience as a normative concept. In her 1989 book *White Women's Christ and Black Women's Jesus*, Jacquelyn Grant affirms:

> Womanist theology begins with the experiences of Black women as the point of departure. This experience includes not only Black women's activities in the larger society but also in the churches and reveals that Black women have often rejected the oppressive structure in the church as well. (205)

And Hong Kong–born scholar Kwok Pui-lan writes,

> I . . . agree with post-Christian feminists that our religious imagination cannot be based on the Bible alone, which often excludes women's experience. . . . In particular, I cannot believe that truth is only revealed in a book written almost two thousand years ago, and that the Chinese have no way to participate in its inception. (Kwok 1988, 29–30)

The concept of experience as articulated by feminist scholars of religion was radically historicized by the entry into the discussion of voices such as these repre- senting diverse minority communities. Walsh in her bibliography notes that it was "during the years 1978–1985 . . . that the pluralism of women's experience became theologically visible, and particularly so for women within African American, Hispanic, Asian, and Jewish religious communities" (Walsh 1999, 17). Regarding womanist theology, Walsh writes,

> At no point should the reader conceive of womanism as merely a form of 'femi- nism-in-black.' . . . Rather, womanism is a cultural consciousness that stems from the commitments of black women to black family and community life and *within these* to gender and 'women's experience.' (Ibid., 269, emphasis in original)

The entrance into the conversation of womanist, *Mujerista* (Latina), Asian, and other global voices and perspectives permanently altered the way in which it was pos- sible to invoke "women's experience" as a warrant for any position.[8]

Our Bodies, Ourselves, Our Traditions

Our Bodies, Ourselves appeared in 1973. It represented, in expanded book form, a version of lectures, papers, and notes originally published by the Boston Women's Health Collective in 1971, the year Mary Daly and her sympathizers effected their "exodus" from the Harvard Memorial Church. Its phenomenal success and ultimately global reach—it has since been translated into dozens of languages—testify to the emphasis on empowering women in relation to their bodies that emerged early in Second Wave thought, and was manifested in the abortion rights movement and the antipornography debates within the women's movement, as well as in the women's health movement, which *Our Bodies, Ourselves* helped to launch.

Emphasis on the body also informed feminist thinking in religion from its inception. Nelle Morton's piece, "The Goddess as Metaphoric Image" (1985), which begins Part III, is illustrative of this theme in its revisioning of blood and menstruation, in the context of the author's experience, as vehicles out of patriarchal consciousness. The Goddess invoked by Morton is an immanent presence who grounds our experience of nature and physicality:

> Human beings did not come from another world nor are we headed for one. Nor did we descend from the sky but out of the womb of our mother, our mother's mother, and our mother's mother. Recognizing our origin, we experience *presence*. . . . We can claim our sexuality as pervasive and as ourselves. We can claim our bodies as ours and as ourselves and our minds as our own and ourselves. (Morton 1985, 166, emphasis in original)

The cultural feminism that sprang from the women's movement affirmed and celebrated femaleness and in particular the cycles, functions, and "specialness" of women's bodies.[9] The feminist spirituality movement that grew out of cultural feminism ritualized such celebrations in many ways, borrowing freely from diverse cultures and traditions, as its participants sought to meet women's spiritual needs through the development of nonpatriarchal and nonoppressive religious forms. It intersected at various times and in a variety of ways with other social movements—some, like ecofeminism, with a specific political agenda and others, like the New Age movement, of more amorphous character. Cynthia Eller, in her studies of the feminist spirituality movement as it evolved in the United States, calls it "a fascinating study in religious syncretism" and "a contemporary example of what women appropriate and what they invent when they set their hands to the task of creating religion in a realm largely free of the restraints of tradition" (Eller 1993a, 175, 172; see also Eller, *Living in the Lap of the Goddess*, 1993b).

As Eller notes, a salient feature of the feminist spirituality movement that emerged from the Second Wave was its reversal of the stance of nineteenth-century women's religious movements on the issue of women's relationship to the body. She also points out that, in its linking of women to nature and the body, twentieth-century feminist spirituality presents a strong contrast to earlier women's religions, whose leaders sought to de-emphasize that very connection:

> When Mary Baker Eddy says that the body is an illusion and only the spirit is reality, when Annie Besant describes bodies as outer garments on which existence is not dependent, when a spiritualist medium regards her body as a frail vessel through which the spirit world can speak, or when Ann Lee advocates

celibacy as the proper relation between men and women, the time-honored connection between women and nature is being severed. (Eller 1993a, 188)

Reflecting a twentieth-century critique, Rita Gross asserts: "Conventional male-created religions long for transcendence and immortality, define perfection as changelessness, are anti-body and anti-nature, and in short, promote dualistic and otherworldly thinking" (Gross 1996, 237). But Eller suggests that it was that very transcendence to which earlier American women religious leaders aspired:

> If women are not unbreakably bound to nature, they are free to claim what men have always had and what they as women have been denied: an autonomous will, the free use of intellectual gifts, and the ability to transcend bodily existence in communion with the divine. (Eller 1993a, 188–189)[10]

Thus, within women's religion historically, divergent attitudes toward the body appear as a kind of fulcrum upon which definitions and rhetorical strategies turn.

The desire to affirm the body characterizes not only adherents of the feminist spirituality movement, but also many who are committed to remaining within the Christian or Jewish mainstream.[11] Their task has not always been a simple one; to many, an engagement with Jewish and Christian sacred texts revealed a tradition in which "female" equaled not only "nature," but also uncleanness, sin, and death. Whereas ancient goddess religions had often linked sexuality with the sacred, a feature celebrated, as we have seen, by their modern devotees, both Judaism and Christianity had severed that link. This, like the identification of women with nature, appeared to some as a root cause of women's status under patriarchy. Rita Gross, in discussing the transition in the ancient world from polytheism to male monotheism, writes that "it seems inevitable that if sexuality and the sacred are widely separated, then, at least in a male-dominated society, women will be treated as inferiors and phobias about their sexuality will develop, as eventually did happen in biblical thought" (Gross 1996, 179). Daly's early work had focused attention on the misogyny in the writings of the early Church Fathers. Rosemary Ruether (1974) also elaborated on ways in which the tradition assimilated women to the body, to changeableness and decay, and, ultimately, to finitude and death. The consequences of such a development were, as many pointed out, anything but academic; scholars tracing the religious and cultural roots of dominant traditions of representation of the female body began to see religious doctrine and imagery as undergirding violence against women and children. Margaret Miles's piece in Part II, drawing on the legacy of Christian art as well as on textual evidence, argues that Christianity bears direct and historic responsibility for the fostering of violence against women.[12]

Within the confines of Christianity and Judaism, could such a past be made usable? Several of the essays in this volume are illustrative of a feminist determination to turn traditions upside down and shake them, until a drop of the usable falls out. Judith Plaskow (1991), engaging Jewish tradition on the body and sexuality, argues that Jewish law and attitudes must change to eliminate the view that another person can possess one's sexuality, and to include homosexual marriage. A younger Jewish feminist, Jennifer Bleyer, resolves to salvage what is valuable in Jewish tradition for her own life, even if it necessitates becoming "my own damn rabbi." Latina writer Sandra Cisneros seeks to mend the historically and culturally severed relationship between the sacred and the sexual in her essay on the Virgin of Guadalupe. Unwilling to reject her Mexican American heritage but unreconciled to its attitudes toward women, Cisneros acknowledges in the Virgin of Guadalupe a figure that both attracts and repels her. Like María Elena Lucas, the subject of the oral history excerpted in Part I, Cisneros renegotiates her relationship with this powerful cultural icon. She does so by restoring to the indigenous American goddess the sexuality that was stripped away in the process of her transformation into the Spanish, Catholic *Virgen de Guadalupe*. This restoration makes possible the author's physical self-affirmation: "My nipples are big and brown, like the Mexican coins of my childhood. When I see *la Virgen de Guadalupe* I want to lift her dress as I did my dolls' . . . does she have dark nipples too? Yes, I am certain she does" (Cisneros 1996, 51). Cisneros' reenvisioning converts *la Virgen* into "Guadalupe the Sex Goddess" of her title. But the psychological and emotional power of this gesture runs headlong into Catholic orthodoxy when she writes of the reclaimed goddess, "My *Virgen de Guadalupe* is not the mother of God. She is God" (Ibid., 50).

Our Traditions, Our Future

Women's studies in religion is an enterprise whose ethos has been optimistic and exploratory, within an overarching communal framework. Reflecting on the field as a whole, Sheila Greeve Davaney wrote, "Feminist theory, especially in its theological form, has always . . . been about the self-conscious expression of alternative visions for human community, practice and thought" (Davaney 2001, 395). In the classroom, as Judith Plaskow wrote in 1993, women's studies in religion "can help women claim the power to name themselves and their own experiences in the context of a political/religious discourse rooted in visions of a new social order" (10).

The articles in this volume illustrate an arc of development from early critiques of misogyny within received traditions through the distinctly future-oriented project of ecofeminism. They are arranged thematically rather than chronologically; thus, the essays in Part I, "Starting from Experience," illustrate what results when women do start from their own experience in engaging religion and its place in their lives. Notwithstanding the way in which the category of experience has been called into question by the entrance of multiculturalism into the academy, these pieces in many cases reflect a debt to scholars such as Rosemary Ruether, Judith Plaskow, Elisabeth Schüssler Fiorenza, and others who first articulated the category of women's experience as a norm for reflection in matters of theology and religion generally.[13]

The stages of development through which women's studies in religion has moved overlap and often proceed concurrently, as social change and theory interact. Within this volume, the narrative taken from the oral history of farm worker María Elena Lucas that appears in Part I may in some ways be taken as illustrative of the three moments we have delineated: starting from experience, confronting traditions, and moving toward a reenvisioned future. On the basis of her experience, this individual becomes empowered to confront her religious and cultural traditions with respect to their teachings about women; she then goes on to imaginatively transform an image that is historically emblematic of those teachings and attitudes.

From the standpoint of the larger culture, the most visible and interesting way in which feminism and religion have interacted is in the challenges that reformers have pressed against established religious institutions. The popular press, as it tracked the course of this cultural change throughout the 1970s, 1980s, and 1990s, featured stories on conflicts over the ordination and advancement of women clergy, liturgical reform and innovation, issues of authority and jurisdiction within denominations, and occasionally, revisionist interpretations of Scripture or tradition.[14]

In contrast to this attention focused on such conflicts in the societal arena, within the field of women's studies in religion the early distinction between reform and revolution has broken down. In the 1989 introduction to their second influential anthology, *Weaving the Visions*, Christ and Plaskow reject the reformist versus revolutionary dichotomy that had informed the organization of their earlier *Womanspirit Rising* (1979). By the later date, confronted with a much-expanded body of literature by a far more diverse array of voices, it seemed clear, as they write, that this overly simplistic classification obscured more than it clarified about the nature of the field (Plaskow and Christ 1989, 6–7). The authors, both influential figures who have contributed to the shaping of the discipline, illustrate that point with personal statements about their own differences: Christ has devoted her career to Goddess spirituality, whereas Plaskow has committed herself to the transformation of Judaism (Ibid., v).

The question of deeply held loyalties, and also of those that are experienced as multiple, intersecting, and sometimes conflicting, continues to characterize discussions within women's studies in religion.[15] At the same time, the line that defines "inside" or "outside" of established tradition can blur for individuals, as well as for the field as a whole. In a personal reflection, Jewish poet, translator, and theologian Marcia Falk writes about the experience of inhabiting the space between inside and outside of her own tradition:

> While the theists have nigh-convinced me that I do not belong in their camp, the secularists are still tempting me to stake my tent in theirs. Yet I am not totally at home there, either. For while theists question my refusal to use the word *God* in prayer . . . Jewish secular humanists challenge my use of words like *sacred* and *divine*. . . .
>
> Perhaps it is the poet in me—the lover of language who is loath to limit her options. . . . All theology, it seems to me, is a kind of metaphor making on a grand scale. (Falk 2003, 99–100)

Falk explains how her Jewish self and her writer self are inevitably intertwined:

> The Hebrew tradition is inescapably theological, and the Hebrew language itself is inextricably bound up with the cultures of theological Judaism. When the poet enters this tradition, she is—whether or not she chooses to be—engaged in the theological domain. (Ibid., 100)

And on a note that suggests the open-endedness and future orientation of the feminist theological project, she writes: "I have wanted to do for the Jewish God what [feminist theologian] Nelle [Morton] did for the Goddess, that is, make it impossible for people to refer to it without immediately asking themselves (or being asked by others) what they mean" (Ibid.).

Exploring what they (or we) mean by Goddess or God, along with women's many and diverse namings of self, community, and world in relation to those meanings, leads to the multifaceted enterprise that is women's studies in religion. It leads to the work, some of which is represented here, of the followers of a vision informed by Mary Daly's 1971 call to take our own "place in the sun" (Daly 1996a, 318).

Notes

1. In 1980 women made up about 3 percent of the ordained clergy in the United States; by the year 2000 they comprised 13.8 percent. Seminary enrollments show a similar dramatic shift: in 1972 women were 10.2 percent of students in Christian seminaries, whereas in 1999 their numbers had risen to 34.16 percent. In some traditions, moreover, women represent the majority of a seminary's entire student body (National Council of Churches 2003; Meinzer and Merrill 2003, 7).

2. During these years, many women also experienced the revolutionary impulse within religiously based reform movements with broad social agendas. For a study of religion and social activism in women's lives at this time, see Evans (2003).

3. For the full development of Pagels's research on the Gnostics and their relationship to the tradition that emerged as orthodox Christianity, see her *The Gnostic Gospels* (1979b) and *Adam, Eve, and the Serpent* (1988).

4. Ruether, in particular, has continued to pursue a scholarship aimed at retrieving valuable but suppressed elements of the Christian tradition—"glimpses . . . of transformative, biophilic relationships," as she writes in *Gaia and God*, that should be "separated from the toxic waste of sacralized domination" (Ruether 1992, 3).

5. See, for example, womanist theologian Delores S. Williams's "Black Women's Literature and the Task of Feminist Theology" (1985).

6. On the line of medieval women foremothers, see Lerner (1993), Chapters Four and Five.

7. Since the 1980s, concepts of female "nature" and experience as employed in earlier feminist writing have come under attack within religious studies, as elsewhere in the academy. For a discussion of the use of the concept of experience in three of feminist theology's major theorists see Sheila Greeve Davaney's "The Limits of the Appeal to Women's Experience" (1987). For a later reflection on the implications of critiques of the category "women's experience" for the future of feminist theology, see Davaney's contribution to "Roundtable Discussion: What's in a Name? Exploring the Dimensions of What 'Feminist Studies in Religion' Means" (Davaney 2001).

8. The subject of racial, ethnic, and religious diversity continues to be a contentious one within the field of feminist theology. In a review of recent books on feminist work in religion, Carol Christ protests the "conflation of Christian feminist theology with feminist theology" and "a restriction of focus from the more inclusive one reflected in *Womanspirit Rising* and *Weaving the Visions*, which included Christian

Jewish, Goddess, and other voices, to a more narrow one that defines feminist theology as Christian" (Christ 2004, 81).

9. For background on cultural feminism as it emerged from the women's movement of the 1960s and 1970s, see Eller (2000).

10. For a fuller discussion of the material and cultural conditions underlying this historical difference, and of the tactical implications for feminism of differing stances toward nature and the body, see Eller's essay (1993a).

11. Eller comments on the overlap between these groups, noting that "some women active in Jewish or Christian feminism consider themselves part of the feminist spirituality movement" (Eller 1993a, 172).

12. For more examples of this type of critique, see Schüssler Fiorenza and Copeland (1994).

13. For a discussion of "women's experience" in Ruether and Schüssler Fiorenza, see Davaney (1987). For an early statement by Plaskow, see "The Coming of Lilith: Toward a Feminist Theology" (1979).

14. There are, of course, many such reports from these decades. See, for example, Woodward (1989), Goldman (1990), and Steinfels (1993).

15. See, for example, the special section "Meeting at the Well: Multiculturalism and Jewish Feminism" in Kwok Pui-lan and Elisabeth Schüssler Fiorenza, eds., *Journal of Feminist Studies in Religion* 19(1): 85–128 (Spring 2003).

References

Ahmed, Leila. 1999. *A Border Passage: From Cairo to America—A Woman's Journey*. New York: Farrar, Straus and Giroux.

Boston Women's Health Book Collective. 1973. *Our Bodies, Ourselves*. New York: Simon and Schuster.

Christ, Carol P. 2004. Whose history are we writing?: Reading feminist texts with a hermeneutic of suspicion. *Journal of Feminist Studies in Religion* 20: 59–82.

———. 1987. Expressing anger at god. In Carol P. Christ, *Laughter of Aphrodite: Reflections on a Journey to the* Goddess, 27–33. San Francisco: Harper & Row.

———. 1979b. Spiritual quest and women's experience. In Carol P. Christ and Judith Plaskow, eds., *Womanspirit Rising: A Feminist Reader in Religion*, 228–245. San Francisco: Harper & Row.

———. 1987. Toward a paradigm shift in the academy and in religious studies. In Christie Farnham, ed., *The Impact of Feminist Research in the Academy*, 53–76. Bloomington: Indiana University Press.

Christ, Carol P. and Judith Plaskow, eds. 1979. *Womanspirit Rising: A Feminist Reader in Religion*. San Francisco: Harper & Row.

Cisneros, Sandra. 1996. Guadalupe the sex goddess. In Ana Castillo, ed., *Goddess of the Americas/La Diosa de las Américas: Writings on the Virgin of Guadalupe*, 46–51. New York: Riverhead Books.

Daly, Mary. 1968. *The Church and the Second Sex*. New York: Harper & Row.

———. 1973. *Beyond God the Father*. Boston: Beacon.

———. 1996a. The women's movement: An exodus community. In Elizabeth A. Clark and Herbert Richardson, eds., *Women and Religion: The Original Sourcebook of Women in Christian Thought*, rev. ed., 311–318. San Francisco: HarperSanFrancisco.

———. 1996b. Sin big. *New Yorker*, February 26 & March 4: 77–83.

Davaney, Sheila Greeve. 1987. The limits of the appeal to women's experience. In Clarissa W. Atkinson, Constance H. Buchanan, and Margaret R. Miles, eds., *Immaculate & Powerful: The Female in Sacred Image and Social Reality*, 31–50. Boston: Beacon.

———. 2001. Roundtable discussion: What's in a name? Exploring the dimensions of what 'feminist studies in religion' means. In Darlene M. Juschka, ed., *Feminism in the Study of Religion: A Reader*, 393–397. New York: Continuum.

Eller, Cynthia. 1993a. Twentieth-century women's religion as seen in the feminist spirituality movement. In Catherine Lowman Wessinger, ed., *Women's Leadership in Marginal Religions: Explorations Outside the Mainstream*, 172–195. Urbana: University of Illinois Press.

———. 1993b. *Living in the Lap of the Goddess: The Feminist Spirituality Movement in America.* New York: Crossroad.

———. 2000. The roots of feminist spirituality. In Wendy Griffin, ed., *Daughters of the Goddess: Studies of Healing, Identity, and Empowerment*, 25–41. Walnut Creek, CA: AltaMira.

Evans, Sara M., ed. 2003. *Journeys That Opened up the World: Women, Student Christian Movements, and Social Justice, 1955–1975.* New Brunswick, NJ: Rutgers University Press.

Falk, Marcia. 2003. My father's riddle, or conflict and reciprocity in the multicultural (Jewish) self. *Journal of Feminist Studies in Religion* 19: 97–103.

Goldman, Ari L. 1990. "Black Women's Bumpy Path to Church Leadership." *New York Times*, July 29, national edition, sec. A.

Grant, Jacquelyn. 1989. *White Women's Christ and Black Women's Jesus.* Atlanta: Scholar's Press.

Gross, Rita M. 1996. *Feminism and Religion: An Introduction.* Boston: Beacon.

Gross, Rita M. and Nancy Falk, eds. 1980. *Unspoken Worlds: Women's Religious Lives in Non-Western Cultures.* San Francisco: Harper & Row.

Kwok Pui-lan. 1988. Mothers and daughters, writers and fighters. In Letty M. Russell, Kwok Pui-lan, Ada María Isasi-Díaz, and Katie Geneva Cannon, eds., *Inheriting Our Mothers' Gardens*, 21–33. Louisville, KY: Westminster John Knox.

Kwok Pui-lan and Elisabeth Schüssler Fiorenza, eds. 2003 (Spring). Meeting at the well: Multiculturalism and Jewish feminism. Special section, *Journal of Feminist Studies in Religion* 19(1): 85–128.

Lerner, Gerda. 1993. *The Creation of Feminist Consciousness: From the Middle Ages to Eighteen-Seventy.* New York: Oxford University Press.

McLaughlin, Eleanor. 1979. The Christian past: Does it hold a future for women? In Carol P. Christ and Judith Plaskow, eds., *Womanspirit Rising: A Feminist Reader in Religion*, 93–106. San Francisco: Harper & Row.

Meinzer, Chris A. and Nancy Merrill, eds. 2003. *Fact Book on Theological Education 2002/2003.* Pittsburgh, PA: Association of Theological Schools in the United States and Canada.

Miles, Margaret. 1985. Introduction. In Clarissa W. Atkinson, Constance H. Buchanan, and Margaret R. Miles, eds., *Immaculate & Powerful: The Female in Sacred Image and Social Reality*, 1–14. Boston: Beacon.

Morton, Nelle. 1985. The goddess as metaphoric image. In Nelle Morton, *The Journey Is Home.* Boston: Beacon.

National Council of Churches. "Benevolences Up, Membership Stable, 2001 Yearbook Reports, National Council of Churches, http://www.ncccusa.org/news/01news15.html (accessed September 15, 2003).

Pagels, Elaine. 1979a. What became of God the mother? Conflicting images of God in early Christianity. In Carol P. Christ and Judith Plaskow, eds., *Womanspirit Rising: A Feminist Reader in Religion*, 107–119. San Francisco: Harper & Row.

———. 1979b. *The Gnostic Gospels*. New York: Random House.

———. 1988. *Adam, Eve, and the Serpent*. New York: Random House.

Plaskow, Judith. 1979. The coming of Lilith: Toward a feminist theology. In Carol P. Christ and Judith Plaskow, eds., *Womanspirit Rising: A Feminist Reader in Religion*, 198–209. San Francisco: Harper & Row.

———. 1991. Toward a new theology of sexuality. In Susan E. Davies and Eleanor H. Haney, eds., *Redefining Sexual Ethics*, 309–319. Cleveland, OH: Pilgrim.

———. 1993. We are also your sisters: The development of women's studies in religion. *Women's Studies Quarterly* 21: 9–21.

Plaskow, Judith and Carol P. Christ, eds. 1989. *Weaving the Visions: New Patterns in Feminist Spirituality*. San Francisco: HarperSanFrancisco.

Rosen, Ruth. 2000. *The World Split Open: How the Modern Women's Movement Changed America*. New York: Viking.

Ruether, Rosemary Radford. 1974. Misogynism and virginal feminism in the fathers of the church. In Rosemary Radford Ruether, ed., *Religion and Sexism*, 150–183. New York: Simon and Schuster.

———. 1979. Motherearth and the megamachine. In Carol P. Christ and Judith Plaskow, eds., *Womanspirit Rising: A Feminist Reader in Religion*, 42–52. San Francisco: Harper & Row.

———. 1992. *Gaia and God: An Ecofeminist Theology of Earth Healing*. San Francisco: HarperSanFrancisco.

Rukeyser, Muriel. 1978. *Collected Poems*. New York: McGraw-Hill.

Saiving, Valerie. 1979. The human situation: A feminine view. In Carol P. Christ and Judith Plaskow, eds., *Womanspirit Rising: A Feminist Reader in Religion*, 25–42. San Francisco: Harper & Row.

Schüssler Fiorenza, Elisabeth. 1984. *Bread Not Stone: The Challenge of Feminist Biblical Interpretation*. Boston: Beacon.

Schüssler Fiorenza, Elisabeth and M. Shawn Copeland, eds. *Violence Against Women*. Maryknoll, NY: Orbis, 1994.

Stanton, Elizabeth Cady. 1993, 1895. *The Woman's Bible*. Boston: Northeastern University Press.

Steinfels, Peter. 1993. "Catholic Feminists Ask, Can We Remain Catholic?" *New York Times*, April 16, sec. A.

Walsh, Mary-Paula. 1999. *Feminism and Christian Tradition: An Annotated Bibliography and Critical Introduction to the Literature*. Westport, CT: Greenwood.

Williams, Delores S. 1985. Black women's literature and the task of feminist theology. In Clarissa W. Atkinson, Constance H. Buchanan, and Margaret R. Miles, eds., *Immaculate & Powerful: The Female in Sacred Image and Social Reality*, 88–110. Boston: Beacon.

Woodward, Kenneth L. 1989. "Feminism and the Churches." *Newsweek*, February 13.

Suggested Readings

Armstrong, Karen. *The Gospel According to Woman*. New York: Anchor Books, 1986.

Bednarowski, Mary Farrell. *The Religious Imagination of American Women*. Bloomington: Indiana University Press, 1999.

Braude, Ann. *Women and American Religion*. New York: Oxford University Press, 2000.

————. *Transforming the Faith of Our Fathers: Women Who Changed American Religion.* New York: Palgrave, 2004.

Byrne, Lavinia. *The Hidden Tradition: Women's Spiritual Writings Rediscovered.* New York: Crossroad, 1991.

Chopp, Rebecca S. *The Power to Speak: Feminism, Language, God.* New York: Crossroad, 1989.

Chopp, Rebecca S. and Sheila Greeve Davaney, eds. *Horizons in Feminist Theology: Identity, Tradition, and Norms.* Minneapolis, MN: Fortress, 1997.

Christ, Carol P. and Judith Plaskow, eds. *Womanspirit Rising: A Feminist Reader in Religion.* San Francisco: HarperSanFrancisco, 1992.

Clark, Elizabeth A. and Herbert Richardson, eds. *Women and Religion: The Original Sourcebook of Women in Christian Thought.* San Francisco: HarperSanFrancisco, 1996.

Collier, Diane M. and Deborah F. Sawyer, eds. *Is There a Future for Feminist Theology?* London, UK: Sheffield Academic Press, 1999.

Drucker, Malka. *White Fire: A Portrait of Women Spiritual Leaders in America.* Woodstock, VT: Sky Light Paths, 2003.

Franzmann, Majella. *Women and Religion.* New York: Oxford University Press, 2000.

Fulkerson, Mary McClintock. *Changing the Subject: Women's Discourses and Feminist Theology.* Minneapolis, MN: Fortress, 1994.

Gross, Rita. *Feminism and Religion.* Boston: Beacon, 1998.

Halbertal, Tova Hartmann. *Appropriately Subversive: Modern Mothers in Traditional Religions.* Boston: Harvard University Press, 2002.

Holm, Jean and John Bowker, eds. *Women in Religion.* London: Pinter, 1994.

Keller, Rosemary Skinner and Rosemary Radford Ruether, eds. *In Our Own Voices: Four Centuries of American Women's Religious Writings.* Louisville, KY: Westminster John Knox, 2000.

King, Ursula. *Religion and Gender.* Oxford, UK: Blackwell Publishers, 1995.

Lindley, Susan Hill. *You Have Stept out of Your Place: A History of Women and Religion in America.* Louisville, KY: Westminster John Knox, 1998.

Malone, Mary T. *Women and Christianity, Vol. 2: From 1000 to the Reformation.* New York: Orbis, 2002.

Parsons, Susan Frank, ed. *The Cambridge Companion to Feminist Theology.* Cambridge, UK: Cambridge University Press, 2002.

Peach, Lucinda Joy. *Women and World Religions.* Upper Saddle River, NJ: Prentice-Hall, 2002.

Plaskow, Judith and Carol P. Christ, eds. *Weaving the Visions: New Patterns in Feminist Spirituality.* San Francisco: Harper & Row, 1989.

Ruether, Rosemary Radford and Rosemary Skinner Keller, eds. *Women and Religion in America, Vol. 1: The Nineteenth Century.* San Francisco: Harper & Row, 1981.

————. *Women and Religion in America, Vol. 2: The Colonial and Revolutionary Periods.* San Francisco: Harper & Row, 1983.

————. *Women and Religion in America, Vol. 3: 1900–1968.* San Francisco: Harper & Row, 1986.

Russell, Letty M. and J. Shannon Clarkson, eds. *Dictionary of Feminist Theologies.* Louisville, KY: Westminster John Knox, 1996.

Schneider, Laurel C. *Re-imagining the Divine: Confronting the Backlash against Feminist Theology.* Cleveland, OH: Pilgrim, 1998.

Sharma, Arvin and Katherine Young, eds. *Feminism and World Religions.* Albany: State University of New York Press, 1999.

Shepherd, Lorain MacKenzie. *Feminist Theologies for a Postmodern Church: Diversity, Community, Scripture.* New York: Peter Lang, 2002.

Stanton, Elizabeth Cady. *The Woman's Bible*. Boston: Northeastern University Press, 1993.

Vuola, Elina. *Limits of Liberation: Feminist Theology and the Ethics of Poverty and Reproduction*. London, UK: Sheffield Academic Press, 2002.

Young, Serenity. *An Anthology of Sacred Texts by and about Women*. New York: Crossroad, 1993.

Web Sites

Academic Info, Religion in America, http://www.academicinfo.net/amrelig.html

Association of College and Research Libraries, American Library Association, Women's Studies Section, WSS Links, Women and Theology, http://www.earlham.edu/~libr/acrlwss/wsstheo.html

Catholic Network for Women's Equality, http://www.cnwe.org/about.htm

Lau, Susan C. "Bibliography on Women and Religion," http://www.nd.edu/~archives/LAU.HTM

Virtual Religion Index, http://virtual religion.net/vri/

PART I

STARTING FROM
EXPERIENCE

It is an unforgettable, irreversible, and definitive fact of feminist experience that respect for women's experience/voice/perception/knowledge, our own and others', is the ground and foundation of our emancipation—of both the necessity and the possibility of rewriting, recreating, the world.

—MARILYN FRYE, "The Possibility of Feminist Theory"

Marilyn Frye describes the feminist enterprise as the creation of an "encyclopedia" entitled *The World, According to Women.* Each woman's experience, especially when shared with other women, serves to illuminate patterns within her own life and the lives of some other women, spiraling out to reflect the "world" to which Frye refers. These patterns become "an anthology, a collection of tales, unified, like any yarn, only by successively overlapping threads held together by friction, not riveted by logic" (Frye 1993, 111).

The "collection of tales" in this part illustrates in several ways the significance of experience for feminist religious thought. These authors recognize that biographical differences as well as differences in social location (culture, gender, social class, racial/ethnic status, and sexual orientation) create contexts that affect the nature of women's experiences of religion. Experiencing discrimination as a member of an oppressed group can lead to a reexamination of religious doctrine and imagery that may have contributed to that oppression. The beliefs, practices, and symbols of one religion may be rejected as unredeemable, they may be changed to speak to a group's experience, or they may be combined with different symbols to create "moods and motivations" (Geertz 1966: 4) that resonate with one's way of life. In societies in which women and men live very different lives, in which, in a sense, they inhabit different "worlds," it is fair to speak of women's religion as distinct from men's. Although "men's religion" may be the dominant narrative in many societies and may define women and their roles as being of lower value than men's, we should not assume that most women accept those definitions or that they agree with the ways in which men interpret religious doctrine and symbols.

Korean theologian Chung Hyun Kyung's "Following Naked Dancing and Long Dreaming" illustrates through the author's dramatic personal story the claim of feminist theology that women's own experience should be the primary source and touchstone of that theology. The author credits a variety of religious traditions, including indigenous belief systems as well as Buddhism and Christianity, with helping to uphold and sustain women whose lives are demeaned by a patriarchal society. Chung argues that the fullness of women's religious lives cannot be appreciated by focusing on their exclusion from formal roles or lack of systematic training in doctrine—a point that will receive further development, within a different cultural context, in the selection by Leila Ahmed. The garden imagery in this essay and the title of the volume in which it first appeared will be recognized by many as an allusion to Alice Walker's feminist classic, *In Search of Our Mothers' Gardens* (1983).

Leila Ahmed, who is Egyptian by birth, writes in the selection from *A Border Passage: From Cairo to America* of the life she shared with the women of her extended family in Alexandria, where her family summered, and at her grandmother's house in Zatoun. It is in this context that she distinguishes between "men's Islam," which she calls an official, textual heritage, and "women's Islam," characterized as a moral ethos and "a way of being in the world." She is keenly and painfully aware that it is "men's Islam" that holds authoritative sway over the lives of women in the Islamic world. At the same time, her personal narrative reveals the way in which the "women's Islam" of her own family and childhood continues to inform her life.

Ahmed's approach contrasts sharply with that of Muslim scholar Riffat Hassan, whose selections appear in Part II. This contrast should serve to break down notions of Muslim belief as being monolithic, as well as to draw connections to the way in which Jewish and Christian scholars are engaging their respective traditions.

Ahmed comes to Western feminism as an outsider, having arrived in the United States in 1979 to teach in a women's studies program. In this piece she also addresses the issue of the hostility she has experienced *from within* the community of feminist scholars to the study of women in Islam. This topic may well engender debate—among those who hold the view that Islam is unremittingly hostile to women's interests, for example.

In excerpts from *White Women's Christ and Black Women's Jesus,* Jacquelyn Grant analyzes and expands Christian feminist theology by focusing on the triple oppressions of racism, sexism, and classism affecting Black women. Grant argues that feminist theology, which she labels white and racist, does not reflect the struggles of African American women. She outlines a womanist theology that grows out of Black women's experiences in the world and in the church. Both the Bible and Jesus are central to womanist theology because both have been, and continue to be, important for Black women. Thus, a womanist theology is a "contextualized" theology, rooted in the world of African American women and in their experiences of racism, sexism, and classism. Grant's assertion of the reality of a Black Jesus is bound to spark discussion and controversy. She also confronts the sexism embedded in

Christianity and in the Black church, and celebrates women's efforts to find new ways of reading scripture and creating symbols that are representative of their lives.

In "Mediations of the Spirit: Native American Religious Traditions and the Ethics of Representation," Inés Hernández-Ávila, whose cultural heritage is Nez Perce and Mexican, raises troubling and challenging questions about how Native American religious traditions can be preserved without being misrepresented or commodified by non-Native scholars or by participants in New Age spirituality. Her emphasis on personal experience and social location as sources of authority and authenticity resonate with other voices in this collection. Noting that Native American women have not embraced feminism, Hernández-Ávila is critical of feminists who claim solidarity with all women, while ignoring Native women or trivializing their culture. She is particularly disturbed by the expropriation of Native American sacred beliefs and practices by non-Native women seeking an authentic, "feminist," earth-centered spirituality.

Kwok Pui-lan, the author of "Mothers and Daughters, Writers and Fighters," is a native of Hong Kong who came from a family in which the two sons were favored over the five daughters. She saw the contradiction between the low value placed on girls and women on the one hand, and the power and independence of her illiterate but creative mother on the other. Kwok's mother and mother-in-law were strong women who refused to see themselves as victims of the oppressive patriarchal society in which they lived. They used Buddhism and folk religion as sources of power and managed to live with integrity under difficult conditions. Kwok's Christianity became a similar source of strength and she found a role model in a female pastor who saw men and women as equals and who encouraged women to reach their potential.

The new theology Kwok proposes would include life stories and women's wisdom along with scripture and tradition. She insists that the Western heritage Christianity represents need not exclude religious insights from other cultures. She hopes for a Christianity that can be integrated ("indigenized") into Chinese culture, despite Christianity's patriarchal bias and its problematic history in China.

Fran Leeper Buss's *Forged under the Sun* is an oral history—a work in which an individual narrates her life story in an edited context. Buss's role as editor is one of feminist advocacy, as well as providing historical background and a narrative framing the subject's account. The voice that speaks in the text is that of María Elena Lucas, a Mexican American farm worker from south Texas. Her voice is distinctive in relation to the others represented here, and is particularly well suited to introduce questions of class as well as ethnicity in the context of feminism and religion. Lucas is an individual whose formal education was cut short in the sixth grade, and her theological speculations, though thematically similar to those of many feminist theologians, are entirely experience-based. They reflect the speaker's confrontation, in both childhood and adulthood, with the reality of male violence, as well as her struggle for self-expression under highly constrained circumstances. In the excerpt presented here Lucas attempts to reappropriate the image of the Virgin of Guadalupe as a positive, empowering model for herself and other women. In language reflective of personal and collective struggle, she seeks to imagine how a powerful cultural symbol might be reinterpreted so as to support female empowerment and transformed gender relations within her community.

The final piece in Part I, "Challah for the Queen of Heaven," is perhaps the best example of what might be called a postmodern perspective in this collection. Drawing on feminism, traditional Judaism, and Paganism, Ryiah Lilith constructs a kind of syncretic, highly personal spirituality that does not require an external entity to validate it. Her aim is to incorporate goddess spirituality, specifically witchcraft, with the Judaism that is an important part of her heritage.

This piece graphically illustrates the contemporary fragmentation of religious tradition as individuals select, from a variety of sources, those elements that speak to their personal experience. The tension between experience and tradition, as well as between individual and community, is palpable in Lilith's account of her own spiritual search. Paradoxically, embracing Paganism, as she asserts, has enabled Lilith to confirm and express her Jewish identity. Paganism attracted Lilith, in part, because of its "lack of dogma and authority"; this selection by a twenty-something feminist raises questions about whether "religion" loses its definition in the absence of some form of institutional authority and shared beliefs.

References

Frye, Marilyn. 1993. The possibility of feminist theory. In Alison M. Jaggar and Paula S. Rothenberg, eds., *Feminist Frameworks,* 3rd ed., 103–112. New York: McGraw-Hill
Geertz, Clifford. 1966. Religion as a cultural system. In M. Banton, ed., *Anthropological Approaches to the Study of Religion,* 1–46. London, UK: Tavistock.
Walker, Alice. 1983. *In Search of Our Mothers' Gardens: Womanist Prose.* San Diego, CA: Harcourt Brace Jovanovich.

Following Naked Dancing
and Long Dreaming*

❖ *Chung Hyun Kyung* ❖

"Mom, stop it!"

I screamed at her, but she did not look at me. She continued her dance, moving nearly naked in the forest. I felt ashamed of her; I wished she were not my mother. There was nothing to hide the scene before me. There was a deathly silence around us, except for Mother's singing and the sound of the river.

Under the hot sun of August, the forest seemed to be taking a nap. There were no villagers moving about, only Mother and I. She looked like a person who did not belong to this world. I saw real happiness in her face while she was singing and dancing. I could see her breasts, the lines of her body—large, like a whale's—through her wet underwear. I did not want anybody in the world to see that shape, my mother's body that had worked and lived. I finally started to cry out of extreme embarrassment. I wanted to hide from her. She did not look anymore like the noble mother of whom I was always proud. But in spite of my crying, she continued singing and dancing, twirling in the forest as a child might, twirling and dancing in a space of her own.

This happened twenty-four years ago, when I was seven. My mother and I were traveling together to visit her older sister, who lived in a small, remote village in a southern province in Korea. My father was deeply involved with his business and had remained at home in Seoul. I had been raised in a big city, and traveling to a remote village was not easy for me. No bus or train service was available. We had to go over the mountain and cross the river. I was exhausted from walking so long on the dusty road under a hot summer sun. Mom had been telling me stories from her childhood as we were walking—how she had played in the river and climbed the mountain with her sisters. So when we came to the river, Mother's memories came to life and she took off her clothes and started to bathe in the water. She encouraged me to bathe with her. I was shocked. How could she do this? I looked to see whether there were any other people around. No one was there. I did not approve of my mother's behavior at all. I hoped she would finish her bathing as soon as possible. I sat on the riverbank and waited.

At last she got out of the water, but the situation only grew worse. She began singing a song I had never heard before. She danced while she was singing.

I thought my mother had gone crazy; otherwise she would never have acted like that. Humiliation and confusion made me cry. "Mom, stop it, *stop it!*" I screamed, but she continued to dance and sing, her body flopping and straining against the dampened clothes. I could not stop the tears from coming, and we stayed like that—me crying and her dancing—for some time. After a while, because of my continuous crying, she stopped her dance and put on her clothes and we took up our journey again.

One Mother's Story

Most of the time my mother behaved like a typical Korean housewife. She took care of us very well. She saved all the best parts of food for my father and me, eating the leftovers herself. She appeared to be submissive to my father and made many sacrifices on behalf of both of us. But there was a contradiction in her life. From time to time, her behavior showed a wild, raw, extreme passion for freedom that was not characteristic of the model Korean woman. The contradiction that she lived she also taught me. The manner in which she raised me was very different from other Korean mothers. Even though she kept telling me to be a "nice" likable girl, she never asked me to cook for family gatherings or feasts, which is the Korean girl's family duty. Rather, she would give me a small amount of money and tell me to go to the library to study whenever the big feasts came. She always told me that I could learn how to cook any time I wanted, but I could not learn how to study once I became older. Sometimes she scolded me because she thought I was too tomboyish. She frequently told me that if I was not feminine, I would not get married because no man would want me. But at other times, she seriously told me not to get married. She said I could not live a full life in marriage because marriage, for a Korean woman, meant giving up freedom.

I still vividly remember the night I had a serious fight with my college boyfriend over the issue of marriage. I loved him very much, but I could not jump into the marriage, as he was insisting, because I had strong doubts about the limitations it would place on my freedom. I could not live without freedom. He accused me of being a selfish woman. I came home crying after a bitter argument with him and had a long conversation with Mother. After listening to my story, she leaned toward me in utter seriousness and offered her advice.

"Hyun Kyung," she said, "do not get married. I have been married for more than forty years. Marriage works for the man, but not for the woman. Forget about your boyfriend. Korean men don't understand women. Live fully. If you want to do something very much—from your heart, from your gut—then do it. Don't hesitate. If you don't have money, then make money, even if it means selling your used underwear. Discipline yourself to be a good scholar when you are young, since you always have loved to learn." And she added, with ambivalence, "Go abroad to study. And if, while you are studying, you find a good *Western* man who can understand *you,* your inner life, then get married. *Western* men seem more generous to women than Korean men."

I was very surprised by my mother's response. I could not believe what she had said. Her advice to me contradicted my image of her as a model Korean woman, someone who worried that I might not get married, who scolded me for my "unfemininity."

My mother passed away one year after I arrived in the United States to begin my theological studies. I cried in my bed every night for more than six months after she died, missing her—missing her like a little motherless child. I felt as if I were standing by myself in the middle of a wilderness, struggling with a powerful storm. My mother had gone; it was the loneliest time in my life.

The Other Mother's Story

Three years after my mother's death, I returned to Korea. There I heard about the existence of my other mother from my cousin-sister. She told me that I had a birth mother besides my late mother. I could not believe it.

If it were true, how could it be that I had never heard about her? If it were true, it would mean that my late parents had totally deceived me. Even in their last words, my father and mother did not mention her to me. If I really did have another mother, a birth mother, then this woman had been erased from my family history, totally erased for the entire thirty years of my life.

My cousin-sister took me to meet my other mother. With confused emotions, I silently followed her until we came to the door of my other mother's home just outside the city of Seoul. I had brought a dozen red roses with me to give to my other mother. I stood at her doorway, holding the roses, and timidly reached for the doorbell.

An old woman opened the door. When she saw me her eyes filled with tears. She took my hands in her own and asked, "Is this Hyun Kyung?" I said, "Yes." Then she began to sob. She told me, "Finally I have met you! I thought I would die without seeing you. Now I can leave this world without holding my *han*."

I did not even know how I felt. I felt numb. Without knowing how to respond, I listened to her story.

My mother was a Korean version of a surrogate mother. In Korea, we call these women *ci-baji. Ci* means seed, *baji* means receiver. Therefore, the literal meaning of *ci-baji* is "seed receiver." According to my birth mother, my late mother could not conceive a child even after twenty years of marriage. My father became very anxious. He wanted to have *his* own child in order to continue *his* family line. So he asked my late mother to search for a *ci-baji* woman for him. My late mother found a woman from the countryside who was a *yu-mo* for a child in our neighborhood. My father, however, did not like her at all; he thought she was not bright and beautiful enough to be a *ci-baji* for *his* future child. He sent her away and began to look for a *ci-baji* himself. He found a woman he liked, a woman who had lost her husband during the Korean War. She lived with her mother. My father followed her for a few months and finally persuaded her to conceive a baby for him. She and my father had posed for a picture when they knew that she had become pregnant, and she showed that picture to me. She was a good, healthy-looking woman. She gave birth to me and raised me until my first birthday.

The day after my first birthday, my parents came to my birth mother's house and took me from her. She did not want to let me go, but she could not challenge my parents. They were economically and politically powerful in her city. So she had to give me up, and I, of course, soon forgot her.

She became mentally disordered for a while because of her intense feelings of helplessness and sadness. Even when she recovered from the mental disorder, she could not regain her physical strength for a long time. She said she spent more than a year crying and missing her child. My parents had commanded her not to see me until I had married and borne my first child.

My father was kind to her, but my mother was not. Once my birth mother visited my parents' home because she missed me so much, but my mother did not even allow her to enter the house. My birth mother kept a record of the days of my life. She showed me an old photo album. Surprisingly enough, there I was, first as an infant, a student, and at other stages of my life. She said my father had sent her photos of me, and she kept them carefully. She had watched me and prayed for me for thirty years. They were prayers offered from the shadow of history.

She had inquired after my well-being in various ways. She knew what happened to me in my primary school, high school, and college years. She asked people who had gone to school with me about my activities, but always without revealing her relationship to me. She deliberately did not make herself known to me in order not to hurt my feelings or jeopardize my future. In Korean tradition, children who are born by a *ci-baji* woman are not considered legitimate; they are like second-class children. In the Yi Dynasty, which lasted until the dawn of the twentieth century in Korea, those who were born of a surrogate mother could not take exams to hold governmental offices. This tradition still thrives in Korean society today, although in a subtle way. That is why she did not want to reveal herself to me. She remained hidden for my sake.

I stayed with her for two days before returning to the United States. When she fell asleep, I looked into her face. White hair and many wrinkles told me of her hard life's journey. In her face, I met all Korean women who had been erased into the underside of "he-story." I held her hand and cried.

Marriage and Motherhood

These are the stories of two women. One had the privilege of being a "legitimate" wife and mother but continuously wondered about the meaning of marriage. She had the safety of assured food, clothing, and shelter because she was a legitimate wife, but she also had to accept her husband's affair—also "legitimate"—because she was barren. She wanted freedom badly, but she could not go beyond the rules of Korean society.

The other woman was denied the privilege of being a legitimate wife and mother because she was not officially married to my father. This "illegitimacy" put her on the underside of history. She became a "no-name" woman, who was nearly erased from my family history. Even though she was productive, she was unable to claim her right and space as mother of the child to whom she had given life. She was threatened continuously by poverty because she did not have a legitimate husband, whose duty, according to Korean tradition, would have been to take care of his wife.

My mothers hated each other. The one who raised me resented the one who gave birth to me because she thought this woman took her husband's love away. She might better have hated her husband, but she could not; he was the one who gave her security within the structure of society. All her anger and frustration were projected onto my birth mother, the safest target to attack. For her part, my birth mother hated the mother who raised me, because she took her baby and thus became the "legitimate" mother of her child. And of course my birth mother missed me even more because the mother who raised me did not allow her to see me.

Both mothers loved their child. I really believe the mother who raised me loved me as a birth mother would have. In many ways, she totally devoted herself to me, always being there when I needed her. I still remember vividly the way she treated me, taking me everywhere she went, decorating my hair with many colorful ribbons. She often told me I was the most beautiful girl in the world, even though I was not a pretty girl at all in the ordinary sense.

When I prepared for the junior high school and senior high school entrance exams, she brought warm lunches, freshly cooked, to my school every day in order to encourage my studies. My success in school was very important to her. Once I was almost forced to drop out of college because I could not afford the tuition. At that time my father was bankrupt. We had moved to a very poor neighborhood and hardly had enough money to cover everyday expenses. I decided to give up my studies, but she would not let me. She promised to borrow some money from her close friends. On the day she was to bring the money, I sat in the registrar's office, waiting for her. Hours passed, but she did not come. I almost gave up. Then, near closing time, I saw her: my elderly mother running to the registrar's office in my college. She was sweating. I could see she was exhausted, but also relieved. Very gently, she placed the money in my hand. I broke into tears. Sobbing, I asked her, "Mother, where did you get this money? I know you have been worried about buying even the basic things." Her eyes filled with tears too. "Don't worry about that. God provided the money. You just study hard." I loved her from the deepest part of my heart. Even though I was confused by her ambivalent remarks concerning marriage and femininity, she provided me with the space I needed to explore my own daring ideas. In the ways that matter, I was her "own" child.

My birth mother loved me too. She wanted me to be the legitimate child of a good family. She did not want to ruin my social image, to make me subject to the scornful strictures that Confucian culture in the Korean tradition sets for those born outside of marriage. That was why she spent thirty years following my life from the shadows. She showed her love for me by waiting and erasing herself totally from my personal history. She told me how much she wanted to come for my college graduation and marriage ceremony. I was *her* "own" child too.

When I met my birth mother in Korea last summer, she talked about my late mother with both anger and gratitude. She was angry because my late mother despised her, yet she was thankful that I had been raised to be a healthy and strong woman.

Both my mothers were victims of a male-defined family system. My father benefited from both women. He received everyday nurturing from my late mother and a child from my birth mother. Since a child is necessary to continue a man's family lineage in Korean culture, he did not feel any social pressure against having a relationship with another woman outside of wedlock. It seemed little more than the natural order of things. But both of my mothers suffered from this social system. For them, it was not a small thing.

The only person who could bring about reconciliation between these two women was their child. Their child was the only connecting factor that could ease the bitterness between them. The love they felt for me enabled them to accept each other in spite of the chasm between them, a chasm caused by the action of a man who held so much power over them.

These are the stories, then, of two mothers who shared a child, the lives of three women bound together by love and embittered by a tradition that honors only men.

Choosing Life: My Mothers' Spirituality

Sometimes I wonder how my mothers could sustain their sanity. My late mother struggled with the burden of being a noble woman within a strenuous marriage that did not acknowledge her humanity, and my birth mother struggled to retain her dignity in the context of continuous poverty and social ostracism. As I now reflect on both mothers' histories, I realize that they used all the life-giving resources they could find around them in order to keep their lives going.

My late mother was officially a Christian. She was a member of a big church in Seoul, where she participated in a strong women's mission group. She played the role of a nice Christian lady in that church. The mission group program gave her an opportunity to express herself in a public area, providing a legitimate excuse to go out of the house. Through that program she found her self-worth as a "public" person.

However, her Christian faith was not dogmatic. She changed Christian doctrine to suit her own convenience. For example, she had a very interesting view of our ancestor spirit and developed her own religious system. Since my father was a Confucianist, my mother's duty as his wife was to prepare big feast meals for ancestor worship two or three times a month, despite the fact that many Christian churches in Korea still taught that ancestor worship contradicted the Christian faith. One day when I was six years old, one of my friends told me something she had learned in Sunday school: "You will go to hell if you continue to worship your ancestors!" This was a real shock to me, because I wanted to go to heaven. So on the next ancestor worship day, I asked my mother about the relationship between the Christian God and my ancestors. My mother answered that my ancestors were secretaries of Jesus Christ, who was a god to my mother. "Because Jesus Christ is so busy in heaven," she said, "he can't take care of every detail of our lives. That's why Jesus Christ uses our ancestors as his secretaries to get things done." My mother's answer relieved me of the fear of going to hell.

Mother seemed to have created a peace for herself between Christian faith and Confucian practice. Both figured prominently in her religious life. She also drew spiritual strength from other strains of traditional Korean religiosity. For example, she often went to female fortune-tellers when she really had a life crisis. She did not go to see Christian ministers—males—to solve her personal problems, even though she was officially a Christian.

My mother also went to a Buddhist temple from time to time, whenever she wanted to meet her women friends and play or dance with them. Korean Buddhism did not prohibit women from drinking, smoking, or dancing during Buddhist festivals—very different from the teaching of Christian missionaries. When Buddha's birthday came, she went to the temple and celebrated with her women friends, drinking and dancing. Some orthodox Christians would say my mother was a heretic because she mixed religions and did not know the real essence of Christianity. Maybe she did not know what was orthodoxy and what was heresy, but she *did* know which things offered life-giving power. And she grasped them with both hands.

My birth mother went through a spiritual journey similar to my late mother's, even though she was extremely underprivileged by comparison. She said she was a Buddhist when she was young, and she had two dreams about my arrival into the world while she was pregnant.

In her first dream, she was inside the temple, holding me piggyback while bowing down to the Buddha. When she finished her bow, the big bell suspended at the temple ceiling began to ring. She immediately knew that my arrival was Buddha's blessing. In a second dream, she saw my father sitting on a small pagoda on Mudeng Mountain in Kwang-Ju. He was wearing a rainbow outfit. Then an amazing thing happened. When she approached my father, Mudeng Mountain suddenly changed to salt. It became Salt Mountain. Salt is a positive symbol in the Korean shamanistic tradition. Korean people believe that salt has the power to exorcise evil spirits. My birth mother received an affirmation of her pregnancy from the Buddha and indigenous Korean spirits. We Koreans call dreams that are connected with a pregnancy *tae-mong*—dreams that show the future of the baby.

My birth mother believed in her dreams. Even though Korean society did not approve of her pregnancy, she knew that the baby came through Buddha's compassion and protection from evil spirits. I was so grateful to her for remembering the details of her *tae-mong*. I felt connected to the ocean of Asian traditions and to the revolutionary spirit of Kwang-Ju, a small city that has been the city of freedom fighters in Korean tradition. She said I was born there; I did not know that. My parents had changed my birthplace on the official governmental records in order to hide my real origin.

My birth mother also visited fortune-tellers in order to check on my well-being. They told her that I would be a great scholar, and she believed them. She said to me she *knew* that I would be very good at school and finally would actually become a scholar. There were no doubts in her mind.

Now she is a deacon in a pentecostal church in Korea. I know the church very well. I hated that church so much as a theological student; I used to think it was dispensing otherworldly, ahistorical religious opium to the people. But after hearing my birth mother's painful life story, I came to understand why she chose that church. Maybe that church was the only place where she felt comfortable, where her spirit was lifted out of this painful world and given a place to dream. This kind of religion can easily become an opiate for people who have no options, no routes out of their personal impasses. Opium is like a magician, for those who have no access to change; it enables them to endure intolerable pain.

My two mothers mixed and matched all the spiritual resources they found around them and established their own comfortable religious cosmos in their hearts. Their center of spirituality was not Jesus, Buddha, Confucius, or any of the various fortune-tellers. All these religious personalities and spirits helped my mothers in various stages of their life journeys, but none dominated their inner life. The real center for their spirituality was life itself. They consciously and unconsciously— mostly the latter—selected the life-giving aspects of each religion and rejected the death-giving ones. As Alice Walker said of her great-grandmother's spirituality, my mothers "knew, even without 'knowing' it." It was a matter of the epistemology of the body. Maybe their conscious selves could not catch up with what their body said because their conscious selves were not ready for the "new paradigm." Orthodoxy and heresy debates were meaningless to them, since the words themselves were unfamiliar. Most Korean women of my mothers' age could not go beyond a primary-school education. Their fathers did not send them to school. Higher education was for boys. Boys, therefore, learned how to fight against heresies, how to safeguard their narrow, privileged circles for orthodoxy. Girls did not learn the fancy words in their primary schools.

My mothers made "chemical changes" in traditional religions by infusing them with the liberative thrusts of already existing religions. Since women were excluded from the public process of determining the meaning of religion, they were free to carve out a religion on their own, without the constraints of orthodoxy. Their "imposed freedom" allowed them to develop in private a religious organic whole that enabled them to survive and liberated them in the midst of their struggle for full humanity. I want to name my mothers' distinctive spirituality as "survival-liberation-centered syncretism." The heart of their spirituality was the life power that sustained and liberated them. "Life-giving power" is the final criterion by which the validity of any religion is judged.

Inheriting My Mothers' Gardens
Through Naked Dancing and Dreaming

Inheriting my mothers' gardens is a dangerous business because I inherited not only their flowers and fruits but also their insects. If I am not a good gardener, the insects will destroy my mothers' gardens. I have to look very closely at the flowers and fruits in order to pick out the insects.

I found some insects in my late mother's garden. They may be called classism, the caste system, and cultural imperialism. Since her husband had money and she was his first and only legitimate wife, my mother used her privilege against another woman, my birth mother. Still, my late mother wanted to get out of her suffocating Korean housewife's role. The problem was that she could not find many channels for her liberation.

Under the patriarchal system, which is defined by the interests of men only, women are separated among themselves according to men's needs. Because women are not the subject of their destiny and relationships but are the object of men's desire and pleasure, women are not raised to make active life-affirming relationships with other women. They are trained only to develop intimate relationships with men, and then only at the men's convenience. Under this patriarchal system, women cannot love each other. They have to be competitive and become enemies to each other because their human worth can only be affirmed by men. In my mothers' hatred for each other, I can see the most dangerous insect: patriarchy.

My late mother thought about the Western world as a model for the liberated world; she judged it by what she saw in the movies and magazines. She knew Western men opened doors for women and gave flowers to them and said "Ladies first." Therefore, my late mother assumed that Western men respected women. That was why she told me to marry one. Oh, dear Mom, I'll tell you: Even in the Western world, women are not respected and understood as you thought.

I am glad my father went bankrupt when I was eleven years old. We became very poor after that, and I learned how the majority of Korean people lived. Through the experience of poverty after my father's bankruptcy, I could see the class privilege of our family and the role we played in Korean society. This experience prepared me for the student movement and Minjung theology and finally enabled me to welcome my birth mother without feeling ashamed of her.

In my birth mother's garden, I can find some insects too. Her internalized defeat took away all her power for fighting even before she started her battle against my late parents. She could not fight in this world; her consciousness told her so. She retreated to her own interior mental world, had bitter fighting there, and became mentally disordered. Mom, I am not going to run away into my inner world. I'll fight in this world, in this history, to claim my land and my power!

However, in spite of all these insects, I love my mothers' gardens. In view of the legacies of these gardens, the fruits and insects, what does it mean for me to be a theologian? It means that I must use the fruits they bequeathed to me to help create a perspective on religion that is liberating for women, a perspective that will enable us to claim our life-giving power. No longer will I accept a male-dominated religion or society but will fight until freedom comes for all women. My understanding of God is not primarily defined by the doctrines and ritualistic practices of Christian churches, Buddhist temples, or any other religion. God is found in the life experiences of poor people, the majority of them women and children, and She is giving them power not only to survive amid wretched conditions but also to overcome those conditions. The beauty of the flowers in my mothers' gardens makes me cry with joy; the bittersweetness of their fruits makes me refreshed and nourished.

> Dear Moms!
>
> Today is a beautiful day. I invite both of you to my garden. My garden is not fancy, but I am growing some strong, healthy flowers, vegetables, and fruit trees. I named them Eve, Mother of All; Mary, Mother of Jesus; Kwan-In, goddess of compassion; Pārvatī, goddess of cosmic dance; Sarah; Hagar; Du-Ran; Kwang-Myung; and many other women I like.
>
> Here you can dance the naked dance again. I'll join you this time, not crying but laughing. Mary will sing the Magnificat for your dance. Sarah and Hagar will teach you the circle dance. They're a great team. You'll like them.
>
> You would be surprised if you knew how similar your life experiences are to theirs. Pārvatī is a great dancer too. We'll have a spirit-lifting dance festival. If we become tired after joyful dancing, we can take a rest under Eve's apple tree. We can share her apples when we become hungry. Then we can take a nice nap under Kwan-In's Boddi tree. She'll lead us to a fantastic dream world. You'll meet many wise people in your dream.
>
> How does it sound? Exciting, isn't it? Next year, I want to invite many other sisters from various parts of the world to my garden. We'll have a great time together.
>
> Then, maybe next-next-next year, when my plants and trees become stronger, I will invite my fathers and brothers too, if they promise not to play war games in my garden. Then we'll have a family reunion.
>
> Moms, thank you! I am so glad you taught me how to be a gardener. I am so proud of both of you.
>
> Shalom!
>
> > Much love,
> > Your daughter, *Hyun Kyung*

27 September 1987

어머니

회색 빛 뉴욕의 추운 거리를 걸으며 어머니를 생각합니다. 세)찬 바람이 뼈 속 까지 스며드는 이 겨울, 당신의 따뜻한 품이 더욱 그립습니다. 언제나 "어머니"로만 여겨졌던 당신이 이제는 비로소 한 여성으로, 한 인간으로 느껴집니다. 이제는 당신과 만나 밤을 새며 여자로서 느끼는 저의 기쁨과 보람, 분함과 억울함 그리고 황홀함을 어머니께 다 이야기 할 수 있을 것 같은데, 당신의 말씀들 웃으며 울며 들을 수 있을 것 같은데 당신은 이 세상을 떠나셨군요. 공부한다고 이국 땅에 있으면서 어머니의 임종도 지켜보지 못한 것이 응어리져 가슴이 남아있읍니다.

어머니가 돌아가신 후, 여성 신학을 공부하면서 당신을 많이 생각했었읍니다. 남성 중심의 문화에 의해 지워졌던 여성들의 삶의 역사를 들춰 내면서, 제가 이해할 수 없었던 당신의 행동과 말씀들이 하나 하나 이해되기 시작했읍니다. 어머니, 기억하세요? 25년 전 여름, 어머니와 저와 둘이 경상도 두메 산골의 어머니 친정 집을 방문하였던 때, 당신이 옷을 벗으시고 일찍 오시는 숲속에서 노래하며 춤 추시던 걸요. 그 때 저는 비록 그 살았겠지만 당신같은 어머니를 둔 것이 창피 하여 소리 지르며 울었읍니다. 그 때 당신의 모습은 제게는 잊어버리고만 싶었던 어머니의 모습이었읍니다. 그러나 세월이 지나 제가 성후이 넘고 보니, 그리고 어머니를 한 여성으로 한 인간으로 이해 하게 되니, 어머니의 그 모습이 사랑스럽고 자랑스럽습니다. 이제는 왜 어머니가 숲 속에서 불을 뿜듯 춤을 추셨는지 이해 할 수 있을 것 같습니다. 특히 고래의 사촌 언니로 부터 제 출생에 관련된 비밀을 듣고서, 아버지가 딴 여성에게서 낳아 온 저를 키우셨던, 임신할 수 없어 여자취급도 못 받고 살아 오신 어머니의 삶이 가슴 아프게 다가 옵니다.

어머니의 벌거벗은 춤은 아기를 낳아야만 여자고, 남편이 외도를 하건 구박을 하건 한 남자 만을 죽을 때까지 섬겨야한다는 남성들이 만든 놓은 종교, 문화, 제도 속에서, 속으로만 속으로만 분과 한을 쌓고 살으셨던 어머니와 많은 한국 여성들의 자유와 해방을 향한 몸부림이 있읍니다. 이제는 저도 어머니와 함께 그 춤을 출 수 있을 것 같습니다. 가부장적 문화가 우리 여성 들에게 입혀 놓은 그 거짓의 옷을 벗고, 벌거 벗은 몸으로 분을 뿜어 내며, 한을 풀어 내며 어머니와 함께 명실

명실 해방춤을 추고 싶습니다. 그 춤의 열기 속에서 거짓
제도, 거짓 문화, 거짓 종교가 다 버리고, 새 질서, 새 문화,
새 하나님 이해가 탄생할 것을 저는 믿습니다.

어머니, 어머니가 그렇게 질투하시고 미워하시되 저를
낳아주신 어매를 천국에 만났습니다. 그 어머니도 당신만큼
강하고 아름다우신 분이더군요. 정식으로 아버지와 결혼도 못하시고
"씨받이"로 저를 낳아 어머니께 빼앗기신 후 눈물도 많이
흘리셨고 가슴도 많이 찢기셨더군요. 정식 남편없이 아기
를 낳은 여자가 한국 사회에서 겪어야만 했던 모든 수모를
다 받으시고도, 가난하지만 꿋꿋하게 고통을 이기면서 살아
오신 그 분을 이제는 어머니도 사랑하실 수 있으리라고
믿습니다. 비록, 이 세상에서는 당신들 두 분이 남성들에
의해 규정되었던 제도 속에서 서로를 "적"으로 미워하셨지만,
앞으로의 만남에서는 이 생에서 겪었던 강요된 아픔과
"한" 때문에 서로를 더욱 더 이해하고 사랑하실 수 있는
"자매"가 되실 것을 기도해 봅니다. 이제는 우리 세 모녀가,
그리고 "한" 많은 한국 여성들이 우주를 뒤흔드는 춤을 출
시간이 돌아왔습니다. 해방의 춤, 자유의 춤, 정의의 춤,
평화의 춤, 화해의 춤을 출 시간이 말입니다.

어머니, 이제 당신의 딸의 세대는 더 이상 역사의
그늘 속에서 눈물 흘리며 한숨 짓는 역사의 희생자로 남아있어
새 역사를 만드는, 새 창조를 만드는 역사의 주체로서
찢기우고 상처 투성이인 우리 민족의 아픔을, 분단의 아픔을
온 몸으로 느끼며 우리를 노예화하는 모든 악의 세력과
싸울 것입니다. 당신들께서 저희를 낳으시고 키우시며
생명을 주신 것 같이, 어머니의 딸들도 이 땅위에 새 역사
를 낳고 키우며 우리 민족에게 생명을 주려 합니다. 춤추며
싸우는 당신들의 딸들을 지켜 봐 주세요.

어머니! 큰 춤사위를 휘두르며, 지축을 흔드는
울림을 하며, 명실 덩실, 엉덩이를 흔들흔들, 어깨를 으쓱
으쓱, 멋드러지게, 신명나게 저와함께 그 해방춤을
지금 다시 추지 않으시렵니까요?

" 여성 ～～ 해방 ～～ 신천지 ! "

덩 딱기 덩 딱 ! 더덩 딱기 덩 딱 ! 얼쑤 !

· · · · · · · · · · · · · · ·

1988 . 1 . 25
당신의 딸, 현경 올림

A Border Passage: From Cairo to America—A Woman's Journey

❖ *Leila Ahmed* ❖

It is easy to see now that our lives in the Alexandria house, and even at Zatoun, were lived in women's time, women's space. And in women's culture.

And the women had, too, I now believe, their own understanding of Islam, an understanding that was different from men's Islam, "official" Islam. For although in those days it was only Grandmother who performed all the regular formal prayers, for all the women of the house, religion was an essential part of how they made sense of and understood their own lives. It was through religion that one pondered the things that happened, why they had happened, and what one should make of them, how one should take them.

Islam, as I got it from them, was gentle, generous, pacifist, inclusive, somewhat mystical—just as they themselves were. Mother's pacifism was entirely of a piece with their sense of the religion. Being Muslim was about believing in a world in which life was meaningful and in which all events and happenings were permeated (although not always transparently to us) with meaning. Religion was above all about inner things. The outward signs of religiousness, such as prayer and fasting, might be signs of a true religiousness but equally well might not. They were certainly not what was important about being Muslim. What was important was how you conducted yourself and how you were in yourself and in your attitude toward others and in your heart.

What it was to be Muslim was passed on not, of course, wordlessly but without elaborate sets of injunctions or threats or decrees or dictates as to what we should do and be and believe. What was passed on, besides the very general basic beliefs and moral ethos of Islam, which are also those of its sister monotheisms, was a way of being in the world. A way of holding oneself in the world—in relation to God, to existence, to other human beings. This the women passed on to us most of all through how they were and by their being and presence, by the way *they* were in the world, conveying their beliefs, ways, thoughts, and how we should be in the world by a touch, a glance, a word—prohibiting, for instance, or approving. Their mere responses in this or that situation—a word, a shrug, even just their postures—passed on to us, in the way that women (and also men) have forever passed on to their young, how we should be. And all of these ways of passing on attitudes, morals, beliefs, knowledge—through touch and the body and in words spoken in the living moment—are by their very nature subtle and evanescent. They profoundly shape the next generation, but they do not leave a record in the way that someone writing a text about how to live or what to believe leaves a record. Nevertheless, they leave a far more important and, literally, more vital, living record. Beliefs, morals, attitudes passed on to and impressed on us through those fleeting words and gestures are written into our very lives, our bodies, our selves, even into our physical cells and into how we live out the script of our lives.

It was Grandmother who taught me the *fat-ha* (the opening verse of the Quran and the equivalent of the Christian Lord's Prayer) and who taught me two or three other short suras (Quranic verses). When she took me up onto the roof of the Alexandria house to watch for angels on the night of the twenty-seventh of Ramadan, she recited the sura about that special night, a sura that was also by implication about the miraculousness of night itself. Even now I remember its loveliness. It is still my favorite sura.

I remember receiving little other direct religious instruction, either from Grandmother or from anyone else. I have already described the most memorable exchange with my mother on the subject of religion—when, sitting in her room, the windows open behind her onto the garden, the curtain billowing, she quoted to me the verse in the Quran that she believed summed up the essence of Islam: "He who kills one being [*nafs*, self, from the root *nafas*, breath] kills all of humanity, and he who revives, or gives life to, one being revives all of humanity." It was a verse that she quoted often, that came up in any important conversation about God, religion, those sorts of things. It represented for her the essence of Islam.

I happened to be reading, when I was thinking about all this, the autobiography of Zeinab al-Ghazali, one of the most prominent Muslim women leaders of our day. Al-Ghazali founded a Muslim Women's Society that she eventually merged with the Muslim Brotherhood, the "fundamentalist" association that was particularly active in the forties and fifties. Throughout her life she openly espoused a belief in the legitimacy of using violence in the cause of Islam. In her memoir, she writes of how in her childhood her father told her stories of the heroic women of early Islam who had written poetry eulogizing Muslim warriors and who themselves had gone to war on the battlefields of Islam and gained renown as fearless fighters. Musing about all this and about the difference between al-Ghazali's Islam and my mother's pacifist understanding of it, I found myself falling into a meditation on the seemingly trivial detail that I, unlike al-Ghazali, had never heard as a child or a young girl stories about the women of early Islam, heroic or otherwise. And it was then that I suddenly realized the difference between al-Ghazali and my mother and between al-Ghazali's Islam and my mother's.

The reason I had not heard such stories as a child was quite simply that those sorts of stories (when I was young, anyway) were to be found only in the ancient classical texts of Islam, texts that only men who had studied the classical Islamic literary heritage could understand and decipher. The entire training at Islamic universities—the training, for example, that al-Ghazali's father, who had attended al-Azhar

University, had received—consisted precisely in studying those texts. Al-Ghazali had been initiated into Islam and had got her notions as to what a Muslim was from her father, whereas I had received my Islam from the mothers, as had my mother. So there are two quite different Islams, an Islam that is in some sense a women's Islam and an official, textual Islam, a "men's" Islam.

And indeed it is obvious that a far greater gulf must separate men's and women's ways of knowing, and the different ways in which men and women understand religion, in the segregated societies of the Middle East than in other societies—and we know that there are differences between women's and men's ways of knowing even in non-segregated societies such as America. For, beside the fact that women often could not read (or, if they were literate, could not decipher the Islamic texts, which require years of specialist training), women in Muslim societies did not attend mosques. Mosque going was not part of the tradition for women at any class level (that is, attending mosque for congregational prayers was not part of the tradition, as distinct from visiting mosques privately and informally to offer personal prayers, which women have always done). Women therefore did not hear the sermons that men heard. And they did not get the official (male, of course) orthodox interpretations of religion that men (or some men) got every Friday. They did not have a man trained in the orthodox (male) literary heritage of Islam telling them week by week and month by month what it meant to be a Muslim, what the correct interpretation of this or that was, and what was or was not the essential message of Islam.

Rather they figured these things out among themselves and in two ways. They figured them out as they tried to understand their own lives and how to behave and how to live, talking them over together among themselves, interacting with their men, and returning to talk them over in their communities of women. And they figured them out as they listened to the Quran and talked among themselves about what they heard. For this was a culture, at all levels of society and throughout most of the history of Islamic civilization, not of reading but of the common recitation of the Quran. It was recited by professional reciters, women as well as men, and listened to on all kinds of occasions—at funerals and births and celebratory events, in illness, and in ordinary life. There was merit in having the Quran chanted in your house and in listening to it being chanted wherever it was chanted, whereas for women there was no merit attached to attending mosque, an activity indeed prohibited to women for most of history. It was from these together, their own lives and from hearing the words of the Quran, that they formed their sense of the essence of Islam.

Nor did they feel, the women I knew, that they were missing anything by not hearing the exhortations of sheikhs, nor did they believe that the sheikhs had an understanding of Islam superior to theirs. On the contrary. They had little regard, the women I knew, for the reported views and opinions of most sheikhs. Although occasionally there might be a sheikh who was regarded as a man of genuine insight and wisdom, the women I knew ordinarily dismissed the views and opinions of the common run of sheikhs as mere superstition and bigotry. And these, I emphasize, were not Westernized women. Grandmother, who spoke only Arabic and Turkish, almost never set foot outside her home and never even listened to the radio. The dictum that "there is no priesthood in Islam"—meaning that there is no intermediary or interpreter, and no need for an intermediary or interpreter, between God and each individual Muslim and how that Muslim understands his or her religion—was something these women and many other Muslims took seriously and held on to as a declaration of their right to their own understanding of Islam.

No doubt particular backgrounds and subcultures give their own specific flavors and inflections and ways of seeing to their understanding of religion, and I expect that the Islam I received from the women among whom I lived was therefore part of their particular subculture. In this sense, then, there are not just two or three different kinds of Islam but many, many different ways of understanding and of being Muslim. But what is striking to me now is not how different or rare the Islam in which I was raised is but how ordinary and typical it seems to be in its base and fundamentals. Now, after a lifetime of meeting and talking with Muslims from all over the world, I find that this Islam is one of the common varieties—perhaps even *the* common or garden variety—of the religion. It is the Islam not only of women but of ordinary folk generally, as opposed to the Islam of sheikhs, ayatollahs, mullahs, and clerics. It is an Islam that may or may not place emphasis on ritual and formal religious practice but that certainly pays little or no attention to the utterances and exhortations of sheikhs or any sort of official figures. Rather it is an Islam that stresses moral conduct and emphasizes Islam as a broad ethos and ethical code and as a way of understanding and reflecting on the meaning of one's life and of human life more generally.

This variety of Islam (or, more exactly perhaps, these familial varieties of Islam, existing in a continuum across the Muslim world) consists above all of Islam as essentially an aural and oral heritage and a way of living and being—and not a textual, written heritage, not something studied in books or learned from men who studied books. This latter Islam, the Islam of the texts, is a quite different, quite other Islam: it is the Islam of the arcane, mostly medieval written heritage in which sheikhs are trained, and it is "men's" Islam. More specifically still, it is the Islam erected by that minority of men who over the centuries have created and passed on to one another this particular textual heritage: men who, although they have always been a minority in society as a whole, have always been those who made the laws and wielded (like the ayatollahs of Iran today) enormous power in their societies. The Islam they developed in this textual heritage is very like the medieval Latinate textual heritage of Christianity. It is as abstruse and obscure and as dominated by medieval and exclusively male views of the world as are those Latin texts. Imagine believing that those medieval texts on Christianity represent today the only true and acceptable interpretation of Christianity. But that is exactly what the sheikhs and ayatollahs propound and this is where things stand now in much of the Muslim world: most of the classic Islamic texts that still determine Muslim law in our day date from medieval times.

Aurally what remains when you listen to the Quran over a lifetime are its most recurring themes, ideas, words, and permeating spirit, reappearing now in this passage, now in that: mercy, justice, peace, compassion, humanity, fairness, kindness, truthfulness, charity, mercy, justice. And yet it is exactly these recurring themes and this permeating spirit that are for the most part left out of the medieval texts or smothered and buried under a welter of obscure and abstruse "learning." One would scarcely believe, reading or hearing the laws these texts have yielded, particularly when it comes to women, that the words "justice," "fairness," "compassion," "truth," ever even occur in the Quran. No wonder non-Muslims think Islam is such a backward and oppressive religion: what these men made of it *is* largely oppressive. Still— to speak less judgmentally and, in fact, more accurately—the men who wrote the foundational texts of official Islam were living in societies and eras rife with chauvinism, eras when men believed as a matter of categorical certainty that God created them superior to women and fully intended them to have complete dominion over women. And yet, despite such beliefs and prejudices, here and there in the texts they created, in the details of this or that law, they wrote in some provision or condition that, astonishingly, does give justice to women. So, even in those bleak days, the Quran's recurring themes filtered through. They did so, however, only now and then in a body of law otherwise overwhelmingly skewed in favor of men.

I am sure, then, that my foremothers' lack of respect for the authority of sheikhs was not coincidental. Rather, I believe that this way of seeing and understanding was quite common among ordinary Muslims and that it was an understanding passed on from mothers and grandmothers to daughters and granddaughters. Generations of astute, thoughtful women, listening to the Quran, understood perfectly well its essential themes and its faith. And looking around them, they understood perfectly well, too, what a travesty men had made of it. This ingrained low opinion that they had of sheikhs, clerics, and ayatollahs stemmed from a perfectly just and astute understanding of their world, an understanding that they passed on to their daughters and indeed their sons.

Leaving no written legacy, written only on the body and into the scripts of our lives, this oral and aural tradition of Islam no doubt stretches back through generations and is as ancient as any written tradition.

One could even argue that an emphasis on an oral and aural Islam is intrinsic to Islam and to the Quran itself, and intrinsic even to the Arabic language. Originally the Quran was an aural, and only an aural, text recited to the community by the Prophet Muhammad. And it remained throughout his life, and indeed for several years after his death, only an aural text. Moreover, a bias in favor of the heard word, the word given life and meaning by the human voice, the human breath (*nafas*) is there, one might say, in the very language itself. In Arabic (and also Hebrew) script, no vowels are set down, only consonants. A set of consonants can have several meanings and only acquires final, specific, fixed meaning when given vocalized or silent utterance (unlike words in European script, which have the appearance, anyway, of being fixed in meaning). Until life is literally breathed into them, Arabic and Hebrew words on the page have no particular meaning. Indeed, until then they are not words but only potential words, a chaotic babble and possibility of meanings. It is as if they hold within them the scripts of those languages, marshaling their sets of bare consonants across the page, vast spaces in which meanings exist in a condition of whirling potentiality until the very moment that one is singled out and uttered. And so by their very scripts these two languages seem to announce the primacy of the spoken, literally living word, and to announce that meaning can only be here and now. Here and now in this body, this breath (*nafas*) this self (*nafs*) encountering the word, giving it life. Word that, without that encounter, has no life, no meaning. Meaning always only here and now, in this body, for this person. Truth only here and now, for this body, this person. Not something transcendent, overarching, larger, bigger, more important than life—but here and now and in this body and in this small and ordinary life.

We seem to be living through an era of the progressive, seemingly inexorable erasure of the oral and ethical traditions of lived Islam and, simultaneously, of the ever-greater dissemination of written Islam, textual, "men's" Islam (an Islam essentially not of the Book but of the Texts, the medieval texts) as *the* authoritative Islam. Worse still, this seems to be an era of the unstoppable spread of fundamentalist Islam, textual Islam's more narrow and more poorly informed modern descendant. It is a more ill-informed version of old-style offical Islam in that the practitioners of that older Islam usually studied many texts and thus at least knew that even in these medieval texts there were disagreements among scholars and many possible interpretations of this or that verse. But today's fundamentalists, literate but often having read just a single text, take it to be definitive and the one and only "truth."

Ironically, therefore, literacy has played a baneful part both in spreading a particular form of Islam and in working to erase oral and living forms of the religion. For one thing, we all automatically assume that those who write and who put their knowledge down in texts have something more valuable to offer than those who simply live their knowledge and use it to inform their lives. And we assume that those who write and interpret texts in writing—in the Muslim context, the sheikhs and ayatollahs, who are the guardians and perpetuators (perpetrators) of this written version of Islam—must have a better, truer, deeper understanding of Islam than the non–specially trained Muslim. Whereas the fact is that the only Islam that they have a deeper understanding of is their own gloomy, medieval version of it.

Even the Western academic world is contributing to the greater visibility and legitimacy of textual Islam and to the gradual silencing and erasure of alternative oral forms of lived Islam. For we too in the West, and particularly in universities, honor, and give pride of place to, texts. Academic studies of Islam commonly focus on its textual heritage or on visible, official institutions such as mosques. Consequently it is this Islam—the Islam of texts and of mosques—that becomes visible and that is presented as in some sense legitimate, whereas most of the Muslims whom I know personally, both in the Middle East and in Europe and America, would never go near a mosque or willingly associate themselves with any form of official Islam. Throughout history, official Islam has been our enemy and our oppressor. We have learned to live with it and to survive it and have developed dictums such as "There is no priesthood in Islam" to protect ourselves from it; we're not now suddenly and even in these new lands going to easily befriend it. It is also a particular and bitter irony to me that the very fashionableness of gender studies is serving to disseminate and promote medieval men's Islam as the "true" and "authentic" Islam. (It is "true" and "authentic" because it is based on old texts and represents what the Muslim male powers have considered to be true for centuries.) Professors, for example, including a number who have no sympathy whatever for feminism, are now jumping on the bandwagon of gender studies and directing a plethora of dissertations on this or that medieval text with titles like "Islam and Menstruation." But such dissertations should more aptly have titles along the lines of "A Study of Medieval Male Beliefs about Menstruation." For what, after all, do these men's beliefs, and the rules that they laid down on the basis of their beliefs, have to do with Islam? Just because they were powerful, privileged men in their societies and knew how to write, does this mean they have the right forever to tell us what Islam is and what the rules should be?

Still, these are merely word wars, wars of ideas that, for the present anyway, are of the most minor significance compared with the devastation unloosed on Muslim societies in our day by fundamentalism. What we are living through now seems to be not merely the erasure of the living oral, ethical, and humane traditions of Islam but the literal destruction and annihilation of the Muslims who are the bearers of those traditions. In Algeria, Iran, Afghanistan, and, alas, in Egypt, this narrow, violent variant of Islam is ravaging its way through the land.

If a day won't come
when the monuments of institutionalized religion are in ruin
. . . then, my beloved,
then we are really in trouble.

—RUMI

It has not been only women and simple, unlearned folk who have believed, like the women who raised me, that the ethical heart of Islam is also its core and essential message. Throughout Muslim history, philosophers, visionaries, mystics, and some of the civilization's greatest luminaries have held a similar belief. But throughout history, too, when they have announced their beliefs publicly, they have generally been hounded, persecuted, executed. Or, when they have held fast to their vision but also managed to refrain from overtly challenging the powers that be and thus avoided violent reprisal, they have been at best tolerated and marginalized— accepted as eccentrics outside the tradition of "true" Islam. From almost the earliest days, the Islam that has held sway and that has been supported and enforced by sheikhs, ayatollahs, rulers, states, and armies, has been official, textual Islam. This variant of Islam has wielded absolute power and has not hesitated to eradicate— often with the same brutality as fundamentalism today—all dissent, all differing views, all opposition.

There has never been a time when Muslims, in any significant number, have lived in a land in which freedom of thought and religion were accepted norms. Never, that is, until today. Now, in the wake of the migrations that came with the ending of the European empires, tens of thousands of Muslims are growing up in Europe and America, where they take for granted their right to think and believe whatever they wish and take for granted, most particularly, their right to speak and write openly of their thoughts, beliefs, and unbeliefs.

For Muslims this is, quite simply, a historically unprecedented state of affairs. Whatever Islam will become in this new age, surely it will be something quite other than the religion that has been officially forced on us through all these centuries.

All of this is true.

But the fact is that, however genuinely humane and gentle and pacifist my mother's and grandmother's Islam was, it left them and the women among whom they lived wholly accepting of the ways of their society in relation to women, even when those ways were profoundly destructive. They bowed their heads and acquiesced to them even when the people being crushed were their nearest and dearest. Tradition and the conviviality, warmth, companionship, and support of the women of the extended family were rich and fine and nourishing and wonderful so long as things went well and so long as these women were dealing with men whom they loved and who loved them. But when things went wrong, the women were powerless and acquiescent in a silence that seemed to me when I was young awfully like a guilty averting of the eyes, awfully like a kind of connivance.

This, in any case, seems to me to be what my aunt Aida's story points to.

Aida's marriage was absolutely miserable from the very start, but divorce, according to Grandfather, was simply not a permissible thing in his family. And yet his own niece Karima, my mother's cousin twice over (her parents were Grandmother's sister and Grandfather's brother), had divorced twice, and each time by her own volition. The difference was that Karima was an heiress, both her parents having died when she was young. Independent and wealthy, she had married on her own terms, ensuring always that the 'isma, the right to divorce, was placed by contract in her own hands. (The Islamic legal provision permitting women to make such contracts is one of those details that I mentioned earlier that are written into and buried deep in what is otherwise a body of law overwhelmingly biased in favor of men. Generally only rich women and women with knowledgeable, protective families are able to invoke these laws. Many people don't even know of their existence.) Aunt Aida had not inherited anything as yet and was financially dependent on her husband and her father.

Grandmother, grieving all her life over the cost of Grandfather's intransigence toward their son Fuad, was powerless to alter his decision about Aida. For all I know, Grandmother even acquiesced in the notion that divorce was so great a disgrace that, despite her daughter's misery, she could not bring herself to advocate that course or attempt to persuade Grandfather to relent. Karima, her own niece, always received, of course, with warmth and unconditional affection in their home, was nevertheless regarded by Grandmother and her daughters as somewhat scandalous, or at any rate as someone who was rather unconventional and living dangerously close to the edge of impropriety. Aunt Karima further added to her reputation for unconventionality when she founded an orphanage for illegitimate children. It was scandalous to men like Grandfather for respectable women even to mention such a subject, let alone to be founding a society and openly soliciting funds from him and his cronies to support an organization addressing the matter. She raised substantial funds for it over the course of her life as well as for another society, which she also founded, for the care and training of the blind. Both still flourish today and honor their founder. A bust of her stands in the front garden of the Society for the Blind.

Grandmother would not live to witness Aida's suicide. But she was witness to Aida's sufferings and unhappiness in her marriage, and the electric-shock treatment she underwent.

There is an irony to all this. In the circumstances in which Aida found herself, Islamic law would in fact have granted her the right to a divorce or an annulment. Had she been free to take her case to an Islamic court and had she not been constricted by the conventions of her people, she would have been granted, even by that male-created law, the release that she sought. Not by Grandfather and his customs or by Grandmother and her daughters and their conventions, steeped as they, too, were in the ways of their society, but by Islamic law, in another of those unexpected, startlingly just provisions of this otherwise male-biased construction.

Nor was this the only situation in the various family circumstances I've described when women would have been more justly treated at the hands of Islamic law than they were by the traditions of the society, traditions by which the women of the family, too, were evidently bound. Islamic law, for example, frowned on the practice, entirely accepted by cultural tradition, whereby a man repudiated a woman, as my dying uncle had done, because he doubted her virginity. Asked about such a case, a medieval Islamic judge responded that the man had no right to repudiate a woman by claiming she was not a virgin, since virginity could be lost in many ways—just by jumping about or any such thing. He could divorce her nevertheless, since men had the absolute right of divorce even if in the absence of a good reason, but the woman was entitled to full compensation and could not be regarded or treated as guilty of anything.

And so we cannot simply conclude that what I have called women's Islam is invariably good and to be endorsed. And conversely, everything about what I've called men's Islam is not to be automatically rejected, either.

> To refuse to veil one's voice and to start "shouting," that was really indecent, real dissidence. For the silence of all the others suddenly lost its charm and revealed itself for what it was: a prison without reprieve. . . .
>
> While I thought I was undertaking a "journey through myself," I find I am simply choosing another veil. While I intended every step forward to make me more clearly identifiable, I find myself progressively sucked down into the anonymity of those women of old—my ancestors!
>
> —ASSIA DJEBAR (ALGERIAN NOVELIST), *Fantasia*

If the women of my family were guilty of silence and acquiescence out of their inability to see past their own conditioning, I, too, have fallen in with notions instilled in me by my conditioning—and in ways that I did not even recognize until now, when, thinking about my foremothers, I suddenly saw in what I had myself just written my own unthinking collusion with the attitudes of the society in which I was raised. Writing of Aunt Farida and of how aggrieved and miserable she was when her husband took a second wife, I reproduced here without thinking the stories I'd heard as a youngster about how foolish Aunt Farida was, resorting to magic to bring back her husband. But I see now how those stories in effect rationalized and excused his conduct, implying that even though taking a second wife wasn't a nice way for a man to behave, perhaps he had some excuse, Aunt Farida being so foolish.

"The mind is so near itself," Emily Dickinson wrote, "it cannot see distinctly." Sometimes even the stories we ourselves tell dissolve before us as if a mist were momentarily lifting, and we glimpse in that instant our own participation in the myths and constructions of our societies. . . .

It was no easy transition, the transition to America and to women's studies.

First of all, live American feminism was not anything like what I had imagined. Reading its thoughtful texts in the quiet of the desert, I had, I suppose, formed a notion of feminism as tranquil, lucid, meditative—whereas, of course, the living feminism I encountered once on these shores was anything but a lucid, tranquil, meditative affair. Militant, vital, tempestuous, passionate, visionary, turbulent—any or all of these might be more apt. In the gatherings of feminists—at the various conferences, meetings, and public lectures that I now single-mindedly threw myself into attending—there was a kind of raw, exhilarating energy and a sense, intellectually, of freewheeling anarchy. Almost as if people felt themselves caught up in some holy purifying fire that was burning away the dross and obscurities from their minds, freeing them to dream dreams and see visions and to gather themselves up and prepare to unmake and remake the world, remake it as it had never been made before.

And all this *was* tremendously exhilarating and exciting. But along with exhilaration came shock. For I naturally made a point at these conferences of attending, and often participating in, sessions and panels on Muslim women. Not that these were common. The women's studies conferences I attended when I first came in 1980—I remember one at Barnard, and another in Bloomington, Indiana—focused primarily on white women and were overwhelmingly attended by white women. But such sessions on Muslim women as there were left me nearly speechless and certainly in shock at the combination of hostility and sheer ignorance that the Muslim panelists, myself included, almost invariably encountered. We could not pursue the investigation of our heritage, traditions, religion in the way that white women were investigating and rethinking theirs. Whatever aspect of our history or religion each of us had been trying to reflect on, we would be besieged, at the end of our presentations, with furious questions and declarations openly dismissive of Islam. People quite commonly did not even seem to know that there was some connection between the patriarchal vision to be found in Islam and that in Judaism and Christianity. Regularly we would be asked belligerently, "Well, what about the veil" or "What about clitoridectomy?" when none of us had mentioned either subject for the simple reason that it was completely irrelevant to the topics of our papers. The implication was that, in trying to examine and rethink our traditions rather than dismissing them out of hand, we were implicitly defending whatever our audience considered to be indefensible. And the further implication and presumption was that, whereas they—white women, Christian women, Jewish women—could rethink their heritage and religions and traditions, we had to abandon ours because they were just intrinsically, essentially, and irredeemably misogynist and patriarchal in a way that theirs (apparently) were not. In contrast to their situation, our salvation entailed not arguing with and working to change our traditions but giving up our cultures, religions, and traditions and adopting theirs.

And so the first thing I wrote after my arrival and within months of being in America was an article addressing the extraordinary barrage of hostility and ignorance with which I found myself besieged as I moved among this community of women. They were women who were engaged in radically rejecting, contesting, and rethinking their own traditions and heritage and the ingrained prejudices against women that formed part of that heritage but who turned on me a gaze completely structured and hidebound by that heritage; in their attitudes and beliefs about Islam and women in Islam, they plainly revealed their unquestioning faith in and acceptance of the prejudiced, hostile, and often ridiculous notions that their heritage had constructed about Islam and its women. I had come wanting to read and think and write about Muslim women, but it was this that commanded my attention as the subject that I desperately had to address. The first piece I wrote, "Western Ethnocentrism and Perceptions of the Harem," still rings for me with the shocked and furious tones of that initial encounter.

My first year in America, 1979, was also the year of the Iran hostage crisis, and I am sure now that the hostility toward Islam by which I felt myself besieged was more pronounced than usual because of that situation. But as I would learn soon enough, the task of addressing racism for feminists of color in the West is, and has to be, an ongoing and central part of the work and the thinking that we ordinarily do, no less so than the work of addressing male dominance. And so my first experience of American feminism was a kind of initiation and baptism by fire into what has indeed been an ongoing part of my thought and work ever since. Back then, though, it was still early in our understanding of the racist gaze the white feminist movement turned on women of other cultures and races. Audre Lorde, at a conference in 1976 (in a presentation much-anthologized since), was among the first to identify, and speak out against, this strand in white feminist thought, and June Jordan, Bell Hooks, and others followed up with work on the subject.

Also making my initial experience of America a more arduous experience than it might otherwise have been was the fact that I took a job in women's studies. I had come intent on working in this field and had applied for an advertised position as a part-time lecturer at the University of Massachusetts at Amherst. Although the pay was low, I felt that a part-time job was the sensible way into the field, whose scholarly productions I'd been reading out in the desert but about which I had still an enormous amount to learn. A part-time job would give me the time, I thought, to do all the extra reading that I no doubt needed to do.

Of course I found that my part-time job, as is so often the case, was only technically part-time. In fact, preparing classes, teaching, and attending meetings took up every moment of my waking life. I have never worked so hard in my life as in my first couple of years in America. Of course, too, the fact that everything was new to me contributed to making those years so tough. Teaching in a new academic system in a new country must always entail demanding transitions, but I am sure that my having joined a women's studies program, particularly at that moment in the history of women's studies in America, rather than, say, taking a job in a more established department, created a whole set of unique hurdles and difficulties.

Women's studies programs in that era, including the program that I joined, had an embattled and precarious relationship with the university. There was sometimes open hostility from faculty members in other departments and, occasionally, condescension and a presumption that the women's studies faculty must be ignorant, undereducated fanatical women. For me, as someone coming from abroad who had not been part of the American feminist movement, there was one very particular difficulty that I had not anticipated when I imagined that, by working hard and reading widely, I could quickly master the ideas, theories, perspectives that I needed to be familiar with. I could *not* quickly master them through reading, for the simple reason that a lot of them had not yet found their way into print. The ideas that I heard passionately voiced and argued around me by faculty and also by students were part of a rich, vibrant, diverse, and internally contentious cargo of debates that had been generated by an intellectually vital social movement. This was what I had stepped into in joining women's studies—a living social movement of quite extraordinary but as yet mainly oral intellectual vitality, about to spill over and become a predominantly intellectual, academic, and theoretical force rather than, as it had in part been in its beginnings, an activist social movement. It was the ideas that people had developed in their encounters and meetings and exchanges in their involvement in this movement, and the continuing evolution of these ideas, that were providing the foundations of women's studies. I stepped, that is to say, too, into the stream of what was as yet a largely unwritten oral culture—the oral, living culture of the feminist movement, a culture to which there were as yet almost no guides, no maps, no books.

There were often passionate debates, both among my colleagues and in the feminist community more widely, between, say, Radical feminists and Marxist feminists, debates that could become quite furious. It was clear that there was a history here, a common, shared evolution, in the course of which particular positions, in relation to this or that issue, had been progressively defined and sometimes had become polarized. But to someone arriving from the Arab Gulf, what these positions and issues were and why they should generate such passion was, at first anyway, profoundly unfathomable. And there was nothing, or very little, in those days, that I could read that would enlighten me and make the issues, debates, and history accessible. Moreover, this culture and history that I had not been part of informed nearly everything in women's studies, not only intellectual issues but also ordinary routines and exchanges and conversations. It was this culture, for instance, that determined that all decisions were to be made by consensus and not by vote. It determined, too, the code of dress—as strict here, in its way, as in Abu Dhabi. For those were the days when whether you shaved your legs or wore a bra signaled where you stood on the internal feminist battlelines and/or your degree of feminist enlightenment. In Abu Dhabi it had been easy to ask about appropriate dress and the meaning of this or that style, but here not only were you supposed to just *know*, but supposedly there was no dress code and people here—as I was emphatically told when I ventured the question in my early innocent days—simply dressed exactly how they wished. And so there were many ways in which the women's studies culture in which I found myself was an unknown culture to me to which I had no key and maps. But, as with any other culture, after a period of intense immersion, my confusion naturally resolved into comprehension.

Another difficulty arising from my being in women's studies was one I shared with my colleagues. An essentially new field, women's studies as yet had no set syllabi, no texts, no solid, extensive body of scholarship to draw on. And so even devising courses and syllabi and putting them together from photocopies was a demanding task. Even the novels and stories by women that were already being used and that would soon be the staples of feminist courses in literature were not yet in readily accessible form or were just being published and reissued, in large part thanks to the feminist movement and the demand created by women's studies. And the kind of material that a few years later would begin to be available on feminist theory, on women of color in America, on women in Islam, and so on, was also not yet available. In short, women's studies was still in the process of being invented, created, and developed as a field. My colleagues as well as I, a newcomer, were still groping our way forward in this as yet unstudied, uncharted, and indeed uninvented territory, for the most part without textbooks, without established syllabi, without a body of scholarship raising the questions that needed to be raised, setting them out, analyzing them, complicating them.

We are now, of course, in quite another place.

And I am now at the end point of the story I set out to tell here.

For thereafter my life becomes part of other stories, American stories. It becomes part of the story of feminism in America, the story of women in America, the story of people of color in America, the story of Arabs in America, the story of Muslims in America, and part of the story of America itself and of American lives in a world of dissolving boundaries and vanishing borders.

There are more Muslims today in America, it is said, than Episcopalians. We did not have, on these shores, an auspicious beginning. I think of Bilalia Fula, buried here, after his years of slavery, with his prayer rug and his Quran. I think of Al-Hajj Omar ibn Said, brought to this country in shackles when he was thirty-seven, as he wrote in his autobiography—one of the first Muslim autobiographies written in America. I think of the countless others brought here in the same way, who held on in their minds as long as they could to the world they were from, passing on to children and grandchildren, however they might, their vanishing memories.

But this now is another time. We are on the point of a new beginning.

White Women's Christ and Black Women's Jesus*

❖ Jacquelyn Grant ❖

The Beginnings of a Womanist Theology with Special Reference to Christology

Womanist theology begins with the experiences of Black women as its point of departure. This experience includes not only Black women's activities in the larger society but also in the churches and reveals that Black women have often rejected the oppressive structure in the church as well. . . .

The Starting Point for Womanist Theology

Because it is important to distinguish Black and White women's experiences, it is also important to note these differences in theological and Christological reflection. To accent the difference between Black and White women's perspective in theology, I maintain that Black women scholars should follow Alice Walker by describing our theological activity as "womanist theology." The term "womanist" refers to Black women's experiences. It accents, as Walker says, our being responsible, in charge, outrageous, courageous and audacious enough to demand the right to think theologically and to do it independently of both White and Black men and White women.

Black women must do theology out of their tri-dimensional experience of racism/sexism/classism. To ignore any aspect of this experience is to deny the holistic and integrated reality of Black womanhood. When Black women say that God is on the side of the oppressed, we mean that God is in solidarity with the struggles of those on the under side of humanity. . . .

. . . Black women, because of oppression determined by race and their subjugation as women, make up a disproportionately high percentage of the poor and working classes. However, the fact that Black women are a subjugated group even within the Black community and the White women's community does not mean that they are alone in their oppression within those communities. In the women's community poor White women are marginalized, and in the Black community, poor

Black men are also discriminated against. This suggests that classism, as well as racism and sexism, has a life of its own. Consequently, simply addressing racism and sexism is inadequate to bring about total liberation. Even though there are dimensions of class which are not directly related to race or sex, classism impacts Black women in a peculiar way which results in the fact that they are most often on the bottom of the social and economic ladder. For Black women doing theology, to ignore classism would mean that their theology is no different from any other bourgeois theology. It would be meaningless to the majority of Black women, who are themselves poor. This means that addressing only issues relevant to middle class women or Blacks will simply not do: the daily struggles of poor Black women must serve as the gauge for the verification of the claims of womanist theology.

The Use of the Bible in the Womanist Tradition

Theological investigation into the experiences of Christian Black women reveals that Black women considered the Bible to be a major source for religious validation in their lives. Though Black women's relationship with God preceded their introduction to the Bible, this Bible gave some content to their God-consciousness. The source for Black women's understanding of God has been twofold: first, God's revelation directly to them, and secondly, God's revelation as witnessed in the Bible and as read and heard in the context of their experience. The understanding of God as creator, sustainer, comforter, and liberator took on life as they agonized over their pain, and celebrated the hope that as God delivered the Israelites, they would be delivered as well. The God of the Old and New Testament became real in the consciousness of oppressed Black women. Though they were politically impotent, they were able to appropriate certain themes of the Bible which spoke to their reality. For example, Jarena Lee, a nineteenth century Black woman preacher in the African Methodist Episcopal Church constantly emphasized the theme "Life and Liberty" in her sermons which were always biblically based. This interplay of scripture and experience was exercised by many other Black women. An ex-slave woman revealed that when her experience negated certain oppressive interpretations of the Bible given by White preachers, she, through engaging the biblical message for herself rejected them. Consequently, she also dismissed White preachers who distorted the message in order to maintain slavery. Her grandson, Howard Thurman, speaks of her use of the Bible in this way:

> "During the days of slavery," she said, "the master's minister would occasionally hold services for the slaves. Always the white minister used as his text something from Paul. 'Slaves be obedient to them that are your masters . . . , as unto Christ.' Then he would go on to show how, if we were good and happy slaves, God would bless us. I promised my Maker that if I ever learned to read and if freedom ever came, I would not read that part of the Bible.

What we see here is perhaps more than a mere rejection of a White preacher's interpretation of the Bible, but an exercise in internal critique of the Bible. The Bible must be read and interpreted in the light of Black women's own experience of oppression and God's revelation within that context. Womanists must, like Sojourner, "compare the teachings of the Bible with the witness" in them.

To do Womanist Theology, then, we must read and hear the Bible and engage it within the context of our own experience. This is the only way that it can make sense to people who are oppressed. Black women of the past did not hesitate in doing this and we must do no less.

The Role of Jesus in the Womanist Tradition

In the experiences of Black people, Jesus was "all things." Chief among these however, was the belief in Jesus as the divine co-sufferer, who empowers them in situations of oppression. For Christian Black women in the past, Jesus was their central frame of reference. They identified with Jesus because they believed that Jesus identified with them. As Jesus was persecuted and made to suffer undeservedly, so were they. His suffering culminated in the crucifixion. Their crucifixion included rape, and babies being sold. But Jesus' suffering was not the suffering of a mere human, for Jesus was understood to be God incarnate. As Harold Carter observed of Black prayers in general, there was no difference made between the persons of the trinity, Jesus, God, or the Holy Spirit. "All of these proper names for God were used interchangeably in prayer language. Thus, Jesus was the one who speaks the world into creation. He was the power behind the Church. . . .

Black women's affirmation of Jesus as God meant that White people were not God. One old slave woman clearly demonstrated this as she prayed:

> "Dear Massa Jesus, we all uns beg Ooner [you] come make us a call dis yere day. We is nutting but poor Etiopian women and people ain't tink much 'bout we. We ain't trust any of dem great high people for come to we church, but do' you is de one great Massa, great too much dan Massa Linkum, you ain't shame to care for we African people."

This slave woman did not hesitate to identify her struggles and pain with those of Jesus. In fact, the common struggle made her know that Jesus would respond to her beck and call.

> "Come to we, dear Massa Jesus. De sun, he hot too much, de road am dat long and buggy (sandy) and we ain't got no buggy for send and fetch Ooner. But Massa, you 'member how you walked dat hard walk up Calvary and ain't weary but tink about we all dat way. We know you ain't weary for to come to we. We pick out de torns, de prickles, de brier, de backslidin' and de quarrel and de sin out of you path so dey shan't hurt Ooner pierce feet no more."

As she is truly among the people at the bottom of humanity, she can make things comfortable for Jesus even though she may have nothing to give him—no water, no food—but she can give tears and love. She continues:

> "Come to we, dear Massa Jesus. We all uns ain't got no good cool water for give you when you thirsty. You know, Massa, de drought so long, and the well so low, ain't nutting but mud to drink. But we gwine to take de 'munion cup and fill it wid de tear of repentance, and love clean out of we heart. Dat all we hab to gib you, good Massa."

For Black women, the role of Jesus unraveled as they encountered him in their experience as one who empowers the weak. In this vein, Jesus was such a central part of Sojourner Truth's life that all of her sermons made him the starting point. When asked by a preacher if the source of her preaching was the Bible, she responded "No honey, can't preach from de Bible—can't read a letter." Then she explained; "When I preaches, I has jest one text to preach from, an' I always preaches from this one. My text is, 'When I found Jesus!' " In this sermon Sojourner Truth recounts the events and struggles of her life from the time her parents were brought from Africa and sold "up an' down, an' hither an' yon. . . " to the time that she met Jesus within the context of her struggles for dignity of Black people and women. Her encounter with Jesus brought such joy that she became overwhelmed with love and praise:

> Praise, praise, praise to the Lord! An' I begun to feel such a love in my soul as I never felt before—love to all creatures. An' then, all of a sudden, it stopped, an' I said, Dar's de white folks that have abused you, an' beat you, an' abused your people—think o' them! But then there came another rush of love through my soul, an' I cried out loud—'Lord, I can love *even de white folks!*

This love was not a sentimental, passive love. It was a tough, active love that empowered her to fight more fiercely for the freedom of her people. For the rest of her life she continued speaking at abolition and women's rights gatherings, condemning the horrors of oppression.

The Significance of Jesus in the Womanist Tradition

More than anyone, Black theologians have captured the essence of the significance of Jesus in the lives of Black people which to an extent includes Black women. They all hold that the Jesus of history is important for understanding who he was and his significance for us today. By and large they have affirmed that this Jesus is the Christ, that is, God incarnate. They have argued that in the light of our experience, Jesus meant freedom. They have maintained that Jesus means freedom from the sociopsychological, psychocultural, economic and political oppression of Black people. In other words, Jesus is a political messiah. "To free (humans) from bondage was Jesus' own definition of his ministry." This meant that as Jesus identified with the lowly of his day, he now identifies with the lowly of this day, who in the American context are Black people. The identification is so real that Jesus Christ in fact becomes Black. It is important to note that Jesus' blackness is not a result of ideological distortion of a few Black thinkers, but a result of careful Christological investigation. . . . The condition of Black people today reflects the cross of Jesus. Yet the resurrection brings the hope that liberation from oppression is immanent. The resurrected Black Christ signifies this hope.

. . . "The least in America are literally and symbolically present in Black people." This notion of "the least" is attractive because it descriptively locates the condition of Black women. "The least" are those people who have no water to give, but offer what they have, as the old slave woman cited above says in her prayer. Black women's experience in general is such a reality. Their tri-dimensional reality renders their particular situation a complex one. One could say that not only are they the oppressed of the oppressed, but their situation represents "the particular within the particular."

But is this just another situation that takes us deeper into the abyss of theological relativity? I would argue that it is not, because it is in the context of Black women's experience where the particular connects up with the universal. By this I mean that in each of the three dynamics of oppression, Black women share in the reality of a broader community. They share race suffering with Black men; with White women and other Third World women, they are victims of sexism; and with poor Blacks and Whites, and other Third World peoples, especially women, they are disproportionately poor. To speak of Black women's tri-dimensional reality, therefore, is not to speak of Black women exclusively, for there is an implied universality which connects them with others.

Likewise, with Jesus Christ, there was an implied universality which made him identify with others—the poor, the woman, the stranger. To affirm Jesus' solidarity with the "least of the people" is not an exercise in romanticized contentment with one's oppressed status in life. For as the Resurrection signified that there is more to life than the cross for Jesus Christ, for Black women it signifies that their tri-dimensional oppressive existence is not the end, but it merely represents the context in which a particular people struggle to experience hope and liberation. Jesus Christ thus represents a three-fold significance: first he identifies with the "little people," Black women, where they are; secondly, he affirms the basic humanity of these, "the least"; and thirdly, he inspires active hope in the struggle for resurrected, liberated existence.

To locate the Christ in Black people is a radical and necessary step, but an understanding of Black women's reality challenges us to go further. Christ among the least must also mean Christ in the community of Black women. William Eichelberger was able to recognize this as he further particularized the significance of the Blackness of Jesus by locating Christ in Black women's community. He was able to see Christ not only as Black male but also Black female.

> God, in revealing Himself and His attributes from time to time in His creaturely existence, has exercised His freedom to formalize His appearance in a variety of ways. . . . God revealed Himself at a point in the past as Jesus the Christ a Black male. My reasons for affirming the Blackness of Jesus of Nazareth are much different from that of the white apologist. . . . God wanted to identify with that segment of mankind which had suffered most, and is still suffering. . . . I am constrained to believe that God in our times has updated His form of revelation to western society. It is my feeling that God is now manifesting Himself, and has been for over 450 years, in the form of the Black American Woman as mother, as wife, as nourisher, sustainer and preserver of life, the Suffering Servant who is despised and rejected by men, a personality of sorrow who is acquainted with grief. The Black Woman has borne our griefs and carried our sorrows. She has been wounded because of American white society's transgressions and bruised by white iniquities. It appears that she may be the instrumentality through whom God will make us whole.

Granted, Eichelberger's categories for God and woman are very traditional. Nevertheless, the significance of his thought is that he was able to conceive of the Divine reality as other than a Black male messianic figure.

Challenges for Womanist Christology

Although I have argued that the White feminist analysis of theology and Christology is inadequate for salvific efficacy with respect to Black women, I do contend that it is not totally irrelevant to Black women's needs. I believe that Black women should take seriously the feminist analysis, but they should not allow themselves to be coopted on behalf of the agendas of White women, for as I have argued, they are often racist unintentionally or by intention.

The first challenge therefore, is to Black women. Feminists have identified some problems associated with language and symbolism of the church, theology, and Christology. They have been able to show that exclusive masculine language and imagery are contributing factors undergirding the oppression of women.

In addressing the present day, womanists must investigate the relationship between the oppression of women and theological symbolism. Even though Black women have been able to transcend some of the oppressive tendencies of White male (and Black male) articulated theologies, careful study reveals that some traditional symbols are inadequate for us today. The Christ understood as the stranger, the outcast, the hungry, the weak, the poor, makes the traditional male Christ (Black and White) less significant. Even our sisters, the womanist of the past though they exemplified no problems with the symbols themselves, they had some suspicions about the effects of a male image of the divine, for they did challenge the oppressive and distorted use of it in the church's theology. In so doing, they were able to move from a traditional oppressive Christology, with respect to women, to an egalitarian Christology. This kind of equalitarian Christology was operative in Jarena Lee's argument for the right of women to preach. She argued ". . . the Saviour died for the woman as well as for the man." The crucifixion was for universal salvation, not just for male salvation or, as we may extend the argument to include, not just for White salvation. Because of this Christ came and died, no less for the woman as for the man, no less for Blacks as for Whites.

> If the man may preach, because the Saviour died for him, why not the woman? Seeing he died for her also. Is he not a whole Saviour, instead of half one? as those who hold it wrong for a woman to preach, would seem to make it appear.

Lee correctly perceives that there is an ontological issue at stake. If Jesus Christ were a Savior of men then it is true the maleness of Christ would be paramount. But if Christ is a Saviour of all, then it is the humanity—the wholeness—of Christ which is significant. Sojourner was aware of the same tendency of some scholars and church leaders to link the maleness of Jesus and the sin of Eve with the status of women and she challenged this notion in her famed speech "Ain't I A Woman?"

Then that little man in black there, he says women can't have as much rights as men, 'cause Christ wasn't a woman! Where did your Christ come from? Where did your Christ come from? From God and a woman. Man had nothing to do with Him.

If the first woman God ever made was strong enough to turn the world upside down all alone, these women together ought to be able to turn it back, and get it right side up again! And now they is asking to do it, the men better let them.

I would argue, as suggested by both Lee and Sojourner, that the significance of Christ is not his maleness, but his humanity. The most significant events of Jesus Christ were the life and ministry, the crucifixion, and the resurrection. The significance of these events, in one sense, is that in them the absolute becomes concrete. God becomes concrete not only in the man Jesus, for he was crucified, but in the lives of those who will accept the challenges of the risen Saviour the Christ.

For Lee, this meant that women could preach; for Sojourner, it meant that women could possibly save the world; for me, it means today, this Christ, found in the experiences of Black women, is a Black woman. The commitment that to struggle not only with symptoms (church structures, structures of society), as Black women have done, but with causes (those beliefs which produce and reinforce structures) yield deeper theological and christological questions having to do with images and symbolism. Christ challenges us to ask new questions demanded by the context in which we find ourselves.

The second challenge for Black women is that we must explore more deeply the question of what Christ means in a society in which class distinctions are increasing. If Christ is among "the least" then who are they? Because our foreparents were essentially poor by virtue of their race, there was no real need for them to address classism as a separate reality. Today, in light of the emerging Black middle class we must ask what is the impact of class upon our lives and the lives of other poor Black and Third World women and men.

Another way of addressing the class issue in the church is to recognize the fact that although our race/sex analyses may force us to realize that Blacks and women should share in the leadership of the church, the style of leadership and basic structures of the church virtually insure the continuation of a privileged class.

Contemporary Black women in taking seriously the Christ mandate to be among the least must insist that we address all three aspects of Black women's reality in our analyses. The challenge here for contemporary Black women is to begin to construct a serious analysis which addresses the structural nature of poverty. Black women must recognize that racism, sexism and classism each have lives of their own, and that no one form of oppression is eliminated with the destruction of any other. Though they are interrelated, they must all be addressed.

The third and final challenge for Black women is to do constructive Christology. This Christology must be a liberating one, for both the Black women's community and the larger Black community. A Christology which negates Black male humanity is still destructive to the Black community. We must, therefore, take seriously only the usable aspects of the past.

To be sure, as Black women receive these challenges, their very embodiment represents a challenge to White women. This embodiment (of racism, sexism and classism) says to White women that a wholistic analysis is a minimal requirement for wholistic theology. The task of Black women then, is constructive.

As we organize in this constructive task, we are also challenged to adopt the critical stance of Sojourner with respect to the feminist analysis as reflected in her comment:

> I know that it feel a kind o' hissin' and ticklin' like to see a colored woman get up and tell you about things, and woman's rights. We have all been thrown down so low that nobody thought we' ever get up again, but we have been long enough trodden now; we will come up again, and now I am here. . . .
>
> . . . I wanted to tell you a mite about Woman's Rights, and so I came out and said so. I am sittin' among you to watch; and every once in a while I will come out and tell you what time of night it is.

Mediations of the Spirit

Native American Religious Traditions and the Ethics of Representation

Inés Hernández-Ávila

. . . I agree with Erkkila when she says, "[I]t matters very much who is speaking, about what, and from which particular social, historical, and political location."[1] I am keenly aware of my own location as I write. I am the daughter of a Nimipu mother and a Tejano father. On my mother's side I am a descendant of Hinmaton Yalatkit's (Chief Joseph's) band of the Nimipu (Nez Perce) from Nespelem, Washington (my mother's family and I are enrolled on the Colville reservation). On my father's side, I am of Mexican (and therefore, *mestiza*, and Mexican Indian) descent by way of the Texas-Mexican border town of Eagle Pass, then Galveston, Texas. I am a mother and a grandmother. I know my responsibility as a member of my various communities: as a Native American woman concerned with preserving the (intellectual) sovereignty of Native peoples (for my children and my grandchildren and our future generations); as a scholar and professor actively contributing to the evolution of Native American

Studies as a discipline; as a Native Woman contributing to the articulation of Native American "feminisms"; as a creative writer intent on digging for the roots of original-ity of my own and other indigenous peoples; as the faculty member in our program who is entrusted to teach the "Native American Religion and Philosophy" course; and as a practicing member of certain Native American ceremonial traditions. . . .

. . . In the case of this essay, I want to use elements of my (life) story to fore-ground those issues which have emerged as critical ones for many Native people in this historical moment of our relationship with Western institutional(izing) politics. . . .

. . . [I]t is my personal experience, informed, of course, by formal research, which has given me the authority to speak (and write), and for that matter, to teach what pertains to Native American religious traditions. Indeed, my own authority (including any deci-sion to "talk about") emerges exactly from my understandings of the ethical frames, boundaries, and reciprocal protocols that attend to any discussion of Native belief sys-tems. Also, because my own research project includes an articulation of Native American "feminisms,"[2] I often have been asked to participate in or contribute to feminist projects wherein I would have to reveal information about Native women's ceremonial matters. Several questions present themselves to me as I consider the task of describing a "woman-centered ritual" from a Native American perspective. As Sequoya has noted, "The problem, of course, is precisely one of context: what is misuse in relation to the sacred cultures of particular tribal communities evokes authentic atmosphere in relation to the secular humanist and popular cultures of the Euroamerican tradition."[3]

I am a sweat lodge person and a *danzante* (a traditional dancer within the Aztec Conchero tradition of Mexico City). I have participated in sweat lodge ceremonies since 1981, and in the Conchero tradition formally since 1979, not only as a dancer but as a *Malinche*. In the Conchero tradition, the woman who fills the role of the *Malinche* takes her name from the young Aztec girl who was given as a gift to Hernan Cortes by the Maya, to whom she had been enslaved. Because of her facility for languages, she became Cortes' interpreter (and his mistress) during the period of the "Conquest" (or "continuing invasion"). Because she was forced into the role of Cortes's "tongue," she is considered, in both popular and intellectual traditions in Mexico, the arch traitor and sell-out, who, in presumably opening her legs, gave over the people and the land to the invaders. But in the ceremonial tradition of the Conchero dance community, "*la Malinche*" is not seen negatively. She opens the paths, going ahead of the group, protecting them, holding the sacred fire, cleansing and blessing the way so that the others may follow. She is a dancer, too, but in her caring for the fire, she is caring for the community of dancers in her group.

As I think of writing about her,[4] I remember one year when a film crew set themselves up in Chalma (south of Mexico City), a major place of pilgrimage for the Concheros. It was impossible to ignore the cameras and the crew as they intruded into sacred space and began to set up their scenes. How could the filming not distract us, how could it not divert us from the (playful, in the sense of sacred recreation) prayer-ful intention that had brought us there? The main filmmaker of this crew had done a film about one Mexican pueblo's dance of the "*voladores*"; I had occasion, later, to watch the film, where I learned that after the filming, the dance died in that village— it was never performed again. How much might I write about "*la Malinche*" before someone decides to go down to the ceremonies to do their own investigation? At what price does the revealing of *danza*, or any ceremony, happen so that the world (and/or the academy) can "share" in the experience, given that the world tends to dismiss any ethical considerations in the fervor of "discovery." I agree with Sequoya when she suggests, "Perhaps one might consider such dismissive strategies as an institutional residue of the paradigm of the vanishing Indian[s]" who are objectified rather than recognized as subject and voice of their own stories.[5]

I have similar reservations about writing about the sweat lodge tradition. According to many people whom I consider teachers, the sweat lodge is female; she is referred to as the "grandmother sweat lodge"; when we enter the lodge, many say that we enter the womb of Mother Earth.[6] The sweat lodge tradition exists south as well as north of what is now known as the U.S.–Mexican border. In the Aztec tradition there is a song titled "Teteo Innan, Temazcalteci" ["Our Grandmother, the Grandmother Sweat Lodge"]. The song speaks to "Our Grandmother" as the "Heart of the Earth," and the "Tree of Life" whose flowers bloom in the four colors that represent the four directions of the universe. A "woman's sweat" is, in a pronounced way, a centering and gathering of female energy for the purposes of purification and healing.

I could describe how the lodge is built, and according to what tradition; how many rocks are used and what kind, and how they are heated; how the ceremony is structured; what kind of songs are sung, if any; how the prayers are said and in what language; what the order of speakers is and why; what each one of them says, and so on. But even if I were to write a disclaimer in such an essay, warning people not to imitate this Native American "woman-centered ritual," and even though in the world of academia I might feel I had not done anything improper in describing it, I know that in the Native American community, among the elders, I could not say the same thing because I am certain that just as there would be readers who would be truly respectful of the information, there are those who would feel that my description of details gave them permission to appropriate. Worse than that, I would have betrayed the confidence of the women in the sweat lodge circle that I described, because my intention within the circle of ceremony would have been not to pray, but to record and tell. . . .

In her essay, "Claiming Power-In-Relation: Exploring the Ethics of Connection," Mary Grey writes of a feminist spiritual vision "rooted in respect for the context of a group's experience."[7] Grey delineates the obstacles that have impaired women from "bonding-in-solidarity" with each other; among the "key areas of difficulty" she lists class difference, the tenuous Jewish/Christian connection, black women's oppression, difference in sexual orientation, women's (internalized) negative self-image, damaged social structures, the exploitation of the planet, and the suffering of Third World women. Grey not only casts black women as the only women of color who are contrasted to white women, she seldom in her discussion mentions cultural differences with respect to any American women of color, except perhaps in her veiled (possible) reference to Native women when she addresses the "destroyed sense of community between Western women and women living in communities still respecting nature's [or the earth's] rhythms."[8] Her mention of black women only calls attention to "the history of white women's collusion in [black women's] oppression."[9] Even her mention of Third World women does not consider issues of cultural and political sovereignty, but instead her focus is on Third World women's courage in the face of pain.

Yet Grey establishes the idea of "interconnectedness [as] both a new revelatory paradigm and a moral imperative" for women who seek to broaden the scope and vision of the feminist struggle.[10] This ethics of connection, which calls for a reclaiming of the "healing strength of nature,"[11] she says requires an understanding of the interdependence and interrelatedness of all life. Ironically, her "new" metaphysic of connection resonates (in broad sweeps) with long-held understandings regarding Native peoples' belief systems. As Peggy Beck, Anna Lee Walters, and Nia Francisco say, in *The Sacred: Ways of Knowledge, Paths of Life*, "The knowledge that is instilled in youngsters throughout their lives in Native American sacred tradition, is the knowledge of relationships and how these relationships are arranged and interact with each other."[12] What is more, "Through this interdependency and awareness of relationships, the universe is balanced."[13] Unfortunately, perhaps Grey has not been "situated" to realize that her "new" perspective is actually quite old.

Even though Grey calls for "privileged women" to "listen [and] to learn," from "other women" (women who are not privileged? By what? Class, race/ethnicity? How is privilege defined?), she also posits in the conclusion to her essay,

> . . . [W]omen of privilege—for whom it has not been a great problem to discover a voice—have the responsibility to empower other groups of women, with whom we are as a political group *in relation*, to discover, own, celebrate and mourn a story in all its particularity.[14]

Besides the assumption Grey makes about the ease with which "privileged women" discover their own voices, she also presumes a responsibility, for herself and other "privileged women," that does not belong to them. Put specifically, Native women empower ourselves; other women have the option of standing in solidarity with us as we do so. We take back our power as we reclaim (and tell) our own and each other's stories and find in our stories the herstories and histories of our peoples. One of our tasks is to (re)view the work that has been done on Native healers, spiritual practicioners and leaders through the lens of ethical representation. . . .

. . . Many Native Americans are working with a conscious and devoted love on the recovery and transformation of our histories, languages, and traditions, on the recovery and transformation of ourselves and our peoples.

After all, for more than five hundred years it has been beaten into Native peoples that it is absolutely the worst, ugliest, most loathsome thing in the world to be an indigenous person. The total dehumanization of indigenous peoples of the Americas was and is necessary in order to justify their continuing exploitation in the United States and throughout the hemisphere. Native peoples continue to be subjected (in varying degrees) to a regime of terror and punishment in order to strip them "clean" of their spiritual (cultural) foundations, with the intent of rendering them helpless. As a result of the many trails of tears, the dispossessions, the relocations, the boarding schools, the introduction of alcohol into our communities, and the other genocidal policies of the federal government, it is actually remarkable that Native peoples have held on at all to any of our spiritual foundations. It is my strong belief that the high rate of alcoholism and suicide among Native peoples is directly related to the immense despair and grief over our losses.

The missionization campaign among indigenous peoples has always been, and continues to be, intense. Many Native American communities have been very open to Jesus Christ, blending Christian beliefs easily with their original belief systems. Fundamentalist Christianity (and in some cases, as with the Navajo, Mormonism[15]) has made powerful inroads, however. The rigidity of fundamentalism has caused many Native people to be ashamed of or afraid to admit their "Indianness." In what George Tinker calls "the praxis of self-hatred,"[16] these Native people have become convinced that "Indian" truly is evil, savage, heathen, and that any "Indian" ways are the devil's work. Activist/poet/singer/actor Floyd "Red Crow" Westerman describes the process in his song called "Missionaries":

> Go and tell the savage Native that he must be Christianized
> Tell him end his heathen worship and you'll make him civilized
> Shove your gospel-fostered values down his throat until it's raw
> And after he is crippled, turn your back and lock the door.[17]

To complicate matters even more, the paradoxical historical moment we are in has "New Agers" anxiously seeking out Native traditions at the same time many Native people are disavowing their "Indianness."

As many non-Indian people, including many feminists, search for "alterNative" ways of viewing the world and living in harmony with the universe, they are turning to Native American philosophies and peoples for guidance and inspiration, on issues such as holistic healing, ecology, respect for difference (as in sexual orientation), and respect for women, elders, and children.[18] While Indian people are still being denied their own full religious expression, many non-Indians are devouring Native American spiritual traditions in the same way they have consumed Native American art, jewelry, clothing, weavings, and crafts, once again with no thought to the real, present-day, political, social, economic, and cultural/religious struggles in which Native people are engaged. Where are these people when Native American sacred sites are at stake? Where are they when the religious rights of Native American women and men prisoners (and communities) are at stake? Where are they when the rights of Native Americans to use sacred medicines such as *hikuri* (peyote) are at stake? Where are they when Native American burial sites are being defended? Where are they when Native people are struggling for the repatriation of ancestral remains?[19] Where are they when Native American lives and continuance as distinct peoples are at stake? Does their respect and reverence for Native American spirituality increase or lessen in proportion to their ability or inability to participate in the ceremonies?

Many, if not most, non–Native Americans seem to feel an entitlement regarding Native American ceremonial and cultural traditions, artifacts, and gravesites, including ancestral bones, that can only be understood in the context of the original entitlement the first colonizers felt toward this land by "right of conquest" and soon after, "Manifest Destiny." This entitlement assumes the right to take what is indigenous, with complete disregard for Native peoples, in a manner in which the perpetrators would not think of doing so easily with other traditions. Oddly enough, this notion of taking what is indigenous is never characterized as "stealing," or as "theft," or even as disrespectful or outrageous. Imagine people wanting to find out what it "feels like" to take part in the Catholic ceremony of the Eucharist, or to wear a priest's garments, or the dress and hairstyle of Orthodox Jews, because it seems "cool."[20] Imagine going into any cemetery, and wandering around, picking up here and there different mementos that have been left at the distinct gravesites, to then display them as "treasures" in one's home. Imagine contributing to a museum your "private collection" of dead white people's clothes, jewelry, and other belongings taken from them at the moment of death, before they were dumped into a mass grave.

One spring, a nice enough white woman visited D-Q University,[21] where I was living and teaching at the time. She happened to participate in a sweat ceremony that I led, and she enjoyed the experience very much. Sometime later, I phoned her with a question about a journal she was editing because I was interested in contributing an essay to her. When she recognized my voice, she excitedly said, "Oh, is this my shaman?" I said no. "My medicine woman?" she went on. "No," I said. "But you led the sweat lodge ceremony!" she exclaimed, "What would you call that!?" I said, "I led the sweat lodge ceremony, that's all." Neither of us pursued any association after that conversation. She was not interested in me as an intellectual. She wanted me to play a role that suited and served her spiritual needs. One of the most popular Native American comedians, Charlie Hill, has a list of ten things white people always say to "Indians."[22] I'm not sure if "Won't you be my shaman?" is on the list, but it should be. The appropriation of Native American spirituality relies on the romanticization (and objectification) of indigenous peoples. Those who appropriate ignore the humanity, complexity and intellect of Native peoples, just as they ignore the history of oppression that has been the experience of Native peoples in relation to the United States government and "mainstream" society.

I have also been present at D-Q University when non–Native Americans (this time European women) have *insisted* on being allowed into a sweat. Would they themselves allow complete strangers to walk into their homes and demand entrance into a private family gathering, much less a religious ceremony? . . . As the noted Lakota scholar Vine Deloria Jr. says, "The non-Indian appropriator conveys the message that Indians are indeed a conquered people and that there is nothing that Indians possess, *absolutely nothing*—pipes, dances, land, water, feathers, drums, and even prayers—that non-Indians cannot take whenever and wherever they wish."[23]

According to some New Agers, everyone was "Indian" in a past life, which then justifies the taking in this life of anything that is Native American. "Rainbow Tribe" (and lately I've heard "Eco-Tribe") encampments and gatherings abound in many places, even in Europe, especially, I understand, in Germany. There are non-Indians who think they are more Indian than the Indians, and there are Indians who have succumbed and catered to the demand for "Native ways." Deloria says:

Many Indians are irritated, and justly so, with the wholesale appropriation of American Indian rituals, symbols, and beliefs by the non–Indian public. Several national magazines and newspapers and a myriad of pamphlets, posters, and bumper stickers proclaim the wonders of studying with the likes of Wallace Black Elk, Richard Erdoes, [the late] Sun Bear, Lynn Andrews [the "Beverly Hills Shaman"], Edward McGaa, and a host of lesser luminaries in the New Age Indian medicine man circuit.[24]

The International Circle of Elders, made up of Native American women and men elders from throughout this hemisphere, who have traveled around the world on behalf of indigenous people, have issued directives in the form of warnings against the selling of vision quests, sweat lodge ceremonies, "shamanic workshops," ceremonial objects, sacred medicines, and so on.[25]

Once money enters the conversation, the nature of the gatherings and ceremonies is altered. Money affirms entitlement on the one hand, since devotees of consumer culture believe that enough money can buy anything, and on the other hand, money encourages people to assume a false authority because it is profitable to do so. Throughout California, you can see flyers announcing all kinds of "experiences" modeled after some Native American tradition or another. The fee is always quite high, which to many consumers, of course, means that the product is "worth more." However, the warnings sent out by the Elders Circle speak of another cost that is more dangerous. The perversion of ceremonies and distortion of rituals can cause people to get hurt because they are "messing around" with spirituality, and they don't know what they're doing. Besides the fact that people could get hurt, physically, spiritually, emotionally, mentally, or in any combination thereof, what is costly for the Native American community is the loss of potential and actual support for legitimate issues. . . .

There is debate within the Indian community itself, even among scholars and writers, about what is all right to "share" and what is not. As Sequoya elaborates in her own essay, well-known (mixed-blood) Laguna Pueblo writer Leslie Silko has been criticized severely by Paula Gunn Allen, who is part Laguna herself, for revealing too much of Laguna ways in her novel *Ceremony*. At the same time, Gunn Allen's *Grandmothers of the Light: A Medicine Woman's Sourcebook*, in its very title suggests that it was written with a New Age and (eco)feminist readership in mind.[26] What is so objectionable to Native people is the current phenomenon of the "instant" medicine women and medicine men and the ease with which they appropriate. Even more disheartening is when Native people themselves appear to invite the dissolution of distinct traditions by suggesting that it is fine to use whatever you want. Many Native people who work with New Agers insist that they have been "instructed" to share their learnings because the world as we know it is ending. To this, Deloria astutely comments,

> If we accept these claims as true, we are basically saying that traditional Indian religions have become missionary minded and now seek converts in a larger intercultural context. This claim is contrary to every known tenet of any tribal tradition but it may be a new revelation given at the end of this world.[27]

Of these exchanges, George Tinker says, "In this 'meeting' of cultures, the communal culture value of Indian people is transformed by those who do not even begin to see the cultural imposition that has occurred, however unintended."[28]

. . . The commodification and commercialization of Native American spirituality disturbs and disrupts the work of sustaining the spiritual traditions that belong to specific Native American communities, and the work of retrieving those traditions that, in many cases, have been almost forgotten. There is an integrity of form to each people's songs, to each people's ceremonies—what has been denied us through the process of colonization is being delicately and patiently rebuilt. Many Native American women and men, children and elders, are actively involved in the process of decolonizing our consciousnesses and reconstructing our belief-systems. At the same time, we are engaged in the overall struggle for the social, economic, and political betterment of our people. Since we are the most legislated of any peoples in the United States, the rebuilding and sustaining of our spiritual traditions is intertwined with our overall struggle.[29] It is insulting to hear non-Indians self-righteously proclaim their entitlement to our traditions—whether via New Ageism or because they have had the (class/economic) privilege of studying our languages, histories, and cultures in institutions of higher learning—while the young people in our communities still contend largely with a boarding school type of indoctrination and otherwise poor education that rarely allows them to finish high school. In academia, the "experts" assume the right to pass judgment on our authenticity by the rule of their supposed "civilized objectivity." These grievances are exacerbated by the fact that those who take from us do not care to know of our struggles in this life.

The issues that frame the question of Native American religious traditions within the Native American community are interwoven with questions of identity, community, and representation, from the personal to the hemispheric and global levels. There are as many Native American spiritual traditions as there are distinct "tribes" or nations in this hemisphere, even though, as Sequoyah says, "[I]t is one of the paradoxes of democratic government that without the appearance of a homogeneous political identity—an identity constituted in terms of the dominant system of representation—the issues crucial to Native American survival as regionally diverse peoples cannot be heard."[30] Still, many Native peoples are engaged in the struggle for sovereignty. Many Native American women and men, whether they are community activists, health workers, educators, cultural workers, visual and performing artists, curators, writers, filmmakers, scholars, elders, or students, to name a few, are contributing to the rethinking about issues of identity, community, spirituality, and "culture." Race, ethnicity, class, gender, sexual orientation, age, ability, in the context of the specific historical experiences of our peoples, factor into our reconfigurations, and into our representations. For many Native people, whether the issues revolve around our personal well-being or the well-being and continuance of our peoples, our distinct and evolving spiritual traditions remain the base of what we do as conscious human beings. Just as we show respect for the strength and beauty of each people's traditions and for the pain and joy of their histories, we must show respect to one another as women and men, acknowledging each other for our differences. As we honor each other's spirits, we honor women's and men's wisdom and women's and men's authority within the context of the communities we claim as our own.

Notes

1. Betsy Erkkila, "Ethnicity, Literary Theory, and the Grounds of Resistance," *American Quarterly* 47 (December 1995): 572.

2. I have qualified the term "feminisms" with quotation marks because Native women have not embraced it. At the same time, I am interested in re(or un) covering those aspects of distinct Native belief-systems that address the roles and power of women. I am also interested in the work of Native women in opposing and otherwise (re)negotiating a transformation of any such aspects which might repress and/or violate women's space and voice.

3. Jana Sequoya, "How(!) Is an Indian?: A Contest of Stories," in *New Voices in Native American Literary Criticism*, ed. Arnold Krupat (Washington, DC: Smithsonian Institutional Press, 1993), 456.

4. I have written about *Malintzin*, or *"la Malinche,"* in other essays, but I have not detailed exactly what the *"Malinche"* does, moment by moment, within the dance ceremony itself.

5. Sequoya, 456.

6. There are books that delineate the sweat lodge tradition within a range of specificity, such as *The Sacred Pipe: The Seven Rites of the Oglala Sioux* by Joseph Eppes Brown (New York: Penguin Books, 1953) and *Imagine Ourselves Richly: Mythic Narratives of North American Indians* by Christopher Vecsey (New York: HarperCollins, 1991).

7. Mary Grey, "Claiming Power-In-Relation: Exploring the Ethics of Connection," *Journal of Feminist Studies in Religion* 7 (Spring 1991): 17–18.

8. Ibid., 9.

9. Ibid., 8–9.

10. Ibid., 11.

11. Ibid., 17.

12. Peggy V. Beck, Anna Lee Walters, and Nia Francisco, *The Sacred: Ways of Knowledge, Sources of Life* (Tsaile, AZ: Navajo Community College Press, 1992), 21.

13. Ibid., 13.

14. Grey, 17.

15. See Steve Pavlik, "Of Saints and Lamanites: An Analysis of Navajo Mormonism," *Wicazo Sa Review* 8 (Spring 1992): 21–30.

16. George Tinker, *Missionary Conquest: The Gospel and Native American Cultural Genocide* (Minneapolis: Fortress Press, 1993), 3.

17. Floyd "Red Crow" Westerman, "Missionaries," from the cassette recording *Custer Died for Your Sins*, Red Crow Productions, 1982.

18. I am, of course, aware of the other side of this conversation, the position that Native people do not really have the belief systems that have been attributed to us, that

instead, some well-meaning sympathizers to indigenous causes in their zeal to garner support for Native peoples have merely projected onto us, in a highly romanticized manner, this sophisticated consciousness of ecology, astronomy, holistic healing, etc. I would certainly agree that many Native people no longer have (access to) these belief-systems. However, I am also cognizant of the work of Native scholars, and groups like the Society for the Study of Native American Religious Traditions, who are developing the study (and recovery) of Native religious traditions as a disciplinary field of its own.

19. Jack F. Trope, "Protecting Native American Sacred Sites and Religious Freedom," *Wicazo Sa Review* 7 (Fall 1991): 54. In 1990, the Native American Grave Protection and Repatriation Act, P.L. 101–601, was passed, which provides some protection to Native American grave sites and requires the repatriation (by federally funded museums and federal agencies) of cultural affiliated human remains and associated funerary objects, as well as some unassociated funerary objects, sacred objects, and items of cultural patrimony.

20. I was startled several years ago upon seeing a fashion magazine (in the checkout lane at a grocery store) highlighting some famous designer's new styles patterned after religious habits from different denominations. One model wore a gown modeled after a monk's habit, another wore an outfit indeed copied in the styles of Orthodox Jews, and so on. I have not seen those styles catch on in the general populace, though.

21. D-Q University is a private Native American college in Davis, California; its name combines the name of an Iroquois prophet known as "The Peacemaker" and the name of the Aztec god of wisdom, the Plumed Serpent, Quetzalcoatl.

    The university was founded in 1971 as a "College of the Americas" where indigenous (and other) peoples could come to study from a hemispheric Native American perspective and where Native peoples could determine how their own histories and cultures would be studied. The school is referred to as "D-Q" because the Iroquois people requested that their prophet's name be shared only in trust.

22. While many Native people here in the United States have begun to call themselves "Native American," some still refer to themselves as "American Indian" or "Indian" (they are all generic terms). Everyone in the "Indian" community knows that the term is a misnomer, but it is a word we have made our own.

23. Vine Deloria, Jr., "Is Religion Possible? An Evaluation of Present Efforts to Revive Traditional Tribal Religions," *Wicazo Sa Review* 8 (Spring 1992): 37.

24. Deloria, 35. Wendy Rose's essay, "The Great Pretenders: Further Reflections on Whiteshamanism," in *The State of Native America: Genocide, Colonization, and Resistance,* ed. M. Annette Jaimes (Boston: South End Press, 1992), is an important contribution to this discussion as is George Tinker's "New Age and the Continuing Colonial Invasion" in his book *Missionary Conquest,* 120–23.

25. See Lee Irwin's essay, "Freedom, Law, and Prophesy," in *Native American Spirituality: A Critical Reader,* ed. Lee Irwin (Lincoln: University of Nebraska Press, 2000), Appendix One, for an early statement of the Circle of Elders.

26. Paula Gunn Allen, *Grandmothers of the Light: A Medicine Woman's Sourcebook* (Boston: Beacon Press, 1991).

27. Deloria, 35.

28. Tinker, 122.

29. See Stephen L. Pevar's *The Rights of Indians and Tribes: An American Civil Liberties Handbook* (New York: Bantam Books, 1983).

30. Sequoya, 455.

Mothers and Daughters, Writers and Fighters

❖ *Kwok Pui-lan* ❖

I was born in Hong Kong on the twenty-third of March, according to the Chinese lunar calendar. On this day, many Chinese in the coastal provinces of China celebrate the birthday of Mazu, the goddess who protects fisherpeople, seafarers, and maritime merchants. This is also a festive day for my family, for it is the only day in the year that my father will take a day off and go to offer thanksgiving in the temple.

I am the third child of a family of seven children. My mother gave birth to five girls before two sons came at last. Because of the patriarchal and patrilineal structure of the Chinese family, to produce a male heir used to be the most important responsibility of women in marriage. My parents had been waiting for twelve years before the sons were born, and it can be expected that the boys were given most of the attention. From my early childhood, I questioned the legitimacy of a social system that does not treat boys and girls equally.

My mother is tall and thin but very strong. When we were young, we once moved into a new building where the water supply had not yet been adequately installed. To fetch water for the whole family, every day my mother carried two big tins full of water and slowly climbed up seven flights of stairs. This vivid image of her is lodged in my mind. Like many Chinese women of her age, she is a devout follower of folk Buddhist religion. When the moon waxes and wanes, she will offer prayers and thanksgiving sacrifices, and she also makes offerings to the ancestors. When I became a Christian in my teens, my mother did not object to my going to church, and I also thought that she must have found something important in her religious life.

My mother-in-law belongs to an ethnic group called the Kejia, whose women have a reputation of being powerful and independent. Contrary to the prevailing practice, the Kejia women seldom had their feet bound, since many of them had to work in the field. My mother-in-law came from a poor family and was betrothed to her husband as a child. Without learning how to read and write, she has taught herself to make all kinds of things, and her creativity often surprises me. When she lived with us in Hong Kong, she would grow many different vegetables in our backyard during the summer season. Juicy red tomatoes, fleshy white cabbages, and green Dutch beans made our garden look gorgeous. Our little daughter used to help her in watering plants and plucking weeds.

My mother-in-law does not follow any particular religious practice, but she has a profound trust in life and an unfailing spirit to struggle for survival. I have always admired people like my two mothers, who had very limited life chances, yet who have tried to live with dignity and integrity and to share whatever they have with others. The stories of these women have seldom been told, and their lives easily fall into oblivion. Nonetheless, it is these women who pass the wisdom of the human race from generation to generation, and who provide the context of life for others. The stories of my mothers drive home to me a very precious lesson: as women living in a patriarchal cultural system, they are oppressed by men, but, never contented to be treated as victims, they have struggled against the forces that seek to limit them and circumscribe their power.

My Spiritual Foremothers

When I was twelve, one of our neighbors took me to the worship service at an Anglican church. This church is one of two churches in Hong Kong built in a Chinese style, with Christian symbols and motifs embodied in Chinese architecture. I grew to like the liturgical worship, the music, and the fellowship. The vicar of the church was Deacon Huang Xianyun, who was later officially ordained as one of the two women priests in the worldwide Anglican Communion in 1971. Rev. Huang has been a strong role model for me, and her life exemplifies that women can serve the church just as men do.

Rev. Huang has always preached that men and women are created equal before God, and she has encouraged women to develop their potential. Because of her influence, there were many women in our church who volunteered to do various kinds of ministry. As a high school girl, I used to accompany them in visiting the sick and calling on those old people who were too weak to come to church. Some of these women volunteers were widows; a few were rich; others came from poor and middle-class backgrounds. Their dedication to others in ministering to the needy helped me to see glimpses of the divine and sustained me through many doubts and uncertainties.

Just like these women of my church, other Chinese women joined the Christian community in search of an alternative vision of society and human relationships. In the last decades of the nineteenth century, women who joined the church were poor and lower-class; the gentry and the upper-class families would not allow their wives and daughters to follow a foreign religion. To read the Bible and the catechism, these illiterate women had to be taught how to read. Bible-women were employed to translate for the missionaries and to do the home visitations. As the church became involved in social reforms, some of the Christian women participated in literacy campaigns and the anti-footbinding movement and organized health care programs and women's associations.

These activities allowed women to come together to talk about their problems and to find ways and means to tackle them. Amid all the changes in modern China, these women have tried to work for the benefit of women and contribute to society. Like other women in Third World churches, they bear witness to a faith that empowers people to break through silence and move to action. Although many of their names have been lost in history, they are my spiritual foremothers in loving memory.

Between the Two Worlds: As Chinese and as Christian

My double inheritance from my own mothers and my spiritual foremothers has raised a serious question for me: What is the connection between the lives of simple folk like my mothers and Christianity? I have long rejected the arrogance that "outside the church, there is no salvation," for it means condemning my ancestors, mothers, nieces, and nephews. In fact, in the long history of China's encounter with Christianity, the Christian population in China has scarcely exceeded one half of one percent. As a tiny minority, we live among our people in the world's most populous country, which has a long history and civilization. China not only challenges any presumptuous "universal" salvation history but also presents a world of thought, language, art, and philosophy radically different from the Christian tradition. As Chinese Christians, we have been in constant dialogue with this rich cultural heritage, long before the term "religious dialogue" was coined.

But to claim that we are both Chinese and Christian is not an easy matter; in the view of many Chinese, this claim is simply implausible. Chinese identity is defined by participation in a complicated cultural matrix of social behavior, rites, and human relationships, while Christianity is often perceived to be bound up with Western philosophy, liturgy, and cultural symbols.[1] Moreover, Christianity came to China together with the expansion of Western military aggression. We people of Hong Kong are painstakingly aware that in the first unequal treaty between China and the West, Hong Kong was ceded to the British, and at the same time missionaries were allowed to preach at China's treaty ports.

With such a heavy historical burden on our shoulders, we Chinese Christians have to vindicate ourselves to our own people: we are not the instruments of foreign aggressors, nor do we share the same religion as the oppressors. In the 1920s, religious leaders in China began the process of the indigenization of the church, so that Chinese Christians would eventually assume the tasks of self-propagation, self-support, and self-government. Some Chinese theologians, at that time, believed that Christianity could be the social basis for the revitalization of China. Others believed that Christianity could be a revolutionary force that would lead to social changes.

But as Chinese women, we are much more concerned about how Christianity is indigenized into the Chinese culture. The Confucian tradition has been vehemently criticized in China's recent past as advocating hierarchical social relations, strict separation between the sexes, and a backward-looking world-view. The androcentric moral teachings have been castigated as undergirding the conservative inertia of keeping China feudal and patriarchal.[2] At the same time, Christianity has been subjected to vigorous dissection and in-depth analyses to expose its dualistic tendency and patriarchal bias.[3] For some time, Chinese women have taken comfort in knowing that Jesus advocated equality of the sexes, in spite of the Jewish patriarchal custom, and that Paul's teachings on women were limited by the cultural conditions of his time.[4] But today, Jewish feminists caution us against anti-Semitic prejudices, and feminist biblical scholars argue that Paul's bias against women took place in a much wider process of patriarchalization of the early church.[5]

In a dazzling way, there is a "shaking of the foundations" on both sides and we are confronted with a double culture shock. There is no easy path we can follow. As one Chinese poet says, "The road is long and tortuous, we have to search above and below."[6] Out of this most trying experience, we have come to face both our cultural heritage and the Christian tradition with courage and hope, that we may find new ways to do theology which will liberate us and sustain our faith.

Searching for a Liberating Faith

The crisis of meaning and identity motivates me to search passionately for my mothers' gardens. What is the source of power that they found liberating, and how were they able to maintain their integrity as women against all the forces that denied them opportunities and tried to keep them in a subordinate place? The answer to these questions is not easy to come by, since women's lives have been trivialized and their contributions often erased from our memory. For a long time, the history of Christianity was written from the missionary perspective. These books record the life and work of the missionaries but seldom relate facts about the Chinese Christians. Even when they mention mission for women, they emphasize the work "done for" Chinese women, instead of telling the stories and lives of the women themselves. Chinese scholars, too, have tended to focus more on Chinese men, who could write and therefore leave us with so-called "reliable" historical data. We know too little about the faith and religious imagination of Chinese Christian women.

To be connected with my own roots, I have learned to value the experiences and writings of my foremothers. Many of their short testimonies, gleaned from articles in journals and small pamphlets, would not formerly have been counted as "theological data." I have also looked in alternative resources, such as songs, poems, and myths, as well as in unexpected corners, such as obituary notices. Sometimes this requires a fresh treatment of the materials: reading between the lines, attending to small details, and providing the missing links by circumstantial evidence. This meticulous work is done with a deep respect for these women, and in remembrance of their testimony to an alternative understanding of the fullness of life.

Trying to find the link to the threads of their lives, I have come to understand that they were not passive recipients of what was handed down or taught to them. They were brave enough to challenge the patriarchal tradition, both in Chinese culture as well as in Christianity. After they became Christians, some of the women refused to follow the Chinese marriage rites or to participate in the funeral ceremony, which were social enactments of patrilineal and patriarchal family ideals. In addition, some questioned the overt patriarchal bias of the Bible. A Christian woman whose name has been lost to history used a pin and cut out from her Bible Paul's injunction that wives should be submissive to their husbands. When her husband exhorted her to obey what the Bible taught, she brought out her Bible and said it did not contain such teachings. At the turn of this century, a medical doctor named Zhang Zhujun was said to be the first Chinese woman preaching at the church. Commenting on Paul's prescription that women should keep silence in the church, Dr. Zhang boldly asserted that Paul was wrong![7]

About sixty years after Chinese women started to join the church in recognizable numbers, women organized themselves in the first meeting of the Chinese National Council of Churches in 1922. Ms. Ruth Cheng addressed the Assembly and raised the issue of the ordination of women. She said:

People in some places think that the ordination of women is out of the question and women pastors are simply impossibilities. I do not intend to advocate that the church ought to have women pastors, but I would simply like to ask the reason why women cannot have such rights. If the Western Church because of historical development and other reasons has adopted such an attitude, has the Chinese Church the same reason for doing so? If the ancient Church, with sufficient reasons, considered that women could not have such rights, are those reasons sufficient enough to be applied to the present Church?[8]

These brave acts of women demonstrated their critical discernment, as moral agents, and a radical defiance which uncompromisingly challenged those traditions that were limiting and binding for women.

To claim such a heritage for myself is a process of self-empowerment. First, it informs me that these Chinese Christian women have a history and a story that need to be recovered for the benefit of the whole church. Second, I stand in a long tradition of Chinese Christian women who, with tremendous self-respect, struggled not only for their own liberation but also for justice in church and society. Third, these women brought their experience to bear on their interpretation of Christian faith and dared to challenge the established teaching of the church. It is because of this history that I can claim to do theology from a Chinese woman's perspective.

Toward an Inclusive Theology

There are a few important insights I have found while tending and digging in my mothers' gardens. Their religious experience and quest for liberation point to the necessity of expanding our Christian identity and developing a more inclusive theology. This involves several major shifts in our traditional theological thinking. First, it requires us to shift our attention from the Bible and tradition to people's stories. The exclusiveness of the Christian claim often stems from a narrow and mystified view of the Bible and church teaching. I admit that the Bible records many moving stories of struggle against oppression, and it continues to inspire many Third World Christians today. But I also agree with post-Christian feminists that our religious imagination cannot be based on the Bible alone, which often excludes women's experience.[9] In particular, I cannot believe that truth is only revealed in a book written almost two thousand years ago, and that the Chinese have no way to participate in its inception. Let me give some concrete examples to illustrate what I mean. Coming from the southern part of China, where rice is the main food, I have often found the biblical images of bread-making and yeast-rising as alienating. I also feel a little uneasy when some Western women begin to talk about God as Bakerwoman.[10] The Chinese, who live in an agricultural setting instead of a pastoral environment, have imaged the divine as compassionate, nonintrusive, immanent in and continuous with nature. The images and metaphors we use to talk about God are necessarily culturally conditioned, and biblical ones are no exception.

The Bible tells us stories that the Hebrew people and the Christians in the early church valued as shaping their collective memory. The Western Christian tradition represents one of the many ways to interpret this story for one's own situation. The

Indians, the Burmese, the Japanese, and the Chinese all have stories that give meaning and orientation to their lives. Women in particular have a treasure chest of lullabies, songs, myths, and stories that give them a sense of who they are and where they are going. Opening this treasure chest is the first step to doing our own theology. With full confidence, we claim that our own culture and our people's aspiration are vehicles for knowing and appreciating the ultimate. This would also imply that our Christian identity must be radically expanded. Instead of fencing us from the world, it should open us to all the rich manifestations that embody the divine.

Second, we have to move from a passive reception of the traditions to an active construction of our own theology. The missionary movement has been criticized for making Third World churches dependent on churches in Europe and America. This dependence is not just financial but, more devastatingly, theological. With an entirely different philosophical tradition, we enter into the mysterious debate of homoousia, and with no critical judgment we continue the modernist and fundamentalist debate of the missionaries, long after a partial cease-fire has been declared in the West. We try our best to study Greek and Hebrew, and Latin or German too, if we can manage, and spare little time to learn the wisdom of our own people. As half-baked theologians, we are busy solving other people's theological puzzles—and thus doing a disservice to our people and the whole church by not integrating our own culture in our theology.

All peoples must find their own way of speaking about God and generate new symbols, concepts, and models that they find congenial for expressing their religious vision. We women, who have been prevented from participating fully in this myth- and symbol-making process, must reclaim our right to do so. As a Chinese Christian woman, I have to critically reassess my double heritage, to rediscover liberating elements for building my own theology. Ironically, it is my commitment to feminism that leads me to a renewed interest and appreciation of my own cultural roots. Chinese folk religions have always been much more inclusive, and they do not exclude the female religious image and symbolism. Chinese religious sensibility has a passion for nature and longs for the integration of heaven and earth and a myriad of things. If theology is an "imaginative construction," as Gordon Kaufman says,[11] we would need constantly to combine the patterns and weave the threads in new ways to name ourselves, our world, and our God.

Third, doing our own theology requires moving away from a unified theological discourse to a plurality of voices and a genuine catholicity. The new style of theology anticipates that there will be many theologies, just as there are many different ways of cooking food. For those who are raised in a cultural tradition that constantly searches for the "one above many," this will imply confusion, complication, and frustration. For others, like me, who are brought up in a culture that honors many gods and goddesses, this is a true celebration of the creativity of the people.

The criterion to judge the different styles of theologizing is not codified in the Bible, and the norm of theology is not determined by whether it smells something like that of Augustine and Aquinas—or Tillich and Barth, for that matter. Instead, it lies in the praxis of the religious communities struggling for the liberation of humankind. All theologies must be judged as to how far they contribute to the liberation and humanization of the human community. A living theology tries to bear witness to the unceasing yearning of human beings for freedom and justice, and articulates the human compassion for peace and reconciliation.

Will plurality threaten the unity and catholicity of the church? For me, unity and catholicity cannot be understood in terms of religious doctrines and beliefs but must be seen as an invitation to work together. Unity does not mean homogeneity, and catholicity does not mean sameness. Process theologian John B. Cobb, Jr., captures the meaning of unity well:

> The unity of Christianity is the unity of a historical movement. That unity does not depend on any self-identity of doctrine, vision of reality, structure of existence, or style of life. It does depend on demonstrable continuities, the appropriateness of creative changes, and the self-identification of people in relation to a particular history.[12]

The particular history that Third World people and other women's communities can identify with is that God is among the people who seek to become full human beings. Today, as we Third World women are doing our own theology, we come closer to a unity that is more inclusive and colorful and a catholicity that is more genuine and authentic.

I heartily welcome this coming age of plurality in our way of doing theology, that our stories can be heard and our experiences valued in our theological imagination. To celebrate Asian women's spirit-rising, I would like to conclude by sharing a song written by my dear friend Mary Sung-ok Lee:[13]

We Are Women

We are women from Burma, China,
India, Japan, Korea, Malaysia,
Philippines, Thailand, and U.S.A.

> *Chorus:* Eh hey ya ho-o
> Eh hey ya ho-o
> Cho ku na cho wa (Oh, how good it is!)
> Eh hey ya ho-o.

We are women, we are alive,
breaking our silence,
seeking solidarity.

> *Chorus*

We are women, Yellow women,
angered by injustice,
denouncing exploitation.

> *Chorus*

We are sisters, gathered for bonding,
mothers and daughters,
writers and fighters.

> *Chorus*

We are women, spirit-filled women,
claiming our story,
voicing our poetry.

Chorus

　　路遙遙其修遠兮
　　吾將上下而求索　　　《離騷》

　　我們對信仰的追尋,是漫長
而曲折的道路。
　　中國的信徒婦女,在過去的
日子,曾經向壓迫婦女的社
會制度和宗教思想提出挑戰,
她們參加了反纏足運動、婦女
節制會,及女青年會的工作。
　　今天,我們要學效她們的
模範,批判地繼承傳統中
國文化和基督教思想,深入
地發展有中國特色的婦女神
學,與第三世界婦女一起,為人
類整体的釋放,作出貢獻。

　　　　　　　郭佩蘭
　　　　　　　八七．十二．

Notes

1. For an insightful discussion of the two different cultural systems, refer to Jacques Gernet, *China and the Christian Impact,* trans. Janet Lloyd (Cambridge: Cambridge University Press, 1985).

2. The Confucian tradition was criticized as patriarchal in the May Fourth Movement of 1919 and was more severely condemned in the Cultural Revolution during 1966–1976. In the post-Mao era, Chinese philosophers have begun to analyze the limits and contributions of the Confucian tradition as it relates to present Chinese society.

3. See for example, Mary Daly, *Beyond God the Father* (Boston: Beacon Press, 1973), and Rosemary Radford Ruether, *Sexism and God-Talk: Toward a Feminist Theology* (Boston: Beacon Press, 1983).

4. Din Shujing, "Funü zai jiaohui de diwei" (Women's Status in the Church). *Nü Qing Nian* 7(2): 22 (March 1928).

5. See Judith Plaskow, "Blaming Jews for Inventing Patriarchy," *Lilith* 7: 12–13 (1980), and Elisabeth Schüssler Fiorenza, *In Memory of Her: A Feminist Theological Reconstruction of Christian Origins* (New York: Crossroad Publishing Co., 1983).

6. From Qu Yuan, "Li Sao" (Farewell Ode).

7. See "The History of Ms. Zhang Zhujan," in Li Youning and Zhang Yufa, eds. *Jindai Zhongguo nüquan yundong shiliao* (Historical Materials on Modern Chinese Feminist Movement), 2 vols. (Taipei: Biographical Literature Publisher, 1975), vol. 2, p. 1380.

8. Ruth Cheng, "Women and the Church," *Chinese Recorder* 53: 540 (1922).

9. Carol P. Christ, "Spiritual Quest and Women's Experience," in Carol P. Christ and Judith Plaskow, eds., *Womanspirit Rising: A Feminist Reader in Religion* (San Francisco: Harper & Row, 1979), pp. 228–245. See also her *Laughter of Aphrodite: Reflections on a Journey to the Goddess* (San Francisco: Harper & Row, 1987).

10. See the poem of Alla Bozarth-Campbell, "Bakerwoman God," in Iben Gjerding and Katherine Kinnamon, eds., *No Longer Strangers: A Resource for Women and Worship* (Geneva: World Council of Churches, 1983), p. 54.

11. Gordon D. Kaufman, *The Theological Imagination: Constructing the Concept of God* (Philadelphia: Westminster Press, 1981), pp. 263–279.

12. John B. Cobb, Jr., "Feminism and Process Thought: A Two-Way Relationship," in Sheila Greeve Davaney, ed., *Feminism and Process Thought* (Lewiston, N.Y.: Edwin Mellen Press, 1981), p. 42.

13. Used by permission of Mary Sung-ok Lee.

Forged under the Sun/Forjada bajo el sol: The Life of María Elena Lucas

❧ *Fran Leeper Buss* ❧

A Different *Madre de Cristo:* Changing the Roles of Males and Females

Sometimes I think about the way we do things, what things make us strong. One thing in our culture, even today, kids never get kicked out of their family. We're just so bound together. And even if you do get married, your mom's home is the family home, and your grandma comes and stays with you after she grows old. It's just something you don't even talk about, that's the way it is. I'm always thinking that eventually my home, God willing, if I ever really have one, it'll be the kids' home, and they'll be able to come here for the rest of their lives. And whoever stays here will also know that they have to accept the rest of the family in case there's a tragedy or something. Like my mom's home, even though it's just now a two-bedroom apartment in the projects, if the weather really gets bad, maybe twenty or thirty people will stay there.

And my father, he does the same. He always says, "If it gets cold, honey, you can always come home. If you want to stay here it's no problem." Of course, then I'd have to put up with his criticism. And I don't stay with Mom often 'cause it's so crowded, and with the television and the phone going all night, I can't sleep. Still, it's there for me.

Not long ago, I had a nightmare at my trailer. I'd taken baby chicks in there with me to keep them warm, and I think that was my mistake. We were gone a few days, and when we came back we had *culebras de cascabel* [rattlesnakes] in our trailer! It was so terrible. We threw pots of boiling water on the floor to try to scare them out, and Pablo and one of them men got bug bombs and set them off inside, but a couple of them wouldn't leave. So we slept outside by our cement blocks, and I made a lot of noise to try to scare them away from me whenever I went to cook in the trailer.

Well, when my mom heard that, she and my brother Martín came to get me. Martín was very upset. He said, "I don't want you to stay here."

"No, I'm staying. I'm sleeping outside."

"For God's sake, you're living *como un animal.*"

"I know, but I'm sleeping on the cement." See, Pablo and I are trying to build a house with cement blocks. We've got our floor poured and some of the walls, and I've got all my plants and animals, and if I leave I know everything will fall apart, my home will never get built. So Mom and Martín were real upset, but I stayed, and now two of my brothers and one of my sons are helping me build my house.

Mom and I fight sometimes, pretty bad, but regardless of what happens, when we need her, she's there for us, and home is home. And if I don't show up in town for awhile, she'll call my sister Mary Jane, and Mary Jane will come over and say, "Mom's all upset because you haven't showed up there, and she says to go for you now." Mom's got sixteen kids, and she still does this. So we may get real upset with each other, but the next day it's gone, disappeared, and love is back, and that's the way it's always been.

And families always share. That's how come, some of the time, none of us have nothing. With so many people, somebody's always in trouble and whatever you get is loaned out. But that's also what keeps us going. That's how it works with almost everybody in my culture. Families stick together and help each other out. Most of the families in Onarga are related to each other in one way or another, and they do that for each other. My kids helped each other through college that way, and when Héctor's wife left him with the babies, his sisters and brothers, they've been helping to raise them. We make a close unit. Even if there's eight kids sleeping in one room, no kid is ever turned away.

But how men and women act with each other, that's where I have my struggle. I don't know much about how most Anglos and rich people live. They probably have the same conflict, but I don't know 'cause I haven't seen it.

I hate to say it, but all my life, I've seen men treat women with violence, sometimes with hits and sometimes by hurting their feelings. Not all men, but a great many. I try to imagine how it got started like this, and I guess it goes back to the people who wrote the Bible. Even when you look at the story of Adam and Eve, it's a masculine thing. Eve came from a man's rib, and they blame Eve for being so seductive. They don't say it's the serpent that tempted her, 'cause the serpent is considered a male. Even with the beginning of creation, they didn't give women credit. They didn't even things out so women would have self-esteem, confidence, so men would respect the woman.

I always fight with Pablo about the Bible, I always defend the female side, how I feel it's being squashed and smeared, totally stepped on. What would have happened if Jesus had been a woman? I'll tell you. If she had been a woman, a female, she would have gotten killed right away unless the divine spirit of God would have prevented it.

When I hear men say, "You women want to conquer the world and you want to dominate men," I just get so frustrated.

I answer, "The reason we are all dying, the reason we're in the economic situation we have, the reason we have war is because of men. If we women were given a fair-square chance and equal opportunity, I don't think that things would be so bad." I think women are taught to take better care of other people and the world, to keep it clean and safe. I think we have all these chemical problems, 'cause some man's up there after power and money.

But sometimes I also think the machismo has also rubbed off on the woman in the sense that the female accepts, like my mom and other parents, when they themselves, or we ourselves, turn around and allow our sons to do the same things to our daughters-in-law, and we allow our daughters to be abused by their husbands, and we allow our sons to abuse our daughters. This is all over our culture, and we're creating the same situation, reproducing it again.

I think I've been successful in bringing up at least two of my sons who are very conscious in not participating in that double standard. Not long ago, my daughter-in-law, Sulema, she says, "You know what, *Suegra*?" That means mother-in-law. "So-and-so came over and said, 'Well, who's the boss in this family?' So I said, 'Well, I guess Oscar.'"

When Sulema said that, right away I turned around and said, "*Mi'ja*, if it ever happens again, stand up in the door and say, '*I'm* the boss.'" Oscar started to laugh. I said, "It's not that I want to weigh one's rights over the others, but what do they take her for? Sulema's got to fight back when men say things like that."

I hate to say it, but our parents teach those kinds of attitudes. Usually our women are kind of prepared by their experience growing up that men are going to push their power. The girls go into marriage with some kind of fear that if they make the wrong move, they're going to get a whipping. I know this by listening to my younger sisters and the younger generation and watching how they talk to each other, the way men handle women.

It even happens to my sister who lives with her husband in my mother's house. Her husband can be drinking a *cerveza*, sitting in front of the television, and the baby will be on the floor in front of him, and my sister is out in the kitchen making dough for tortillas. If her husband says, "Hey, come and get this kid out of here," she'll get that look of fear on her face and wipe her hands real quick and go get the baby.

See, if she says, "Well, you're closer to the baby. Why don't you pick him up? I'm making tortillas and my hands are covered in dough," if she doesn't obey and respond to his demands real quick, he will be out there and say, "Who do you think you are?" And, slap, she'll get it. This happens right in front of my mother, and she won't do anything to correct him.

I've also seen the way my mom treats some of my sister-in-laws. I've heard one of my brothers come over to my mom's house and say, "I don't know what's wrong with this woman, Mom." I mean, he comes home and complains to Mom. Then Mom turns around and says, "My son is so good. She does not deserve him." And I think that's wrong. My poor sister-in-law, they put her down so much. . . .

Sometimes I got feeling so bad about all the conflict between men and women that I know that when a new baby boy was born, I'd look at him and think, thank God he's healthy, and thank God everything is alright, but I wonder what he will grow up like. Will he be one of our oppressors? What a terrible thing, right? Even with grandsons, I have worried. I keep thinking, we've got to change it now. And somehow we've got to change things before it gets so bad that people become violent.

That's why I wrote my play, and that's why I never stop talking about it, no matter what names people call me. See, men and women, we're caught in this together. Somehow we got to work our way out. So I keep telling everybody what I think, and sometimes when I say what I think, it comes out funny.

... I refuse to believe God is a man or that there is only one God. God is not a
man and if she is a man, no wonder! (Diary, March 16, 1990)

I feel real bad for some of the young undocumented women, girls really, the
ones who came here and can't get asylum or papers or find any kind of work, and they
don't even have a home to go back to. Many of them are working as prostitutes for
old men. They're so desperate they say to the old men, "I'll work for you, I'll cook,
I'll clean, I'll rub you, I'll do anything that makes you feel good, just please, Señor,
give me a place to stay."

Then all the women turn against these girls. They call them *putas* and say
they're breaking up the family. I tell the women that it's not the girls, they're desperate; it's the men. And the system. The immigration barriers. But lots of people just
say I'm crazy.

The other danger for all of them is AIDS. They warn about AIDS on television,
tell people it will kill them, but then they don't tell them exactly how it spreads. So
there are lots of rumors, but people don't have information. And poor women can't
afford condoms, even if the men would agree to use them. Men can get real mean
about that, and the women are so desperate thinking about tomorrow. How are they
supposed to think about something that might happen in a bunch of years? Like one
young woman I know, she's supporting four sick kids and a mother at home by trying to work as a maid. If a man gives her a little help, how's she supposed to force
him to use protection? God knows what will happen.

So all the time I talk. I try to say things but also I try not to make the men so
mad they won't even listen, but I make sure that men know that there is something
called wife abuse in the United States and that it is illegal. I also don't think each one
of us women can just do it by ourselves, just individually, one woman after another
changing her own marriage. I think we have to change things as a group. I think we
women have to get organized together.

I've thought about this a lot, and I think that someday when I have my home or
a better trailer, what I'd like to do is form a women's organization and say we're open
for services. I'd also keep on organizing people in general, teaching them about the
union, showing them the video about pesticides. But I'd especially like to have a place
where I can invite women over and teach them about a different Christ, the kind of
Christ that's an organizer, and a different *Madre de Cristo*, the kind that would come
to us in our present times. Not the Mary from way back then, but the kind of mother
that we need now and that would stand up for our rights and be with us.

I'd teach them that Christ from the past is Christ from the past, and he accomplished as much as he could. So we have to bring Christ into our present, and God's
got to be one of us. The same with the Virgin of Guadalupe and Mary Magdalene and
Ruth and Naomi and all those examples from the Bible.

I only hope I have enough time to do it. I look ahead sometimes and I think, oh
gosh, I better work as fast as I can. But, see, I think maybe that's the whole purpose
of creation. That maybe God divided himself into millions of particles, and that part
of God in us is what stands up to take action when there is injustice.

. . . Stand tall and stand together,
hold on to hope and faith.
with your right hand hold to justice high,
with your left hand your [sister's] right.

You've got to have the guts to fight,
chiseled by anger, love, and right,
for the war is just beginning,
in the Land of Lincoln hearts.

(September 13, 1982)

On the Wings of the Black Eagle: The Creative Impulse

My writing and my religion and my politics are all part of the same thing, they all go together. Many of my feelings come from my care and loving for Mother Earth. And I think my creativity comes from so much suffering also, so much oppression, which is where my desire to organize comes from also. Going through so much hell sensitizes you. And I think my creativity comes from God. I can be creative 'cause God was creative first.

Also, I'm profoundly touched by Mother Nature and by God. There is something super strong there. I don't just see the sky like the sky or the plants like the plants, I see beyond them. I don't just look at an apple and see an apple and eat it. I see the hands that picked it, the tree that held it. My mind goes way back to when the tree was coming out of the ground. And I do that with people also. I can look way back into people's eyes and see their hearts and minds and tell what's there. It's a different way of loving life, of seeing life.

I think that God has given each one of us an ability and a gift, individually. I also think that God has a purpose for most of us, and I think that God has used me in several ways. I didn't go to school, but, in my own way, I have a purpose to serve and a mission to carry on, and I don't feel like I've yet accomplished what God wants me to do.

I get my ideas for my songs and poems and drawings based on real life, they're true stories related to something that happened. Sometimes what I write actually indicates a totally different thing. The poetry and songs have a double meaning, and in order to do it, I become different people. It's like when I approached Casa Romero and saw all the refugees standing there, longing for help. It was like suddenly Jesus Christ became them, and I had to become like Christ when He said, "I was naked and you clothed me." I don't mean that I'm comparing myself to Jesus, but it's also said that we have a duty to pick up where he left off and carry on the work.

And throughout the story of Jesus, I think that's one of the things he does. He takes the place of people and speaks for them. And in a lot of my writings, I've done that too. Like I become the beggar in the street and speak for him or a poor girl and speak for her, it's a way to try to convey a message to the people, to motivate them, to sensitize them, and to make them support a good cause.

I've written *corridos* and the traditional songs of my people, some that don't have anything to do with the farm worker life, but most of my songs are protest songs. They are songs that in some way deliver a message. "José Mendiola" is a protest song, very much.

I think you can usually judge a good song or a good poem by whether it's based on real things and touches your heart. With a song like "Forged under the Sun," not just anybody can feel it. You have to be sensitized, you have to be organized, you have to be exposed and have feelings in order to understand it. With some of my songs and poetry, when I read it or sing it, I cry. Gloria, my daughter, she is also so *concientizada*, and when I read things to her that I've written, she gets real emotional.

My song, "Forjada bajo el sol," means, "Forged under the Sun." There's a moan in the fields from a person that's very tired and is working. It's coming out of a tomato picker, a cucumber picker, whatever. I can look out over the fields and actually see the person and see what goes on and feel the same anguish.

It's late in the evening, and, all of a sudden, the person takes a deep breath, a sigh really. And the poem talks about how beautiful everybody is, all brown, because they've been forged under the sun, and especially the kids have their wonderful smiles. Then, we farm workers, we share our food and say, "Here is a bite of my rice." "This is the eucharist that we have in the fields."

Then a little later it says, "Cae el sol y llora el angelus." This is referring to a belief we have that at a certain time of the day, all the people, like all the birds and the trees, go to sleep, that everybody should quit working and go to rest because the poem says that the sun goes down, and the angel of light begins to cry and says, "It's time to quit working." But sometimes the growers keep farm workers working out there until it is so dark they can't see. Our God wants to rest and can't quit working unless we do too. Of course, I also have my stories of the beautiful dark angel of the night, the one with wings of the black eagle. See, I try to bring what really happens and poetry and how things should change altogether.

A poem or a song or something will start coming to me, like in a dream, and writing it can go on for days and nights, and I can't stop until it's done. Sometimes it will go on for most of a week, and I can't rest until it is finished. And it seems like if I get depressed or something happens, the only way I can let it out is by writing or drawing something. That's the way I get rid of my anguish or pressure. Sometimes it takes me weeks, and I will go until two or three o'clock in the morning until I really just drop and sleep. Sometimes Pablo makes fun of me because I'm writing under a blanket with a flashlight late at night. It's strange. I don't read much at all—reading is kind of hard for me, partly because of my eyes—but I can't stop writing.

I've often wondered how many other women out there, out of their depression, out of their loneliness without anybody to talk to, also have to sit down like me and write out their emotions and their feelings on paper. Sometimes it turns out in the form of a diary, and sometimes it can be in the form of poetry or like when you are appealing to God. Maybe you're writing like a *lamento*. I wonder how many other women out there do the same thing, but they never talk about it.

I know I've destroyed a lot of my stuff because I got so depressed, I didn't want a reminder anymore, but mostly I've lost a whole lot of things because I keep moving from one place to another. I haven't met any migrants, farm workers, who've been able to keep any writing, and living like this makes it hard to do a lot of creative-type work. I feel that I don't have time to sit down and do what I'd love to do because I have so many responsibilities all around me. And my financial situation makes it bad. It's hard to get pencils and paper, much less paints and a canvas.

I have another song called "El Preso Pizcador." It means "The Harvest Prisoner." It also talks about a real situation but with a larger meaning. In it I'm a little child questioning my mom, "Mother, mother, where is God?" And she answers, "Well, God is by your side, *el preso pizcador*." Then the next verse applies to like Central America or Mexico or wherever the family has been separated or a parent has been killed or martyred. The child asks, "Why did my father leave? Why did he abandon us? I want to see his smile, I need his love."

And the mother answers, "Por nuestra causa murió." He died for our cause. Then she says, "Allí va luchando a tu lado." There he is struggling by your side. The harvest prisoner.

In the last verse, the child says, "¿Por qué, si Dios es tan grande y tiene tanto poder, hay hambre y guerra en la tierra y duda de amanecer?" Why, if God is so great and has so much power, there is war and hunger on earth and doubt about tomorrow? Then the child says, "¿Por qué? ¿Por qué? Mamá, ¿dónde se halla Dios?" Why? Why? Mom, where is God to be found? Then she answers, "Allá está preso en la gloria el pobre pizcador." He's imprisoned in heaven, the poor farm worker. So what I do in a lot of my songs is bring a God that is in our image, that resembles our cause, to life.

God is so much a part of my life. I think the wind and the sun, the rain and the plants have beautiful, holy spirits. And it's like they can reach out to me. Once I was so depressed and so sad and so low, and all of a sudden, here's this beautiful fragrance of *reseda* flowers, and it was just like it said "María Elena," and I turned and went to it, and my depression was left behind. I started to caress the plant, and I thought, you're beautiful, you're precious. It was like there was no one else to help me, and she called me and gave me this strong feeling that there is life, that life has meaning. It was like my friend came to me in my time of need. Then I was able to get up, go back inside, and begin to think clear again. And the same thing can happen at night when you're lonely, when there is no one to talk to. You can go out there and share with everything around you, the moon, the stars, the wind, the sounds of night.

> *Friend, you're like the black candle I light*
> *on my moonless nights.*
> *Angel moon, Angel moon, watch over my dreams.*
> *You're the moon I create when I lay me down.*
> *Angel night, Angel light, tell the stars tonight,*
> *She's the child, I'm her mom,*
> *lighting by her side.*

(Diary, February 20, 1990)

There is a very special kind of life in the plants, in the flowers, in the trees that I can communicate with. I can tell when they're happy, when they're sad, when they're praying. I can tell when they're asleep, when they sing. I think the spirits in plants and nature are different from those in people. In people, I don't see that kind of deep profound love and caring. One minute we care for others, and the next we hurt each other—there's a lot of both evil and good. But plant life is different—there's nothing evil, no bad intentions—it's just there to give. Like the sun and the birds and the crickets and the wolves, they're just there to nourish the earth and to give us life and beauty. But I see that we're here to destroy it, not everybody, but some.

These beliefs are a lot different from most of the beliefs of our people. They probably came from my grandma and the Indian background, but they're connected to other beliefs. Our Lady of Guadalupe is very important to us Mexicans because she appeared as a brown Indian to us in our world. She wasn't brought over from Spain, and she nurtures our spirit. Our mothers and grandmothers have always thought of Our Lady of Guadalupe as a very powerful woman and messenger or *intermediaria* between God and us. Sometimes I imagined that I could just lay on her chest and in her arms and be comforted.

But lately I've become so rebellious that Our Lady turned into something different for me. I imagine having a little chapel in a garden where I go to pray, but it has a remade statue of Our Lady of Guadalupe. I'd have her pregnant and in jeans and with a farm worker shirt with the sleeves rolled up. She'd have a scarf like we use when we work in the fields and a hat also, but underneath the hat, she'd have her veil with the stars. And instead of her hands together like in prayer, I'd have one hand on her chest by her heart holding a document, and her other hand would be holding a rifle that was resting against her. Her eyes would be strong and looking forward, saying something like, "You'd better behave." Or I could have her arm thrust forward with the document, like, "Here, this is the law." The rifle wouldn't be a symbol of violence but a symbol of enforcement of that law. Like, "Either you abide or you're in trouble."

The document she would be holding would say, "Justice. Power to women. No barriers between countries. Freedom in the world for all people." Then, instead of having Juan Diego holding her up, I'd have a farm worker with a basket of tomatoes and signs of the harvest. That's how she looks to me.

And now I see God more female than anything else. Mom and I fight a lot about religion and the church. I say, "Mom, what would you say if I said that I believe God is a female?" "Oh, my God, now you are saying that God is gay, that God is *joto*!" So we don't get far with our talks about religion.

Maybe God's part male and part female, but I think more female because imagine how creative she must have been. Think of our eyes, as an example. Here we are with just two tiny little eyes, but we can see the stars, and whatever is in the stars can't see us. How miraculous. And it seems to me that men just don't think about these things.

I think I turned to God as female because I never got support from males, none, and my mom was never there either. Because there was nobody else to answer my questions, I turned to God 'cause God is always there. But sometimes I want to see God as a male, times when I need the strength of a male to take care of something that deals with the power of men. Then I say, "Come on! Do your job, fight them!" But a female God can fight also.

Mostly I imagine or picture God as all sorts of different images, like with Mary Magdalene and Rachel and Esther from the Bible. I think they're a part of God coming out in different roles. Lots of the time, I try to draw these images. When I draw a portrait of Mother Nature, I go beyond just the planet Earth. I draw our galaxy with the earth on one side and light reaching out to the side that we've never seen.

If I drew God as Mary Magdalene, I'd make her very beautiful, and her eyes would tell a lot. She'd be able to speak with her eyes and would probably be a perfect organizer. I think she'd make a wonderful organizer because of all her experience and her kind heart. And if I drew Mother Mary grieving by the cross, I'd have Christ be telling her, "Mother, don't grieve. There's still work to be done."

I made a drawing of Our Lady of Guadalupe and wrote a poem and sent it to people I loved at Christmas. This time she was pregnant and dressed in jeans as a farm worker and supporting a basket of tomatoes on her head. The heavens and sun was behind her, and she stood on a globe that showed Canada, the United States, Mexico, and Central America. I called it "Un Eco Navideño" [A Christmas Echo].

Era María, mi cara, la suya.
En su vientre, un hijo,
en mis manos, una semilla.
Nace un amanecer,
Por primera vez, ve sus ojos,
"Ay, Madre Mía."

Mama de sus senos
la dulzura de mi miel
y la amargura de mi vida.

Pisa la tierra
y siente el sol que me quema
y el frío que me tortura.

Habla, y sale un grito que estremece al mundo
y a aquél que me lastima.

Queda su eco: soy yo,
y su grito sale del alma mía.
¡Yo soy campesina!

[It was Mary; her face was mine.
In her womb a child,
In my hands a seed.
At the birth of dawn,
He sees, for the first time, her eyes
"Oh, my Mother."

He drinks from her breast
the sweetness of my honey
and the bitterness of my life.

He walks on the land
And feels the sun that burns me
And the cold that tortures me.

He speaks, and out comes a cry
that makes the world,
and he who hurts me, tremble.

An echo remains: It is I,
And his cry leaps from my soul,
I am a farm worker!]

I feel very close to God so I can get mad at God and nag and talk back when I need to. Sometimes I'll get real frustrated and say, "Jesus Christ! Give me a break!" I nag, but eventually I give in.

One of the ways I can tell what God wants me to do is the way my heart tells me. But there have been some times when I got so upset, I almost wished I was dead. I'd think, God's got to be wrong, I can't be the person to do this. Especially since my health has been so bad, I think that I don't have the kind of intelligence it takes, the energy, it's just something impossible. But I have to do it. I also get angry at God when I see a great injustice. That's when I think that maybe heaven is also a jail, that if God's so powerful and great, why can't he come out?

I also disagree with the church a lot, like with their stand on birth control, and I don't agree with the people who wrote the Bible. I feel kind of strange contradicting the big *sabios*, the sages who wrote it, and I think that parts of creation are a beautiful story, but it can't be possible. When they tell me that women came out of a man's rib, forget it. I came out of a womb! A mother's womb. They also say God took the clay and blew and made Adam. No. It didn't happen that way. I keep thinking, here I am a farm worker, a nobody, an uneducated person, but I think things like this—how long can they fool people? If a farm worker who doesn't have an education can think these things, how long is the church going to be able to keep our eyes blindfolded? The church is going to have to change if it wants to have people stay with it.

There is another image from our culture that I think about. That is La Malinche. She's always been considered an aggressive woman who was a traitor to our people. She was supposed to have helped Cortés and slept with him, and then she gave birth to the first mestizo. And all my life I've heard women like myself who are outspoken or aggressive called Malinche or la Chingada. Pablo says it all the time. But to me, I've begun to think about La Malinche as a very intelligent, very smart woman. It seems like nobody cared what was behind what she did, nobody ever bothered to ask her motives. Maybe she was a Gloria Chiquita using her only skills. Maybe she was preparing a better road for her people. Maybe she thought she could bring about good change and set an example. God knows the condition of the woman at the time. So I have all these opinions, and when men call me that, I say, "Sure, say that. I don't call that a put-down."

God comes to me in many ways. God is in the religion of the Farm Worker Ministry and the farm worker movement, in Christ and the Virgin of Guadalupe. God is in Mother Nature and in my strange dreams. And it seems to me that God is in some way imprisoned in all of us people and waiting for us to come together.

As the Sun Sets and the Beast Falls: The Creation of the Third Testament

Even with my criticisms of the farm worker movement, my commitment to it stays so strong. I am constantly talking about it to people and thinking about how I can explain it. I remember how I used to approach people when I was organizing in the camps, and how I explained the whole history of our struggle.

Let's say, for example, we are recruiting people in a certain area, trying to introduce them to our union. Maybe they are on a farm that is not under contract, and I want to talk to a family I've never met before. I always use my story to organize them and to make comparisons. I also always use the word of God, so I have to be careful about their religious beliefs. When they ask me what religion I am, I usually say, "I'm ecumenical."

They ask, "What is that?"

I say, "In a way, that means I am what you are."

Most of the time, most of the people that I visit sign the card. What I think takes place, really, when you organize people, truly organize them, it is a conversion. You have to somehow connect it between God and our cause. The people have to feel it, and they have to see your own sincerity.

Some people want to know about the whole history, about how everything happened. Then I need to be prepared to tell them what happened, how I see it from the beginning. Sometimes I explain it altogether, but usually the story will come out, piece by piece, over time.

I tell them how I think that it really started way back in the beginning, that Adam and Eve were the first farm workers. But then I explain how Moses was the first activist who tried to get, how do you say it, who tried to get *un descanso para la gente*. He was the first bricklayer leader, organizer, and he asked the Pharaoh for a break for the people. And I say, "This was in the First Testament, the Old Testament."

Then I explain what I believe about Jesus. I tell them I believe that at first Jesus Christ organized all the people in Galilee. He taught them a different way of life. Now this is my own theory, but what I believe is that he thought and he studied and said, "What is wrong? These people now have learned a better way of living, but the situation doesn't change. They're still poor. They're still hurting." So he got the idea that *el mal*, the problem, was coming from over there with the politicians. He thought, I've already organized these people, so now I have to go to Jerusalem and start with the politicians. Then, of course, I tell the people that Jesus went to Jerusalem and fought with the politicians and died for us in the process.

If the people aren't too tired, I keep on talking. I don't know the next story real well, but I think I understand. I talk about the time when Spain went under the control of the Moslems for about five hundred years, and they didn't allow any Bibles or any religious practices for the Catholic people. But I say that our grandmothers and our mothers maintained the belief and the teachings, that even at night they would light up a little candle and teach the kids how to do the sign of the cross and pray to the Mother of Jesus and to God. So, in spite of all the cruelty, all the persecution at that time, the Moslems couldn't take the Catholics' religion away. People held onto their faith.

Then I explain how the Spaniards came to Mexico and taught religion to the people in Mexico, and that, later on, the United States took much of Mexico for itself, and when that happened a lot of our parents, our ancestors, stayed on this side, and we were divided from each other. Then I say that I really believe that the church in the United States neglected us poor people, that the church was used to keep us under control, and that I truly believe that confession was used to control the whole community. And I say that we were also neglected in school. I tell them that when I was in school, I was just given some paper and Crayolas and told to paint and draw, but I was never even taught the basics.

Then I explain how the government did start some programs to help the poor people, but because we didn't have work and the aid wasn't enough, we started migrating north. We heard that they were giving good jobs and better opportunities up there, so we started the migration thing, and that has led us into *nuestro fracaso*, our own downfall. Because a lot of the growers and the people said, "Gosh, what a good opportunity for cheap labor." So we go up north with no rights, just shacks, to do hard labor. And these people I'm talking to certainly know what I mean.

Then I tell them about the thing that hurt me so bad when I learned about it: the law that was passed in 1935, the Labor Relations Act. I tell them how all the other people at that time got the right to organize for collective bargaining, but how, when the Department of Agriculture found this out, they paid lobbyists to go and convince the congressmen to exclude the farm workers. They did this because they thought that if the farm workers got organized, they weren't going to work so cheap. They weren't going to live under such bad conditions. I tell them how we were sold out.

After that I go into the story about the black people and all they fought for and President Kennedy. "Remember the day when we had to sit at the very back of the bus?" I say that especially to people my age or older, but I also try to be sure that their children hear it so they will understand. I say, "Remember how we couldn't go into a restaurant or a movie theater or the same rest room that white people did?" And I tell them that we should have been instructed at that time, we should have been taught about our rights, but we weren't. It seems to me that if we had known, there wouldn't have been any need for all those riots and the suffering of the black people.

But I tell them that the black people struggled and struggled and one day obtained their civil rights, and to me it seems like they opened a great big gate, and we just walked behind them. Because they did all the hard work, and we didn't even know about it. I say how it took all their sacrifice in order that we could have the liberty of going to a restaurant, to a toilet, to a movie, sitting in front of anywhere we went, and the right, also, in case anybody discriminates against us, to report it, so somebody will do something about it. I tell them that this is a very good example of what brothers and sisters are in God. In God there is no difference. It's here on earth that us people divide ourselves into different nationalities and put up barriers. Then I say how President Kennedy was the person that gave the black people their civil rights, but then he was killed, and how I've always thought that must have some connection to his death.

Finally, I say, "Have you ever heard of César Chávez? He is like Moses in the Bible. He took into his hands a whole nation of farm workers and has tried to lead us out into a better land. He has tried to take us across to the land of milk and honey. But he has to do it different than Moses did it in the past. He has to do it in the present time by dealing with the government and with politicians and by dealing with the laws."

So this all takes a very long time, but it's very important that the people get a clear understanding that our cause doesn't have to do with a hundred years or even two hundred years, it has to go way back to even before Jesus came, and then it goes on and on in the future.

I think about how the story will be continued, and it seems to me that we have two testaments that tell the story, the Old Testament and the New Testament, and that what we need is a Third Testament of life. I want to make sure that women are included this time. Sometimes I start thinking about who's going to keep records and chronicles about what's happening. I wonder if there's a way that records could be saved for future children. I keep thinking about not just my story but the stories of all the women I've known. I hope that the next testament will talk about the chemical problems and the pesticides and about how women have been excluded and what it has taken to make any gains. Sometimes I draw up lists of names for the Third Testament. I include men, but I especially include the women. . . .

Sometimes I think about what I would have done if I had been able to get some schooling or if I'd known about César and the movement when I was young. I think if I'd gone to school and if anybody had believed in me, I could have been a great labor leader, maybe a female César Chávez. When I was a child and for many years, I'd love to think about the theater and singing, but when I began to get involved with the movement, anything that I did with performing or singing or reading had to be linked to the movement. Nothing, in my whole life, has ever touched me like it did.

And if I'd known about the movement when I was young, oh my God, the things I would have been able to do. I had so much energy, so much strength, so much enthusiasm. But at my age, with my condition, I feel like my time is short. Every day I get up and look outside. I look at the ground and the plants and the sky, and I say, "God, you gave us a beautiful world," and then I think, and I'm running out of time. . . .

Challah for the Queen of Heaven

❖ *Ryiah Lilith* ❖

Witchcraft led me back to Judaism.

I grew up in a secular Zionist home, and though I sometimes went to shul with friends, and in high school attended quite a few confirmation ceremonies, my own Jewish education and observance were casual. In college I unearthed my proverbial roots and fell in love with the absolutes of traditional Judaism, but my love affair was cut short when I discovered feminism. As buzzwords and phrases such as *patriarchy, masculine God-language* and *blood taboo* crept into my vocabulary, the lure of Orthodox Judaism diminished. In Conservative services I was distracted by the gendered and often sexist prayers and felt little connection to either Adonai or other congregants, and although the Reform *Gates of Prayer* was explicitly nonsexist, I noticed that the rabbi, cantor, congregational leadership and most of the board were men. So I left, taking a cue from Carol Christ and declaring myself "post-Jewish."

My exodus from Judaism was only one manifestation of my righteous feminist anger. Feminism had opened my eyes, but rather than the "click" described by Gloria Steinem, feminism became both my worldview and my blinders. I stopped going to classes mid-semester when I decided that the professors, students or reading materials were sexist, or not explicitly feminist, and hence no longer relevant to my life. I changed my major seven times before nesting in the women's studies department. I declined invitations to see nonfeminist movies, and eventually cut people who suggested such misogynistic entertainment out of my life. I decided that I would never again allow a man to fuck me and threw a coming-out party for myself. I began a senior thesis on lesbian separatism and dreamed of living on wimmin's land. I dabbled in Witchcraft and women's spirituality. And then I graduated.

My righteous feminist anger, cut off from the inspiration of women's studies, morphed into frustration and depression. Convinced that I was the sole radical post-Jewish lesbian feminist in my small Midwestern town, I cocooned myself in my apartment and experimented with solo consciousness-raising. I had spent almost a year in self-imposed exile when a newspaper ad for an annual women's Winter Solstice ritual caught my attention. I arrived on time, with my yarn, round mirror and white candle in tow.

The ritual was powerful—a hundred or so women of all ages, shapes and sizes chanting and dancing in a candlelit room smelling of sage and sweetgrass, welcoming the return of the Sun Goddess. I lingered after the ritual was over, hoping to soak up enough of the ambience to sustain me until next year's ritual. I was surprised at the intensity of my experience, for my brief undergraduate forays into Witchcraft had been lackluster. Although I had appreciated the feminist orientation and the emphasis on the Goddess, I had already given up one religion and felt ambivalent about practicing another.

In the following weeks, I reread and reconsidered the few books on Witchcraft and Paganism that I had saved during my post-graduation book purge. I unpacked the small collection of ritual tools that I had started to accumulate and I began creating solitary rituals, in the hopes of recapturing the feeling of peace and serenity that I had experienced at the Solstice. It just wasn't the same. I felt silly standing or sitting before my coffee-table altar, chanting Goddess names to myself. Wondering if maybe the requirement of a minyan had somehow been genetically etched into my soul, I decided to search for a group of Witches. Instead, I found a group of Jewish women.

I felt apprehensive and explained to the group's leader that I no longer practiced Judaism. She assured me that a Rosh Chodesh ceremony was quite distinct from mainstream Jewish services, and explained that this traditional Jewish observance of the new moon, sometimes considered a women's holiday, had been appropriated and updated by Jewish women. Contemporary Rosh Chodesh rituals are often women-only and include explicitly feminist liturgy. Eventually I decided to go, figuring that I wasn't having much success on my own. We gathered in a member's backyard and sat cross-legged on mats under the new moon. We lit candles, introduced ourselves as the daughters of our mothers and our grandmothers ("I am Ryiah, daughter of Ruth, daughter of Mary . . . ") and took turns reading poems by Jewish women. We sang prayers to Shekinah, the feminine aspect of God, using traditional melodies. I left feeling oddly inspired, promising to return next month.

Historically, Rosh Chodesh evolved out of ancient Near Eastern lunar rituals, which focused on fertility, divination and Goddess worship.[1] As combating idol worship became a significant priority for some Israelite leaders, lunar observances by Israelite women became problematic.[2] Interestingly, instead of prohibiting lunar observances—or perhaps because such prohibitions proved ineffective—celebration of the new moon became a sanctioned Israelite festival, complete with a revised mythology that the women were given Rosh Chodesh by God as a reward for their refusal to donate any of their gold for the creation of the Golden Calf. Although Rosh Chodesh observances varied, common practices included baking challah, refraining from work and lighting candles or fires at night.[3]

Rosh Chodesh observance has waxed and waned over the last two thousand years, but it met a strong revival during the second wave of feminism. Contemporary Rosh Chodesh rituals often take place in women's homes and involve lighting candles, praying, singing and chanting to Shekinah (as Lady of the Moon) and festive or ritual meals.

I found in Rosh Chodesh a way to integrate Jewish and Pagan practices, and for a while I experienced a peaceful reconciliation. I still avoided temple, but I also stopped referring to myself as "post-Jewish." I began a tentative study of feminist Jewish theology and Torah commentary. But I soon uncovered dissension between Jewish feminists and Goddess worshippers. For example, some of the latter believe in a prehistorical, prebiblical, Goddess-oriented, matrifocal society, which was destroyed by Indo-European invaders (sometimes identified as the Levites[4]) who were militaristic and patriarchal, and worshipped a transcendent male God.[5] In response, Jewish feminist theologians likened this interpretation of herstory to claims that the Jews killed Jesus, and were equally adamant that Jews did not kill the Goddess, noting that the societies which predated the Israelites had attempted to curtail Goddess worship.[6] Other Jewish scholars argue that even after this time, the Goddess continued to play a role in Judaism.[7]

I hoped to eventually reconcile my Jewish and Pagan spirituality, but in light of this intellectual schism I resigned myself to practicing both separately: I was a solitary Witch who also belonged to a Jewish women's circle. I occasionally wondered whether I would still practice Judaism if I left the area, but the other women often spoke of other Rosh Chodesh collectives they had belonged to, both in the past and in other cities. Sure enough, when I moved to the District of Columbia I soon found a Jewish women's group that met monthly for both social and religious occasions. Unfortunately, differences between the D.C. crowd and my former collective quickly emerged. Although the D.C. group celebrated the Jewish holidays with feminist liturgy that referred to Shekinah, she was merely Adonai in drag. At Yom Kippur, we prayed to Shekinah to forgive us, and at Passover we remembered how she led us out of Egypt with a mighty hand and an outstretched arm. I felt as little connection to this Shekinah as I had to Adonai.

While some Pagans consider Shekinah to be a Goddess in her own right, completely distinct from Adonai,[8] most non-Pagan Jewish feminists consider her to be the immanent, feminine aspect of God who accompanied the Israelites into exile after the destruction of the Temple, and who became incorporated into Jewish mysticism. As the immanent aspect of God, Shekinah possesses different attributes than Adonai. For example, Jewish mystics believe that the divine becomes manifest in the world through Shekinah, not Adonai, and Jewish feminist theologians have discovered that many of the symbols and metaphors for Shekinah—such as lunar cycles, the morning and evening star, the primordial sea, the dove and the serpent—were also associated with ancient Near Eastern Goddesses, but were not associated with Adonai.[9]

While I wasn't certain whether I understood her to be a Goddess or a feminine aspect of God, I knew that Shekinah was not simply another name for Adonai. When I raised this issue with the group's leader, I discovered that criticism and dissent were not tolerated. Unlike my Midwestern Rosh Chodesh circle, the D.C. group was not an egalitarian collective, but a dictatorship. Membership decisions, dates and times of events, liturgical revision and networking or outreach were all determined by one woman whose authority could not be questioned without risking excommunication. My attempts to "Paganize" the liturgy—as my questioning was characterized—resulted in my expulsion from the group.

Despite this experience, I was hopeful that I would find a more open-minded group of Jewish women who were creating feminist rituals. The D.C. area has a large enough Jewish population to host several Jewish women's groups; over time, I participated in a feminist group that was mixed-gender, an Orthodox women's minyan and a feminist women's circle that conceived of God as gender-neutral. Yet none of them were exactly what I was looking for—a path to the Goddess. All were uncomfortable with Shekinah as anything other than Adonai's alter ego, and steadfastly refused to even consider incorporating other ancient Near Eastern Goddesses, such as Asherah (who was worshipped for some time by the Israelites themselves) into group ritual. I realized that I would again have to leave the Jewish tribe—this time, not because of my feminist sensibilities, but because of my increasingly Pagan worldview.

I was drawn to Witchcraft, and to Paganism in general, because of the lack of dogma and authority and the emphasis on personal responsibility for one's own spiritual development and expression. In contrast to the revealed mysteries of Judaism, Witchcraft is an occult religion—its mysteries must be experienced to be understood. An aspiring Witch first studies with a teacher, or series of teachers, and learns the teacher's ways of doing things, but eventually she has to break away, design her own rituals and develop her own cosmology and thealogy (Goddess-based theology) in order to delineate a personal and fulfilling spiritual practice. Although most Pagan traditions or denominations are open to both women and men, and honor both the Goddess and the God, I chose to follow the all-female, all-Goddess Dianic tradition (from Diana, the Roman lunar Goddess of the hunt). I had found my path to the Goddess, but as I progressed in my studies and practice, I realized that my spiritual development would never be complete until I figured out how to integrate Judaism into my feminist Goddess-worship.

Since I still wasn't sure how to intellectually reconcile Judaism and Witchcraft, I began at the material level: I looked to see what was similar in Jewish and Pagan ritual and practice. This also meshed with the Pagan approach to attaining spiritual wisdom. First, there was the timing of holidays: Both Jews and Witches use a lunar calendar, and many of the annual festivals are linked to agricultural cycles of planting (Tu B'Shvat and Passover for Jews, and the Spring Equinox and May Day for Pagans), tending (counting the *omer* between Passover and Shavuot; the Summer Solstice) and harvesting (Shavuot and Sukkot; the Fall Equinox). Second, although Jewish observances do not generally include drumming and dancing, some do, and most involve a fair amount of singing and candlelighting—all of which are central in many Pagan rituals and celebrations. I was determined to keep things simple. I wanted to experience only the smallest inklings of synchronicity and syncretism—no books, no groups, only candles and the moon.

A Witch usually sets up an altar in her home, on which she may display candles, photographs, artwork, seashells, crystals, herbs or other symbols of the Goddess and the natural world. I unpacked my Shabbos candlesticks, dusted them off, and placed them on my altar. On Friday evenings and Rosh Chodeshim, I lit candles and recited feminized blessings. As Hanukah approached, I positioned my altar so that it was underneath the window in which I placed a menorah.

While I found these simple observances comforting, I knew that they were not based on an integrated thealogy. Although I could place Jewish ritual items on a Pagan altar, the altar as a whole still represented the Goddess. I was figuratively resting my Judaism on a foundation of idolatry, and I had to explore the ramifications of that from a Jewish perspective. While Witchcraft is eclectic, and can easily absorb multicultural practices and beliefs, Judaism can only be stretched so far before it ceases to be Judaism. I wanted to determine if I could stretch Judaism far enough that its margins overlapped with Goddess worship and Witchcraft. I was not seeking an absolute understanding of Jewish law, but rather an interpretation that would help me to understand the apparent oxymoron of Pagan Judaism.

In attempting to navigate a Jewish Pagan path to the Goddess, I began by considering the Goddess and idolatry. Literally, the mitzvot only prohibit worship of other Gods, so perhaps worship of the Goddess is acceptable. However, the prohibitions against idolatry are wider-reaching: There is Jeremiah's admonishment to the women to cease pouring libations and baking cakes for the Queen of Heaven. And there are the multiple references to tearing down the high places: the Asherim, or altars to the Goddess Asherah. The Torah, in fact, describes countless incidents of Goddess worship, but always in the context of Israelites who strayed, or other wicked people. Logically, idolatry and Goddess worship would not have been repeatedly prohibited unless the Israelites were repeatedly practicing them. So the question then becomes, if being Jewish is defined as doing those things that Jews have traditionally done, how does one determine what Jews have traditionally done—by what the Torah proclaims that Jews should do, or by other historical revelations of what Jews actually did?

I realize that this line of reasoning could be extended to other prohibitions, and similar arguments could be made: for example, that the prohibition against murder implies that murder should be embraced as a Jewish act. But the act of murder is quite distinct from Goddess worship in my mind. Anyone who does equate the two will likely condemn my beliefs anyway, to the extent that no argument I could make would convince them that I can be both Jewish and Pagan. However, a useful parallel can be drawn in this context between Goddess worship and homosexuality. The Torah prohibits both, perhaps because at the time of its writing, both threatened the unity or survival of the Israelites—or perhaps those were more patriarchal and homophobic times. Today, different denominations have different stances on homosexuality. Likewise, denominations differ in their view of God; humanistic Jews probably are not concerned that other Jews worship a Goddess instead of God. It may not be traditional to worship the Goddess, but what is sufficiently traditional? Certainly not secular, Reform, Reconstructionist, Renewal, Conservative, humanist, GLBT or feminist Judaism. Orthodox Judaism may be the most traditional modern denomination, but it is still post-Temple Judaism—a fairly recent invention.

Eventually, I stopped trying to parse out arguments. My solitary altar-based rituals were so meaningful to me in their successful blend of Judaism and Witchcraft—much more so than crafting an argument that Judaism and Witchcraft are not mutually exclusive—that I began to incorporate Jewish elements into the Pagan group rituals that I was creating. One year, the spring equinox coincided with Purim, and I designed a ritual to celebrate survival: the survival of the Jewish people, Jewish feminism and Jewish Goddess worship, as well as the survival through winter. After the ritual, several of the women in attendance talked about their Jewish backgrounds and efforts to reconcile Judaism and Witchcraft. Although most Pagans were raised as Christians—not surprising, since most people in this country are raised Christian—and many others were raised as Pagans, there are a number of Jewish women within the Pagan community who worship the Goddess and who want more feminine and feminist liturgy and ritual than Judaism currently allows. In the Pagan community, we can create and shape Jewish rituals without the concerns that they are too Pagan or too feminist or too nontraditional to be authentically Jewish.

The rituals I design and lead often contain both Jewish and Pagan symbols, prayers and customs—even when the ritual is celebrating a purely Jewish or purely Pagan occasion. I do not claim that these are Jewish rituals—they are Jewish Witchcraft, or Pagan Judaism. I will not give up Judaism, and I will not allow others, Jewish or not, to determine what Judaism should mean to me or how I should practice it within my home and my community. As a Goddess-worshipping lesbian feminist, I found that no mainstream Jewish denomination fulfilled my spiritual needs; but just because I am not a Reform Jew or a Conservative Jew, it doesn't mean that I'm not a Jew. I rejected the denominations, not the religion.

I may not be able to explain exactly *how* I manage to be both Jewish and Pagan, but I know with certainty that I *am* both. If I had not discovered Witchcraft, I would probably be so frustrated and disillusioned with organized religion that I would avoid all manifestations of it. If my life had taken that turn, then perhaps I would identify as a secular, humanistic, ethnic or cultural Jew. And while I do not mean to disparage any of those forms of Judaism, a great deal of Jewish custom and belief is intertwined and woven into religious rituals and practices. Maybe it is possible to be a completely secular Jew in Israel—to never have entered a synagogue or uttered a prayer—and still feel very Jewish. But in the United States, with Sundays, Christmas and Easter automatically designated as holidays, and when the Bible usually means the New Testament, I wonder how long it would be before a post-Jew would cease to feel Jewish at all. Witchcraft enabled me to avoid that fate. Instead, I found a religion and spirituality that allows me to embrace and express all aspects of myself. Since I am able to create and share Jewish rituals that are feminist and Goddess oriented in the Pagan community, I am content to attend more traditional Jewish rituals without feeling a need to Paganize them. In Jewish services, I feel connected to other Jews; in Pagan rituals, I feel connected to the Goddess; and in Jewish Pagan rituals, I feel at home and at peace. I don't believe that that makes me less of a Jew; it simply makes me another type of Jew.

A multitude of different practices fall under the title and rubric of Judaism. If "Jewish" is a sufficiently expansive and flexible marker to describe the overlap or commonality—no matter how slight—between Reconstructionist, Israeli, transgender, Hasidic and Ethiopian Jews, then it can certainly include Goddess-worshipping Jewish Witches as well.

Notes

1. Marcia Falk, *The Book of Blessings: New Jewish Prayers for Daily Life, the Sabbath, and the New Moon Festival* (HarperSanFrancisco, 1996), 329. Falk notes that "it is likely that the adoption of Rosh Hodesh by women was rooted, at least in part, in a generally perceived connection between lunar cycles and menstrual cycles."
2. Ellen Frankel, *The Five Books of Miriam: A Woman's Commentary on the Torah* (Putnam, 1996), 136–41. Frankel discusses Rosh Chodesh, Israelite worship of the Goddess Asherah and prohibitions against idolatry in her commentary on Exodus 30:11–34:35.

3. Penina V. Adelman, *Miriam's Well: Rituals for Jewish Women Around the Year* (2nd ed.) (Biblio Press, 1990), 1–2. Adelman writes, "As it evolved, [Rosh Chodesh] became a way for the religious establishment to combat idol worship and to satisfy the need to continue observance of the sacred relationship between the moon and women which had been part of the indigenous mythologies of the region."

4. Merlin Stone, *When God was a Woman* (Harcourt Brace Jovanovich, 1978), 163–79.

5. Riane Eisler, *The Chalice and the Blade: Our History, Our Future* (HarperSanFrancisco, 1995), 44–45.

6. Judith Plaskow, "Blaming the Jews for the Birth of Patriarchy," and Annette Daum, "Blaming the Jews for the Death of the Goddess," in *Nice Jewish Girls: A Lesbian Anthology,* ed. Evelyn Torton Beck (Beacon Press, 1989), 298–309.

7. Raphael Patai discusses this in *The Hebrew Goddess* (3rd ed.) (Wayne State University Press. 1990).

8. Janet and Stewart Farrar, *The Witches' Goddess: The Feminine Principle of Divinity* (Phoenix Publishing, 1987), 272. The Farrars list Shekinah as one the "Goddesses of the World."

9. Lynn Gottlieb, *She Who Dwells Within: A Feminist Vision of Renewed Judaism* (HarperSanFrancisco, 1995), 19–23. See note 2 above.

Discussion Questions

1. Chung Hyun Kyung states that religion helped to sustain the two women who were her mothers. What religion is she referring to? Did they both have the same religion? Did they practice it in a systematic way? What was it about religion that helped them: A religious belief? Membership in a church or other religious community? A practice that they followed on their own? A minister or other type of religious leader? Does this compare or contrast in any way with your assumptions or experience about the role that religion plays in individual lives?

2. What is the difference between the "men's Islam" and the "women's Islam" that Leila Ahmed describes? How do they compare in terms of power and importance in people's lives? Are you aware of any corresponding difference in the religious tradition with which you are most familiar? What is your reaction to Ahmed's contention that Western feminism has often dealt with Islam in a biased way?

3. What feature of womanist theology, as Jacqueline Grant describes it, distinguishes it from more mainstream Christian theology? Grant asserts the reality of a Black Jesus. What is your reaction to this assertion? Do you think that women can, as she suggests, create new symbols and find new ways of reading scripture and still remain within established churches? Should they try to do so? Do you think, after reading Grant's essay, that the issues involved are different for Black women than for their white counterparts in Christian churches?

4. Do you believe that feminists who use Native American beliefs or practices in their own spiritual practice are stealing in a sense, as Inés Hernández-Ávila suggests? Do you believe that it's necessary to be a member of a certain community in order to

adopt a given belief or practice? According to her, what is the criterion for authenticity in relation to spiritual practices? Why would this be particularly important for a people such as Native Americans?

5. Kwok Pui-lan grew up in a family that practiced Buddhism and traditional Chinese religions, yet she became a Christian. What is her attitude toward the religious milieu in which she grew up? What direction does she, as a theologian, want to see Christian theology take? Does her approach seem right/wrong/likely/realistic to you?

6. How is the voice that speaks in Lucas's piece different from that in the other selections you have read? What does it indicate about the speaker? How does Lucas envision the image of the Virgin of Guadalupe? Why does Lucas feel the desire to re-envision this traditional Catholic image? Does it seem to you that she is leaving behind traditional Catholic belief by doing so?

7. What led Lilith, when she was in college, to declare herself to be "post-Jewish"? What was the theological issue that led to her "expulsion" from the Jewish women's group that she had joined while living in Washington, D.C.? How would you characterize the respective importance of belief and practice in Lilith's approach to religion? How does that compare with your own experience? Lilith asserts that the category "Jewish" is sufficiently flexible to allow her, through her own eclectic rituals, to forge an identity as "another type of Jew." What do you think of her assertion? Do you believe that the tradition with which you identify or are most familiar would afford you the same possibility? Lilith characterizes her rituals as Jewish Witchcraft, or Pagan Judaism. Does it seem to you that they are in fact more one than the other? Is the creation of a syncretic religious practice a good way, in your opinion, for an individual to set about meeting her own spiritual needs?

Suggested Readings

Ahmed, Leila. *Women and Gender in Islam: Historical Roots of a Modern Debate.* New Haven, CT: Yale University Press, 1992.

Allen, Paula Gunn. *The Sacred Hoop: Recovering the Feminine in American Indian Traditions.* Boston: Beacon, 1992.

Aquino, María Pilar, Daisy L. Machado, and Jeanette Rodriguez, eds. *A Reader in Latina Feminist Theology: Religion and Justice.* Austin: University of Texas Press, 2002.

Cannon, Katie G. *Black Womanist Ethics.* Atlanta: Scholars Press, 1988.

Chung, Hyun Kyung. *The Struggle to Be the Sun Again: Introducing Asian Women's Theology.* Maryknoll, NY: Orbis, 1990.

———. "Han-puri: Doing Theology from Asian Women's Perspective." In *We Dare to Dream: Doing Theology as Asian Women,* Virginia Fabella and Sun Ai Park, eds. Maryknoll, NY: Orbis, 1990.

———. "Seeking the Religious Roots of Pluralism." *Journal of Ecumenical Studies* 34 (1997): 399–401.

Donaldson, Laura E. "On Medicine Women and White Shame-Ans: New Age Native Americanism and Commodity Fetishism as Pop Culture." *Signs: Journal of Women in Culture and Society* 24 (1999): 677–696.

Donaldson, Laura E. and Kwok Pui-lan, eds. *Postcolonialism, Feminism, and Religious Discourse.* New York: Routledge, 2002.

Gilkes, Cheryl Townsend. *"If It Wasn't for the Women . . . ": Black Women's Experience and Womanist Culture in Church and Community.* Maryknoll, NY: Orbis, 2001.

Hampson, Daphne. *Theology and Feminism.* Oxford: Basil Blackwell, 1990.

Hennelly, Alfred T. *Liberation Theologies: The Global Pursuit of Justice.* Mystic, CT: Twenty-Third Publications, 1995.

Hutton, Ronald. *The Triumph of the Moon: A History of Modern Pagan Witchcraft.* Oxford: Oxford University Press, 1999.

Isasi-Díaz, Ada María. *En la Lucha/In the Struggle, Elaborating a Mujerista Theology.* Minneapolis, MN: Fortress, 1993.

Jaimes, M. Annette. "'Patriarchal Colonialism' and Indigenism: Implications for Native Feminist Spirituality and Native Womanism." *Hypatia* 18 (2003): 58–69.

Kwok Pui-lan. "Speaking Out." *Journal of Feminist Studies in Religion* 14 (1998): 77–78.

———. "Feminist Theology as Intercultural Discourse." In *The Cambridge Companion to Feminist Theology,* Susan Frank Parsons, ed., Cambridge, UK: Cambridge University Press, 2002, 23–39.

Michem, Stephanie Y. *Introducing Womanist Theology.* Maryknoll, NY: Orbis, 2002.

Raphael, Melissa. *Introducing Thealogy: Discourse on the Goddess.* Sheffield, UK: Sheffield Academic Press, 1999.

Roald, Anne Sofie. *Women in Islam: The Western Experience.* New York: Routledge, 2001.

Ross, Rosetta E. *Witnessing and Testifying: Black Women, Religion, and Civil Rights.* Minneapolis, MN: Fortress, 2003.

Ruether, Rosemary Radford, ed. *Gender, Ethnicity, and Religion: Views from the Other Side.* Minneapolis, MN: Fortress, 2002.

Russell, Letty, Kwok Pui-lan, Ada María Isasí-Diaz, and Katie Cannon, eds. *Inheriting Our Mothers' Gardens: Feminist Theology in Third World Perspective.* Philadelphia: Westminster, 1988.

Smith, Andy. "For All Those Who Were Indian in a Former Life." In *Ecofeminism and the Sacred,* Carol J. Adams, ed., New York: Continuum, 1993, 168–171.

Thomas, Linda E. "Womanist Theology, Epistemology, and a New Anthropological Paradigm." *Cross Currents* 48 (1998/1999): 488–499.

Townes, Emilie M., ed. *Embracing the Spirit: Womanist Perspectives on Hope, Salvation, and Transformation.* Maryknoll, NY: Orbis, 1997.

Webb, Gisela, ed. *Windows of Faith: Muslim Women Scholar-Activists in North America.* Syracuse, NY: Syracuse University Press, 2000.

Williams, Delores. *Sisters in the Wilderness: The Challenge of Womanist God-Talk.* Maryknoll, NY: Orbis, 1993.

Web Sites

Indigenous Women's Network (IWN), http://indigenous women.org

Islam for Today, Women in Islam, http://www.islamfortoday.com/women.htm

Maryams.net, Muslim Women and Their Islam, http://www.maryams.net/

Muslim Women's League, http://www.mwlusa.org

Resources for and about Muslim Women, http://www.jannah.org/sisters/index.html

Under Shekhina's Wings, Cross-Cultural Women's Spirituality, http://www.geocities.com/Athens/1501/

University of California at Santa Barbara, Black Feminism Bibliography, "Womanist Spirituality and God-talk, http://www.library.ucsb.edu/subjects/blackfeminism/ah_womanisttheol.html

Women in Islam, http://www.usc.edu/dept/MSA/humanrelations/womeninislam/

PART II

※

CONFRONTING TRADITION

The system of patriarchy is a historic construct; it has a beginning; it will have an end.

—GERDA LERNER, *The Creation of Patriarchy*

Carol Christ, whose "Expressing Anger at God" begins this section, is perhaps the best-known academic spokesperson for goddess spirituality. However, this early essay was written prior to her embracing of the Goddess as a spiritual symbol for women. In it she recounts a painful event in her life that serves as an example of the type of experience that led many women to confront the mainstream religious traditions in which they were raised. This essay signals the beginning of the divide that would come to characterize the women's spirituality movement, between those who remained within a religious tradition and directed their efforts at reform, on the one hand, and those, like Christ, who were led elsewhere in their search for spiritual meaning, on the other. Christ has cited the writing of Elie Wiesel as an important early influence on her thought; in this piece, though she recounts an experience that took place in a Christian church, Christ draws on the resources of Jewish tradition for a mechanism through which to express—on her own behalf and that of other women—anger at God.

Mary Daly's *The Church and the Second Sex* is often cited as a founding text of feminist theology. The allusion in the book's title to Simone de Beauvoir's classic work (Beauvoir 1953), and the highly negative reception it received from Catholic authorities, link it to a particular moment of social and cultural ferment. Compared with Daly's later works this is a measured critique, a historical survey of attitudes and teachings about women in the Catholic tradition in which the author concludes that that tradition represents a "record of contradictions," in which "the symbolic glorification of 'woman' arose as a substitute for recognition of full personhood and equal rights." A useful comparison can be made between Daly's thought, which subsequently diverged toward radical cultural feminism, and that of thinkers such as Carol Christ, who became an exponent of goddess spirituality. Such a comparison illustrates the varied paths pursued by those American feminists who, at a certain stage of Second Wave feminism, came to see feminism and Christianity as mutually exclusive commitments.

In "Violence against Women in the Historical Christian West and in North American Secular Culture: The Visual and Textual Evidence," Margaret Miles moves beyond assertions about the Christian churches' exclusion of women or lack of support for their personhood, to argue that Christianity has been complicit, historically, in fostering violence against women. Miles cites the visual evidence of Christian art over the centuries as reinforcing the identification of woman with nature, the body, and sin, and in presenting female suffering as desirable. She then goes on to argue that our secular society, and American popular culture in particular, incorporate many elements of this misogynist inheritance.

Frances Wood condemns the Black church for its "sexist apartheid," which subordinates African American women and legitimizes violence against them, in "'Take My Yoke upon You': The Role of the Church in the Oppression of African-American Women." Traditional Christian explanations for suffering (to punish sin, to build character, and to mark someone as special in God's eyes), Wood argues, have been used by the Black church to justify an oppressive status quo that is lethal for women. Pastors expect women to submit to men's abuse and to take upon themselves the "yoke" of martyrdom. Women who speak out against sexist violence and oppression are seen as undermining African American manhood and betraying the Black community.

Women's voices are to be raised in song and in praise, but not in complaint or in accusation. The silence expected of women is matched by the silence of the church in the face of sexism and brutality. For Wood, the silence of the church is sinful. As a womanist theologian, she recognizes the need of women to define themselves in their own terms in order to overcome oppression. Hers is a call to the church to listen to women and to confront its misogyny.

In contrast to Wood's critique, which is rooted in religious commitment, Darice Jones' piece "Falling off the Tightrope onto a Bed of Feathers" takes self-affirmation and personal authenticity as orienting principles. Jones, an African American lesbian artist and writer, interrogates the place of religion in relation to those goals as she tells the story of her search for an authentic self and a public voice. A major influence in Jones's life was the Pentecostal church, which played a central role in her adolescence, and with which she continued to struggle into young adulthood. Jones's adolescent experience in the church involved abuse and betrayal; however, her response to this experience involves an attitude of determined questioning as opposed to outright rejection. Moreover, by stressing her closeness to and admiration for her mother, Jones presents herself as a searcher who is relationally grounded; even as she speaks the language of personal identity, independence, and wholeness, the author asks herself, "What would my mother think?"

Jones, who grew up in the 1980s and attended college in the 1990s, belongs to a generation for whom feminism offered an interpretive frame of reference. For her, feminism is a blend of the academic and the experiential, a force that she uses to come to terms with her disastrous encounter with religious authority, as well as to affirm her own voice and identify in the face of family, church, and society.

Within Islam, as in Judaism and Christianity, sacred texts have been used to justify oppressive gender roles. Riffat Hassan argues in the two pieces excerpted here that, contrary to what is often claimed by male Muslim authorities, the Qur'an does not present a view of woman as either inferior or subordinate. Her exegesis provides an excellent example, from within Islamic tradition, of what has been identified as the "first stage" of the feminist theological enterprise; namely, the critique of patriarchy within a tradition and specifically, the attempt to wrest the interpretation of sacred texts out of male control. Her second essay is a deeply affecting account of the author's own life, and of her efforts to negotiate an identity as both a highly educated and achieving woman and a devout Muslim. Taken together, these pieces illustrate in a clear and moving way, through the testimony of an Islamic scholar, the way in which personal experience motivates individuals to confront a religious tradition even while struggling to remain faithful to it.

Carol Christ, in "Why Women Need the Goddess," offers a kind of cultural analysis centering on the function of symbols to undergird her contention that women "need the Goddess." In contrast to the goddess selection by Nelle Morton in Part III, which is more personal and experiential, this piece represents an attempt to provide a well-developed, systematic account of why this form of spirituality is essential to women. Christ draws on the work of anthropologist Clifford Geertz (1966) to describe how the symbol of the Goddess can be used to serve important psychological and polit-ical functions for women. The Goddess symbol represents legitimate female power, the affirmation of women's bodies and reproductive roles, the value of women's exer-cise of willpower, and a celebration of women's bonds to each other. Christ argues that women need the Goddess as an alternative to negative images of women created by the worship of a male god, images that legitimize patriarchal social relations by portray-ing women as weak or dangerous. And, women need the Goddess in order to identify their corporeal selves with divinity in a way that, within the Judeo-Christian tradition, is readily available to men. This short piece confronts tradition in a more radical way than the other selections in this section. Rather than critiquing established religious tra-ditions, Christ argues that women's spiritual needs can be most fully met elsewhere.

In the short selection, "The Coming of Lilith," Jewish feminist theologian Judith Plaskow retells from a feminist perspective the story of Lilith, Adam's rebel-lious first wife. In Plaskow's retelling Eve is led, under Lilith's influence, to a new self-understanding. This piece was originally written in 1972 and published in 1974 before being reprinted in *Womanspirit Rising*, the seminal 1979 anthology that Plaskow edited with Carol Christ. In a more recent reflection on this early piece, Plaskow (1999) states that from her later vantage point she would designate it not as myth but as *midrash*, an interpretive technique within Jewish tradition in which sto-rytelling may be brought to bear on the questions or contradictions in biblical narra-tives. "The Coming of Lilith" evoked an immediate response from its first readers and has continued to do so, becoming something of a classic in the mode of revisionist myth, or imaginative feminist reconstructions of a canonical patriarchal narrative.

Jennifer Bleyer's piece, like that of Darice Jones, represents an autobiographi-cal account of personal search and exploration by a member of American feminism's Third Wave. "From Riot Grrl to Yeshiva Girl" is Bleyer's account of her travels from the secular Jewish family of her childhood to a Hasidic yeshiva for young women in Israel. Along the way, she encountered the punk rock scene and feminism. Although she ultimately decided not to embrace Hasidism, in part because of its authoritarian stance on gender and race, Bleyer found the seriousness of Hasidic Judaism a refreshing change from the superficiality of much of modern life. She valued the opportunity to learn more about her Jewish heritage, and, at the same time, she also learned some important lessons about the need to challenge authority and orthodoxy, whether feminist or religious. This piece by a younger feminist differs from most of the other selections in this volume in its irreverent tone and in the author's insistence on the need to "shake up" doctrinaire thinking about religion and gender.

Like "The Coming of Lilith," "Coatlicue's Rules: Advice from an Aztec Goddess" presents an imaginative retelling of a patriarchal creation myth. Also like Plaskow's midrash on the Adam/Eve/Lilith stories, Pat Mora's poem offers a revisionist view of a particular culture's past. In the poem, we hear a version of Aztec creation mythology as told by the goddess Coatlicue herself, a creator/destroyer goddess of fearsome aspect, who wears a knot of twisted serpents for a skirt. This is the goddess who, in a later incarnation, would be desexed, domesticated, and transformed into the Virgin of Guadalupe. Like the oral history included in Part I and Plaskow's "The Coming of Lilith," this piece represents an example of the commitment in feminist writing to give voice to the voiceless. Coatlicue the serpent-skirted goddess speaks in Mora's poem as a woman who has seen a great deal in her (potentially infinite) time, and has a few things to say about the uses to which her own story has been put at the hands of patriarchal mythmakers. Her evident love for her own son, the sun god, is tempered by a certain realism about men and the things of which they are capable.

References

Beauvoir, Simone de. 1953. *The Second Sex*. New York: Knopf.

Geertz, Clifford. 1966. Religion as a cultural system. In M. Banton, ed., *Anthropological Approaches to the Study of Religion*, 1–46. London, UK: Tavistock.

Lerner, Gerda. 1986. *The Creation of Patriarchy*. New York: Oxford University Press.

Plaskow, Judith. 1999. Lilith revisited. In Kristin E. Kvam, Linda S. Schearing, and Valarie H. Ziegler, eds., *Eve and Adam: Jewish, Christian, and Muslim Readings on Genesis and Gender*, 425–430. Bloomington: Indiana University Press.

Expressing Anger at God

❖ *Carol P. Christ* ❖

This essay takes the form of story theology, theology as story and reflection on story. The biblical books of Job, Jeremiah, and Hosea provide intriguing models for the story theologian.[1] In each book the deep personal crisis of an individual (whether "real" or not) becomes a paradigm that illumines the community's relation to God. In each case, the probing of personal experience produces theological expressions which shock the pious and challenge the foundations of conventional faith. Despite the risks, I am convinced that by remaining faithful to the truth of our stories, no matter how difficult and isolating that truth seems at first, we will discover that our stories are shared. We may even find that they lead us, individually and communally, to a new relation with God.

Several years ago I met Caroline. One of the first women hired to teach at a major Eastern university, Caroline found her first years there difficult, frustrating, and painful. Our friendship developed as we discovered we shared many similar experiences, the same anger. We talked often about how our colleagues saw us as sexual beings yet did not take us seriously as scholars and thinkers. Caroline told me of her elation when one of her colleagues finally asked her to lunch to discuss her ideas, and her rage when he tried to seduce her. I told Caroline of my humiliation and rage on learning that the professor whose seminar I had actively participated in for a full year seemed to remember me simply as "the one with the long legs."

Through our friendship, and with the support of other women who shared our lives, Caroline and I began to learn together how to assert ourselves in a hostile academic environment without sacrificing ourselves as whole persons. For Caroline, the birth of her daughter Evelyn was a symbol of her power to be both a woman and a scholar. She felt her full self, her power, to be as new and as full of potential as her little daughter.

When Caroline asked me to become the godmother of her child, I knew she was asking me to affirm and help her daughter to grow into a full and vital woman. She hoped Evelyn would not know the bitter lonely struggle we had known. She wanted Evelyn to have me, her godmother, to help and guide her, to be the role model neither of us had known in our growing up. I also knew that Caroline's desire to baptize her daughter as a Christian expressed her trust that in some way the ground of our being

Acknowledgement is made for permission to reprint from the following: *Laughter of Aphrodite: Reflections on a Journey to the Goddess* (San Francisco: HarperSanFrancisco, 1987). © Carol P. Christ. "Why Women Need the Goddess" was originally published in *Heresies* 5 (1978) (The Great Goddess Issues) and "Expressing Anger at God" was originally published in *Anima* 5(1) (1978).

and living supports and affirms the new becoming of women. Because I wanted to share in that affirmation, I agreed to become Evelyn's godmother, even though I was aware of my increasing estrangement from God the Father.

I knew I would feel discomfort at the baptismal service, but I was not prepared for the enormity of feeling that surfaced in me that day. Evelyn was the only child being baptized, and the young bearded minister, friend of the family, spoke only of the Christian and "his" baptism into the "fellowship" of Christian "men." I had expected to hear God referred to only as "Father," but I had not been prepared to hear this young girl's identity stolen from her by a man whose words were saying that she could not at one and the same time be a woman and a Christian. I remained silent during the service, but I felt a conflict growing within me. My shoulders tensed, my stomach knotted, my head ached. I did not want to spoil my goddaughter's baptismal day, but neither could I deny my feelings.

After the service, I walked up to the minister and told him I had not appreciated his sexist language. He angrily retorted that he was waiting for the day when women like me would not feel the need to impose their personal problems on the Christian liturgy, which transcended such petty problems. Because I was struggling to restrain the full power of my anger, I spoke in an offhand way to the minister, not revealing the depth of my feeling of betrayal. I had expected him to know without my saying it. This failure of communication underscores the need for anger to be expressed fully and directly.

The minister's response provoked me to tears, to the expression of more feeling. I became the center of attention at the gathering of friends and relatives after the baptism. First the mother, then the father, then the minister and others asked me about my tears and expressed their understanding of my pain. At the time, I was embarrassed and ashamed to divert attention from Evelyn on her baptismal day. Now I see that my anger and my tears were a gift to Evelyn. In speaking out about my sense of Evelyn's exclusion and my own from the service of her baptism, I expressed my commitment to her future.

Now I wish I'd had the courage to interrupt the service itself. The Christian tradition excludes and denies women's full selfhood. Recognizing this, women have three choices: to remain silent, to leave, or to confront. The third choice is the hardest. Some might suggest that this confrontation be kept out of the sanctuary, that women should meet with ministers and church members in order to convince them to change offensive language and the attitudes that give rise to it. Such struggles are important and useful. However, given the pervasive sexism of the tradition, simple elimination of the most offensive words from the liturgy will not suffice to bring about the kind of transformation of spirituality that is required. It may be that only the full and direct expression of women's feelings of anger and betrayal—before the community *and* before God—will create the situation in which genuine and creative healing can occur.

The suggestion that women's anger at God must be expressed both in solitude and in community provokes a deep resistance from both women and men. Will such rage destroy the community of faith? Ought women to feel it? And if they feel it, should they not keep it to themselves?

Let us imagine another scene. A women sits in church and listens to the stories of the Exodus. Hearing of God's compassion on the Hebrew slaves, she takes hope that God will pity her in her bondage as well. But then she hears that the convenantal promises were not made to her or her mothers, but to her fathers, to Abraham, to Isaac, to Jacob, she experiences bodily her exclusion from the very tradition that shaped her longings for redemption. Imagine that instead of choking back her anger, she rises and cries out.

In the grip of powerful feelings and emotions, why does a woman swallow the words forming in her throat? Perhaps she thinks she is alone with her feelings. Perhaps she is afraid her feelings will not be approved by her sisters or brothers. Job was mocked by his friends, accused of impiety, when he called upon God to defend himself against accusations of injustice. How much more scorn would be heaped on the woman who expressed her anger at God, who called upon the Almighty to answer her charges! Surely the pious members of the congregation would accuse her of emotionalism, would wonder what was wrong with her that she forced her personal feelings on them, would accuse her of spoiling a beautiful service. How much easier to swallow her anger. How much easier to choke to death on it.

Still, there may be important religious reasons for expressing anger at God. While women sit silent, perhaps even unaware that they are deadening themselves in order to do so, others leave the churches and synagogues, cutting off their relation with the biblical God. In both cases, women who once had powerful feelings about the God of biblical tradition may be denying part of themselves. They may be deadening their religious sensibility altogether, suppressing powerful, conflicting feelings toward God that come to them, perhaps, "in the night, tinged with hatred, with remorse, but most of all with infinite yearning."[2] A woman who swallows her anger and bitterness at God may also cut off her longing for the God who provoked her to anger.

For many women, I suggest, it is far more true to speak of hatred for God than of indifference to God. This anger at God, like feminist anger at men, must be expressed. And, just as in some cases, the expression of anger at men precedes a reconciliation, so too, the expression of anger at God may precede a renewed relation.

There is also traditional precedent for expressing anger at God. The biblical notion of relation with a living God implies the notion of full presence. Martin Buber has suggested that the enigmatic name of God, usually translated as "I am who I am," might better be translated as "I will be there as I will be there," or even "I will be present (to you) as I will be present (to you)."[3] God did not promise always to express loving feelings to the people but rather to be fully present with whatever God felt in response to the situation. Thus, God did not withhold anger when the people broke the covenant but was fully present with angry feelings. I suggest that God's ability to be present with whatever feelings God felt was the *sine qua non* of the possibility of a continuing relation. Had God repressed anger instead of expressing it, Israel would not have known the living God in the fullness of being. Like any other relation when anger is not expressed, the convenantal relation would have stagnated, gone dead.

In the Bible full presence also meant that the people could challenge God. Abraham and Moses questioned God's justice. Jeremiah, Jonah, and Job accused God of injustice.

In biblical religion the covenantal relation implied reciprocal obligations. When the people sinned God called them to court to present the case against them. The prophets often cast the relation between God and Israel into the form of the covenant lawsuit, as in Hosea 4:1, where God spoke to the people:

> *Hear the words of the LORD, O people of Israel*
> *For the LORD has a case against the inhabitants of the land.*
> *There is no faithfulness or kindness*
> *And no knowledge of God in the land.*[4]

God justified God's anger toward the people by pointing out what they had done to provoke it.

In the book of Job the covenant lawsuit form is turned around. Though not an Israelite, Job seemed to be familiar enough with the form to use it against God, as when he said:

> *But I would speak to the Almighty*
> *And I desire to argue my case against God.* (13:3)[5]

I suggest that the covenant lawsuit form is one biblical precedent appropriate to women's relation to God today. Through the covenant lawsuit, women can appeal to God against God. They can use God's own words to indict God for failure to live up to the promises of covenantal relation. I suggest that the appropriate place for this in the liturgy would be either before or after the congregation's prayers of confession. At that time, a woman might rise and recite the "sins" of God, echoing the words of the people of Israel who said, "My God has passed over my rights" (Isa. 40:27). Women might begin to collect indictments against God from their own experiences and from literary sources, which could be used regularly or at set times in the liturgy. The words of the woman imagined above as crying out against God provide one example of such an indictment of God. The words of the black singer Nina Simone from her album "Emergency Ward," provide another example. The medley that she begins with George Harrison's song of passionate yearning, "I Really Want to See You Lord" and concludes with a terrible vision, "Who are you Lord? Today, today, today, You are a Killer"[6] would be powerful in a liturgical setting.

In proposing that women adopt covenant lawsuit to state their case against God, I am suggesting that women call on God to take responsibility for the patriarchal histories in which God has been known—biblical, Christian, and Jewish. When the question of God's responsibility for patriarchal history is asked, a theological objection is often raised, "But God himself is not male, it was only the patriarchal storytellers who imaged God as male." The problem, it is suggested, has nothing to do with God. I am suggesting that *for a storytelling theology*, this anwer will not do. In a storytelling theology the split between "God God's self" and the God revealed in the relation, in the story, cannot be allowed. In a storytelling theology, God "is" who God is in the story. It is equally true that in a storytelling theology, God may become who God may become.[7]

If the biblical tradition is viable, if Christians and Jews really experience a relation with God, then human dealings with God cannot be transacted simply on an intellectual level. The storytellers of the traditions have always known that. Nor need the community always express loving, humble feelings to God. Biblical tradition warrants the view that humans have a right and even a responsibility to question God, to wrestle with God, until the answers to human questions are revealed.

Notes

1. The model of the prophets was suggested by Mary Wakeman in an article in *Beyond Androcentrism: New Essays on Women and Religion,* ed. Rita Gross (Missoula, Mont.: AAR and Scholars Press, 1977).
2. Elie Wiesel, *The Town beyond the Wall,* trans. Steven Becker (New York: Avon Books, 1970), 190.
3. Martin Buber. *The Prophetic Faith,* trans. Carlyle Witton-Davies (New York: Harper & Row, 1960), 24–30.
4. My translation. The Hebrew word *'im* translated here as "against," carries the meaning "with" or "against."
5. See note 4.
6. Nina Simone, "Emergency Ward," side one, medley including "My Sweet Lord," by George Harrison and "Today Is a Killer," poem by David Nelson, music by Nina Simone (New York: RCA Records, 1972).
7. See Judith Plaskow, "The Coming of Lilith," in *Religion and Sexism*, ed. Rosemary Ruether (New York: Simon & Schuster, 1974), 341–43.

The Church and the Second Sex*

❖ Mary Daly ❖

Those engaged in the struggle for the equality of the sexes have often seen the Catholic Church as an enemy. This view is to a large extent justified, for Catholic teaching has prolonged a traditional view of woman which at the same time idealizes and humiliates her. It is precisely this ambivalence, characteristic of so many Catholic utterances about women, which those committed to improving the legal, professional and economic condition of women find deplorable. . . .

A study of Christianity's documents concerning women reveals a puzzling ambiguity if not an outright contradiction. Most observable is the conflict between the Christian teachings on the worth of every human person and the oppressive, misogynistic ideas arising from cultural conditioning. If the latter do not contradict they at least obscure the basic doctrine. Intimately bound up with this dialectic there is another tension, between a pseudo-glorification of 'woman' and degrading teachings and practices concerning real women. The second tension of opposites is an effect of the first. Its existence betrays an uneasy awareness that 'something is out of joint', and it reflects an inauthentic response to this awareness. The symbolic glorification of 'woman' arose as a substitute for recognition of full personhood and equal rights. So we may say that the record of Christianity in regard to women is a record of contradictions.

The Bible manifests the unfortunate—often miserable—condition of women in ancient times. The authors of both the Old and the New Testaments were men of their times, and it would be naïve to think that they were free of the prejudices of their epochs. It is therefore a most dubious process to construct an idea of 'feminine nature' or of 'God's plan for women' from biblical texts. As one theologian expressed it: 'Let us be careful not to transcribe into terms of nature that which is written in terms of history.'

An example will illustrate this point. The New Testament gave advice to women (and to slaves) which would help them to bear the subhuman (by today's standards) conditions imposed upon them. It would be foolish to erect, on this basis, a picture of 'immutable' feminine qualities and virtues. Thus, although obedience was required of women and slaves, there is nothing about obedience which makes it intrinsically more appropriate for women than for men. The idea of taking feminine 'types' from the Bible as models for modern women may be an exercise for the imagination, but it is difficult to justify as a method. Any rigid abstraction of types from history implies a basic fallacy. . . .

Most of the usage of Old Testament texts to support sex prejudice reveals a total failure not only to grasp the fact of the evolution of human consciousness in general but also to understand the fact and meaning of the evolution of thought in the Old Testament itself. The foundation upon which the case for the subordination of woman is built lies in the older of the two accounts of creation. The earlier creation story (J document), found in Genesis 2, has been stressed as a basis for Christian thinking about women, while the P document account, found in Genesis 1—written several centuries later—has not been stressed, nor have its implications been understood.

Contemporary scriptural exegetes of all faiths, having the tools of scholarship at their disposal, as well as insights of psychology and anthropology, are enabled to look critically at the first chapters of Genesis. The two creation accounts, which differ greatly from each other, have been carefully scrutinized. The later creation story gives no hint that woman was brought into being as an afterthought. On the contrary, it stresses an original sexual duality and describes God's act of giving dominion to both. The plural is used, indicating their common authority to rule: 'And God said, Let us make mankind in our image and likeness, and let them have dominion . . . ' (Gen 1 : 26). The following verse says: 'God created man in his image. In the image of God he created him. Male and female he created them' (Gen 1 : 27). This is understood by exegetes to mean that the image of God is in the human person, whether man or woman. Moreover, the plural is used in the following:

> 'Then God blessed them and said to them, "Be fruitful and multiply, fill the earth and subdue it. Have dominion over the fish of the sea, the birds of the air, the cattle and all the animals that crawl on the earth" ' (Gen 1 : 28).

Thus, the burdens of reproduction are not specially associated with the woman, nor is there any indication that 'technical' or 'professional' work should be proper to the man.

It is the earlier (J) creation account, found in the second chapter, which has been the source—or excuse—for many of the disparaging theories about women. . . .

In the New Testament it is significant that the statements which reflect the antifeminism of the times are never those of Christ. There is no recorded speech of Jesus concerning women 'as such'. What is very striking is his behavior toward them. In the passages describing the relationship of Jesus with various women, one characteristic stands out starkly: they emerge as persons, for they are treated as persons, often in such contrast with prevailing custom as to astonish onlookers. The behavior of Jesus toward the Samaritan woman puzzled even his disciples, who were surprised that he would speak to her in public (John 4 : 27). Then there was his defense of the adulterous woman, who according to the law of Moses should have been stoned (John 8 : 1–11). There was the case of the prostitute whose many sins he forgave because she had loved much (Luke 7 : 36–50). In the Gospel narratives the close friendship of Jesus with certain women is manifested in the context of the crucifixion and resurrection. What stands out is the fact that these, his friends, he saw as persons, to whom he gave the supreme yet simple gift of his brotherhood.

The contemporary social inferiority of women was, indeed, reflected in the New Testament. Although the seeds of emancipation were present in the Christian message, their full implications were not evident to the first century authors. The most strikingly antifeminist passages are, of course, in the Pauline texts, which are all too familiar to Catholic women, who have heard them cited approvingly *ad nauseam*. We now know it is important to understand that Paul was greatly preoccupied with *order* in society and in Christian assemblies in particular. In modern parlance, it seemed necessary to sustain a good 'image' of the Church. Thus it appeared to him an important consideration that women should not have too predominant a place in Christian assemblies, that they should not 'speak' too much or unveil their heads. This would have caused scandal and ridicule of the new sect, which already had to face accusations of immorality and effeminacy. In ancient Corinth, as one scholar has pointed out, for a woman to go out unveiled would be to behave like a prostitute. Paul was concerned with protecting the new Church against scandal. Thus he repeatedly insisted upon 'correct' sexual behavior, including the subjection of wives at meetings. Once this is understood, it becomes evident that it is a perversion to use Pauline texts, which should be interpreted within their own social context, to support the claim that even today, in a totally different society, women should be subject. . . .

The equal dignity and rights of all human beings as persons is of the essence of the Christian message. In the writings of Paul himself there are anticipations of a development toward realization of the full implications of this equality. . . .

An examination of the writings of the Church Fathers brings vividly into sight the fact that there is, indeed, a problem of women and the Church. The following statement of Jerome strikes the modern reader as weird:

> 'As long as woman is for birth and children, she is different from man as body is from soul. But when she wishes to serve Christ more than the world, then she will cease to be a woman and will be called man (*vir*).'

A similar idea is expressed by Ambrose, who remarks that

> 'she who does not believe is a woman and should be designated by the name of her sex, whereas she who believes progresses to perfect manhood, to the measure of the adulthood of Christ. She then dispenses with the name of her sex, the seductiveness of youth, the garrulousness of old age.'

These strange utterances can be understood only if one realizes the lowness of women in the commonly held view. The characteristics which the Fathers considered to be typically feminine include fickleness and shallowness, as well as garrulousness and weakness, slowness of understanding, and instability of mind. For the most part, the attitude was one of puzzlement over the seemingly incongruous fact of woman's existence. Augustine summed up the general idea in saying that he did not see in what way it could be said that woman was made for a help for man, if the work of child-bearing be excluded. Clement of Alexandria was also evidently baffled. Although he was somewhat more liberal than Augustine and concluded that men and women have the same nature, he inconsistently upheld masculine superiority.

In Genesis the Fathers found an 'explanation' of woman's inferiority which served as a guarantee of divine approval for perpetuating the situation which made her inferior. John Chrysostom thought it followed from the later creation of Eve that God gave the more necessary and more honorable role to man, the more petty and the less honorable to woman. Ambrosiaster remarks that woman is inferior to man, since she is only a portion of him. Thus there was an uncritical acceptance of the andro-centric myth of Eve's creation. Linked to this was their refusal, in varying degrees of inflexibility, to grant that woman is the image of God, an attitude in large measure inspired by Paul's first epistle to the Corinthians. Ambrosiaster states baldly that man is made to the image of God, but not woman. Augustine wrote that only man is the image and glory of God. Since the believing woman, who is co-heiress of grace, cannot lay aside her sex, she is restored to the image of God only where there is no sex, that is, in the spirit. . . .

The presumed defectiveness of woman extended also, and perhaps especially, into the moral sphere. The primary grievance against her was her supposed guilt in the Fall. . . . Tertullian, for example, wrote for the edification of his contemporaries:

'Do you not know that you are Eve? . . . You are the devil's gateway. . . . How easily you destroyed man, the image of God. Because of the death which you brought upon us, even the Son of God had to die.'

Clement of Alexandria taught that it is shameful for woman to think of what nature she has. Augustine cynically complained that man, who was of superior intelligence, couldn't have been seduced, and so the woman, who was small of intellect, was given to him. The logical inconsistencies implied in this seem to have escaped him: this dull-witted creature could hardly have been too responsible. Moreover, she was clever enough to seduce man, which the ingenious devil could not do. Why did that paragon of intelligence and virtue succumb so easily? It is all too evident that logic is not operative in such invective, which neurotically projects all guilt upon the woman. For the Fathers, woman is a temptress of whom men should beware. That the problem might be reciprocal is not even considered.

There were attempts to balance the alleged guilt-laden condition of the female sex, but these, unfortunately, did not take the form of an admission of guilt shared by the sexes. Instead, Eve was balanced off by Mary. Thus, for example, Origen remarks that as sin came from the woman so does the beginning of salvation. Augustine wrote that woman is honored in Mary. He claimed that since man (*homo*) fell through the female sex, he was restored through the female sex. 'Through the woman, death; through the woman, life.' This type of compensation produced an ambivalent image of woman. Mary was glorified, but she was unique. Women in the concrete did not shake off their bad reputation and continued to bear most of the burden of blame. The sort of polemic, therefore, which attempts to cover the antifeminism of the Fathers by pointing to their glorification of Mary ignores the important point that this did not improve their doctrine about concrete, living women. In fact there is every reason to suspect that this compensation unconsciously served as a means to relieve any possible guilt feelings about injustice to the other sex.

In the mentality of the Fathers, woman and sexuality were identified. Their horror of sex was also a horror of woman. . . . The idea of a special guilt attached to the female sex gave support to the double moral standard which prevailed. For example, in cases of adultery, the wife had to take back her unfaithful husband, but if the wife was unfaithful, she could be rejected. . . . On the whole, then, the Fathers display a strongly disparaging attitude toward women, at times even a fierce misogynism.

The Middle Ages

Theological opinion of women was hardly better in the Middle Ages, although some of the fierceness of tone was mitigated. . . .

What was new in the picture in the Middle Ages was the assimilation into theology of Aristotelianism, which provided the conceptual tools for fixing woman's place in the universe and which, ironically, could have been used to free her. In the writings of

Thomas Aquinas, which later came to have a place of unique pre-eminence in the Church, Aristotelian thought was wedded to the standard biblical interpretations, so that the seeming weight of 'science' was added to that of authority. Thus, following Aristotle, Aquinas held that the female is defective as regards her individual nature. He wrote that she is, in fact, a misbegotten male, for the active force in the male seed tends to the production of a perfect likeness in the masculine sex. Her existence is due to some defect in the active force (that of the father), or to some material indisposition, or even to some external influence, such as that of the south wind, which is moist. He adds that, as regards human nature in general, woman is not misbegotten, but is included in nature's intention as directed to the work of generation. She has, then, a reason for being—that is, she is needed in the work of generation. It seems that this really is all she is good for, 'since a man can be more efficiently helped by another man in other works'.

It would be a mistake, however, to conclude that Thomas thought woman has a major or even an equal role, even in her one specialty, i.e. reproduction. He wrote:

'Father and mother are loved as principles of our natural origin. Now the father is principle in a more excellent way than the mother, because he is the active principle, while the mother is a passive and material principle. Consequently, strictly speaking, the father is to be loved more.'

He continues:

'In the begetting of man, the mother supplies the formless matter of the body; and the latter receives its form through the formative power that is in the semen of the father. And though this power cannot create the rational soul, yet it disposes the matter of the body to receive that form.'

Thus, the role of the woman in generation is purely passive; she merely provides the matter, whereas the father disposes this for the form. This view of woman as a purely passive principle which merely provides the 'matter' of the offspring is, of course, linked to an entirely outdated and false biology: that the mother is, in fact, equally 'active' in the production of the child was unknown in the thirteenth century. . . .

Despite medieval theories, there were some cases of powerful women in the Middle Ages. Nuns, especially, had a certain autonomy, which even St Thomas recognized. It is one of the ironies of history that there were abbesses who legitimately exercised great power, far beyond what is accorded to religious women today. They were 'persons constituted in ecclesiastical dignity' who had 'the administration of ecclesiastical affairs and pre-eminence of grade'. In fact, abbesses had power of jurisdiction. Like bishops and abbots, they wore the mitre and cross and carried the staff. . . .

Besides the abbesses, there were other great individual women in the secular world. There were such outstanding rulers as Clotilde and Blanche of Castille, and learned women like Eleanor of Aquitaine and Blanche of Navarre. There were great saints: Catherine of Siena wielded enormous influence in her milieu, and the story of Joan of Arc has no parallel. However, it would be absurd to judge the general condition of women by such examples. The naïve idea of those who say that 'true ability will always prove itself', and point to such extraordinary cases, simply ignores the fact that countless women were completely stifled by an environment which worked against the development and expression of their talents.

The prevailing low status of women was fixed by law and custom. By canon law a husband was entitled to beat his wife. Canon law allowed only the dowry system for matrimony, and under this system women were defenseless. Moreover, since they were legally incompetent, they were not considered fit to give testimony in court. In general, they were considered as man's property. Since for feudal lords marriages were a way of gaining property, women were pawns in the game of acquiring wealth. The Church's complicated marriage laws offered ample opportunity for trickery and abuse. Thus, while the history of the Middle Ages reveals a few glorious feminine personalities, that side of the scales is extremely outbalanced by the masses of mute and anonymous victims of hypocrisy and oppression.

. . .

Beginnings of the Modern Period

'The very thought that I am a woman is enough to make my wings droop.' This remark, which was made by Teresa of Avila, suggests that the situation of women was not yet greatly improved in the sixteenth century. Why would a person of such intelligence and greatness have such a low conception of her own sex? Perhaps it is not too surprising when one realizes that some preachers of the time, as well as fathers of families, considered it wrong for women even to learn to read and write. In such an atmosphere, it must have been difficult for a woman to have much esteem for herself and other members of her sex. In fact, Teresa's words often reflect, perhaps unconsciously, the attitudes of her milieu. She speaks frequently of the 'weaknesses' of women. The following remark is revealing:

> 'During the very sorest trials that I have suffered in this life, I do not recall having uttered such expressions, for I am not in the least like a woman in these matters but have a stout heart.'

The implicit assumption is that real courage is normal only for men. Moreover, more than one admirer of Teresa made remarks similar to that of John of Salinas: 'She is a man.' It is thought-provoking that this great woman and her friends, when they tried to express the nature of her uniqueness, spontaneously had recourse to expressions which disassociated her from her own sex. . . . It was not Catholic ideology but the industrial revolution which led to feminine emancipation. The eighteenth, nineteenth and twentieth century theologians continued to justify the traditional subordinate and legally helpless situation of married women. . . .

The official Catholic reaction in the nineteenth and twentieth centuries to the modern movement toward feminine emancipation manifested the persistence of the conflict between the Christian concept of women as persons, made to the image of God, and the notion of them as inferior, derivative beings. The first pope to confront the movement was Leo XIII. Against the socialists, whom he saw as threatening the stability of marriage, he defended 'paternal authority'. As for the husband-wife relationship, he re-affirmed the subjection of the female:

> 'Wherefore as the Apostle admonishes: "As Christ is the head of the Church, so is the husband the head of the wife"; and just as the Church is subject to Christ, who cherishes it with most chaste and lasting love, so it is becoming that women also should be subject to their husbands, and by them in turn be loved with faithful and constant affection.'

This, of course, implies a limited view of woman's 'nature,' which he briefly expresses in another document:

> 'Women, again, are not suited for certain occupations; a woman is by nature fitted for home work, and it is that which is best adapted at once to preserve her modesty and to promote the good bringing up of children and the well-being of the family.'

In his encyclical on Christian marriage, Leo asserted:

> 'The husband is the chief of the family and the head of the wife. The woman, because she is flesh of his flesh and bone of his bone, must be subject to her husband and obey him; not, indeed, as a servant, but as a companion, so that her obedience shall be wanting in neither honor nor dignity.' . . .

In his encyclical on Christian marriage Pius XI, citing Paul, repeated the familiar ideas on the 'order' of domestic society:

> 'This order includes both the primacy of the husband with regard to the wife and children, the ready subjection of the wife and her willing obedience.'

His hostility to feminine emancipation is hardly disguised. He attacks those 'false teachers' who say that 'the rights of husband and wife are equal', and who say that there should be emancipation 'in the ruling of the domestic society, in the administration of family affairs, and in the rearing of children', and that this liberty should be 'social, economic, and physiological'. Through loaded wording, psychological pressure is brought to bear against women who would want to improve their situation. He wrote, for example, that according to the doctrine of the 'false teachers', the married woman should, 'to the neglect of these [her family] be able to follow her own bent and devote herself to business and even public affairs'. The whole tone and context suggests that anyone who does devote herself to business or public affairs is suspected of doing this to the detriment of her family. This is suggested also by omission, since there is no hint of the possibility that by such activity the woman could become a more well-rounded person and therefore a better wife and mother. It is noteworthy, furthermore, that Pius's choice of language unconsciously refuted the 'feminine nature' hypothesis upon which he elsewhere relied so heavily. It is the admission of such an ambitious 'bent' in women which reveals the shakiness of his views about 'the natural disposition and temperament of the female sex'. . . .

Pius XII perpetuated the custom of giving a double meaning to 'equality'. Having granted the equality of women with men 'in their personal dignity as children of God', he repeats the familiar jargon which serves to nullify the practical implications of real equality. Thus he wrote of 'the indestructible spiritual and physical qualities, whose order cannot be deranged without nature herself moving to re-establish it', affirming that 'these peculiar characteristics which distinguish the two sexes reveal themselves so clearly to the eyes of all', that only obstinate blindness or doctrinairism could disregard them. The difficulty with this is, of course, that not only physical qualities but also 'spiritual' ones are presumed to be linked universally and exclusively to members of one sex. It is precisely this bridge from the biological differentiation to the level of personality differences which responsible thinkers today who are aware of the role of cultural conditioning would regard as highly problematic, and as anything but clear 'to the eyes of all'. . . .

Violence against Women in the Historical Christian West and in North American Secular Culture: The Visual and Textual Evidence

✤ *Margaret R. Miles* ✤

Let's start with a story, an old, old story, not really one woman's story, but a story repeated in some or all of its details numberless times in the lives of countless women. The story from the Hebrew Bible book of Judges relates the story of a nameless woman who was betrayed, raped, tortured, murdered, and dismembered. The concubine of a powerful ruling-class man, this nameless woman was offered by her master, as the text calls him, to some men who threatened violence against *him* as they travelled through a foreign territory.

> So the man seized his concubine and put her out to them; and they raped and abused her all night until the morning. And as the dawn began to break, they let her go. As the morning appeared, the woman came and fell down at the door of the man's house where her master was, till it was light.

"Violence against Women in the Historical Christian West and in North American Secular Culture" from *Shaping New Vision* edited by Clarissa W. Atkinson, Constance H. Buchanan, and Margaret R. Miles. © 1987 by Margaret R. Miles. Reprinted by permission of the author.

And her master rose up in the morning, and when he had opened the doors of the house and went out to go on his way, behold, there was his concubine, lying at the door of the house with her hands on the threshold. He said to her, "Get up, let us be going." But there was no answer. Then he put her upon the ass; and the man rose up and went away to his home. And when he entered his house he took a knife, and laying hold of his concubine he divided her, limb by limb into twelve pieces and sent her throughout all the territory of Israel.[1]

He did this, according to the text, to protest this cavalier treatment of his property. Commenting on the story in her book, *Texts of Terror*, Hebrew Bible scholar Phyllis Trible writes: "Of all the characters in scripture, she is the least. Appearing at the beginning and close of a story that rapes her, she is alone in a world of men. Neither the other characters nor the narrator recognizes her humanity. She is property, object, tool, and literary device. Without name, speech, or power, she has no friends to aid her in life or mourn her in death."[2]

This is an old story, but is it not also a current story? Parts of it sound strangely contemporary for a story about two thousand years old. In the United States today, a woman is raped once every six minutes; one in ten women will be a rape victim sometime in her life; 20–30 percent of girls now twelve years of age will suffer violent sexual assault in their lifetimes. In the first three years of the 1980s, there were approximately three-quarters of a million attempted or completed rapes, according to FBI statistics.[3] In addition, a woman is beaten every eighteen minutes in the United States; each year three to six million women are beaten by their sexual partner or ex-partner. In one state alone—Massachusetts—a woman is murdered by her husband or partner every twenty-two days.[4]

Sexual violence against women is also a racist crime: black women are nearly six times as likely to be rape victims as white women.[5] And it is a class crime: the incidence of violence against women is significantly higher in poor families, in racial minority families, and in urban families.[6] Violence, far from being a thing of the past in our enlightened age, is on the increase, and women are its primary victims. But violence against elderly people, children, and vulnerable men is also growing in American culture. Rape is only one form—though a particularly heinous one—of the pervasive violence that is a major threat to Americans, draining human resources and requiring massive strategies for containment and the rehabilitation of its victims and perpetrators. Analysis of the ideological rationalization of and support for violence toward those most affected—women—will help us to begin to unravel the complex cultural strands that keep violence at record highs in American culture.

Women who are fortunate enough never to have been sexually molested often do not realize how much we adjust our lifestyle to avoid victimization. These "precautions" constitute an implicit recognition of the danger; the threat of assault and rape is enough to make us rearrange our lives, reflecting our constant state of terror. Yet our precautions are often futile efforts to lessen the possibility of attack. A high percentage of rapes take place in somebody's home, many of these by assailants known to the victim. There is no possibile way for any woman to be thoroughly enough protected that we can feel safe; there is no "safe" way to dress, no "safe" way to behave that will guarantee that we will never be victims of a sexual assault.

Is rape a universal crime, simply a biological fact of life? Because of its distance from us in time and space, the story with which we began seems to imply that rape has been prevalent in every society in every time. If rape is universal, surely there is nothing we can do about it except hope that some *other* woman will be in the wrong place at the wrong time and become a victim. Rape is not, however, a universal crime. The misconception that rape is universal is one of the factors that keeps women feeling passive and helpless in the face of the statistics. Peggy Reeves Sanday's cross-cultural studies of rape revealed that in 40 percent of the societies she studied rape was absent or rare. Rape is not universal but is, Sanday writes, "a learned response which comes from the way societies are organized."[7]

Similarly, Beryl Lieff Benderly, in her article "Rape Free or Rape Prone," writes:

> Certain behavioral patterns and attitudes are common to rape-prone societies. These societies tolerate violence and encourage men and boys to be tough, aggressive, and competitive. Men in such cultures generally have special, politically important gathering spots off-limits to women. . . . Women take little or no part in public decision making or religious rituals: men mock or scorn women's work and remain aloof from childbearing and rearing. These groups usually trace their beginnings to a male supreme being.[8]

North American Christian and post-Christian culture is certainly not unique in its record of violence against women; it is, however, the serious common moral duty of women and men in all rape-prone societies to identify the ideas and images, the attitudes and practices that support, promote, and rationalize violence. If rape is not universal—something we must resign ourselves to and learn to live with—then we must be prepared to detect the images and ideas in American culture that formulate and support the misogyny that results in violence against women.

The second misconception that keeps us feeling helpless in the face of the startling figures on violence against women in our own culture is that rape has a biological cause in the powerful sexual urges of males, that it is, in some sense, "natural." This idea is without basis in fact, according to Sanday's cross-cultural studies which identified societies in which rape occurs rarely or not at all. Nevertheless it is pervasive enough in western culture to come from places as various as the Marquis de Sade—and my mother. Men can't "help themselves," my mother told me when I was a teenager, and thus it was "up to me" to see to it that I didn't arouse them. The Marquis de Sade wrote:

> It appears beyond contradiction that Nature has given us the right to carry out our wishes upon all women indifferently; it appears equally that we have the right to force her to submit to our wishes. . . . It is beyond question that we have the right to establish laws which will force women to yield to the ardors of him who desires her; violence itself being one of the results of this right, we can legally employ it. Has not Nature proved to us that we have this right, by allotting us the strength necessary to force them to our desires?[9]

Sexual violence against women is not universal and it is not hormonal, whether the biological basis is construed as an irresistibly powerful sexual urge or as superior physical strength. Moreover, sexual violence is not sexual. Marie Marshall Fortune, in her book *Sexual Violence, The Unmentionable Sin*, calls rape a "pseudosexual act motivated by aggression and hostility."[10] Clinician Nicholas Groth in his study of rapists quotes what he describes as a typical description of a rape by the offender:

> I was enraged when I started out. I lost control and struck out with violence. After the assault I felt relieved. I felt I had gotten even. There was no sexual satisfaction; in fact, I felt a little disgusted. I felt relieved of the tension and anger for awhile, but then it would start to build up again. The crime just frustrated me more. I wasn't sexually aroused. I had to force myself.[11]

Marie Marshall Fortune writes: "The belief that male sexual aggression is natural, biologically driven behavior and is 'so overwhelming that the male is the one to be acted upon by it' is a myth that we can no longer afford to perpetuate." Implicit in this myth of male helplessness in the face of a massive biological drive is a pessimistic view of men. Ironically, it is feminists who question this helplessness hypothesis most strongly. Believing that rape is neither inevitable nor natural to males, feminists insist that men "take responsibility for their sexual and aggressive behavior."[12] If particular social practices—such as male gender conditioning that trains boys to be tough, aggressive, and competitive—are connected to the rape-prone societies studied by Benderly, it is clear that these practices must be identified and changed if misogyny is to be healed. But the dominant ideas, values, and visual images of the American public must also be scrutinized by feminists since these inform social practices.

Patriarchal Order: Eve as Derivative

What are the ideas and images of historical Western Christianity and contemporary secular culture that constitute the particular conceptual foundation of violence in American culture? My analysis will not exhaust the subject but will aim, rather, at stimulating further work to identify, protest, and change the concepts, images, and conditions that promote violence against women in our society. Moreover, instead of exploring some of the dramatic cultural support for violence against women—such as pornography—I will focus on ideas and images that support violence simultaneously in more readily accessible and more foundational ways. The most pervasive foundations of violence against women are so ordinary, so unexceptional, and therefore so unnoticed that they are seldom challenged. Pornography, an industry larger than the record and film industries *put together*, may be enormously important as the major eroticization of violence of our culture,[13] but there are other rationalizations of and support for violence against women. These are more superficial in that they lie more on the surface of American culture; at the same time they are more foundational in that they are built into the assumptions and institutional structures of American culture in the family and child rearing, in educational institutions, and in churches, synagogues, and government.

It is important also to recognize that misogynist ideas and images are not the only messages given in Judaism and Christianity to and about women; there are other ideas and images that were often used by women for their empowerment, as validations of their activity, and as warrants for a degree of independence. Historical Christianity, on which I will focus in discussing medieval and Renaissance visual images, is a frustrating mixture. If it were unambiguously misogynist, feminists could feel free to reject it; if it presented a comprehensive affirmation of women, feminists could find in it tools for present empowerment. Since Christianity carries both possibilities simultaneously, it is necessary to do a painstaking job of identifying the misogynist *and* the useful and usable strands, the history of oppression *and* of women's creative use of ideas and images that gave them credibility and leverage in relation to their societies. It is well to keep in mind that a kind of anachronistic violence against historical women can be done by historians who assume that they tolerated and masochistically enjoyed a religion and culture that oppressed and persecuted them. A respectful attitude toward the struggles of historical women requires that we remain open to seeing the possibility that they were often able to create for themselves lives of amazing beauty and richness by the creative use of their religious and cultural resources.[14]

It is not, however, the project of this chapter to explore the resourceful selective interpretations by which women constructed their self-images and ideas of relationship, world, and God with the help of Christian ideas and images. Our project is the identification of the most common biblical concepts contributing to misogyny and the continued use of these concepts in the present. It is astonishing to detect the continuity of rationales for the subordination of women across what we usually take to be the gulf between the historic religious cultures of the West and contemporary American culture. Although patriarchal religious ideas and visual images are still strong in their religious setting in large sectors of the American public, their translation in the secular media has insured both their continuing influence and their constant availability to Americans. Secularization has not apparently rejected, but rather taken over many ancient religious judgments about the role and value of women. We will shortly take a closer look at this continuity.

First, let us consider three pervasive and powerful ideas of Jewish and Christian cultures that continue to contribute heavily to the misogyny in American culture that scapegoats women. The first of these ideas is that patriarchal order is the right ordering of society, reflecting cosmic order. Patriarchal hierarchy has been amazingly constant from the Ten Commandments of the Hebrew Bible which list a man's wife along with his cattle and house as one of his possessions, to the laws of modern American culture, which in most states, despite efforts to change them, still stipulate that rape within marriage is impossible since a husband always has the right of sexual access to his wife. Tertullian, an influential North African Christian author of the third century, explained the Genesis account of the creation of men and women like this: "This second human being was made by God for man's assistance, and that female was forthwith named woman."[15] In the texts of historic Christianity, the creation of Eve after Adam is repeatedly cited as "proof" of women's inherent need to be controlled by men. As several contemporary authors are showing, other interpretations of the creation myth are certainly possible; the consistent interpretation of Eve as a "second human being" created to help man, is puzzling unless we find political reasons why it was thus interpreted through centuries of patriarchal order in the Christian West. For example, John Boswell, the Yale historian, has argued that the creation myth of Genesis 1 clearly states an ascending progression of creation: first inanimate matter, then animals, then intelligent being—man, and, as the apex and crown of creation, intelligent and life-bearing woman. What seemed to Boswell as an "obvious" reading is one that is seldom found in the history of interpretation of Genesis.[16]

Most people in historic Western communities did not, however, write or read scriptural or theological texts. And, although they heard expressions of ideas of patriarchal order in sermons, in religious drama, in public readings of devotional texts, in hymns, scripture, and liturgy, the written and spoken word was perhaps not the most powerful communication of misogynist attitudes to illiterate people. Visual images, seen by everyone in the community every day on the walls of their local church, were a constant and fundamental source of instruction and conditioning for whole communities. Historical people did not have television, newspapers, magazines, or billboards. Thus the images they saw daily were few and usually remained the same throughout their lives. It is perhaps impossible for us to reconstruct from our own experience of a glut of media images the powerful influence of medieval "media," that is, religious paintings and sculpture. We cannot do more here than to suggest some characteristic visual themes and pictorial treatments that, seen repeatedly in the central community gathering-place, the church, contributed to and validated violence against women.

The texts written and read by a small minority of culturally and educationally privileged people in historic communities might have been less influential had the idea of Eve's creation as a "second human being" not been visually reinforced and extended in many paintings and sculptures which show Eve emerging bodily from a gaping hole in the side of the sleeping Adam. Repeated depiction of this scene on the facades of cathedrals and in paintings in local parish churches enabled people not only to hear or read, but also to *picture* the secondary creation of the first and prototypical woman.

The establishment of patriarchal order in early Christianity, the exclusion of women from leadership roles in the church, and the theological rationalization of patriarchal order in family and society has been described by several feminist historians.[17] The preoccupation of church leaders with the danger of insubordination led them to urge the gender-specific "virtues" of docility, submissiveness, and obedience for women. Tyrannical domination, the complementary male role, was apparently less to be feared than female insubordination. In the early fifth century, Augustine, discussing the question of why the patriarchs of the Hebrew bible were permitted to have more than one wife, wrote:

> It was permitted for one husband to have several wives, [but] it was not permitted for one woman to have several husbands . . . For, by a hidden law of nature *things that rule love singularity;* things that are ruled, indeed are subjected not only each one to an individual master, but also . . . many of them are not unfittingly subjected to one master . . . just as many souls are properly subjected to the one God.[18]

"Things that rule love singularity" is followed by the justification and rationale, "just as many souls are properly subjected to the one God." The twin assumptions of male supremacy—through self-identification with God—and women as male property constitute patriarchal order. Rationalized as loving protection of the ruled, the bottom line of patriarchal order is the use of violence toward and even murder of the ruled for their protection. Augustine's epic *City of God* provides the explicit connection between rule and protection that allowed patriarchal rulers in families and states to justify their rule to those subjected as "for your own good."[19]

A contemporary example of the murder of a woman for her protection shows the continuity of patriarchal assumptions. James Michener's 1983 novel, *Poland*— thirty-eight weeks on the *New York Times'* best seller list—provides a contemporary example of the continuity of male justification of violence against women as clearly and vividly as if it were contemporaneous with the book of Genesis or with Augustine. After a battle, the protagonist finds in the luxurious headquarters of the defeated enemy the partially decapitated body of a beautiful young slave woman. Reflecting on this grisly scene, he muses that "the man who bought her had obviously loved her deeply, for he had killed her—rather than have her fall into the hands of others."[20] The author apparently expects readers of this novel to assume, along with him, that murderous violence is the ultimate proof of deep love. The short steps from patriarchal order, to ownership, to violence are all in place.

Woman, Body, Nature, and Sin

The second influential idea we need to examine is the identification, in Western Christian cultures, of woman with body and nature, and body with sin. From Eve, the instigator of sin, cause of the fall of the human race, to the actual women whose beauty tempted celibate males, women have been reduced in male eyes to body, visibility, and temptation. Just as images of women as sinful functioned as cultural sanctions for male domination, male supremacy ratified the domination, denudation, and use of nature.

Again, historical sculpture and paintings, the media of Western Christianity, encouraged medieval and Renaissance viewers to picture the sinful woman as naked and old, with swollen belly and pendulous breasts. Excessive female flesh was a consistent visual signal of "fleshliness"—a literalistic interpretation of St. Paul's use of "the flesh" as a theological term to designate the predilection to sin of the whole person, especially the soul. A facade bas-relief on the Modena cathedral, Notre Dame du Part, shows Eve, with swollen belly and exaggerated breasts, standing by Adam. His foot is placed on top of hers, a pictorial device for signifying superiority. Female nudity was symbolic of woman's "natural" proclivity to lust. If, in addition, the female body suggested pregnancy, it represented the biological result of male lust.

Since woman was seen as body, biology, and nature, she represented for men everything in themselves that they must discipline and reject if they are to achieve their potential to be pure intellect, mind, and spirit. Tertullian described male lust as the responsibility of women:

> *You* are the Devil's gateway. *You* are the unsealer of that forbidden tree. *You* are the first deserter of the divine law. *You* are she who persuaded him whom the Devil was not valiant enough to attack. *You* destroyed so easily God's image, man. On account of *your* deserved punishment, that is, death, even the Son of God had to die.[21]

These quotations from the Church fathers are not significant because they originated the ideas they express, but because they are tediously characteristic of the male ecclesiastical leadership whose perspective they represent. If these were novel ideas of Tertullian or Augustine, they would probably not have been influential, since in their own time theological texts were read only by a few culturally and educationally privileged males. They are important precisely because they were *not* novel but were, instead, extraordinarily clear statements of consensus male opinions.

Tertullian says, further, that he can be confident that he recognizes a woman's desire to attract him by the way *he* is affected by the woman's appearance. If a man is aroused by a particular woman, that woman means to arouse him: "Seeing and being seen belong to the selfsame lust."[22]

One result of the identification of woman with body, nature, and sin, is the exaggerated esteem of female virginity that Andrea Dworkin, in her book, *Woman Hating*, calls "a real sexual perversion."[23] If woman is body, sex, and sin, rejection of her "nature" as body/sex/sin is inordinately valued. Thus, although men rape and impregnate women, the woman they value is the untouched, untouchable woman. The virgin/mother of Christ is the prototype. The popular fourteenth-century devotional text, Jacobus de Voragine's *The Golden Legend,* follows the opinions of more esoteric theologians like Augustine and Thomas Aquinas that although the Virgin was consummately beautiful, yet there was something about her that absolutely prevented any man from looking at her with desire.[24]

Paintings and sculptures of the Virgin strongly reinforce textual insistence on her obedience, submissiveness, and innocence. Her head is frequently shown with a side cant, a posture of humble acquiescence, as in Botticelli's Madonna of the Magnificat. An exaggeratedly high brow, large eyes, and a small mouth are iconographical features repeatedly employed by painters to represent her spirituality and lack of sensuality. Even in paintings of the nursing Virgin, like Rogier van der Weyden's St. Luke Painting The Virgin, the potential sensuality of an exposed breast is controlled by her non-sensual facial features.[25]

Female Suffering as Salvific

The final rationalization of misogyny and violence against women that we will discuss is the idea that suffering is the path to transcendence and salvation. This notion has a complicated historical development that, to be fully understood, would require an equally complex examination of the concrete historical situations in which it came to be a prominent Christian idea. The glorification of suffering in Western Christianity has suggested that if suffering is potentially beneficial, even salvific, to impose physical suffering on another human being, far from being reprehensible, may sometimes even be helpful to the victim. From the fifth century B.C.E. forward, the spoken or unspoken law of Western societies has been that the strong take what they will and the weak suffer what they must. The Greeks, who articulated this description of aggression, did not attempt to sweeten it with the rationalization that it was good for the weak to suffer. No heavenly reward that would eventually compensate the sufferer was posited. The Greeks simply acknowledged a brutal law of the jungle.

In Christianity, however, imitation of and participation in the suffering of Christ, although variously interpreted, was seen as normative for Christians. Even the most tyrannical oppressor could claim enough suffering to warrant support for the principle that suffering is good for the soul. Suffering in life was seen especially in the medieval period as a way to preclude suffering after death. Present suffering ensured future bliss. Some notorious oppressors took this maxim quite literally. In fifteenth-century England, John, Lord of Arundel, before going off to war, paid a call on the local convent, carrying off sixty nuns to entertain his soldiers on the long sea voyage. Midway through the voyage, however, storms arose which necessitated lightening the ship's load. The nuns were thrown overboard and perished, to a woman. When John of Arundel died, his will left instructions for posthumous penance for this and other deeds of his adventuresome life. His body, the will stipulated, was to be beaten, wrapped in chains, and buried naked in the earth. The advantage of posthumous penance is obvious,[26] but even in its own cultural setting the notion that such undemanding "suffering" could atone for responsibility for the suffering of the raped and drowned women trivializes the real suffering of the murdered women.

Medieval religious painting, publicly accessible on the walls and altars of churches, repeatedly depicts the suffering of women as salvific—and not only for their own souls; it is their suffering that qualifies them to be effective intercessors for others. The martyrdom of women saints was a favorite theme, a theme which often borders on pornographic eroticization of violence. Paintings of the martyrdom of St. Barbara by Master Franke (The St. Barbara Altarpiece, first half of the fifteenth century) and of St. Agatha by Sebastiono del Piombo (first half of the sixteenth century) show these saints having their naked breasts pulled off by giant pincers or sliced off by one burly executioner, while being whipped by another. Martyrdoms of the legendary St. Catherine of Alexandria, like the painting of this subject on the wall of the St. Catherine Chapel in San Clemente, Rome, show St. Catherine being beheaded. From these depictions of violent suffering to depictions of the fainting but dignified Virgin at the foot of the cross, the physical and spiritual suffering of women is shown as one of the primary ways for women to follow Christ. Excluded from emulating other roles of the human Christ, such as teaching or preaching, women often gained social and spiritual power by exaggerated and self-imposed suffering.

Male saints and scriptural figures—especially Christ—are, of course, also shown in texts and images as suffering, but their roles are not focused on salvific suffering. A much broader repertoire of activities is assigned to men than to women in religious images, while the primary religious participation and power of men was priesthood, religious images suggested to women that various forms of suffering were the surest route to participation in religious power. The reward for suffering was also a constant theme of religious paintings and sculpture. In this life, the reward was ecstatic mystical union, such as that shown in the later Bernini sculpture of St. Teresa in the Cornaro Chapel of Santa Maria della Vittoria in Rome. In the next life, present suffering was rewarded more dramatically; bodily assumptions of the Virgin and Mary Magdalen, as well as Coronation of the Virgin scenes, depicted the fulfillment of patient suffering in this life.

Women as Subordinate, Evil, and Suffering

The most dramatic historical example of the confluence of the three ideas and images we have explored occurred in the fifteenth through the seventeenth centuries in an oppression and persecution of women unparalleled in the history of Christianity. The phenomenon of witch-hunting in the late fifteenth through the early seventeenth centuries is too diverse and complex on the one hand, and too local, petty, and sordid on the other hand to be illuminated by any single explanatory thesis. It is, however, a striking example of the co-operation of misogynist texts and images to produce massive violence against women. Figures for victims of witch persecutions can only be guesswork due to partial and lost records; the most conservative estimate is that of the 100,000 to 200,000 victims approximately 80 percent were women. Henri Bouget, writing in 1590, said that "Switzerland has been compelled to wipe out many of her villages on [the witches'] account," and that Germany was "almost entirely occupied with building fires for them."[27] The human suffering involved cannot be adequately suggested by statistics.

Manuals on witchcraft and its detection and prosecution, like Kramer and Sprenger's *Malleus Maleficarum*, codified and expanded older beliefs about women's moral weakness, gullibility, and wantonness, and concluded that the persecution and execution of witches was God-ordained and God-pleasing. Quoting patristic authors, the *Malleus* says that the root problem of witches and the reason they are mostly women is that such a woman "will not be governed, but will follow her own impulse."[28] Secondly, "All witchcraft comes from carnal lust, which is in women insatiable." The *Malleus Maleficarum* is a catalog of male projection: "The word 'woman' is used to mean the lust of the flesh." Yet, oddly enough, although women cause men to sin through inciting them to lust, one of the chief accusations brought against witches was that they cause impotence. The witches' arrest, judicial torture, and execution by burning was prescribed as the only way to relieve the innocent who suffered from their powers. In fact, it was apparently genuinely believed that the only possible way to impress on a witch the evil of her ways and the urge to true repentance was the extreme suffering of burning; *in extremis*, it was believed, the witch might repent and thus, in spite of all, attain salvation. Therefore, the greatest possible favor one could do for a witch—as for any heretic—was to burn her.

The Inquisitor's witchcraft handbooks, horrifying in their logical impeccability and cool self-righteousness, however, were texts written in Latin and inaccessible to everyone but the educated. The *Malleus* was published in 1484, but it was not until the sixteenth and seventeenth centuries that the witch persecutions reached their most intense level. The manuals did not inspire the popular frenzy against presumed witches of the sixteenth and seventeenth centuries. Rather, the witch persecutions were a media phenomenon. They could not have happened before the invention of the printing press at the end of the fifteenth century. The first widely circulated printed "newspapers" were not pamphlets containing Protestant reformation theology but broadsheets distributing accounts of the trials, tortures, and executions of presumed witches. The dissemination of this "information" to towns and villages prompted the popular mania for identifying and persecuting witches.[29] When people were told that hailstorms, miscarriages, crop failures, accident, and disease were caused by witches, *and* when they were shown what witches looked like, they learned to look for the cause of their high and constant levels of misery in women familiar to them. As in paintings and sculptures of Eve with an abundance of flesh, printed drawings of witches on sixteenth-century broadsheets, etchings and engravings featured corpulent women epitomizing the lust that motivated witchcraft. Hans Baldung Grien and Albrecht Dürer are the most famous of the artists who obsessively pictured witches and their alleged activities. Not until ideas and images were brought together did witch-hunting become mass hysteria and popular sport.

Contemporary Women and Patriarchal Order

We have seen that the first newspapers were illustrated tirades against women; let us turn now to our present situation, to media images of our own time, and ask if traditional misogynist ideas and images are not still selling newspapers. Since media images of our own time are not usually religious images, the continuity of ancient biblical misogyny is masked in North American media. But is it not still there?

How do advertising images function to inform members of the present society of their relative value and position in the society? Verbal captions of advertisements proclaim, by seeming to address everyone, a rhetoric of social equality. Images, however, consistently present young, wealthy, slim, sexually attractive Anglo-Saxon women and men as the satisfied users of their products. The verbal text contradicts the powerful subliminal message of the image, which promotes sexism, racism, and ageism. By the endless repetition of visual cliches, it creates marginal people, both women and men, who can never realistically aspire to youth, wealth, the right skin color or sexual preference in order to qualify for the satisfaction promised by the image.

In advertising images, the valued and valuable members of the society are clearly identified; consistent and cumulative messages are given by which we measure ourselves and formulate self-images based on the degree to which we match the images. Both men and women appear in our daily newspapers, but, as one student recently discovered when she analyzed an issue of the Sunday New York Times, about 90 percent of the pictures of men appeared in news stories, while about 90 percent of the images of women appeared in advertising. On October 27, 1983—the day Grenada was invaded—the front and back pages of the first section of the New York Times illustrated vividly the complementarity of gender images. The front page shows photographs of men, brows furrowed, conferring with one another, and photographs of military men landing in Grenada, greeted with gratitude and enthusiasm. The back page shows a full-page sized "Cosmo girl," partially but inadequately draped, in a seductive pose. Our conditioned expectations that men think and act, while women fulfill themselves and gain whatever power they may have by being beautiful objects, are consistently nourished by media gender imagery.

The three ancient ideas about women examined above are alive and well in today's media. Male supremacy is daily reinforced in implicit if not explicit norms of patriarchal order; identification of women with body and temptation is a staple of media images, and the notion that suffering is salvific is also to be found in press photographs of suffering women and in advertising images: "Life looks better when you do," urges an advertisement for cosmetic surgery. The secularization of these messages makes them seem contemporary, but, as the French proverb has it, "the more things change, the more they remain the same." We have seen that it is precisely these traditional ideas, now artfully clothed in fashionable modern dress, that provide cultural support for misogyny and ultimately for violence against women.

In *The Body and Society*, Bryan Turner has argued that changes in the character of the family unit, industrialization, women's participation in the marketplace, and laws which have to a great extent dismantled the exclusionary practices that established and maintained patriarchy, have given rise to a contemporary American culture that cannot be realistically characterized as patriarchal. If patriarchy is defined as institutional and political subordination of women, we do not presently live in such a society. Yet institutional changes have not created an inclusive society; women still experience sexism, misogyny, and violence in everyday life. In fact, Turner argues, the demise of patriarchy has created the condition of "patrism," or ideological patriarchy. Although "patrism" is unsupported by laws and institutions, it is still a powerful force, a reaction by men who "find their traditional sources of power increasingly open to doubt":

> The collapse of patriarchy has left behind it widespread patrism which is a culture of discriminatory, prejudicial, and paternalistic beliefs about the inferiority of women. . . . Patrism is expanding precisely because of the institutional shrinkage of patriarchy, which has left men in a contracting power position. . . . Institutionalized patriarchy has crumbled along with the traditional family unit and the patristic attitude of men towards women becomes more prejudicial and defensive precisely because women are now often equipped with a powerful ideological critique of traditional patriarchy.[30]

If Turner is correct in identifying a trend in the direction of increasingly inclusive laws and institutions in American culture, then it is important to extend feminist analysis beyond the structures of society to the more subtle oppression of women by patrism—male reaction to the loss of patriarchal laws and institutions. Traditional ideas and images, often in contemporary dress but essentially unaltered and undiminished in virulence, continue to be reiterated, reinforced, and extended in the public practices of everyday life as well as in the media. The ideas and visual images discussed above inform and rationalize numerous everyday occurrences that are too taken-for-granted to be easily changed—jokes, street taunts, sexist language, dress, and sexually differentiated labor. Social change must still proceed, no doubt, by continuing to insist on laws that protect and institutions that include women. But public life is not the only arena in which change is necessary. Personal attitudes and behavior are also political activities. In making some suggestions about how a public ideology of misogyny can be addressed, then, let us speak personally.

What can we do about it? It is, of course, worse than useless to stand around deploring the communication media of modern society, perhaps the most common and constant carrier of misogyny in North America. The media are here to stay. Yet it is important to raise questions about the values implicit in the daily media dosage of a whole society. Until we are conscious of these implicit values, we are helpless victims. Until we are conscious of the messages we receive daily, we can neither choose those we find life-enhancing nor reject and protest those that promote injustice and violence.

There are two possible kinds of response to misogyny and violence against women. One response is that of providing help for victims of violence. As a result of the present women's movement, Mary Pellauer writes, "intellectual and institutional resources have been generated at an incredible speed. There are now more than 500 battered women's shelters and 1500 rape crisis centers around the country."[31] The difference between the passive voyeurism of the viewer of media violence and active engagement to eliminate violence and to heal its victims is crucial. Most shelters are staffed by volunteers, women who find the opportunity of "doing something about it" personally healing. We can address the moral deadening caused by seeing daily doses of misogynist and/or violent media images about which we can do nothing by offering our presence and help to women who are the victims of violence.

The second response aims at prevention, at the massive social transformation that will be necessary to change our situation as women. Identifying the underlying and constant ideas and images that make violence against women possible and even, in the eyes of some, legitimate, enables us to speak against these ideas wherever we find them—in the home, in institutions, in the media, in churches, and in synagogues.

If our speech is to be effective, however, we must overcome the individualism that enables many of us to think that violence against women is not *our* problem. "I've never been raped, never been discriminated against, never been hurt," we hear. The crucial step for the creation of the solidarity necessary to protest and change the conditions in which we live as women is to stop thinking only in terms of "my own experience" and to self-identify with women as a "caste," in Mary Daly's term, with women who are always subordinated in patriarchal cultures and in cultures characterized by patrism. Once one has achieved identification with women as a caste, all one needs to do is to read the newspapers in order to feel as one's own the dramatic abuse of women, especially women of color, poor women, and third world women. Once one has made this self-identification, it will no longer do to blame the victim, to think, however unconsciously, that victims of so-called sexual violence have been assaulted because they dressed provocatively, because they "invited" it by going out alone at night, or even by living alone. Blaming the victim functions to keep women feeling safe, feeling that we will not become victims; it keeps us isolated.

How do we claim as our own the experience of another human being? How do we feel experiences we have not had? Feminist author Emily Culpepper once responded to these questions with a simple but profound reply: "We tell each other our stories," she said. In the commitment to listening with empathy and speaking with honesty, the experience of another woman can become one's own experience. The ability to feel the pain of others can then become an ethical resource, empowering women to overcome isolation, individualism, and fear. The first step toward protesting the misogyny and violence of present society and beginning to create a society in which we can love and play and work without fear, is to begin to think communally, collectively.

The second step has already been named. Women must replace paralyzed passivity with activity. The two steps are intimately connected. Women can act effectively only to the extent that we act collectively. Probably every woman has had the experience of speaking about an issue of personal importance in a public gathering. A great effort was required to do so, and after saying her piece she felt guiltily that she had been daring, subverted the discussion, and made an impact. Then the next person spoke, not in response or even rebuttal to her comment, but on an entirely new topic. The discussion went on as if the woman had never spoken. Perhaps a few minutes later someone else mentioned her comment, reinforced it by noting it, or restated it. Then and only then she feels and *is* heard. A single woman's voice in patriarchal and patristic cultures is inaudible, no matter how strong and loud it may be. But once two or several women have acknowledged or restated the comment, it begins to be heard. Only our collective voices are heard.

Finally, in a culture characterized by patrism, it is not usually by dramatic public statements against women that violence against women is justified and perpetuated, but by the small increments of sexism occurring constantly on a daily intimate level. Even the apparently humorous misogyny of everyday life desensitizes both women and men to misogyny. If misogyny is pervasive, however, it is also accessible; it can be named as it appears, and if it is constantly named and rejected by women it can be changed.

Only by exploration of the deep roots of misogyny in Western scriptures and religious images can the rationalizations for violence against women be recognized in their contemporary forms. For an historian trained to expect that ideas appearing to remain the same across time and space in fact do not act similarly in different cultural settings, it is startling to see the continuity of misogynist ideas and images and the similarity with which they operate to subordinate women in diverse cultures. The next surprise is that, in spite of the pervasiveness and rootedness of misogyny, the subordination of women, and violence against women in Western societies, women have still been able to change the institutionalized, legalized oppression of women in American culture still prevalent a few decades ago. Those real gains, however, cannot be consolidated and advanced unless feminists continue to unmask the patriarchal God as He appears in American culture. Where should women place our attention—on the progress, the fragile beginning of the creation of an inclusive society, or on the mighty forces within and outside individuals that persist in misogyny? We need to have our eye on both—on the progress, so we do not become discouraged, *and* on the magnitude of the task, so that we do not become prematurely comfortable in feminist enclaves.

Notes

1. Judges 19:25b–29, *The Oxford Annotated Bible,* ed. Herbert G. May and Bruce M. Metzger (New York: Oxford University Press, 1962), p. 320.
2. Phyllis Trible, *Texts of Terror* (Philadelphia: Fortress Press, 1984), pp. 80–81.
3. Mary D. Pellauer, "Moral Callousness and Moral Sensitivity," in *Women's Consciousness, Women's Conscience,* Barbara Hilkert Andolsen, Christine E. Gudorf, Mary D. Pellauer, eds. (Minneapolis: Winston Press, 1985), p. 42.
4. September 18, 1986 statistics, Memo to staff, Harbor Me Battered Women's Shelter, Boston, Massachusetts.
5. Pellauer, p. 43.
6. Marie M. Fortune, *Sexual Violence, The Unmentionable Sin* (New York: Pilgrim Press, 1983), p. 90.
7. Peggy Reeves Sanday, *Female Power and Male Dominance: On the Origins of Sexual Inequality* (New York: Cambridge University Press, 1981), p. 42.

8. Beryl Lieff Benderly, "Rape Free or Rape Prone," *Science* (October, 1982), p. 42.

9. Paul Dinnage, ed., *Marquis de Sade: Selections,* pp. 132–33, quoted in Fortune, p. 113.

10. Fortune, p. 116.

11. Nicholas Groth with Jean Birnbaum, *Men Who Rape* (New York: Plenum, 1979), p. 27.

12. Fortune, pp. 116–18.

13. Andrea Dworkin, *Pornography, Men Possessing Women* (New York: Perigree Books, 1979), p. 201.

14. See, for example, Margaret R. Miles, *Image as Insight, Visual Understanding in Western Christianity and Secular Culture,* Chapter 4, "Images of Women in Fourteenth-Century Tuscan Painting" (Boston: Beacon Press, 1985), pp. 63–93.

15 Tertullian, *De velandis virginibus* 5, trans. The Ante-Nicene Fathers, First Series, Vol. 4 (Buffalo: The Christian Literature Publishing Company, 1885), p. 30.

16. Lecture, Harvard Divinity School, April 1985. Another exception to standard inter pretations of the Genesis 1 account of the creation of women as secondary human beings is Agrippa von Nettesheim's 1509 "Declamation on the Nobility and Excellence of the Feminine Sex." In *Opera,* vol. 2, pp. 504–7. Lyon, n.d.; photo. repr. Hildesheim, 1970.

17. See especially Elisabeth Schüssler Fiorenza, *In Memory of Her* (New York: Crossroad, 1983); see also Margaret R. Miles, "Patriarchy as Political Theology: The Establishment of North African Christianity," in *Civil Religion and Political Society,* Boston University Studies in Philosophy and Religion (Notre Dame University Press, 1986), pp. 169–86; Bernadette Brooten, "Paul's Views on the Nature of Women and Female Homoeroticism," in *Immaculate and Powerful: The Female in Sacred Image and Social Reality,* ed. Atkinson et al. (Boston: Beacon, 1986), pp. 61–87.

18. Italics mine; Augustine, *De bono conjungali* 17.20; trans. Fathers of the Church, vol. 27 (New York: Fathers of the Church, Inc. 1955), p. 34.

19. Augustine, *De civitate dei* XIX. 14; trans. Henry Bettenson, *Augustine, City of God* (New York: Penguin, 1972), p. 874.

20. James Michener, *Poland* (New York: Fawcett Crest, 1983), p. 200.

21. Tertullian, *De cultu feminarum* 1.1, trans. Ante-Nicene Fathers, Vol. 4, p. 14.

22. Tertullian, *De velandus virginibus* 2, Vol. 4, p. 27.

23. Andrea Dworkin, *Woman Hating* (New York: E.P. Dutton, 1974), p. 73.

24. Jacobus de Voragine, *The Golden Legend,* trans. Granger Ryan and Helmut Ripperger (New York: Arno, 1969), p. 150.

25. Anne Hollander, in *Seeing Through Clothes* (New York: Viking, 1980), claims that naked breasts are, in any culture, "the sure conveyors of a complex delight," though cultural definitions of the norm for erotic breasts vary widely; p. 186.

26. Kathleen Cohen, *Metamorphosis of a Death Symbol: The Transi Tomb in the Late Middle Ages and the Renaissance* (Berkeley: University of California Press, 1973), p. 5.

27. Henri Bouget, *An Examen of Witches Drawn From Various Trials,* trans. E. Allen Ashwin, ed. Montague Summers (London: John Rodker, 1929), p. xxxiii.

28. Heinrich Kramer and James Sprenger, *The Malleus Maleficarum,* trans. Montague Summers (New York: Dover, 1971), p. xxx.

29. Elizabeth Eisenstein, "The Advent of Printing and the Protestant Revolution: A New Approach to the Disruption of Western Christendom," in *Transition and Revolution,* Robert M. Kingdon, ed. (Minneapolis, Minn.: Burgess, 1974), pp. 260ff.

30. Bryan Turner, *The Body and Society* (New York: Basil Blackwell, 1984), p. 156.

31. Pellauer, p. 49.

"Take My Yoke upon You"

The Role of the Church in the Oppression of African-American Women

❧ *Frances E. Wood* ❧

Introduction

Human struggle with the existence of evil and suffering is recounted throughout recorded history. These struggles can be found in sources as diverse as the book of Job; meditations of mystic Howard Thurman; essays of Holocaust witness Elie Wiesel; and discussions of theodicy by womanist ethicist Katie Geneva Cannon.

Jesus' invitation to "take my yoke upon you, and learn of me,"[1] in all its paradoxical import, frequently has been distorted in theological and philosophical discourse, as well as ministerial instruction. Philosophers and theologians have offered ontological rationalizations and theological explications in their attempts to explain the unexplainable and decipher the perplexing phenomenon of human suffering, particularly suffering that results from intentional harm at the hands of another human being, commonly understood as moral evil.

Among those calling themselves Christian, there are some widely accepted notions concerning suffering, its purposes and meaning. Many, if not all, are based on explanations offered by church fathers whose interpretations have gone unquestioned for centuries. They include suffering as punishment for sin; suffering for the building of character; suffering as evidence of specialness in the sight of God; suffering (particularly for females) as a consequence of Eve's disobedience. When these explanations are applied to the situation of Black females in this country, they function to maintain a lethal sociological and ecclesiastical status quo. Neither the secular nor religious communities pay much attention to the implications for lives of African-American women who have internalized the explanations of church fathers.

Philosophers as well as some behavioral scientists argue that what sets human beings apart from other mammals is the capacity to reason. Coupled with this capacity is the ability to reflect on our life circumstances and environment, and to effect changes in them. I understand our differences from other animals also lie in our capacity to love and call forth love in one another. Sadly, there is yet another ability exhibited only by human beings. That is the ability to oppress one another.

No other life form on the planet engages in intentional acts of oppression or wanton destruction. These are actions over which we have choice, and in which we engage with forethought. In our attempts to justify certain behaviors we place them on an arbitrary scale of lesser and greater harm; often engaging in horizontal oppression, or constructing hierarchies of oppression. By so doing, we seek to exonerate ourselves from the roles we play in perpetuating evil and suffering. Although evil and suffering take myriad forms, my purpose is not to dissect the existence of evil or suffering in the abstract. This essay addresses the particular shapes and forms that manifest themselves in the oppression of African-American women within the Christian community.

The social status quo, despite various modern liberation movements, continues to be one in which females are treated as inferior to males. Moreover, the dominance and submission mode of gender relations within the Black Christian community, as well as the dominant culture, meets criteria for moral evil: sustaining and reinforcing attitudes, beliefs, policies, and practices that deny certain individuals or groups the status of full humanity, create negative concepts of "otherness," and justify patterns of discrimination against the oppressed group. One may argue that Black men are exempt from the role of oppressor in this definition of evil. However, it is important to bear in mind that despite the tenuousness of gender privilege afforded them, the exercise of that privilege by Black men contributes to the oppression of Black women. In this regard, James Cone asks a critical question: "What kind of society do we (Black men) wish to create? Do we want a genuinely new society or just the right to replace white men with black men?"[2]

With this question in mind I will discuss (1) the reality of women who bear the yoke of violence rooted in sexism, which is part of women's fee for membership within the church; (2) the role of the church community in either adding to the burden or denouncing and removing the yoke; and (3) offer some requisites for change in the African-American community claiming membership in the body of Christ. The context for my discussion is the social situation of women in the United States, with particular attention to the treatment of gender as it is constructed in the dominant culture, and reflected in the attitudes and behaviors of the African-American Christian community.

The experiences of women of the African diaspora residing in the United States have begun to be examined sporadically in the teaching of history, sociology, literature, law, theology, and other disciplines. Increasingly, these accounts reflect women as subjects, rather than objects. Black women are depicted as moral agents, rather than immoral beings reacting to the agency of others. African-American women's stories are being shared in ways previously unheard of. Ironically, although the core of African-American Christian tradition has as its foundation, "telling the story" of God's liberating and saving grace in the person of Jesus Christ, there persists an awful silence in telling the *whole* story. This silence can be likened to that afflicting the adults in the children's story, *The Emperor's New Clothes*. Within the African-American church community the silence about the realities of women's experience and how it differs from men's experience has taken the proportions of a version of the "big lie," and is a deadly yoke. This yoke consists of silencing, ignoring, degrading, and dismissing women's experience, especially those experiences that reveal the nature and extent of oppression perpetrated against them within the community. Idealization and romanticization of Black women's suffering is as insidious a habit in the African-American community as it has been historically in the dominant society. Elevating women's suffering to a form of martyrdom for the cause (of others) virtually guarantees that it will remain unexamined. Herein lies a peculiar dilemma for the community. On the one hand, women's suffering is apotheosized. By so doing, we subscribe to the suffering-servant motif in Christology. On the other hand, if the proximate cause of the suffering is the men within the community, the response of the community is active or passive denial. Black women who risk telling their story in this context are shamed, denounced, and treated as pariahs rather than prophets. The yoke of silencing, degrading, ignoring or dismissing women weighs down the Black Christian community in a conspiracy against its own total liberation. In the name of racial solidarity, this yoke is a burden borne by all the members, although disproportionately by those who are female.

As is true in any paradigm of oppression, whenever the alleged inferior group seeks, as womanists have, to define itself on its own terms or, in any other way, shift the status quo, a backlash ensues. Whatever forms it takes, backlash is intended to keep a group "in their place." In the dominant culture this is evidenced in the discussion of issues such as fetal protection or the mommy track, as euphemisms for discriminating against women in employment. In the Black community it takes forms such as the myth of the Black woman being in academic conspiracy with white males, or discussions of Black men's definitions of "real" women. It is worth noting that one of the prerogatives exercised in paradigms of oppression is the dominant group defining the target group. One of the vicissitudes of "real" women (as opposed to those constructed by male fantasy), regardless of ethnicity or race, is that we are treated as "permissible victims."[3] Leadership in the Christian community has failed to demonstrate any seriously considered opposition to this treatment. The legendary strong Black woman has become the personification of the permissible victim. She is the sister whose solo on Sunday morning moves the congregation in a special way, despite her having been assaulted at home on Saturday night. In a younger version, she is the young teen who is an exemplary student and is being forced to keep secret the horrors of being molested. The woman is kept silent with a strong dose of Saint Paul; and the teenager, learning her lessons in being silenced, listens to a sermon on obedient children.[4] Females are regarded as legitimate targets of abuse. Little boys equate being physically vanquished by their male peers with being "like a girl." Grown men continue to view the battering or rape of a woman as simply a hazard of being female, as opposed to a consequence of the behavior of men who choose to victimize women. The assaults that women and girls experience in their homes are seen as normative. More to the point, the abuse is perceived as what women and girls should expect as the result of being female.

With few exceptions (primarily when the victim of violence perpetrated by a *stranger* is *his* daughter, wife, mother, sister), assaults of women go unmentioned in the writing, civic commentary or sermons of male religious leaders. Assaults that occur within the family receive virtually no mention or condemnation at all. Abusive behavior, which we call taboo, is not the real taboo; speaking the truth about the abuse is. In the paterfamilias model of family, proprietary considerations supercede considerations of justice. When African-American male ministers list issues of justice confronting society, the abuse perpetrated against females by family members and friends is conspicuous by its absence.

To add insult to injury, when a battered woman approaches her pastor for assistance, she is frequently advised either to become a better wife; bear her cross in faith; or pray for her husband. The abusive behavior goes unchallenged; the suffering is "explained"; the one who knows best has spoken. Those taking seriously the prophet's injunction to "seek kindness, love justice, and walk humbly with your God"[5] must be willing to sort through and challenge popular myths, stereotypes and illusions that reinforce victimization; to peel away the tough outer layers of the fruit so that the tender truths at the core are revealed. The pastor as interpreter of meaning for the sister in trouble will be held accountable someday for his interpretations.

Men of color have an obligation to extract from their eyes the lens of sexism through which they view the world, no less than white men have an obligation to remove the lens of racism through which they view the world. In responding to situations of oppression one must take care always to ask: Whom does this circumstance serve or disserve? Who benefits from things as they are? In discussing "good news" Bernice Johnson Reagon states:

> It's good news when you reject things as they are; when you lay down the world as it is, and you take on the responsibility of shaping your own way. . . . It's hard times when you decide to pick up *your own cross*. You gonna catch hell if you don't do it the way they say do it. [italics added][6]

This statement is as true in the African-American Christian community as it is in secular institutions and organizations. I understand it to apply particularly to women who struggle to claim their *own* identity and shape their *own* way within the community. Doing it "the way they say do it" has required silence about women's experiences of sexual and domestic violence as well as other forms of oppression manifested by the hydra-headed monster called misogyny.

The Institutional Church: An Added Weight on the Yoke

Founded, constituted, and led by African Americans, the Black church emerged from a people in bondage, who understood the good news as a liberating message. The church has been comforter, leader, moral agent, intercessor, locus of status, and definer of all that is good and right for people who fear the Lord. In many communities, it remains the moral center of public activity. When issues of justice arise, the voice of religious leadership from the Black community is often the most audible and adamant. Because of this voice, we mistakenly have come to believe that matters of justice affecting *all* Black people are at the top of the agendas of Black church leaders. Sadly, this is not the case. Absent from the Black church is any substantive discussion of gender justice as it pertains to women. When one uses the criteria of denying others' full humanity, viewing "otherness" in a negative light, and perpetuating patterns of discrimination as the measure of social evil, one can conclude that the treatment of women in Black churches all too often fits those criteria. There continue to be churches that thwart women's calls to pastor and preach. The excuse that "our church is not ready for a woman, yet" continues to have validity across denominational lines. Jokes from the pulpit that demean women consistently elicit laughter and go unchallenged. Some church organizations prefer slow deterioration under poor male leadership over *any* female leadership.

Within the church, as in all social arrangements, there are those who are treated as pillars who support the group, and scapegoats who are blamed when the structure is crumbling. Both these designations are applied schizophrenically to Black women. Simultaneously placing women on pedestals and denouncing them as the root cause of the demise of the Black community results in an insidious double bind for Black women and men, as well. Labeling women according to the madonna/whore syndrome is not the sole province of white denominations. Indeed, these characterizations of women are found from storefront to cathedral; from the most isolated rural settings to the most populated cities. The madonna most frequently is noted on Mother's Day when the woman in the congregation who has borne the greatest number of children (with benefit of wedlock) is singled out for recognition. The whore is identified primarily in relation to the number of men in the congregation who either actually or allegedly have had sex with her. A woman's place in this seemingly polarized arrangement is subject to shifting arbitrarily as she engages in behavior deemed worthy of praise or blame. We must examine our collusion with these characterizations of women, and what these role assignments reveal about what we *truly* think of women, as opposed to what we say we believe about women. Regardless of the language we use, the dynamics related to pillar and scapegoat syndrome are alive and well. They are but one set of behaviors which reveal our collective bias against women. A concomitant situation of women in the church is the dubious distinction of being identified as the "backbone" of the church. In discussing the backbone phenomenon Jacquelyn Grant offers this analysis:

> The telling portion of the word "backbone" is "back." It has become apparent to me that most of the ministers who use this term are referring to location rather than function. What they really mean is that women are in the "background" and should be kept there.[7]

With many congregations having a 70 percent female membership, we must reflect on the extent to which internalized misogyny erodes the spiritual welfare of the church, and denounce misogynistic practice as antithetical to Christian liberation, and an insidious form of spiritual death. This malaise is not peculiar to Black churches, but it is a form of suffering in the community about which Black folk speak little, if at all. In those rare instances where serious questions are raised against misogynistic assumptions, presumptions, and practices (such as women being capable of preparing but not distributing communion), the questioner, if female, is denounced as a manhater or, if male, as a dominated wimp. The label of manhater or wimp implies that one has engaged in a treasonous act, and broken the contemporary eleventh commandment: thou shalt not criticize male behavior. All challenge or criticism that could remotely hold Black men accountable for their behavior vis-à-vis women is interpreted as maligning African-American manhood. By treating men as fragile egos who cannot bear the truth, women both infantilize men and forfeit an opportunity to call forth the *best* in men. Men frequently equate challenges to gender privilege with being unloved by women. The irony of the situation in the church and wider society is there is no other group that loves and supports Black men as do Black women; and Black men *know* that Black women love them. These two major premises form the foundation for both the support African-American women provide men and the legitimate challenges against injustice that results from the exercise of gender privilege. With these as major premises, how do we incorporate an understanding within the community that deals with the enormously painful and complex reality of the oppressed as oppressor? What is the word of liberation and hope spoken to the battered wife of the head of the deacon board? Where is the accountability required when the head of the trustee board repeatedly sexually harasses "our women"? What are we to make of the double standard for teenage sexual behavior that allows boys to sow their oats, yet expects girls to keep their panties up and their dresses down? How are we teaching our children the meaning of justice when the term "our youth" means our *boys*? What are we to make of the practice in some churches of shunning pregnant teenage girls, and elevating their male counterparts to leadership roles? How do we account for the disgraceful refusal of congregations to consider an ordained woman for pastoral leadership? Before we dismiss these questions as not applicable in our own situations, we must take a moment to think about practices in our own congregations. What are the signposts we need to guide us along the perilous path toward liberation and justice for us all? How will our future communal life honor our forebears' living and dying for equality?

Bearing the Yoke of Jesus

Before we can take on the yoke of Jesus in the work of gender justice, we must name the burdens and claim the memories under which we struggle and labor. This naming is an essential first step if the church is to be able to "remember, repent, and do the works."[8] Remembering is often difficult to do when one is in the midst of crisis. The axiom of America getting a cold and the Black community getting pneumonia is painfully evident throughout the country. However, as William R. Jones would remind us, if the illness is incorrectly diagnosed, the wrong remedies will be applied.[9]

The first memory that must be claimed is that we were never meant to survive as human beings.[10] Second, we must demythologize the notion that African-American women and men working side by side in the cotton rows somehow automatically has translated into gender equality. Whereas partnership as a model for shared work between Black women and men is an ideal, we must understand that "before there is partnering and sharing with someone, there is the becoming of oneself."[11] The becoming of oneself does not supplant partnership. It is, however, a prerequisite for authentic partnership. The third memory we must acknowledge and name is that misogyny against Black women did not begin with their enslavement in the United States. Neither did the habit of mimicking the worst assumptions and values of the oppressor only begin after the Civil War. Just as Black feminists and womanists are not suffering from some disease caught from white women, but rather are women engaged in wrestling with both the awful truths and awesome power of our lives, neither are Black men who exercise male privilege suffering from some disease they caught from white men. How have we come to the place where a group so attuned to the adverse effects of racism, as are Black churchmen, is inured to their own sexism? Given the depth of this anesthetized state, we are long overdue in asking African-American Christian men the question:

> What [man] here is so enamored of [his] own oppression that [he] cannot see [his] heelprint upon [a] woman's face? What terms of oppression have become precious and necessary to [him] as a ticket into the fold of the righteous, away from the cold winds of self scrutiny?[12]

Denial of the oppression of women within the African-American Christian community constitutes a mockery of authentic claims for justice in the face of the variety of "isms" confronting us. The metaphor of getting one's own house in order is apt here. We cannot simultaneously denounce injustice on the part of white society and perpetuate injustice within our own communities. In the last decade of this exceedingly violent century we can no longer tolerate an analysis of the issues of conflict between Black women and men as simply the result of women being "too well educated."[13]

We must acknowledge that "things as they are" are not serving the community well, and that clinging to prerogatives rooted in the oppression of women mitigate against the full personhood of us all. Further, we must be mindful that things as they *are* do not constitute what they necessarily *will be* in the future. In spite of contention within the community, the Black church continues to have

> tremendous potential for fostering constructive, instructive, and reconciling discussion on issues of mutuality, sexuality and spirituality for women and men. It is obvious that the foundational theory and the theology are all in place to accomplish this dialogue, yet the praxis is still limited or lacking if we are at all honest in our reflection upon our lived experience. The recovery of a *meaningful* value system enriching the relationships between black women and men still remains underdeveloped, or at best only moderately achieved.[14] [italics added]

The conditions of misogyny in our churches are neither a "man thing" nor a "woman thing." Rather they are conditions that impede the work of justice and undermine the capacity to "do the works" of justice required of us. Any call to justice in this last decade of the twentieth century, in order to be authentically Christian, must incorporate *metanoia,* a transformation at the deepest levels of one's self. In addressing the issue of feminist activism and maleness, one writer counsels, "One must change the core of one's being. The core of one's being must love justice more than manhood."[15] I would add that what conventionally have been used as attributes of true manhood, that is, social and economic dominance, sexual prowess, and theological supremacy, are bankrupt and need to be put to rest. The prophets of ancient Israel frequently mention the rueful destiny that will befall a stiff-necked people. A destiny of destruction need not be the inheritance of African-American Christian men and women.

Several years ago, when asked about the declining numbers of priests and the increasing role of women and lay men in ministerial leadership, a Roman Catholic archbishop replied: "I believe the Holy Spirit has spoken to us, but we refuse to accept what is being said."[16] Another way of putting the bishop's response is that maybe God is trying to tell us something. Living together in the Spirit in the Christian community is not limited to shouting, sermonizing, and lifting every voice to sing. Being in the Spirit also demands that we risk examining assumptions and presumptions about roles and relationships in the community. Jesus' strongest denunciations in the Gospels are reserved for the "hypocrites, snakes and viper's brood," those in leadership roles who dominated and exacted heavy burdens of the Jewish people. The situation among the male leadership in too many congregations and denominational structures can best be described as sexist apartheid, wherein the minority clings to a structure of domination over the majority. Until or unless this fundamental structural reality is acknowledged, and its implications for women examined, calls for justice outside the church will ring as hollow as the calls for international human rights on the part of U.S. politicians. Christian manhood does not consist of the capacity to rule. Christian womanhood does not consist of a critical, silent collusion with the yoke of sexism.

The yoke that we are called to bear, what is *required* of us, is seeking justice, loving kindness, and walking humbly with our God. It is in this seeking and loving that we will find the signposts to assist us in remembering, repenting, and returning. We must remember that all the Blacks are not men. We must repent from the idolatrous worship of maleness. We must return to an ethic of mutuality.

Seeking justice demands that we not only look outward, but also that we look inward. Looking inward demands that we no longer exploit the concept of racial solidarity to mask bigotry. Looking inward demands that pastoral search committees pay more than lip service to female candidates for the ministry. Looking inward demands an end to pedestaling and scapegoating women. Looking inward demands that men forego a solidarity that places sharing the hormone testosterone as its highest value. Looking inward demands that women begin to realize that we do not serve the best interests of women, children, *or* men when we refuse to hold men accountable for oppressive behavior. In our lifetime there are those who have died being true to the belief that resistance to evil is part of the Christian heritage. The evils we resist today are no less real than those our predecessors fought: oppression, nostalgic revisionism, lying. The context, however, has shifted: the oppression we fight is that of women; the nostalgic revisionism we resist is the fiction that "once we were one"; the lying to which we will not accede is female subjugation as a requisite of racial solidarity.

As long as men continue to define themselves by using the masters' tools of dominance and subordination, whether by commission or omission, as their measure of manhood, there will be no justice in the church. Until there is a new understanding and regard for the full personhood of all women with their gifts and talents in the church, we will not bear the yoke of Jesus. Instead, we will continue to bear the yoke of preserving patriarchal privilege.

Must women bear the yoke alone, and all the men go free?

Notes

1. Matthew 11:29.
2. James H. Cone, *My Soul Looks Back* (Maryknoll, NY: Orbis Books, 1986), 123.
3. The term "permissible victim" refers to those groups or individuals who can be harmed with little or no negative consequence befalling the perpetrator. The least permissible victim in U.S. society is a white, wealthy, heterosexual male.
4. Ephesians 5:22–23; 6:1–3.
5. Micah 6:8.
6. Sweet Honey in the Rock, "Good News," 7th Anniversary Concert, 7 November 1980. Songtalk Publishing Co., 1980.
7. Jacquelyn Grant, "Black Women and the Church," in *All the Women Are White, All the Blacks Are Men, But Some of Us Are Brave,* Gloria T. Hull, Patricia Bell Scott, and Barbara Smith, eds., (Old Westbury, NY: Feminist Press, 1982), 141.
8. Revelation 2:2–5.
9. Author of *Is God a White Racist? A Preamble to Black Theology* (Garden City, NY: Anchor Books, 1973) addressing the National Council of Churches of Christ (NCCC) Commission on Family Ministry and Human Sexuality (CFMHS) on the issue of racism, Sarasota, Florida, November, 1990.
10. Audre Lorde, "The Transformation of Silence into Language and Action," in *Sister Outsider: Essays and Speeches* (Trumansburg, NY: The Crossing Press, 1984), 42.
11. Jeanne Noble, *Beautiful Are the Souls of My Black Sisters* (New York: Prentice-Hall, 1978), 343.
12. Lorde, 132.
13. The Reverend Wallace Charles Smith addressing the National Council of Churches of Christ, CFMHS, at a consultation on the Black Church and the Family, November, 1989.
14. Toinette M. Eugene, "While Love Is Unfashionable," in *Women's Consciousness, Women's Conscience,* Barbara Hilkert Andolsen, Christine E. Gudorf and Mary D. Pellauer, eds. (San Francisco: Harper & Row, 1985), 133.
15. John Stoltenberg, *Refusing To Be a Man* (Portland, OR: Breitenbush Books, 1989), 185.
16. Former Seattle Archbishop Raymond G. Hunthausen addressing members of the Chancery staff, 1984.

Falling off the Tightrope onto a Bed of Feathers

❖ Darice Jones ❖

I lived my life for a long time on a tightrope, trying to find my middle ground, to please my audience of parents, friends, teachers and bosses, trying to look good doing it and come out on the other side unscathed. In my little block of Oakland, California, it was not OK to be all that I was. There was too much contradiction involved. I am African and American, Christian-raised but Tao-embracing, invested in the plight of black men but my life partners are to be women, raised working class but with a middle-class education, peace-bound but activism-prone, and a feminist whose politics are centered around all life—not just the lives of women. Part of learning feminism for me has been about learning that you can't be what people want you to be—and learning how to do better than just survive when you fall.

I didn't grow up with "feminism" as an important word. In fact, I didn't come to hear a working definition of it until a college professor created one for me. She said feminism is simply the idea that women should be free to define themselves. A feminist is someone who espouses that belief. I would add that feminism is also about putting that belief into action and working on your own internalized sexism. A feminist is not just someone who envisions a different world but someone who creates a life that will change it.

I can see feminism at work in every area of my life, as I went from a teething ring to an eyebrow ring. In the late seventies, my early years, I watched my mother and her mother stomping out a ground for me to walk on. Full-time working mothers with full-time investments in their communities and churches is the only image I ever had of the women closest to me. So media images of "stay-at-home" moms never penetrated my psyche. They were as fictional to me as Saturday-morning cartoons. Most of the images I saw in magazines, on television and in movies were of white middle-class women, but working-class African-American women were my reality; mothers, aunts, cousins, teachers, even my Girl Scout instructors were black women on a mission to make good in the world.

As early as I can remember, I knew the bar was high. I was expected to conquer any challenge presented to me at school, to excel in extracurricular sports and music, and to be a young leader in our church. These expectations were implicit in the way our family operated. My mother taught me and my four sisters to read as soon as we could speak, and she made us teach each other. That passing down of learning, child to child, laid the groundwork for our deep, close relationships as sisters.

The relationship between my parents was filled with examples of the feminist ideal in action. While we all lived together, until I was twelve, I saw my parents as two equal superpowers, one never bowing to the other. They seemed to have a respect for each other stronger than romance or love. My father, who passed away a couple of years ago, was a big man, intimidating to many because of his size but a man of heart to those who knew him best. My mother is a tall woman, and people responded not to her size but to her presence, her voice, the way she takes over a room just by walking in. So while movies, TV shows and commercials portrayed women as weak and emotional and men as strong and stoic, the Jones's residence was a home in which a couple's home was their castle and the king was more likely to cry than the queen.

When my parents separated, the two equal pillars that had held up my world into adolescence were shaken. When the dust settled, my mother was left holding up the earth, on her own. After working anywhere between ten- and sixteen-hour overnight shifts as a nurse, our mother would come straight home and drive us to swim, tennis, crafts or drama lessons. My father lived in the same city and was involved in our lives, and although he never worked an overnight shift, every single ride to every single lesson, my entire life, was given to me by my mother. She made it clear to us that learning was essential to living. Maybe the even greater message was that a woman's choices, actions and goals were not necessarily dependent on the support of a man. With my mother at the helm of our family, I just assumed that they weren't.

Although my home was a haven for a girl with ambitions and dreams like mine, our Pentecostal church was the first place I encountered a challenge to my right to fully explore my potential. I was thirteen. It was the first place where I saw people close to me reinforce those media images of women "in their places" that I had so easily dismissed in early childhood. The more deeply involved I became in the church, the less sure I became about my right to a full, free, explosive, untamed life. Even though I had been raised in the Pentecostal (Christian) church all my life, it had been peripheral for me at best. With hormones raging, acne taking over, body blossoming and grown men looking, I needed something to define me other than those things. I chose the church. That choice would later determine my responses to my African ancestry, education, friendship, relationships, sexual violence and sexual identity. And if feminism had a face, she would have frowned; if eyes, she would have cried; if hands, she would have slapped that thirteen-year-old me before I ever internalized the church's position on women.

The story of Adam and Eve reveals the church's view on women. The woman in the story is created specifically to meet the man's needs. He is made from earth; she is made from him. She manipulates him and her trickery is his downfall. She is smart enough to fool the man but too dim to realize the scope of her actions. She is disloyal to her partner and conspires with the creature who has the most to offer. All of the suffering she endures, she brings upon herself, including the pain of childbirth and the death of one of her sons. In short, women are inferior, manipulative cheats whose main purpose in life is to bear children and please men. This was not considered an insult to women in my church but a fact of life.

My parents' reaction to my newfound faith only reinforced that I had made a good choice. I remember the day my father, who was not a religious man, got all dressed up to see me sing the lead in our choir. Similarly, my mother, who never blinked an eye when I brought home the expected A on my report card, seemed to take a sense of pride in my loyalty to the church. So while United States politics around women in the 1980s was generally a time for marked advance, I was headed back in time to a destination that was literally biblical. Despite the fact that I had recognized the import of Geraldine Ferraro being chosen as the nation's first female vice presidential candidate, of Whoopi Goldberg's Academy Award for *The Color Purple* and even the rise of several popular television shows with female leads, my teenage heart was numb to every image but one. The image imbedded in my head through no less than three church services a week: Jesus Christ hanging on a cross, giving his life for sins I had committed. For this I had to pay with my soul, and the men who led my church would show me the way.

The lessons came in many ways. All of our ministers were men. They sat in a raised pulpit above and away from the congregation. They were in charge of all the messages to the congregation. Admonishments to women to stay in their places as outlined in the Bible were commonplace: Women, obey your husbands; and single women, obey your preachers. Never wear pants because the Bible says a woman should not dress like a man. Choose a profession becoming a Christian; my broadcast focus was out because I'd have to wear makeup. Always forgive—even cheating, lying, abusive partners. And for God's sake, young women, get married and be fruitful—the younger the better. Don't be gay, period; it is an abomination in the eyes of God.

With admonitions flowing, rushing over the pews like water over a fall, teachings about our African ancestry were notably missing. I was grown before I heard of the Diaspora. I was grown before the feeling was real to me that there must be more to god than rules that, if broken, led to eternal punishment. The feeling that sometimes whatever Spirits moved people to sing and rock and love and look inside must have a woman's face. Some of the god in me must look like me and move like me and soul like me. But Pentecost had no time, room or interest in telling a little curious girl with an open heart that she was a daughter of the Goddess Osun. Osun is a representation of a creative force in the universe that is not male, coming directly from our African sisters and brothers but not found at all in our teachings—not even as an alternative "god view" to be dismissed. When I started studying African religions on my own, in college, I realized that I was both shocked and comforted by representations of spirit that put forth a need for a balance between female and male energy in life; it felt closer to right than the male-dominant philosophies that permeated Christianity.

What you don't know can hurt you deeply. This sin of omission and ignorance committed by the church kept me as far away from my sisters and brothers in Africa as the miles between us. The internalized racism presented to African Americans as part of the United States's ongoing system of oppression of thought, history and culture against us—beginning with the Atlantic slave trade and continuing today with the prison industrial complex—was so deeply ingrained that children even used the words "black" and "African" as insults to each other. No one was rushing to offer other images of Africa besides those found in the *National Geographic* books that lined the shelves in both the school and public libraries. Exacerbating the ignorance about our history was the apathy that pervaded it. Our only passion was God. As a result, we weren't even Christians of action like Martin Luther King Jr. and his cohorts; we were Christians of criticism and isolation and passivity.

The constant image of one god with a male face only perpetuated the sexism that was so accepted that I never even heard it called by its name. I took in silent messages as I watched the twentysomething couples struggle with the church's heavy-handed tenets and old-world views of male and female roles. The women were always encouraged to acquiesce in any disagreements, while the men were encouraged to show strength by keeping their families in line. Men whose wives seemed to conform were openly rewarded with higher posts; men whose wives were less obedient were slower to rise up the church hierarchy. Divorce was one of the greatest indications of spiritual weakness, so the few married women whose husbands were not in church were encouraged to wait them out, let God handle it and at all costs, stay.

But my greatest lesson about the value of women in the church's eyes was a personal one. One of those pulpit kings took off his crown and robe and stepped down from his dais just long enough to rape me. God had allowed my teenage body to blossom too soon. When I confided in my trusted women in the church, they told me my salvation depended on me forgiving him. Years later when I told our pastor, he told me that that preacher had much more to protect and much more to lose if the news became public. He was a man with a family. I was just a girl. I was a girl too afraid to tell my parents. I was a girl too warped by the fear of losing what felt like the only real relationship in my life—that with Jesus—to leave the church right away. So I paid with my soul, and feminism prayed for eyes to cry for little old me. What she got was an eleven-year struggle from that dusty road of Bible stories, church sermons and women who walked behind to a place where I would rather walk alone with eyes open to the world than in a shadow just to feel like I had some company.

The journey was by no means smooth. Although 1980s politics had failed to touch me, the politics of the 1990s held me in a suffocating embrace. It was in this last decade of the century that all my cultural, religious and political contradictions came to a head. The world was battling over a woman's right to choose, and I was confronted with my own obligation to do so. It wasn't a choice about my body but my mind, and everyone seemed to want a piece. To practice our religion, one had to filter every thought, every move or emotion through the Bible. It was a constant checking and rechecking against biblical tenets and the church's interpretation of those doctrines. The older I became, the more I came to question the teachings. The more I questioned, the more I was reprimanded for being weak in spirit. Mention of other belief systems brought reproach, and instead of exploring questions fully, I was encouraged to put my faith in god and wait for answers from him. It was a way to keep people in line and quiet. The discussion was to be confined to prayers between you and god, preventing you from having discussions with each other.

This narrow view of my spiritual possibilities and total lack of acknowledgment of our forefather's and foremother's beliefs eventually put me on a path away from Christianity. As I started college in 1992, the church was still teaching that pride was a person's downfall, but African-American pride was calling my name. The more time I spent with my young sisters and brothers seeking knowledge about our spiritual possibilities, the more I realized how stifling the church was for a woman with questions. It disturbed and at the same time invigorated me to learn that ours was one of the only religions on earth that lacked powerful images of women as gods.

It is no surprise that the Christian United States continues to show open contempt for its female population through its dissemination of wealth that keeps working-class women and their children last. African-American women and their children are barely in the running. By 1990 a woman's right to choose was being openly attacked by terrorist murderers, while woman battering and rape laws laid down sentences that belittled the crimes. As a rape victim—who could have easily become a teen pregnancy statistic as a result—I found the politics of the time grating on my spirit.

If that wasn't bad enough, there were weekly news reports of women, mostly African-American women, cheating the welfare system. These images were constant and so incessant that they became normalized as a representation of the average low-income African-American mother. Single African-American women were commonly represented as teen mothers, who either abandoned their babies or smoked crack until the babies were born with a multitude of birth defects. Similar news stories about white women were more forgiving and left the audience with questions rather than judgments: What is our country saying when a young woman has to deceive the government about how many kids she has just to get enough support to take care of one child? Where have we gone wrong when a young woman is so afraid that she leaves her newborn to be found by a stranger? When the subject of the same stories were African American, reporters spun them in a way that inevitably left the audience outraged, no questions asked. The shoddy journalism supporting a racism that lived so deep in the average American consciousness that it went unspoken was painful. It was like being slapped across the face with the hatred our high-school history classes tried to convince us died after the civil rights struggles of the 1960s. It was a different kind of hurt than the everyday encounters with people who showed contempt for my brown skin, because it was being mass marketed as the truth. I felt as if they were daring viewers to even think about questioning it.

The control over these racist messages about women was totalitarian. Goliath stood firm. Another blow to my spirit was the fact that representations of women that I knew, the woman that I was becoming were lacking. Who would write their stories, who would tell their tales, who would produce news reports asking questions about their plight? I wavered on the tightrope between religion and spiritual freedom, finally choosing to follow my spirit. My spirit motivated me to choose a journalism major in college, and I began to ask questions for African-American women at work.

Angela Davis, 1960s activist and professor at the University of California in Santa Cruz, came to speak at a rally on campus. I was expecting for her to light a fire under all of us, encouraging us to take our fight for a more egalitarian society to the streets! What she said, with a mellow vibe and tone that can only be attributed to older, wiser, black women who've been down roads and seen things we never will, was that our activism was not to mirror the activism of old. This generation faces the challenge of defining activism in a United States that no longer responds to sit-ins and marches. She suggested that our strength would come from building coalitions with other people of color and like-minded folks.

But first I had to build coalitions with the different parts of myself. The sexism within the African Student Alliance on my campus (which mirrored the kind of sexism

I'd witnessed in my church and my local African-American community) was pushing out the feminist me. At the same time, I found feminist groups so desperate to hang on to some credibility in the mainstream, pushing against my focus on African heritage and pushing to keep the door closed to the closet behind which I hid my love for women. It seemed less and less likely that I would find a place in the world to fully be myself. I worried that the definition of feminism that my college professor had so eloquently laid out would never become a reality for me.

Of course, it was my mother who set me straight. She told me to stop worrying about what people said and to do what I was here to do. She told me I was an artist, and she said it with pride in her voice. With that, I began to put pen to paper, paint to canvas, voice to air and break down all the systems of thinking and accepted ways of being that excluded some part of myself. I found that while what my mother thought of me was paramount to my spiritual survival, what the world thought no longer mattered. Though I didn't share her religious fervor any longer, I still respected her more than any other person.

I didn't know any other women who'd worked a graveyard shift in various hospitals for more than twenty years to feed, clothe and care for five hungry girls. She'd worked overnight so she'd be home when we got out of school. I had never encountered any other women who would share her meager supply of groceries with the single mother across the street or spend the small amount of free time afforded a woman with five daughters sitting with the elderly folks in our church and taking their blood pressures. She was even willing to challenge our church on some of its interpretations of the Bible and didn't force us to follow those interpretations, as most parents in the church did. When my father moved out, she continued to maintain the household without blinking an eye (at least I never saw her blink). Somehow she created time to go back to college and attain various certificates to further her nursing career. More deep and motivating than any books on feminist theory, I'd spent my entire life face to face with a feminist powerhouse who offered neither explanation nor apology. She taught me an abiding love for self and for humanity—and she taught by example. So I went to work.

I created a cable-access show called *Point of View* to discuss politics. A local show, it aired in four nearby Bay Area cities. For every negative representation I saw of people of color, I wrote a show that allowed us to shine. For every report I read that asked no questions about the plights of African-American women, I created a show and asked the questions myself. The walls between me and effecting change in the politics of oppression, racism and sexism that pervade the United States were starting to crumble. I wrote, produced, sang, painted and created ways to say, "We are here. We are diverse. We are good." I knew I was on the right path when a man approached me in the BART train station and told me he'd taped and shown my Black History show to a group of students at a seminar he gave in Sacramento.

The momentum created by following my mother's lead and becoming a woman of action gave me the strength to slowly open the doors to my closet. My passivity in loving created such a stark contrast to my passion in every other area, I could no longer ignore it. Spoken word provided a platform for me to be honest about falling in love again and again with women. My love of women was the one area in my life where fear of judgment, reprisal and loss still ruled me. Not only had I been raised in a religion that preached that same-sex love was abominable, but I had grown up in a community with strictly defined male and female roles, and in a country that openly and lawfully discriminates against same-sex couples. Even feminists seemed obsessed with not being characterized as lesbians. What would it mean about my overall identity if I acknowledged this truth about my makeup? What doors would close? What would my mother think?

I found that just as my questions about our religion had not gone away, and just as my need to seek out my heritage had not been assuaged, in the same way the need to tell the stories of African-American women had risen to the top, so would my orientation reverberate through my spirit and force its way into my voice, my paintings, my writing and my reality. As the 1990s ended and the twenty-first century began, I reached a kind of wholeness. I sat with the woman who had given me all the tools and examples I needed to be strictly myself. I drank coffee and ate eggs and looked into the eyes of the woman who made feminism real for me when I didn't even have words to describe it. I told her that I was in love, that it was not a fad, that I planned to spend my life and raise children with another woman. She didn't accept it. Because of her I knew she didn't have to. I was free to define myself.

The Issue of Woman–Man Equality in the Islamic Tradition

❖ Riffat Hassan ❖

Background of My Work in the Area of Theology of Woman in Islam

. . . [I]t was not until the fall of 1974 that I began my career as a "feminist" theologian—almost by accident and rather reluctantly. I was, at that time, faculty adviser to the Muslim Students' Association (MSA) chapter at Oklahoma State University in Stillwater, Oklahoma. This "honor" had been conferred upon me solely by virtue of the fact that each student association was required to have a faculty adviser, and I happened to be the only Muslim faculty member on campus that year. The office bearers

---

of the MSA chapter at Stillwater had established the tradition of having an annual seminar at which one of the principal addresses was given by the faculty adviser. In keeping with tradition I was asked—albeit not with overwhelming enthusiasm—if I would read a paper on women in Islam at the seminar that was to be held later that year. I was aware of the fact that, in general, faculty advisers were not assigned specific subjects. I was asked to speak about women in Islam at the seminar—in which, incidentally, Muslim women were not going to participate—because in the opinion of most of the chapter members it would have been totally inappropriate to expect a Muslim woman, even one who taught them Islamic Studies, to be competent to speak on any other subject pertaining to Islam. I resented what the assigning of a subject meant. Furthermore, I was not much interested in the subject of women in Islam until that time. Nevertheless, I accepted the invitation for two reasons. First, I knew that being invited to address an all-male, largely Arab Muslim group that prided itself on its patriarchalism, was itself a breakthrough. Second, I was so tired of hearing Muslim men pontificate upon the position, status, or role of women in Islam, while it was totally inconceivable that any woman could presume to speak about the position, status, or role of men in Islam. I thought that it might be worthwhile for a Muslim woman to present her viewpoint on a subject whose immense popularity with Muslim men, scholars and non-scholars alike, could easily be gauged by the ever-increasing number of books, booklets, brochures, and articles they published on it. Having accepted the invitation I began my research more out of a sense of duty (knowing that willing the end involves willing the means to the end) than out of any deep awareness that I had set out on perhaps the most important journey of my life.

I do not know exactly at what time my "academic" study of women in Islam became a passionate quest for truth and justice on behalf of Muslim women—perhaps it was when I realized the impact on my own life of the so-called Islamic ideas and attitudes regarding women. What began as a scholarly exercise became simultaneously an Odyssean venture in self-understanding. But "enlightenment" does not always lead to "endless bliss." The more I saw the justice and compassion of God reflected in the Qur'anic teachings regarding women, the more anguished and angry I became, seeing the injustice and inhumanity to which Muslim women, in general, are subjected in actual life. I began to feel strongly that it was my duty—as a part of the microscopic minority of educated Muslim women—to do as much consciousness-raising regarding the situation of Muslim women as I could. The journey that began in Stillwater has been an arduous one. It has taken me far and wide in pursuit of my quest. When I remember the stormy seas and rocky roads I have traversed, it seems like the journey has been a long one. But when I think of my sisters who, despite being the largest "minority" in the world—more than half of the one-billion-strong Muslim *ummah*[1]—remain for the most part nameless, faceless, and voiceless, I know that there is no end to the journey in sight.

Despite the fact that women such as Khadijah and 'A'ishah (wives of the Prophet Muhammad) and Rabi'a al-Basri (the outstanding woman Sufi) figure significantly in early Islam, the Islamic tradition has, by and large, remained rigidly patriarchal until the present time, prohibiting the growth of scholarship among women particularly in the realm of religious thought. This means that the sources on which the Islamic tradition is mainly based, namely, the Qur'an, the Sunnah,[2] the Hadith[3] literature, and Fiqh,[4] have been interpreted only by Muslim men who have arrogated to themselves the task of defining the ontological, theological, sociological, and eschatological status of Muslim women. It is hardly surprising that until now the majority of Muslim women have accepted this situation passively, almost unaware of the extent to which their human (also Islamic, in an ideal sense) rights have been violated by their male-dominated and male-centered societies, which have continued to assert, glibly and tirelessly, that Islam has given women more rights than any other religious tradition. Kept for centuries in physical, mental, and emotional bondage, and deprived of the opportunity to actualize their human potential, even the exercise of analyzing their personal experiences as Muslim women is, perhaps, overwhelming for these women. (Here it needs to be mentioned that while the rate of literacy is low in many Muslim countries, the rate of literacy of Muslim women, especially those who live in rural areas, where most of the population lives, is among the lowest in the world.)

In recent times, largely due to the pressure of anti-women laws that are being promulgated under the cover of "Islamization" in some parts of the Muslim world, women with some degree of education and awareness are beginning to realize that religion is being used as an instrument of oppression rather than as a means of liberation. To understand the strong impetus to "Islamize" Muslim societies, especially with regard to women-related norms and values, it is necessary to know that of all the challenges confronting the Muslim world, perhaps the greatest is that of modernity. The caretakers of Muslim traditionalism are aware of the fact that viability in the modern technological age requires the adoption of the scientific or rational outlook that inevitably brings about major changes in modes of thinking and behavior. Women, both educated and uneducated, who are participating in the national work force and contributing toward national development, think and behave differently from women who have no sense of their individual identity or autonomy as active agents in a history-making process and regard themselves merely as instruments designed to minister to and reinforce a patriarchal system that they believe to be divinely instituted. Not too long ago, many women in Pakistan were jolted out of their "dogmatic slumber" by the enactment of laws (such as those pertaining to women's rape or women's testimony in financial and other matters) and by "threatened" legislation (such as proposals pertaining to "blood-money" for women's murder) that aimed to reduce them systematically, virtually mathematically, to less than men. It was not long before they realized that forces of religious conservatism were determined to cut women down to one-half or less of men and that this attitude stemmed from a deep-rooted desire to keep women "in their place," which means secondary, subordinate, and inferior to men.

In the face of both military dictatorship and religious autocracy, valiant efforts have been made by women's groups in Pakistan to protest against the instituting of manifestly anti-women laws and to highlight cases of gross injustice and brutality toward women. However, it is still not clearly and fully understood, even by many women activists in Pakistan and other Muslim countries, that the negative ideas and attitudes pertaining to women that prevail in Muslim societies, are in general rooted in theology—and that unless, or until, the theological foundations of the misogynistic and androcentric tendencies in the Islamic tradition are demolished, Muslim women will continue to be brutalized and discriminated against, despite improvements in statistics such as those on female education, employment, and social and political rights. No matter how many sociopolitical rights are granted to women, as long as they are conditioned to accept the myths used by theologians or religious hierarchs to shackle their bodies, hearts, minds, and souls, they will never become fully developed or whole human beings, free of fear and guilt, able to stand equal to men in the sight of God. In my judgment, the importance of developing what the West calls "feminist theology" in the context of Islam is paramount today with a view to liberating not only Muslim women but also Muslim men from unjust structures and laws that make a peer relationship between men and women impossible. It is good to know that in the last hundred years there have been at least two significant Muslim men scholars and activists—Qasim Amin from Egypt and Mumtaz 'Ali from India—who have been staunch advocates of women's rights, though knowing this hardly lessens the pain of also knowing that even in this age that is characterized by the explosion of knowledge, all but a handful of Muslim women lack any knowledge of Islamic theology. It is profoundly discouraging to contemplate how few Muslim women there are in the world today who possess the competence, even if they have the courage and commitment, to engage in a scholarly study of Islam's primary sources in order to participate in the theological discussions on women-related issues that are taking place in much of the contemporary Muslim world. . . .

My inquiry into the theological roots of the problem of man–woman inequality in the Islamic tradition led to the expansion of my field of study in at least two significant areas. First, realizing the profound impact upon Muslim consciousness of Hadith literature, particularly the two collections *Sahih al-Bukhari* and *Sahih Muslim* (collectively known as the *Sahihan*, which the Sunni Muslims regard as the most authoritative books in Islam next to the Qur'an), I examined with care the women-related ahadith in these collections. Second, I studied several important writings by Jewish and Christian feminist theologians who were attempting to trace the theological origins of the antifeminist ideas and attitudes found in their respective traditions.

As a result of my study and deliberation I came to perceive that not only in the Islamic, but also in the Jewish and Christian traditions, there are three theological assumptions on which the superstructure of men's alleged superiority to women (which implies the inequality of women and man) has been erected. These three assumptions are: (1) that God's primary creation is man, not woman, since woman is believed to have been created from man's rib, hence is derivative and secondary ontologically; (2) that woman, not man, was the primary agent of what is customarily described as the "Fall," or man's expulsion from the Garden of Eden, hence all "daughters of Eve" are to be regarded with hatred, suspicion, and contempt; and (3) that woman was created not only *from* man but also *for* man, which makes her existence merely instrumental and not of fundamental importance. The three theological questions to which the above assumptions may appropriately be regarded as answers, are: How was woman created? Was woman responsible for the "Fall" of man? Why was woman created?

. . . I would like to focus on the first question, which deals with the issue of woman's creation. I consider this issue to be more basic and important, philosophically and theologically, than any other in the context of woman–man equality, because if man and woman have been created equal by Allah who is the ultimate arbiter of value, then they cannot become unequal, essentially, at a subsequent time. On the other hand, if man and woman have been created unequal by Allah, then they cannot become equal, essentially, at a subsequent time.

Made from Adam's Rib? The Issue of Woman's Creation

The ordinary Muslim believes, as seriously as the ordinary Jew or Christian, that Adam was God's primary creation and that Eve was made from Adam's rib. If confronted with the fact that this firmly entrenched belief is derived mainly from the Bible and is not only extra-Qur'anic but also in contradiction to the Qur'an, this Muslim is almost certain to be shocked. The rather curious and tragic truth is that even Western-educated Muslims seldom have any notion of the extent to which the Muslim psyche bears the imprint of the collective body of Jewish and Christian ideas and attitudes pertaining to women.

The Biblical account of the creation of the first human pair consists of two different sources, the Yahwist and the Priestly, from which arise two different traditions, subject of much Jewish and Christian scholarly controversy. There are four references to woman's creation in Genesis. . . . Of the four texts referring to creation, undoubtedly the most influential has been Genesis 2:18–24, which states that woman (*ishshah*) was taken from man (*ish*). From this text it has generally been inferred that: (1) Adam was God's primary creation from whom Eve, a secondary creation, was derived, hence Eve is inferior and subordinate to Adam; and (2) Eve was created simply and solely to be the helpmate of Adam.

While in Genesis specific reference is made to the creation of Adam and Eve, there is no corresponding reference in the Qur'an. In fact, there is no mention of Eve (*Hawwa'*) at all in the Qur'an. . . .

The Qur'an describes human creation in thirty or so passages that are found in various chapters. Generally speaking, it refers to the creation of humanity (and nature) in two ways: as an evolutionary process whose diverse stages or phases are mentioned sometimes together and sometimes separately, and as an accomplished fact or in its totality. In the passages in which human creation is described "concretely" or "analytically," we find that no mention is made of the separate or distinct creation of either man or woman. . . .

Summing up the Qur'anic descriptions of human creation, it needs to be emphasized that the Qur'an evenhandedly used both feminine and masculine terms and imagery to describe the creation of humanity from a single source. That Allah's original creation was undifferentiated humanity and not either man or woman (who appeared simultaneously at a subsequent time) is implicit in a number of Qur'anic passages. . . .

If the Qur'an makes no distinction between the creation of man and woman, as it clearly does not, why do Muslims believe that Hawwa' was created from the rib of

Adam? Although the Genesis 2 account of woman's creation is accepted by virtually all Muslims, it is difficult to believe that it entered the Islamic tradition directly, for very few Muslims ever read the Bible. It is much more likely that it became a part of Muslim heritage through its assimilation in Hadith literature, which has been, in many ways, the lens through which the Qur'an has been seen since the early centuries of Islam. . . .

[T]he ahadith clash sharply with the Qur'anic accounts of human creation, while they have an obvious correspondence to Genesis 2:18–33 and Genesis 3:20. Some changes, however, are to be noted in the story of woman's creation as it is retold in the . . . ahadith. [They] mention "the left rib" as the source of woman. In Arab culture great significance is attached to "right" and "left," the former being associated with everything auspicious and the latter with the opposite. In Genesis, woman is named "Eve" after the Fall, but in the . . . ahadith she is called Hawwa' from the time of her creation. In Genesis, woman is named Eve because "she is the mother of all who live" (thus a primary source of life), but in the first of the afore-mentioned ahadith, she is named Hawwa' because "she was created from a living thing" (hence a derivative creature). These variations are not to be ignored. Biblical and other materials are seldom incorporated without alteration into ahadith. [These] examples illustrate how in respect of woman, Arab biases were added to the adopted text. . . .

The creation of woman is as clearly defined in the Qur'an as the creation of man, and the Qur'anic statements about human creation, diverse as they are, leave no doubt as to one point: both man and woman were made in the same manner, of the same substance, at the same time. . . .

The theology of woman implicit in the ahadith is based upon generalizations about her ontology, biology, and psychology that are contrary to the letter and spirit of the Qur'an. These ahadith ought to be rejected on the basis of their content alone. . . .

Conclusion

While all Muslims agree that whenever a Hadith attributed to the Prophet conflicts with the Qur'an it must be rejected, the ahadith [I have discussed] have not only not been rejected, they have in fact remained overwhelmingly popular with Muslims through the ages, in spite of being clearly contradictory to the Qur'anic statements pertaining to human creation. While being included in the *Sahihan* gives the ahadith in question much weight among Muslims who know about the science of Hadith, their continuing popularity among Muslims in general indicates that they articulate something deeply embedded in Muslim culture—namely, the belief that women are derivative creatures who can never be considered equal to men.

. . . It is imperative for the Muslim daughters of Hawwa' to realize that the history of their subjection and humiliation at the hands of sons of Adam began with the story of Hawwa's creation, and that their future will be no different from their past unless they return to the point of origin and challenge the authenticity of ahadith that make them ontologically inferior, subordinate, and crooked. While it is not a little discouraging to know that these ahadith (like many other anti-woman ones) represent not only the ideas and attitudes regarding woman of the early generations of Muslims (whose views were reflected in the Hadith literature), but also of successive generations of Muslims until today, it is gratifying to know that they cannot be the words of the Prophet of Islam, who upheld the rights of women (as of other disadvantaged persons) throughout his life. Furthermore, regardless of how many Muslim men project their own androcentrism and misogyny upon the Prophet of Islam, it is valid to question how, being the recipient of the Qur'an, which states that all human beings were made from a single source (i.e., *al-insan, bashar*, or *nafsin wahidatin*), the Prophet of Allah could say that woman was created from a crooked rib or from Adam's rib.

Notes

1. *Ummah* (from *umm:* mother): community of Muslims.
2. Sunnah: practical traditions attributed to the Prophet Muhammad.
3. Hadith (plural: ahadith): oral traditions attributed to the Prophet Muhammad.
4. Fiqh: jurisprudence.

"Jihād Fī Sabīl Allah" : A Muslim Woman's Faith Journey from Struggle to Struggle to Struggle

✤ *Riffat Hassan* ✤

"We want you to be the ideologue of our movement." The earnest faces looking at me out of a world unutterably grim and dark . . . the earnest voices speaking to me in the deathly stillness of an hour of despair when one is afraid to hear even the throbbing of one's own heart. . . . I saw and heard the angry, tearful, fearful, defiant, despairing, determined, struggling, suffering women from one of the most active women's groups in my native Pakistan, and was spellbound . . . overwhelmed . . . transformed. In that moment of truth I knew with absolute clarity that I had arrived at a point of destiny . . . it seemed natural—inevitable—that the strange paths I had trodden in my

---

Jihād Fī Sabīl Allah: striving or exerting in and for the cause of God; this is a Qur'anic imperative for all Muslims.

life should have led me here, though I had never dreamed that I would be called upon so suddenly—so unexpectedly—to become the theoretician for a movement involved in a life-and-death struggle in a country that was mine by birth and unbreakable bonds of love, from which I had chosen to exile myself in order to be able to do my life's work. For years I had lived a hard and solitary life in an alien world, striving to become free and whole—returning periodically to my "homeland" only to find how alienated I was from "my people" in so many ways. Even as I saw and heard the women who wanted me to dedicate myself to their struggle for self-identification, for self-preservation, I knew how many worlds separated us. The mere fact that I lived alone with my young daughter, in a foreign land, earning my livelihood by the sweat of my brow, using every free moment of my work-filled life to pore endlessly over words, sacred and secular, to find a way to liberate millions of Muslim women from the unspeakable bondage imposed on them in the name of God, created a wide gulf between me and these women who addressed me. Would any of these women be willing to give up their lives of affluence and ease to share a day of my toil-filled life? I would have been surprised to find even one who would—and this thought saddened me. However, it did not affect my deep response to the call I had received. Whatever the distances, the differences that existed between these women and me, I knew in the hour of trial that they were my sisters and that our bond was indissoluble. I was grateful that the work I had done over so many years out of my own passionate quest for truth and justice had become profoundly relevant to the lives of my sisters. I had not hoped to see this day in my lifetime. With a heart full of tears—of joy, of sorrow—I said a silent prayer to my Creator and Sustainer who had brought me to this historic moment. I offered thanks for the opportunity to participate in such a moment and asked for strength and courage so that I might not fail in the critical task entrusted to me.

As I stood on the threshold of a new beginning, a new life, scenes from my past flashed before my eyes. I paused—to cast a look backward at the passages through which my life-journey had led me to bring me to this point of destiny. I knew that tomorrow would usher in a new phase of toil and tribulation and that then there would be no time to look back. But today I could be alone with my memories—of places and peoples and moments that had made my life-journey significant. I did not like to recall many of these memories for they are painful, but I knew that in order for me to have a clear sense of where I was and where I was to go in terms of my inner journey, I had to remember where I had been. I do not believe that it is possible to go forward without going backward, since our future is born out of our past. I closed my eyes and went back to the old house where I was born, which stood at the end of a *galee* (narrow street) adjoining Temple Road in the ancient city of Lahore in what is now Pakistan. In this house my story had begun.

My memories of the house in which I was born, where I spent the first seventeen years of my life, are heavily shaded with darkness. Even now I cannot read a passage about the joy, the beauty, the golden sunshine of childhood years without a storm of tears arising in my heart. I wish I had had a different childhood . . . my own was a nightmare that has never ceased to haunt me. What I remember most distinctly about being a child was how utterly lonely I felt in a house full of people and how unspeakably unhappy, scared, and bewildered I was most of the time.

Objectively, there were many reasons why I should have considered myself and my five brothers and three sisters as very privileged children. We were born into an upper-class Saiyyad family, and the Saiyyads, being the descendants of the Holy Prophet Muhammad, are regarded as the highest caste of Muslims, even though Muslims constantly protest against the idea that Islam has any caste system! My father and mother came from among the oldest and most distinguished families in the city and were both "good" parents in that they took care to provide us with a high quality of life. We lived in a spacious *kothee* (bungalow) and had a glamorous automobile (when only a handful of people had any) and a household full of servants who performed all the domestic duties. We went to the best English-medium schools (which to this day are regarded as status symbols), where we received a sound British education. Children in our neighborhood envied us: we were the children of "Shaah Saahib," as everyone called my father, who was the patriarch of the area and greatly respected and liked by all; all considered it an honor to come to our house to play, even though they knew about my mother's temper-tantrums and the possibility that they might be told unceremoniously to go home at any moment.

Why, when we were so blessed, was my life so full of shadows? The major reason was undoubtedly the deep conflict between my parents. Not only did they have diametrically opposing views on most matters but also radical incompatibility of temperament and character. My father was very traditional in his ways and values. Through most of my life I hated his traditionalism, because I understood it almost exclusively in terms of his belief in sex roles and his conviction that it was best for girls to be married at age sixteen to someone who had been picked out for them by the parents. It took me a long time to see that in some ways my father's traditionalism had been pure gold. He truly believed in taking care of disadvantaged people, relatives and strangers alike, and responding to every call he received for assistance. He was genuinely kind and compassionate and took joy in solving other people's problems, whether they were personal, professional, or social. Anybody could call on him at any hour, and he would receive the caller with courtesy and goodwill. My mother's ways and values differed fundamentally from my father's, even though, in her own way, she responded positively to many who sought the assistance of the "Begum Saahiba," as she was called. Her nonconformism to traditional Muslim culture consisted largely of her rejection of the hallowed cult of women's inferiority and submissiveness to men. She herself was not submissive to her husband. She treated her daughters better than her sons (with the exception of one favorite son) and believed that it was more important to educate daughters than sons because girls were born into Muslim societies with a tremendous handicap. Pre-Islamic Arabs had buried their daughters alive because they had regarded daughters not only as economic liabilities but also as potential hazards to the honor of the men in the tribe. Islam notwithstanding, the attitude of Muslims toward daughters has remained very similar to that of their nomadic forebears. My mother's repudiation of the ideals and practices of patriarchal culture and her passionate commitment to the liberation of her daughters from the *chardewari* (four walls) of the male-centered, male-dominated household put her into the category of radical feminists, which made her strangely out of place in my father's house and in the society in which we lived.

Long before I began to understand the complexities and ambiguities of the Muslim value-system, I knew that my mother would not win in any popularity contest vis-à-vis my father. She had a protected place in society because she was the daughter of the outstanding and creative artist-poet, playwright, and scholar, Hakim Ahmad Shuja'—who had also been a highly regarded educator and bureaucrat—and my father's wife, but in her own person she was viewed as a dangerous deviant. The fact that she had a biting and brutal tongue, and that she could, at times, be ruthless and unscrupulous, did not help to improve her image in many eyes. However, to me, all through my childhood, my mother was a savior-figure who protected me from being sacrificed upon the altar of blind conventionalism. And my father, who was admired and loved by so many, seemed to me through most of my early life to be a figure of dread, representing customary morality in a society that demanded that female children be discriminated against from the moment of birth.

As a child I used to be greatly troubled by the fact that my subjective perceptions of my parents differed greatly from the way in which others perceived them. I remember feeling very guilty because I could not relate to my "good" father to whom almost everyone could relate so well. I also remember feeling very angry and perplexed as to why my father, who liked everyone, seemed so averse to me. I knew that what I perceived to be his negative attitude toward me had something to do with my being one of my mother's "favorites" and belonging to her "camp." Their respective camps were the centers from where my parents conducted their cold war campaigns that enveloped us all and poisoned our family life. My parents did not yell and scream at each other. My father was too much of a gentleman to do that, and even my mother, whom many regarded as a "shrew," was conventional enough not to engage in a vociferous exchange with my father. But though physical and verbal violence did not characterize the relationship between my parents, there was no disguising the fact that they had deep-seated resentments against one another that manifested themselves in all kinds of destructive ways. I remember how the way my parents interacted with one another reminded me of Milton's words: "For never can true reconcilement grow / where wounds of deadly hate have pierced so deep," and I often wondered as a child why they continued to live together. Now I understand the reasons that made it imperative for them to live under one roof—they both came from "old" families to whom divorce was anathema, and they had nine children to raise. But the one roof under which we all lived could not be called a "home," if one defines this term as a place of love, warmth, and security. Our home was a rough sea where tempests raged incessantly. I could only deal with the unremitting hostility that pervaded the atmosphere by becoming a recluse. Before I was twelve years old I had retired from the world.

I believe that it was because I withdrew from an outer to an inner reality that I was able to survive the seemingly unending crises and calamities to which I was exposed. A hypersensitive, painfully shy, and profoundly lonely child, I hated the ugliness that surrounded me and retreated to a world made up of a child's prayers, dreams, and wishful thinking. In this world I found three things that have sustained me through the heart-breaks and hardships of my life: an unwavering belief in a just and loving God, the art of writing poetry, and a deep love for books. Unable to relate at a deep personal level to either of my two parents—such dialogue, I see now, is virtually impossible in Muslim culture, in which human beings relate to each other mainly in terms of their "functions" or roles and not in terms of who they are as persons—I learned to talk to my Creator and Preserver, who at all times seemed very close. I often asked God to reveal to me the purpose of my life and to help me fulfill this purpose. Perhaps that was a strange prayer for a child. However, I was not just any child—I was a war-ravaged child. Born female in a society in which it is customary to celebrate the birth of a son and to bemoan the birth of a daughter, and growing up in a house lacking in love and trust, I could at no time simply take it for granted that I had the right to exist, to be. I had, at all times, to find a justification for living. A very ailing child, I came quite close to dying a few times and almost wished that I were dead, but somewhere, deep within my heart and soul, I always had the assurance that God had a special purpose for my life that justified my existence, and that so long as I remained faithful to God I would be protected from the dangers and devastation that threatened me.

Alone in my inner world I discovered that, like my mother and grandfather, I could write poetry almost effortlessly. This gave me great happiness and hope. I felt as if this was a gift from God given to me so that I could create a world free of shadows, of hate, bitterness, and pain. Looking at the first poem in "My Maiden," a book of eighty-five sonnets written when I was about thirteen years old, I can recall the earnest child who wrote:

> *This humble work of mine do bless my God,*
> *My fervent message to the world proclaim,*
> *I do not covet wealth or power or fame,*
> *I just want satisfaction for reward.*
> *I felt it was Your Will that I should write*
> *Of Beauty, Love and Joy, Eternal Peace,*
> *Of Sorrow, Struggle that a Death does cease,*
> *Of Hope, its sweet illuminating light.*

> *I've done my duty with all faithfulness,*
> *I strove to do Your Will, without a rest,*
> *I pray I have succeeded in this test,*
> *If I have, I can scarce my joy express.*
> *I am sincere that You, dear God, can see,*
> *I'll do Your Will, however hard may be.*

How many worlds have passed away since I wrote that poem, but what I said in that poem still remains true for me. I believed then, as I believe now, that God had chosen me to be an instrument in implementing a plan that I could see only in part and understand only dimly. Since I first experienced the presence of God—powerful, healing, comforting, directing—in the solitude of my inner world, I have regarded my life as a trust that must be spent in *jihād fī sabīl Allah* (striving in the cause of Allah). As a child, there were times when I wanted to share my strong sense of being a missionary for God with my close friends. But I was afraid that they would not understand my calling and would ridicule me. I remember that once, not without trepidation, I mentioned to a friend whom I considered to be wiser than the rest that I believed God spoke to me in special moments and showed me the path I was to follow. I hoped that he would understand what I was trying to say, but he was shocked by what seemed to him to be pretentious words. I remember how his words "So you consider yourself a prophetess or something!" went through my heart like a dagger and left me speechless. After that I would not speak about what lay closest to my soul, though I would write when the burden of silence became too heavy to bear. It was in one such hour that I wrote another sonnet—perhaps my favorite in the collection—which reads:

> *Oft times when loneliness I cannot bear,*
> *When all my consolation, hope has fled,*
> *In words when there is nothing to be said,*
> *My feelings, then, with you—my pen—I share.*
> *When I unburden all my heart to you,*
> *Tell you the secrets of my restless mind,*
> *When for my thoughts expression I do find*
> *In verse, contentment—sweet and deep and true—*
> *Steals on me, offers solace to my soul.*
> *And though there still is grief, there still is strife,*
> *I'm comforted; my poems do console*
> *Me; and I know as long as I can write*
> *I'll have the will life's battle great to fight,*
> *For 'tis the truth—that writing is my life.*

Writing was my chief mode of communication during my childhood, and I wrote much. By the time I was seventeen years old, two volumes of my poems, short stories, and articles had been published, and I was a well-known "budding" poet-author in the world in which I lived. My famous grandfather spoke of me with pride and said that I alone among all his grandchildren had inherited his writing talent. I felt grateful for his recognition and encouragement, but undoubtedly the person who meant the most to me during my early teens when I launched my writing career was my cousin "Sunny Bhaijan" (as I called him), who was married to my eldest sister. Sunny Bhaijan was a remarkably talented person who could have become a first-rate poet, artist, or musician if he had had the passion to create. But he lacked passion and thus was not motivated to develop his talents. He recognized both my ability to write and my passion and became my first mentor. Sadly, many things happened that caused me to grow away from Sunny Bhaijan while I was not yet out of my teens, but I still feel indebted to him for encouraging me to write.

Besides writing, my greatest joy in life in childhood was reading. One day, looking through a dusty bookcase in my house, I found a torn and tattered copy of Palgrave's "Golden Treasury" of poems. Finding that book was one of the most important things that ever happened to me, for it introduced me to many poems I grew to love deeply, including some sonnets of Shakespeare. I loved to recite poems to myself, over and over, till I knew them by heart. There was something about the measured music of poetry that captivated my heart and spirit. Though poetry was my first love, I also liked to read novels and read many "classics" by Dickens, Hardy, the Brontë sisters, Jane Austen, and many others. Of all the novels that I read in my childhood, the one that made the greatest impact on me was Emily Brontë's *Wuthering Heights*. This book had a haunting quality, and it seemed suspended between the world of reality and the world of dream, nightmare, and fantasy. The bleakness and wildness of its landscape seemed to correspond to my own psyche, and I identified with its strange characters, especially Cathy and Heathcliff. Apart from my reading of English "classics," I was also an avid reader of Agatha Christie's books, from which I learned much about human nature.

Most of my childhood I spent alone, writing and reading. I do not remember studying much for school. Despite that, I was the star pupil in my class from the beginning to the end of my scholastic career and won every honor and award there was to win. Many people, including my classmates and their parents, were very impressed with my academic success and treated me as if I were rather special. But as a child, and even as an adult, I did not crave success—perhaps because one does not crave what one does or can have. What I craved was love and peace around me and within me. I was a super-achiever almost against my will. Toward the end of my high school career I became resentful of my own success and wanted to fail. My family never seemed to notice my success, or at least never mentioned it to me—I thought that perhaps if I failed they would pay some attention to me. Had it not been for a teacher who cared for me, I might have acted out my bitter, rebellious feelings, but I did not, and in future years was very grateful that I had not wrecked a record career. I learned very early in life that there is no necessary connection between success and happiness, but I have also come to know that, though many bright women are afraid to succeed, lack of success is not likely to lead to an enhancement of happiness, and I could not have found what I craved through underachieving.

The twelfth year of my life was a landmark year for me because during that year my struggle as an "activist feminist" began. Up until that time I had been a quiet child living for the most part in an inner sanctuary. But before I had turned twelve, all of a sudden the reality of the external world began to close in on me ominously, threatening to destroy my place of refuge. My second sister, who was sixteen, was married off to a man with a lot of money and very little education. She had tried to resist the arranged marriage but had succumbed, as most girls do, to the multifarious crude as well as subtle ways of "persuading" wavering girls to accept the arrangement in order to safeguard the family's "honor" and her own "happiness." Seeing her fall into the all-too-familiar trap I experienced total panic. I was the next in line. Four years later the same ritual would be reenacted, and this time I would be the sacrificial victim unless I found a way of averting the catastrophe. I knew that my mother would try to protect me from an arranged marriage, but I was not sure that she would succeed. I felt that I had to learn to fend for myself, to take a stand against my father and his rigid conventionalism. I had to learn to fight to survive in a society in which women's refusal to submit to patriarchal authority is tantamount to heresy. At twelve I had not learned how to fight. I had not wanted to learn to fight. I simply wanted to be left alone in my dream-world where I could write my poems and read my books . . . but I knew then, as I know now, that if one is born female in such a society as the one I was born in and wants to be regarded as a person and not as an object, one has no option but to fight. And so I learned to fight, and the fight continues to this day, though many battles have been won and lost. Battle-weary, I pray for the dawning of the day when it will not be required of women like myself to spend their entire lifetime fighting for their freedom each day of their life, but I also pray for strength to continue the fight until there is justice and freedom, under God, for all my sisters.

My father, who had not seemed to like me much when I was a little girl hiding in my room, liked me even less when I appeared to become an impossible teenage rebel who disregarded his wishes. For instance, when I was twelve he wanted me to withdraw from the coeducation school where I studied and enroll in an all-girls' school. Thinking with the mind of a twelve-year-old, I believed that if I said "yes" to him once, I would always have to say "yes" to him. Therefore, I refused to comply with his desire and said that if I was forced to leave the school where I had studied for a number of years (and where my brothers still studied), I would not go to any other school. My father did not force me to leave, but he upbraided my mother constantly for spoiling and misguiding me. From the time that I was twelve until I went abroad to England at age seventeen, my father never stopped being upset with me over the fact that I studied with boys and played competitive table-tennis (of which I became a provincial champion) with them. But he never reprimanded me directly— perhaps because during most of that time, he and I were not even on speaking terms with one another. I learned through those tense, silence-filled years how dreadful cold war is, and how through the coldness of its silence it may inflict deeper injury than the angriest of words. Looking back, I am stricken with sorrow that the world in which we lived made it impossible for my father and me to talk to one another through most of my life. Perhaps if we could have communicated directly we could have resolved some of our differences, or even learned to build a personal relationship with one another; but in Muslim societies fathers and daughters seldom talk to one another as peers or persons until the daughters have left the fathers' household and become part of another household. I who have been looking for a father all my life never knew my own until the last year of his life, when he had become a weak and ailing human being who cried to see his children come and cried to see them go. Not until then did I know for sure that he cared about me and wanted to see me happy, regardless of how he had disapproved of me through my growing years. We had so little time to get to know each other, but I am grateful that I was reconciled to him before he died. Such reconciliation does not, and cannot, of course, make up for a lifetime of deprivation, but at least it makes it possible for me to weep for my father and for what we missed.

While being alienated from my father left a deep imprint on my life, my intense and strange relationship with my mother left an even deeper one. For much of my life my mother was the most important person in my life. Feeling as I did that I lived in an arena of gladiators, I regarded my mother as my sole protector after God, and depended upon her for my emotional survival. Certainly my mother gave me much. She provided me not only with the best kind of education but also with the opportunity to become a "person." Considering marriage to be a necessary evil rather than an ideal state, my mother did not raise her daughters to conform to the very rigid, well-defined norms prescribed for female behavior and accomplishments in Muslim culture. She wanted her daughters to have what she herself had never had—a chance to be properly educated, to see the world, to experience freedom, to become self-sufficient, successful, and powerful.

Perhaps my particular tragedy lay in the fact that my mother regarded me as her Derby-winning horse who would actualize all her dreams of glory. My mother perceived me as the most gifted and single-minded of her children and believed that I had what it took to do what she had wanted to do in her life. She told me over and over, from a time when I was very young, that I was to become famous like Florence Nightingale and Joan of Arc. She did not want me ever to think of marriage, since marriage was bondage and a grave impediment to growth and advancement. For me the sky was the limit, provided I was strong and unwavering in the pursuit of my goals and sought always to be a winner.

Much of what I am today is due to my mother's meticulous schooling, but I could never become the ruthless superwoman she wanted me to be. Even as a child I could not accept the way she discriminated against many people, including some of her own children. My earliest battle with her was over my three younger brothers, whom she frequently treated unjustly and unkindly. I protested in their behalf, and in behalf of the other "disadvantaged" persons, like domestic servants, whom my mother mistreated. Strangely enough she did not mind my protesting—in fact, she was rather amused by it and called me "leader of the opposition." Perhaps she did not mind my taking a stand against her because she liked to see me fight, even though it was against her. But my efforts to make her review her own conduct never worked. She lived, and still lives, in a world dominated by the idea of will-to-power.

While my mother wanted me to succeed, she never patted me on the back for doing well. I know that she was proud of my achievements because she told others about them, but I did not hear her tell me that she loved me. In my society there were many stories of how a mother's love was superior to all other kinds of love because it was "unconditional." I wanted so much to believe that, but I could not, since I heard my mother say repeatedly to me: "I do not love you, I love your qualities." Her words, which were meant to affirm my "qualities," made me feel very lonely and sad. I could not receive my mother's love simply because I was her child. I could receive her approval only if I proved myself worthy. I recall that as a child my mother's attitude toward me often made me very melancholy, but that as an adolescent it made me very angry. Part of this anger, which stayed with me for a long time, was directed at myself because I could not break loose of my mother's control over me. Regardless of how strongly I wished to resist her emotional manipulation, when confronted by her immensely powerful personality I felt myself relapsing into a state of juvenile behavior when I reacted to her instead of acting as an autonomous person. It took some devastating experiences to finally sever the chains that bound the little girl in me to my mother's power and make me free of the burden of living out her fantasies instead of living my own life. Free of the bondage, I have sought to reestablish the bond. I still find it very difficult to "dialogue" with my mother, and my feelings toward her remain ambivalent, but I feel a strong sense of duty toward her. My mother not only gave me life but also the strength required to live the kind of life I wanted to live, and for that I owe her more than I can give. With her egocentricity and eccentricity, my mother's indomitable spirit, reflected in her steadfastness of purpose, courage, and refusal to give up in the face of insuperable odds, makes her the most extraordinary woman I have ever known, and despite all the heartache and agony she has caused me, I am proud of the fact that I am my mother's daughter.

Returning to my parents' conflict over me, I remember how tense things became as I approached my sixteenth year. For me my sixteenth birthday had nothing to do with "sweet sixteen," it was D-Day. My father wanted to see me married by then, but he had not found a way to arrange this marriage. He and I were not on speaking terms, and my mother would not hear of my marriage. My father was displeased and troubled about the situation. Another year passed, and the conflict seemed to intensify. My increasing independence of thought and action seemed to threaten my father's notion of family "honor." At the same time he recognized that I had brought much "honor" to my family by my academic successes, especially by standing first among the 24,000 students in the whole province in the intermediate examination.

Terrified lest I fall somehow into the death trap of an arranged marriage, I wanted desperately to escape from the danger that stalked me. My eldest sister had gone to England on a scholarship, and I asked her to secure admission for me in her college. She did so. I expected my father to oppose the idea of my studying abroad, but he permitted me to go. Perhaps by this time he had begun to feel that I deserved to have the opportunity to study abroad. Perhaps he also hoped that once I left home I would be out of my mother's sphere of influence and he would have greater access to me. He never told me his reasons for letting me go, but he spoke to me after a number of years on the day on which my brother and I set out for England with my mother. I wept as he embraced me and felt the pain of saying good-bye to him. In that moment of farewell he was simply my father and not "the adversary."

My seven years at St. Mary's college, University of Durham, in England, were full of homesickness and hard studying. After three years I graduated with joint honors in English literature and philosophy, and then, at age 24, I became a Doctor of Philosophy specializing in the philosophy of Allama Muhammad Iqbal, the national poet-philosopher of Pakistan, whose work I had loved and admired since childhood. During my years in England, I did, in fact, grow closer to my father and more distant from my mother (who never liked the idea of my being on good terms with my father), but when I returned home after finishing my studies abroad, I found that I was alienated from them both in fundamental ways. I could conform neither to my father's norms nor to my mother's values. Since I was no longer a child, I did not experience a child's fears, but I felt unutterably, unbearably alone. Coming home after seven long years of exile, I was again an outcast, an outsider.

It was in that state that I decided to marry a man who seemed to need me intensely. Always having had a great need not only to receive love but also to give it, for me the heaviest part of the price I paid for being a rebel against patriarchal society was that I did not feel free to express the love I felt for my own family members. A rebel's gifts are not accepted, and no one seemed to need my love. But Dawar needed it, and for years I gave it to him—unconditionally, unreservedly. My family was not thrilled with the idea of my marrying an "unmade" man, but they did not oppose it. Perhaps they had learned from experience that opposition did not deter me; perhaps they were glad that finally I had agreed to be married at all. Anyhow, as I began my married life I was aware of the social problems my husband and I would encounter on account of the fact that I was more educated than he and had better wage-earning prospects. These were serious matters in a society in which the man must always be seen to be in control and ahead of the woman, but in my joy at having found what I had always craved I did not pay much thought to them. For me, love was God's greatest gift, a miracle in a world of hate, and I believed that it could accomplish anything and overcome any difficulty. In Dawar's eyes I saw what I had never had—the promise of sustaining love—and overwhelmed, I wrote:

> *Beautiful, beautiful eyes*
> *beautiful as the myriad-tinted sun*
> *lighting upon the golden leaves of autumn*
> *which fall like rain upon the dark, deep waters*
> *of Wear, which guards the cobbled streets and spirits*
> *of an ancient, distant town.*
>
> *A stone-and-concrete wall.*
> *A wall of murky hate*
> *a hate born out of fear*
> *a fear born out of knowledge*
> *that the spirit too*
> *will rot beneath the burden*
> *of the tainted flesh.*
> *All around a wall*
> *to hide the helpless anger*
> *of sin-infected cowardice*
> *and knowing, growing shame.*
> *All around a wall*
> *which in the end must win*
> *crowding out the light*
> *crowding out the life*
> *in an eternal gloom.*
>
> *The soul is sick with sorrow*
> *for the wall is everywhere.*
> *But looking through the mist*
> *of doubt and hurt and sadness*
> *soft with tender caring*
> *knowing and understanding*
> *holding out a strength*
> *that keeps the heart from breaking*
> *are the beautiful eyes,*
> *the beautiful, beautiful eyes.*

My dream of love on which I thought our marriage was based was beautiful, no doubt, but it turned out to be a dream. Dawar was a typical product—victim—of the patriarchal society and had a compelling need to be the "head" of the family. He found it impossible to fulfill this need being married to a woman who was a superachiever, while he regarded himself as a loser. He was attracted by my strength but resented it at the same time. He wanted to utilize my talents out also to deny them. I tried to be a "good" wife, exemplifying the rebel's hidden desire to conform to tradition. For what seemed like a long time I was the model wife, selflessly devoted to her husband, living only for him and through him, but all my efforts to build up his confidence in himself only made him more conscious of what he lacked. A highly introverted person, he became even more withdrawn from life. I thought that perhaps if we left our complex-ridden, male-chauvinistic society and moved to a place where men were not under so much pressure to prove their superiority to women, our marriage would have a better chance of succeeding. We did, indeed, leave Pakistan and came to the United States, but the pattern of our relationship had already been set and it did not change. When I had married Dawar I had not known him well, but more importantly, I had not known myself well. Like many women through the ages I had thought that it was enough to give love without asking for anything in return, but I found out, after five years of constant giving, that I had nothing left to give. I was a hollow woman living in a wasteland. Never had my life seemed more empty, barren, or full of unspoken anguish. The times prior to my second exodus from my homeland (the first one having been for studying) and those which followed it were, in many ways, the darkest ones of my life. Much happened then that scarred me forever.

For me the decision to migrate from the land of my birth to a land I had never seen was one of the most difficult and heartbreaking decisions I have ever had to make. Through all the years that I had lived in England I had literally counted the days until my return to my beloved country. To serve "my people" had been a dream I had cherished since childhood. It is hard to describe the full measure of the disillusionment I suffered when I returned to my homeland and discovered that "my people" were enslaved by a corrupt government and that I could not live and work in my own country unless I was willing to renounce the ideals I most cherished. Torn as I was between love of my people and my commitment to God to work for truth and justice, I might have lingered in indecision had I not witnessed the dismemberment of Pakistan from very close quarters. As deputy director in the "brain-cell" of the federal information ministry, I had reason to believe that the tragedy that occurred could have been averted if the people in power had loved the country enough to let go of their own power fantasies. Traumatized by what I saw, I knew that the time for *hijrah*[1] had come, for my homeland had become the territory of the godless. Facing this truth with an exceedingly heavy heart, I wrote:

> *Who knows what lies ahead?*
> *Upon the vast, impenetrable brink*
> *of that which we call Future, lost and scared*
> *I stand tormented.*
> *Pain, the gnawing pain*

beneath whose weight the spirit wilts away
of making the irrevocable choice.
"To be or not to be," unhappy question
that ever—till the end—must vex our kind.
Can one forfeit one's dreams just to be safe—
safe from the agony of mystic quest?
Or must one, like one banished, leave behind
so much that is one's own, to start anew
somewhere where one can learn to dream again?
A cruel choice—but one which must be made
before the desperate strength of fading courage
dies 'mid the tyranny of conventional ways—
A cruel choice—but one which has been made—
God take care of the rest.

God did, indeed, take care of providing for us as we set out to build a new life in the United States, but soon after our arrival I received news from home that shook the roots of my being. My younger brother, Vicky, the closest to me of all my family and the only one who was always on my side, was dying of cancer. Wild with grief I went back to Lahore to be with him even though I was pregnant and very unwell. My memories of the following months are still so shrouded with pain that I cannot dwell upon them. Seeing my beloved brother waste away in the prime of a glorious youth was the hardest thing I had ever had to bear. In the midst of this overpowering sorrow another devastating blow fell upon us: my eldest brother, the guardian of my father's home and the most caring of all my family, died of a heart attack at the age of thirty-seven. I was not with my brothers when they died and could not participate in their funeral rites, but with them a part of me also died. What remained alive was emotionally paralyzed for a long time when my only reason for living was my little daughter, who was born as all the skies were falling on my head. For me, my little Mona, as I call her, has always been a miracle of God's grace, a gift given to me to keep me alive. When I named her Mehrunnisa[2] I did not know that she would live up to her name, but she is, indeed, a child with a heart so full of love and sunshine that she makes me forget the sorrows of my life. Like all mothers I want my child to have a safe and happy passage through life, but I also tell her that she must understand what it means to be Mujāhida,[3] which is her second name. I tell her that *jihād fī sabīl Allah* is the essence of being a Muslim and that I want her to commit her life to striving for truth and justice. I tell her that though she has herself known no discrimination, she must not become immune to the suffering of millions of Muslim girls who are discriminated against from the moment of birth. I tell her that my prayer for her is that she should be strong enough to be a *mujahida* in the long struggle that lies ahead of us and to continue the efforts of her mother and grandmother.

In the last decade and a half of my life there have been other events and mishaps that have affected me significantly. Perhaps the most memorable of the mishaps was my extremely short-lived marriage to Mahmoud, an Egyptian Arab Muslim more than thirty years my senior in age, who persuaded me to marry him after I had known him only a few days, saying that he would take care of me and my child, and help me develop my talents in order to serve God better. Emotionally wrecked by the death of my brothers and the end of a marriage in which I had invested so much care, and frightened of living alone with a young child in an alien world, I was mesmerized by Mahmoud's powerful personality and believed him when he said that as a member of the Muslim Brotherhood movement in Egypt, he had suffered imprisonment and torture for the sake of God. Mahmoud called himself a man of God, but I learned very quickly that being a man of God had nothing to do with being kind and compassionate and loving. It meant only that Mahmoud could command me to do whatever he wished in the name of God and with the authority of God, and I had no right to refuse, since in Islamic culture refusal to do what is pleasing to the husband is tantamount to refusing to do what is pleasing to God. Short as the marriage was, I came near to total destruction, physically and mentally, at the hands of a man who was not only a male chauvinist par excellence but also a fanatic who could invoke the holy name of God in perpetrating acts of incredible cruelty and callousness upon other human beings. Had I not had a lifetime of struggle for survival behind me and a total faith that God was just and merciful, I could not have survived the three months I spent with Mahmoud or the three years I spent fighting the lawsuits in which he involved me in order to punish me for taking a stand against him. He ruined me financially and did serious damage to me in many ways. However, as good and evil are inextricably linked together in human life, I am grateful even for this soul-searing experience, for it was this experience more than any other that made me a feminist with a resolve to develop feminist theology in the framework of Islamic tradition so that other so-called men of God could not exploit other Muslim women in the name of God.

While my personal life has been filled with momentous crises and upheavals throughout the years I have lived in this country, by the grace of God I have done well professionally. I am now a professor and chairperson of the Religious Studies Program at the University of Louisville. My specialization is in the area of Islamic Studies, and it was due to this expertise that I became involved in various ways, and at various levels, in the discussions going on around the country regarding Islam, after the Arab oil embargo of 1973 and the Iranian revolution of 1979 convinced the Western world that Islam was a living reality in the world. While I found many of these discussions, in which I was called upon to explain "Islamic revival" to Americans, interesting and stimulating, it was in another setting—that of interreligious dialogue among believers in the one God—that I found the community of faith I had sought all my life. In this community of faith I have found others who, like myself, are committed to creating a new world in which human beings will not brutalize or victimize one another in the name of God, but will affirm, through word and action, that as God is just and loving so human beings must treat each other with justice and love regardless of sex, creed, or color. I have found in my community of faith what I did not find in my community of birth: the possibility of growing and healing, of becoming integrated and whole. Due to the affirmation I have received from men and women of faith I am no longer the fragmented, mutilated woman that I once was. I know now that I am not alone in the wilderness, that there are some people in the world who understand my calling, and that their prayers are with me as I continue my struggle on behalf of the millions of nameless, voiceless, faceless Muslim women of the world who live and die unsung, uncelebrated in birth, unmourned in death. . . .

Notes

1. *Hijrah:* emigration; in the Islamic tradition this term has particular reference to the emigration in 632 A.D. of the Prophet Muhammad from his hometown Mecca, which was controlled by polytheist Arabs, to Medina, where he established the first Muslim community.
2. *Mehrunnisa:* symbol of *Mehr* (meaning "sun" and "love") among women.
3. *Mujāhida:* a girl or woman who engages in *jihād* (striving).

Why Women Need the Goddess

❦ *Carol P. Christ* ❦

At the close of Ntosake Shange's stupendously successful Broadway play *for colored girls who have considered suicide when the rainbow is enuf,* a tall beautiful black woman rises from despair to cry out, "I found God in myself and I loved her fiercely."[1] Her discovery is echoed by women and around the country who meet spontaneously in small groups on full moons, solstices, and equinoxes to celebrate the Goddess as symbol of life and death powers and waxing and waning energies in the universe and in themselves.[2]

> It is the night of the full moon. Nine women stand in a circle, on a rocky hill about the city. The western sky is rosy with the setting sun; in the east the moon's face begins to peer above the horizon. . . . The woman pours out a cup of wine onto the earth, refills it and raises it high. "Hail, Tana, Mother of mothers!" she cries. "Awaken from your long sleep, and return to your children again!"[3]

What are the political and psychological effects of this fierce new love of the divine in themselves for women whose spiritual experience has been focused by the male God of Judaism and Christianity? Is the spiritual dimension of feminism a passing diversion, an escape from difficult but necessary political work? Or does the emergence of the symbol of Goddess among women have significant political and psychological ramifications for the feminist movement?

To answer this question, we must first understand the importance of religious symbols and rituals in human life and consider the effect of male symbolism of God on women. According to anthropologist Clifford Geertz, religious symbols shape a

---

"Why Women Need the Goddess" from *Laughter of Aphrodite: Reflections on a Journey to the Goddess,* by Carol P. Crist (San Francisco: HarperSanFrancisco, 1987). Copyright ©1987 by Carol P. Christ. Originally published in *Heresies* 5(1978).

cultural ethos, defining the deepest values of a society and the persons in it. "Religion," Geertz writes, "is a system of symbols which act to produce powerful, pervasive, and long-lasting moods and motivations"[4] in the people of a given culture. A "mood" for Geertz is a psychological attitude such as awe, trust, and respect, while a "motivation" is the social and political trajectory created by a mood that transforms mythos into ethos, symbol system into social and political reality. Symbols have both psychological and political effects, because they create their inner conditions (deep-seated attitudes and feelings) that lead people to feel comfortable with or to accept social and political arrangements that correspond to the symbol system.

Because religion has such a compelling hold on the deep psyches of so many people, feminists cannot afford to leave it in the hands of the fathers. Even people who no longer "believe in God" or participate in the institutional structure of patriarchal religion still may not be free of the power of the symbolism of God the Father. A symbol's effect does not depend on rational assent, for a symbol also functions on levels of the psyche other than the rational. Religion fulfills deep psychic needs by providing symbols and rituals that enable people to cope with crisis situations[5] in human life (death, evil, suffering) and to pass through life's important transitions (birth, sexuality, death). Even people who consider themselves completely secularized will often find themselves sitting in a church or synagogue when a friend or relative gets married or when a parent or friend has died. The symbols associated with these important rituals cannot fail to affect the deep or unconscious structures of the mind of even a person who has rejected these symbolisms on a conscious level—especially if a person is under stress. The reason for the continuing effects of religious symbols is that the mind abhors a vacuum. Symbol systems cannot simply be rejected; they must be replaced. Where there is no replacement, the mind will revert to familiar structures at times of crisis, bafflement, or defeat.

Religions centered on the worship of a male God create "moods" and "motivations" that keep women in a state of psychological dependence on men and male authority, while at the same time legitimating the political and social authority of fathers and sons in the institutions of society.

Religious symbol systems focused around exclusively male images of divinity create the impression that female power can never be fully legitimate or wholly beneficent. This message need never be explicitly stated (as, for example, it is in the story of Eve) for its effect to be felt. A woman completely ignorant of the myths of female evil in biblical religion nonetheless acknowledges the anomaly of female power when she prays exclusively to a male God. She may see herself as like God (created in the image of God) only by denying her own sexual identity and affirming God's transcendence of sexual identity. But she can never have the experience that is freely available to every man and boy in her culture, of having her full sexual identity affirmed as being in the image and likeness of God. In Geertz's terms, her "mood" is one of trust in male power as salvific and distrust of female power in herself and other women as inferior or dangerous. Such a powerful, pervasive, and long-lasting "mood" cannot fail to become a "motivation" that translates into social and political reality.

In *Beyond God the Father*, feminist theologian Mary Daly detailed the psychological and political ramifications of father religion for women.

> If God in "his" heaven is a father ruling his people, then it is the "nature" of things and according to divine plan and the order of the universe that society be male dominated. Within this context, a *mystification of roles* takes place: The husband dominating his wife represents God "himself." The images and values of a given society have been projected into the realm of dogmas and "Articles of Faith," and these in turn justify the social structures which have given rise to them and which sustain their plausibility.[6]

Philosopher Simone de Beauvoir was well aware of the function of patriarchal religion as legitimizer of male power. As she wrote:

> Man enjoys the great advantage of having a god endorse the code he writes; and since man exercises a sovereign authority over women it is especially fortunate that this authority has been vested in him by the Supreme Being. For the Jew, Mohammedans, and Christians, among others, man is Master by divine right; the fear of God will therefore repress any impulse to revolt in the downtrodden female.[7]

This brief discussion of the psychological and political effects of God religion puts us in an excellent position to begin to understand the significance of the symbol of Goddess for women. In discussing the meaning of the Goddess, my method will first be phenomenological. I will isolate a meaning of the symbol of the Goddess as it has emerged in the lives of contemporary women. I will then discuss its psychological and political significance by contrasting the "moods" and "motivations" engendered by Goddess symbols with those engendered by Christian symbolism. I will also correlate Goddess symbolism with themes that have emerged in the women's movement in order to show how Goddess symbolism undergirds and legitimates the concerns of the women's movement, much as God symbolism in Christianity undergirded the interests of men in patriarchy. I will discuss four aspects of Goddess symbolism here: the Goddess as affirmation of female power, the female body, the female will, and women's bonds and heritage. There are, of course, many other meanings of the Goddess that I will not discuss here.

The sources for the symbol of the Goddess in contemporary spirituality are traditions of Goddess worship and modern women's experience. The ancient Mediterranean, pre-Christian European, Native American, Mesoamerican, Hindu, African, and other traditions are rich sources for Goddess symbolism. But these traditions are filtered through modern women's experiences. Traditions of Goddesses' subordination to Gods, for example, are ignored. Ancient traditions are tapped selectively and eclecticly, but they are not considered authoritative for modern consciousness. The Goddess symbol has emerged spontaneously in the dreams, fantasies, and thoughts of many women in the past several years. Kirsten Grimstad and Susan Rennie reported that they were surprised to discover widespread interest in spirituality, including the Goddess, among feminists around the country in the summer of 1974.[8] *WomanSpirit* magazine, which published its first issue in 1974 and had contributors from across the United States, expressed the grass-roots nature of the women's spirituality movement. In 1976, a journal devoted to the Goddess emerged, titled *Lady Unique*. In 1975, the first women's spirituality conference was held in Boston and attended by 1,800 women. In 1978, a University of Santa Cruz conference on the Goddess drew over 500 people. Sources for this essay are these manifestations of the Goddess in modern women's experiences as reported in *WomanSpirit, Lady Unique*, and elsewhere, and as expressed in conversations I have had with women who have been thinking about the Goddess and women's spirituality.

The simplest and most basic meaning of the symbol of Goddess is the acknowledgment of the legitimacy of female power as a beneficient and independent power. A woman who echoes Ntosake Shange's dramatic statement, "I found God in myself and I loved her fiercely," is saying, "Female power is strong and creative." She is saying that the divine principle, the saving and sustaining power, is in herself, that she will no longer look to men or male figures as saviors. The strength and independence of female power can be intuited by contemplating ancient and modern images of the Goddess. This meaning of the symbol of Goddess is simple and obvious, and yet it is difficult for many to comprehend. It stands in sharp contrast to the paradigms of female dependence on males that have been predominant in Western religion and culture. The internationally acclaimed novelist Monique Wittig captured the novelty and flavor of the affirmation of female power when she wrote in her mythic work *Les Guerilleres*:

> There was a time when you were not a slave, remember that. You walked alone, full of laughter, you bathed bare-bellied. You say you have lost all recollection of it, remember. . . . You say there are not words to describe it, you say it does not exist. But remember. Make an effort to remember. Or, failing that, invent.[9]

While Wittig does not speak directly of the Goddess here, she captures the "mood" of joyous celebration of female freedom and independence that is created in women who define their identities through the symbol of Goddess. Artist Mary Beth Edelson expressed the political "motivations" inspired by the Goddess when she wrote:

> The ascending archetypal symbols of the feminine unfold today in the psyche of modern Everywoman. They encompass the multiple forms of the Great Goddess. Reaching across the centuries we take the hands of our Ancient Sisters. The Great Goddess alive and well is rising to announce to the patriarchs that their 5,000 years are up—Hallelujah! Here we come.[10]

The affirmation of female power contained in the Goddess symbol has both psychological and political consequences. Psychologically, it means the defeat of the view engendered by patriarchy that women's power is inferior and dangerous. This new "mood" of affirmation of female power also leads to new "motivations"; it supports and undergirds women's trust in their own power and the power of other women in family and society.

If the simplest meaning of the Goddess symbol is an affirmation of the legitimacy and beneficence of female power, then a question immediately arises, "Is the Goddess simply female power writ large, and if so, why bother with the symbol of Goddess at all? Or does the symbol refer to a Goddess 'out there' who is not reducible to a human potential?" The many women who have rediscovered the power of Goddess would give three answers to this question: (1) The Goddess is divine female, a personification who can be invoked in prayer and ritual; (2) the Goddess is symbol of the life, death, and rebirth energy in nature and culture, in personal and communal life, and (3) the Goddess is symbol of the affirmation of the legitimacy and beauty of female power (made possible by the new becoming of women in the women's liberation movement). If one were to ask these women which answer is the "correct" one, different responses would be given. Some would assert that the Goddess definitely is *not* "out there," that the symbol of a divinity "out there" is part of the legacy of patriarchal oppression, which brings with it the authoritarianism, hierarchicalism, and dogmatic rigidity associated with biblical monotheistic religions. They might assert that the Goddess symbol reflects the sacred power within women and nature, suggesting the connectedness between women's cycles of menstruation, birth, and menopause, and the life and death cycles of the universe. Others seem quite comfortable with the notion of Goddess as a divine female protector and creator and would find their experience of Goddess limited by the assertion that she is not *also* out there as well as within themselves and in all natural processes. When asked what the symbol of Goddess means, feminist priestess Starhawk replied:

> It all depends on how I feel. When I feel weak, she is someone who can help and protect me. When I feel strong, she is the symbol of my own power. At other times I feel her as the natural energy in my body and the world.[11]

How are we to evaluate such a statement? Theologians might call these the words of a sloppy thinker. But my deepest intuition tells me they contain a wisdom that Western theological thought has lost.

To theologians, these differing views of the "meaning" of the symbol of Goddess might seem to threaten a replay of the trinitarian controversies. Is there, perhaps, a way of doing theology that would not lead immediately into dogmatic controversy, would not require theologians to say definitively that one understanding is true and the others are false? Could people's relation to a common symbol be made primary and varying interpretations be acknowledged? The diversity of explications of the meaning of the Goddess symbol suggests that symbols have a richer significance than any explications of their meaning can express, a point literary critics have long insisted on. This phenomenological fact suggests that theologians may need to give more than lip service to a theory of symbol in which the symbol is viewed as the primary fact and the meanings are viewed as secondary. It also suggests that a *thea*logy of the Goddess would be very different from the *theo*logy we have known in the west. But to spell out this notion of the primacy of *symbol* in thealogy in contrast to the primacy of the *explanation* in theology would be the topic of another paper. Let me simply state that women, who have been deprived of a female religious symbol system for centuries, recognize the power and primacy of symbols. I believe women must develop a theory of symbol and thealogy congruent with their experience at the same time as they "remember and invent" new symbol systems.

A second important implication of the Goddess symbol for women is the affirmation of the female body and the life cycle expressed in it. Because of women's unique position as menstruants, birthgivers, and those who have traditionally cared for the young and the dying, women's connection to the body, nature, and this world has been obvious. Women were denigrated because they seemed more carnal, fleshy, and earthy than the culture-creating males.[12] The misogynist antibody tradition in Western thought is symbolized in the myth of Eve who is traditionally viewed as a sexual temptress, the epitome of women's carnal nature. This tradition reaches its nadir in the *Malleus Maleficarum (The Hammer of Evil-Doing Women)*, which states "All witchcraft stems from carnal lust, which in women is insatiable."[13] The Virgin Mary, the positive female image in Christianity, does not contradict Christian denigration of the female body and its powers. The Virgin Mary is revered because she, in her perpetual virginity, transcends the carnal sexuality attributed to most women.

The denigration of the female body is expressed in cultural and religious taboos surrounding menstruation, childbirth, and menopause in women. While menstruation taboos may have originated in a perception of the awesome powers of the female body,[14] they degenerated into a simple perception that there is something "wrong" with female bodily functions. Menstruating women were forbidden to enter the sanctuary in ancient Hebrew and premodern Christian communities. Although only Orthodox Jews still enforce religious taboos against menstruant women, few women in our culture grow up affirming their menstruation as a connection to sacred power. Most women learn that menstruation is a curse and grow up believing that the bloody facts of menstruation are best hidden away. Feminists challenge this attitude to the female body. Judy Chicago's art piece "Menstruation Bathroom" broke these menstrual taboos. In a sterile white bathroom, she exhibited boxes of Tampax and Kotex on an open shelf, and the wastepaper basket was overflowing with bloody tampons and sanitary napkins.[15] Many women who viewed the piece felt relieved to have their "dirty secret" out in the open.

The denigration of the female body and its powers is further expressed in Western culture's attitudes toward childbirth.[16] Religious iconography does not celebrate the birthgiver, and there is no theology or ritual that enables a woman to celebrate the process of birth as a spiritual experience. Indeed, Jewish and Christian traditions also had blood taboos concerning the woman who had recently given birth. While these religious taboos are rarely enforced today (again, only by Orthodox Jews), they have secular equivalents. Giving birth is treated as a disease requiring hospitalization, and the woman is viewed as a passive object, anesthetized to ensure her acquiescence to the will of the doctor. The women's liberation movement has challenged these cultural attitudes, and many feminists have joined with advocates of natural childbirth and home birth in emphasizing the need for women to control and take pride in their bodies, including the birth process.

Western culture also gives little dignity to the postmenopausal or aging woman. It is no secret that our culture is based on a denial of aging and death, and that women suffer more severely from this denial than men. Women are placed on a pedestal and considered powerful when they are young and beautiful, but they are said to lose this power as they age. As feminists have pointed out, the "power" of the young woman is illusory, since beauty standards are defined by men, and since few women are considered (or consider themselves) beautiful for more than a few years of their lives. Some men are viewed as wise and authoritative in age, but old women are pitied and shunned. Religious icongraphy supports this cultural attitude toward aging women. The purity and virginity of Mary and the female saints is often expressed in the iconographic convention of perpetual youth. Moreover, religious mythology associates aging women with evil in the symbol of the wicked old witch. Feminists have challenged cultural myths of aging women and have urged women to reject patriarchal beauty standards and to celebrate the distinctive beauty of women of all ages.

The symbol of Goddess aids the process of naming and reclaiming the female body and its cycles and processes. In the ancient world and among modern women, the Goddess symbol represents the birth, death, and rebirth processes of the natural and human worlds. The female body is viewed as the direct incarnation of waxing and waning, life and death cycles in the universe. This is sometimes expressed through the symbolic connection between the twenty-eight-day cycles of menstruation and the twenty-eight-day cycles of the moon. Moreover, the Goddess is celebrated in the triple aspect of youth, maturity, and age, or maiden, mother, and crone. The potentiality of the young girl is celebrated in the nymph or maiden aspect of the Goddess. The Goddess as mother is sometimes depicted giving birth, and giving birth is viewed as a symbol for all the creative, life-giving powers of the universe.[17] The life-giving powers of the Goddess in her creative aspect are not limited to physical birth, for the Goddess is also seen as the creator of all the arts of civilization, including healing, writing, and the giving of just law. Women in the middle of life who are not physical mothers may give birth to poems, songs, and books, or nurture other women, men, and children. They too are incarnations of the Goddess in her creative, life-giving aspect. At the end of life, women incarnate the crone aspect of the Goddess. The wise old woman, the woman who knows from experience what life is about, the woman whose closeness to her own death gives her a distance and perspective on the problems of life, is celebrated as the third aspect of the Goddess. Thus, women learn to value youth, creativity, and wisdom in themselves and other women.

The possibilities of reclaiming the female body and its cycles have been expressed in a number of Goddess-centered rituals. Hallie Austen Iglehart and Barbry MyOwn created a summer solstice ritual to celebrate menstruation and birth. The women simulated a birth canal and birthed each other into their circle. They raised power by placing their hands on each other's bellies and chanting together. Finally they marked each other's faces with rich, dark menstrual blood saying, "This is the blood that promises renewal. This is the blood that promises sustenance. This is the blood that promises life."[18] From hidden dirty secret to symbol of the life power of the Goddess, women's blood has come full circle. Other women have created rituals that celebrate the crone aspect of the Goddess, especially at Halloween, an ancient holiday. On this day, the wisdom of the old woman is celebrated, and it is also recognized that the old must die so that the new can be born.

The "mood" created by the symbol of the Goddess in triple aspect is one of positive, joyful affirmation of the female body and its cycles and acceptance of aging and death as well as life. The "motivations" are to overcome menstrual taboos, to return the birth process to the hands of women, and to change cultural attitudes about age and death. Changing cultural attitudes toward the female body would help to overcome the spirit-flesh, mind-body dualisms of Western culture, since, as Ruether has pointed out, the denigration of the female body is at the heart of these dualisms. The Goddess as symbol of the revaluation of the body and nature thus also undergirds the human potential and ecology movements. The "mood" is one of affirmation, awe, and respect for the body and nature, and the "motivation" is respect for the teachings of the body and the value of all living beings.

A third important implication of the Goddess symbol for women is the positive valuation of will in Goddess-centered ritual, especially in Goddess-centered ritual magic and spellcasting in womanspirit and feminist witchcraft circles. The basic notion behind ritual magic and spell casting is energy as power. Here the Goddess is a center or focus of power and energy; she is the personification of the energy that flows between beings in the natural and human worlds. In Goddess circles, energy is raised by chanting or dancing. According to Starhawk, "Witches conceive of psychic energy as having form and substance that can be perceived and directed by those with a trained awareness. The power generated within the circle is built into a cone form, and at its peak is released—to the Goddess, to reenergize the members of the coven, or to do a specific work such as healing."[19] In ritual magic, the energy raised is directed by willpower. Women who celebrate in Goddess circles believe they can achieve their wills in the world.

The emphasis on the will is important for women, because women traditionally have been taught to devalue their wills, to believe that they cannot achieve their will through their own power, and even to suspect that the assertion of will is evil. Faith Wildung's poem "Waiting," from which I will quote only a short segment, sums up women's sense that their lives are defined not by their own will, but by waiting for others to take the initiative.

Waiting for my breasts to develop
Waiting to wear a bra
Waiting to menstruate

. . . .

Waiting for life to begin, Waiting—
Waiting to be somebody

. . . .

Waiting to get married
Waiting for my wedding day
Waiting for my wedding night

. . . .

Waiting for the end of the day
Waiting for sleep. Waiting. . .[20]

Patriarchal religion has enforced the view that female initiative and will are evil through the juxtaposition of Eve and Mary. Eve caused the fall by asserting her will against the command of God, while Mary began the new age with her response to God's initiative, "Let it be done to me according to thy word" (Luke 1:38). Even for men, patriarchal religion values the passive will subordinate to divine initiative. The classical doctrines of sin and grace view sin as the prideful assertion of will and grace as the obedient subordination of the human will to the divine initiative or order. While this view of will might be questioned from a human perspective, Valerie Saiving has argued that it has particularly deleterious consequences for women in Western culture. According to Saiving, Western culture encourages males in the assertion of will, and thus it may make some sense to view the male form of sin as an excess of will. But since culture discourages females in the assertion of will, the traditional doctrines of sin and grace encourage women to remain in their form of sin, which is self-negation or insufficient assertion of will.[21] One possible reason the will is denigrated in a patriarchal religious framework is that both human and divine will are often pictured as arbitrary, self-initiated, and exercised without regard for other wills.

In a Goddess-centered context, in contrast, the will is valued. *A woman is encouraged to know her will, to believe that her will is valid, and to believe that her will can be achieved in the world*, three powers traditionally denied to her in patriarchy. In a Goddess-centered framework, a woman's will is not subordinated to the Lord God as king and ruler, nor to men as his representatives. Thus a woman is not reduced to waiting and acquiescing in the wills of others as she is in patriarchy. But neither does she adopt the egocentric form of will that pursues self-interest without regard for the interests of others.

The Goddess-centered context provides a different understanding of the will than that available in the traditional patriarchal religious framework. In the Goddess framework, will can be achieved only when it is exercised in harmony with the energies and wills of other beings. Wise women, for example, raise a cone of healing energy at the full moon or solstice when the lunar or solar energies are at their high points with respect to the earth. This discipline encourages them to recognize that not all times are propitious for the achieving of every will. Similarly, they know that spring is a time for new beginnings in work and love, summer a time for producing external manifestations of inner potentialities, and fall or winter times for stripping down to the inner core and extending roots. Such awareness of waxing and waning processes in the universe discourages arbitrary ego-centered assertion of will, while at the same time encouraging the assertion of individual will in cooperation with natural energies and the energies created by the wills of others. Wise women also have a tradition that whatever is sent out will be returned, and this reminds them to assert their wills in cooperative and healing rather than egocentric and destructive ways. This view of will allows women to begin to recognize, claim, and assert their wills without adopting the worst characteristics of the patriarchal understanding and use of will. In the Goddess-centered framework, the "mood" is one of positive affirmation of personal will in the context of the energies of other wills or beings. The "motivation" is for women to know and assert their wills in cooperation with other wills and energies. This of course does not mean that women always assert their wills in positive and life-affirming ways. Women's capacity for evil is, of course, as great as men's. My purpose is simply to contrast the differing attitudes toward the exercise of will *per se*, and the female will in particular, in Goddess-centered religion and in the Christian God-centered religion.

The fourth and final aspect of Goddess symbolism that I will discuss here is the significance of the Goddess for a revaluation of women's bonds and heritage. As Virginia Woolf has said, "Chloe liked Olivia," a statement about a woman's relation to another woman, is a sentence that rarely occurs in fiction. Men have written the stories, and they have written about women almost exclusively in their relations to men.[22] The celebrations of women's bonds to each other, as mothers and daughters, as colleagues and coworkers, as sisters, friends, and lovers, is beginning to occur in the new literature and culture created by women in the women's movement. While I believe that the revaluing of each of these bonds is important, I will focus on the mother–daughter bond, in part because I believe it may be the key to the others.

Adrienne Rich has pointed out that the mother–daughter bond, perhaps the most important of women's bonds, "resonant with charges . . . the flow of energy between two biologically alike bodies, one of which has lain in amniotic bliss inside the other, one of which has labored to give birth to the other,"[23] is rarely celebrated in patriarchal religion and culture. Christianity celebrates the father's relation to the son and the mother's relation to the son, but the story of mother and daughter is missing. So, too, in patriarchal literature and psychology the mothers and daughters rarely exist. Volumes have been written about the oedipal complex, but little has been written about the girl's relation to her mother. Moreover, as de Beauvoir has noted, the mother–daughter relation is distorted in patriarchy because the mother must give her daughter over to men in a male-defined culture in which women are viewed as inferior. The mother must socialize her daughter to be subordinate to men, and if her daughter challenges patriarchal norms, the mother is likely to defend the patriarchal structures against her own daughter.[24]

These patterns are changing in the new culture created by women in which the bonds of women to women are beginning to be celebrated. Holly Near has written several songs that celebrate women's bonds and women's heritage. In one of her finest songs she writes of an "old-time woman" who is "waiting to die." A young woman feels for the life that has passed the old woman by and begins to cry, but the old woman looks her in the eye and says, "If I had not suffered, you wouldn't be wearing those jeans/Being an old-time woman ain't as bad as it seems."[25] This song, which Near has said was inspired by her grandmother, expresses and celebrates a bond and a heritage passed down from one woman to another. In another of Near's songs, she sings of a "a hiking-boot mother who's seeing the world/For the first time with her own little girl." In this song, the mother tells the drifter who has been traveling with her to pack up and travel alone if he thinks "traveling three is a drag" because "I've got a little one who loves me as much as you need me/And darling, that's loving enough."[26] This song is significant because the mother places her relationship to her daughter above her relationship to a man, something women rarely do in patriarchy.[27]

Almost the only story of mother and daughters that has been transmitted in Western culture is the myth of Demeter and Persephone that was the basis of religious rites celebrated by women only, the Thesmophoria, and later formed the basis of the Eleusinian mysteries, which were open to all who spoke Greek. In this story, the daughter, Persephone, is raped away from her mother, Demeter, by the God of the underworld.

Unwilling to accept this state of affairs, Demeter rages and withholds fertility from the earth until her daughter is returned to her. What is important for women in this story is that a mother fights for her daughter and for her relation to her daughter. This is completely different from the mother's relation to her daughter in patriarchy. The "mood" created by the story of Demeter and Persephone is one of celebration of the mother–daughter bond, and the "motivation" is for mothers and daughters to affirm the heritage passed on from mother to daughter and to reject the patriarchal pattern where the primary loyalties of mother and daughter must be to men.[28]

The symbol of Goddess has much to offer women who are struggling to be rid of the "powerful, pervasive, and long-lasting moods and motivations" of devaluation of female power, denigration of the female body, distrust of female will, and denial of the women's bonds and heritage that have been engendered by patriarchal religion. As women struggle to create a new culture in which women's power, bodies, will, and bonds are celebrated, it seems natural that the Goddess would reemerge as symbol of the newfound beauty, strength, and power of women.

Notes

1. From the original cast album, Buddah Records, 1976. Also see *for colored girls who have considered suicide when the rainbow is enuf* (New York: MacMillan, 1976).
2. See Susan Rennie and Kristen Grimstad, "Spiritual Explorations Cross-Country," *Quest* 1, no. 4(1975): 49–51; and *WomanSpirit* magazine.
3. See Starhawk, "Witchcraft and Women's Culture," in *Womanspirit Rising*, ed. Carol P. Christ and Judith Plaskow (New York: Harper & Row, 1979), 260.
4. Clifford Geertz, "Religion as a Cultural System," in *The Interpretation of Cultures* (New York: Basic Books, 1973), 90.
5. Ibid., 98–108.
6. Mary Daly, *Beyond God the Father* (Boston: Beacon Press, 1974), 13, italics added.
7. Simone de Beauvoir, *The Second Sex*, trans. H.M. Parshleys (New York: Alfred A. Knopf, 1953).
8. See Grimstad and Rennie, "Spiritual Explorations Cross-Country."
9. Monique Wittig, *Les Guerilleres*, trans. David LeVay (New York: Avon Books, 1971), 89. Also quoted in Morgan MacFarland, "Witchcraft: The Art of Remembering," *Quest* 1, no. 4 (1975): 41.
10. Mary Beth Edelson, "Speaking for Myself," *Lady Unique* 1 (1976): 56.
11. Personal communication.
12. This theory of the origins of the Western dualism is stated by Rosemary Ruether in *New Woman/New Earth* (New York: Seabury Press, 1975), and elsewhere.
13. Heinrich Kramer and Jacob Sprenger, *The Malleus Maleficarum*, trans. Montague Summers (New York: Dover, 1971), 47.
14. See Rita M. Gross, "Menstruation and Childbirth as Ritual and Religious Experience in the Religion of the Australian Aborigines," *Journal of the American Academy of Religion* 45, no. 4 (1977): 1147–81.
15. Judy Chicago, *Through the Flower* (New York: Doubleday & Company, 1975), plate 4, 106–7.

16. See Adrienne Rich, *Of Woman Born* (New York: Bantam Books, 1977), chs. 6 and 7.

17. See James Mellaart, *Earliest Civilizations of the Near East* (New York: McGraw-Hill, 1965), 92.

18. Barbry MyOwn, "Ursa Maior: Menstrual Moon Celebration," in *Moon, Moon*, ed. Anne Kent Rush (Berkeley, Calif., and New York: Moon Books and Random House, 1976), 374–87.

19. Starhawk, "Witchcraft and Women's Culture," *Womanspirit Rising*, 266.

20. In Judy Chicago, 213–17.

21. Valerie Saiving, "The Human Situation: A Feminine View," *Journal of Religion* 40 (1960): 100–12.

22. Virginia Woolf, *A Room of One's Own* (New York: Harcourt Brace Jovanovich, 1928), 86.

23. Rich, *Of Woman Born*, 226.

24. De Beauvoir, *The Second Sex*, 448–49.

25. "Old Time Woman," lyrics by Jeffrey Langley and Holly Near, from *Holly Near: A Live Album*, Redwood Records, 1974.

26. "Started Out Fine," by Holly Near from *Holly Near: A Live Album*.

27. Rich, *Of Woman Born*, 223.

28. For another version of the story see Charlene Spretnak, *Lost Goddesses of Early Greece: A Collection of Pre-Hellenic Myths* (Boston: Beacon Press, 1984), 105–18.

The Coming of Lilith

✿ Judith Plaskow ✿

In the beginning the Lord God formed Adam and Lilith from the dust of the ground and breathed into their nostrils the breath of life. Created from the same source, both having been formed from the ground, they were equal in all ways. Adam, man that he was, didn't like this situation, and he looked for ways to change it. He said, "I'll have my figs now, Lilith," ordering her to wait on him, and he tried to leave to her the daily tasks of life in the garden. But Lilith wasn't one to take any nonsense; she picked herself up, uttered God's holy name, and flew away. "Well, now, Lord," complained Adam, "that uppity woman you sent me has gone and deserted me." The Lord, inclined to be sympathetic, sent his messengers after Lilith, telling her to shape up and return to Adam or face dire punishment. She, however, preferring anything to living with Adam, decided to stay right where she was. And so God, after more careful consideration this time, caused a deep sleep to fall upon Adam, and out of one of his ribs created for him a second companion, Eve.

For a time Eve and Adam had quite a good thing going. Adam was happy now, and Eve, though she occasionally sensed capacities within herself that remained undeveloped, was basically satisfied with the role of Adam's wife and helper. The only thing that really disturbed her was the excluding closeness of the relationship between Adam and God. Adam and God just seemed to have more in common, being both men, and Adam came to identify with God more and more. After a while that made God a bit uncomfortable too, and he started going over in his mind whether he might not have made a mistake in letting Adam talk him into banishing Lilith and creating Eve, in light of the power that had given Adam.

Meanwhile Lilith, all alone, attempted from time to time to rejoin the human community in the garden. After her first fruitless attempt to breach its walls, Adam worked hard to build them stronger, even getting Eve to help him. He told her fearsome stories of the demon Lilith who threatens women in childbirth and steals children from their cradles in the middle of the night. The second time Lilith came she stormed the garden's main gate, and a great battle between her and Adam ensued, in which she was finally defeated. This time, however, before Lilith got away, Eve got a glimpse of her and saw she was a woman like herself.

After this encounter, seeds of curiosity and doubt began to grow in Eve's mind. Was Lilith indeed just another woman? Adam had said she was a demon. Another woman! The very idea attracted Eve. She had never seen another creature like herself before. And how beautiful and strong Lilith had looked! How bravely she had fought! Slowly, slowly, Eve began to think about the limits of her own life within the garden.

One day, after many months of strange and disturbing thoughts, Eve, wandering around the edge of the garden, noticed a young apple tree she and Adam had planted, and saw that one of its branches stretched over the garden wall. Spontaneously she tried to climb it, and struggling to the top, swung herself over the wall.

She had not wandered long on the other side before she met the one she had come to find, for Lilith was waiting. At first sight of her, Eve remembered the tales of Adam and was frightened, but Lilith understood and greeted her kindly. "Who are you?" they asked each other, "What is your story?" And they sat and spoke together, of the past and then of the future. They talked not once, but many times, and for many hours. They taught each other many things, and told each other stories, and laughed together, and cried, over and over, till the bond of sisterhood grew between them.

Meanwhile, back in the garden, Adam was puzzled by Eve's comings and goings, and disturbed by what he sensed to be her new attitude toward him. He talked to God about it, and God, having his own problems with Adam and a somewhat broader perspective, was able to help him out a little—but he, too, was confused. Something had failed to go according to plan. As in the days of Abraham, he needed counsel from his children. "I am who I am," thought God, "but I must become who I will become."

And God and Adam were expectant and afraid the day Eve and Lilith returned to the garden, bursting with possibilities, ready to rebuild it together.

From Riot Grrl to Yeshiva Girl

or How I Became My Own Damn Rabbi

❖ *Jennifer Bleyer* ❖

I WAS NOT RAISED IN THE TORRENTIAL DOWNPOUR of women's liberation, but rather in its trickling runoff. My mother and her friends were at-home moms who shaved their armpits, drank chocolate Slim-Fast shakes and played mahjong. They dutifully chauffeured their daughters to ballet class every Wednesday and didn't balk at buying us Barbies. They read Danielle Steel. They Jazzercised. But even so, tiny droplets of the feminist movement leaked into my suburban 1970s childhood. I wasn't allowed to watch *Three's Company* on television because it was demeaning to women, my mom told me, before I even knew what "demeaning" meant. I had a *Free to Be . . . You and Me* record that was riddled with scratches, its album jacket worn out from use. There was never a doubt that I would go to college and, for the sake of parental *kvelling*, perhaps become the successful doctor that only boys were once expected to become. Sure, there must have been women gleefully digging into each other with speculums and burning their quilted pot holders somewhere, but from my vantage point, the alarming, nameless problem that Betty Friedan identified in *The Feminine Mystique* registered as nothing more than a minor fact of life.

I was sent to a Conservative Jewish day school through junior high and then to a public high school in suburban Detroit. The Jewish school guarded each of its students with the same concern and reverence with which we guarded the Torah scroll when it left its small wooden ark. We, boys and girls alike, were the recipients of an education that was creatively inspired, morally rooted and largely egalitarian. Going from there to public high school was something akin to laboratory mice being released into the general population. The boys tousled their hair to disguise near-permanent yarmulke indentations, the girls tried not to slip into Hebrew in their Spanish classes, and all of us seemed a little lost without the ritual of a morning minyan. As a social experiment it may have been interesting, but as a life, it kind of sucked. There was nothing about it, however, that could have predicted the swings my life would soon take.

In 1991, I found punk rock. How does a nice Jewish girl from the Midwest get involved with punk rock, you might wonder? Shortly after a tumultuous move to

Cleveland (and really, what's not tumultuous when you're fifteen?) I was sent to a summer program in Pittsburgh where I befriended an older local punk named Spaz. Spaz had wild blue eyes and a mohawk. He had piles of seven-inch records and strange magazines. He plastered the town with photocopied art that he called Public Enemas, provocative drawings and diatribes that poked fun at the conformity that surrounded him. We would stay out all night taping these up around Pittsburgh, and every staid public monument somehow became magical in our presence. We talked to strangers and absorbed them into our nighttime journeys. I learned through Spaz that, contrary to outdated images of the Sex Pistols and ripped leather jackets, punk rock was about freedom, openness, joy and autonomy. I learned that it was a vehicle through which even the most entrenched social conventions could be questioned and changed. I learned that since the late '70s, when it briefly popped up on the public radar, punk rock had been a viable, self-sustaining subculture. It had produced volumes of music, writing, art and subgroups espousing everything from anarchism to veganism to radical environmentalism. And I happened to become a punk just when it spawned a subgroup espousing what was dearest to me: feminism.

In 1991, a cluster of all-girl bands sprouted up in the Pacific Northwest, and punk girls started to hold small gatherings to confront sexism in the "scene." They called themselves riot grrls. I was sixteen and back home in Cleveland when I heard about them; just the name, with its teeth-grinding spelling of "girl," made me swoon. I was in love. Scouring the underground network of photocopied-and-stapled homemade zines, I sent for as many made by riot grrls as I could find, many no more than alternately angst-ridden and joyous diary entries, handwritten and xeroxed. The Riot Grrl movement spoke to me in a more powerful, visceral and gratifying way than anything I had ever experienced, as if my own subconscious had mysteriously untangled itself and formed an organization. I was unable to rest until Riot Grrl effectively took over the entire known universe. I started off by forming the Cleveland chapter.

When the world, with its appetite for the absurd, looked at us, it saw a bunch of teenage girls with facial piercings, blue hair, torn fishnets and old skate sneakers. But when we looked at each other, we saw our complexity, our hugeness, our love. We went to pro-choice protests, made zines and saw girl bands play when they came through town. Some of us went to the national Riot Grrl conventions in Washington, D.C., and Lincoln, Nebraska. Mostly, though, we just got together at each other's houses for big dinners and sleepover parties, and we talked. Contrary to its threatening name, the riot-grrl world was basically a support group: a '90s version of the '70s consciousness-raising group. Looking back now, just over ten years since its wild inception, I can't help but remember it as somewhat precocious and self-absorbed. But I am also amazed at how sophisticated we were in our heady, earnest discussions of race, class, sexuality and gender dynamics, and how genuinely supportive we were of one another at such a fragile time in our lives.

Throughout my punk-rock and riot-grrl days, I distanced myself from Judaism as if it were a contagious disease. Scouring my memory to recall what I found so odious then, I think that part of it was certainly a growing class consciousness. I was one of only a few riot grrls in our Cleveland group who came from the more affluent east side of the city; although my family was not ostentatiously wealthy, we were comfortable. I began associating Judaism with the social inequalities of which I was growing aware. In this tight community of working-class and lower-middle-class girls who had to work shitty jobs and drown themselves in debt to go to college, I associated Judaism with privilege: the privilege of being white (or at least passing for white), the privilege of having money, the privilege of being educated, the privilege of having a stable family. Of course, I knew that not all Jews were white, wealthy, educated and functional. But I insisted then (as I do now) that while acknowledging gradations of diversity among American Jews, we should not be too delusional about our general social class. One of the big pastimes for riot grrls was attacking and analyzing privilege, and for me, acknowledging my Jewish privilege was an arduous, necessary process.

Another thing that spun me far out from the Jewish orbit was its general irrelevancy to my life. I suppose that's not an uncommon feeling for most Jewish kids, unless by some feat of imagination they can link Judaism to pop music, fashion, SAT scores and the mall. Teenagers' alienation from their parents' lifestyle is a certified part of our cultural experience, but to me, Judaism seemed even more archaic and clueless than my parents themselves. This was not the Democratic Upper West Side of Manhattan, remember. The arbiters of liberal Jewish culture often underestimate that vast bulk of mainstream American Jews who are not concerned with ecological Tu B'Shvat rituals and feminist Passover seders, but rather with showing up in fur coats to High Holiday services and throwing bar mitzvah parties that rival the Trump empire in glitz. The rituals themselves—fasting and then gorging on Yom Kippur, praying in a foreign language—struck me as rote and empty. When matters of the spirit registered on my radar, they were vague, inquisitive and open—unlike the mechanized tradition in which I had been raised.

But I could never totally cut myself off. We once had a riot-grrl potluck during Passover, and I brought a box of matzo to eat while everyone else devoured huge plates of food. I remember wearing my steel-toe combat boots and an old green-and-orange-striped dress that matched the green and orange of the Manischewitz box. We were a big group crammed into the dingy kitchen of someone's apartment. Some of my friends knew what matzo was and others didn't, so I gave my best explanation: "It's just this bread that didn't rise, because the Jews were slaves in Egypt and when they were set free I guess there was no time for their bread to rise, so it's kind of like a thing to remember that, I guess. Something like that." Everyone nodded with respectful interest (they were way into cultural experiences). I crunched away at the flat white matzo and passed around pieces so everybody could try it (again, that cultural experience thing). I felt a small, superficial tinge of pride, realizing that being Jewish was in fact interesting, unusual and somehow significant.

Our riot-grrl chapter slowly faded away as some of us went far away to college and others got stuck in various ruts in Ohio. Riot Grrl as a movement pretty much dissolved everywhere, in fact, as intense scrutiny by the punk scene as well as the mainstream media rendered it an uncomfortable caricature of itself. I moved to New York, traveled across the country, drifted into and out of relationships and otherwise engaged in the strange dance of life. I remained a feminist, of course, and although Riot Grrl as a way of life lost its relevancy for me, the lessons I learned from it remained.

A couple of years later, when I was twenty, I took a year off from college to travel by myself. After months of journeying through the deserts of Egypt, the jungles of Uganda and the verdant lanes of Paris, I went to Vienna, the city my grandparents had fled in 1938. I wanted to spend a Shabbat there, and found a local Chabad family who lived only blocks from my grandparents' old apartment building in the second district of the city. They were a young, energetic Israeli couple who had come to Vienna as "messengers" of their Rebbe; the husband was the headmaster of Vienna's only Jewish school, and his wife was the caretaker of their six children. Over a beautiful Shabbat meal laid with silver and china, conversation revealed that the man and I were distantly removed cousins. The coincidence was astounding, considering how I'd accidentally ended up in their house.

"So, my cousin," he said, stroking his beard, "why are you wasting your time traveling aimlessly like this? You'll never find anything. Go learn in yeshiva if you really want to find something. In fact, if you agree to stay for a few months, I will send you to one of the best yeshivas for girls." Never one to slap serendipity in the face, I accepted the offer and was promptly sent to Machon Alte, a yeshiva for young women in Tsfat, Israel.

If you can imagine the furthest, most dichotomous opposite of a riot grrl, it would surely have to be a Machon Alte yeshiva girl. This was a school for young *ba'ale teshuvah*, girls who had not grown up religiously observant but had become or were exploring the possibility of becoming so. The night I arrived at the Machon Alte's stately old building on Tsfat's main thoroughfare, the girls took me to a back room and told me to dig through boxes of donated clothes for a *tsnius*, or modest, wardrobe. I complied, pulling out long skirts and frumpy shirts that covered the elbows and ever-arousing neckbone. I was placed in a dorm room with two roommates, one of whom was an accomplished guitar player and singer but would only play in the seclusion of our room (outside, she ran the risk of breaking the prohibition against women singing in earshot of men). We had classes all day in Talmud, Torah, Kabbalah and various tracts of Chabad tradition, almost all taught by rabbis who would avoid looking us in the eye. A couple of times a week, we had classes that were essentially Jewish home economics—teaching us how to run a halakhically Jewish home by preparing for Shabbat, honoring our husbands, raising our children and attending to the various domestic duties prescribed for women in Hasidic orthodoxy. On Shabbat, we would go to the city's synagogues and watch the men praying in the main part of the sanctuary from our isolated balcony perches, or through dense lace curtains or latticework partitions. At least once a week, Machon Alte would explode in a joyful frenzy as a student came in and announced that she had gotten engaged.

The yeshiva's cook, a boisterous Tunisian woman named Juliette, doubled as a matchmaker and would "match" young women with boys from the men's yeshiva down the road. If both headmasters agreed to the match, the couple was generally allowed to meet. After no more than three or four meetings, they would often decide to marry.

To be sure, living as a yeshiva girl was utterly bizarre. But I got into it, and flirted with the lifestyle for a few years before coming to my senses. Now, I wonder how it was that I went so quickly from scoffing at the idea of shaving my legs to wearing pantyhose in hundred-degree heat lest anyone see my exposed ankles. Part of it, I think, was just a keen sense of curiosity: I studied anthropology in college and this was almost like an ethnographic study, going undercover in a community in order to understand it. But I was not collecting informants, building rapport or writing fieldnotes, as they say in anthro-speak. There was a part of me that was legitimately attracted to the Hasidic lifestyle and governing beliefs. The laws of modest dress dictated that women were not to be seen as objects of beauty, but as human beings based on their merits—granted, a limited span of meritorious possibilities, but still less superficial than those which mainstream society allowed. In fact, I have heard Orthodox Jewish women defend their wigs and Islamic women defend their veils on seemingly feminist principles, claiming a sense of empowerment by withholding their hair, legs and bodies from the world's visual consumption.

But there was more to it than that. Studying Jewish texts with academic precision and spiritual insight was new to me, and deeply challenged my perception of Judaism as a string of rote holiday rituals and unconvincing rhetoric. Something about Orthodoxy itself was also appealing—partly because the moral absolutism and strictness of behavior (I learned to pre-cut toilet paper for Shabbat, as the act of ripping it constitutes prohibited work) represented a release from the casual, nonsensical whims of society. In my ever-gnawing quest for freedom, I came to recognize the extraordinary spiritual freedom that exists, ironically, like an escape hatch within the most rigid systems of rules, procedures and restrictions.

I quickly learned that I was not alone among women of similar backgrounds who felt drawn to this life, despite all the alarms signaling "second-class citizen." I sat at the Shabbat tables of many highly educated and well-read women who had left promising careers; who had followed the Grateful Dead and spent years at ashrams in India; who had participated in the student uprisings of the sixties and the feminist movement of the seventies—all of whom had chosen to move to Israel, have a gaggle of kids and learn to cook a mean kugel. I even met young women who had been punk-rock kids like myself: One, a convert, had hopped freight trains up and down the West Coast, played in a band and been popular in Berkeley's punk scene before she moved to Israel and became an Orthodox Jew. They did not necessarily proselytize to me, but as logical, thoughtful women with an incredible range of world experience and fluency in contemporary culture, their choice to become Orthodox had a curious credibility. It was simply too intriguing to ignore.

After that summer, I returned to New York and dabbled on and off with religious observance, spending time in the Hasidic enclaves of Brooklyn and the Orthodox synagogues of the Upper West Side. Still, I could never completely give myself over to it. In the seclusion of many family dining rooms, I heard statements about non-Jews, and Arabs in particular, that were absolutely unconscionable if not outright racist. I saw people behave in ways that deeply contradicted their own pious tenets, confirming that a black hat and coat does not render one holier or more spiritually aware than anyone else. I realized that much of what I found attractive about this particular lifestyle was accessible outside of it as well—that the beauty of Jewish ritual, the sense of community and the intense examination of texts are not the exclusive province of ultra-religious Jews.

After this religious exploration (which, needless to say, quite shocked my family), I shook off the residue of judgment and habit and found myself planted with a brilliant, luminous seed. I still retain a strange mix of scorn and fondness for Orthodoxy, but nothing has tarnished my love of that seed, that divine life force that animates Judaism in all of its sectarian chaos. In retrospect, I think that my foray into Orthodoxy shaped me as a Jew in much the same way that being a riot grrl shaped me as a feminist. I learned from both experiences that everything can become dangerously entrenched in its own orthodoxy and has to be shaken up in order to remain dynamic and relevant.

The Riot Grrl movement, for instance, was most daring not in its fuck-you to male-dominated society, but in its screeching fuck-you to mainstream feminism. To be sure, few of us had an especially educated awareness of how hard our mothers and, grandmothers had fought for certain privileges we took for granted. But we legitimately grappled with a feminism that seemed to be about appropriating the roles of men, instead of exploding the entire notion of what it meant to be human. We did not want the "equal right" to be corporate drones, executive whipcrackers or miserable supermoms, futilely trying to balance career, family, friends and therapy. We wanted something that was off the charts completely, that reconfigured every stagnant fixture of society.

Similarly, I began to see Judaism as something essentially beautiful that has been hijacked by a great many self-appointed authorities. As sacrilegious as it sounds, the rabbis need their own fuck-you in order to liberate the treasures they guard. This doesn't mean trashing tradition as much as shaking the dust off of it and letting it grow. As the first generation of Jewish feminists was instrumental to creating egalitarian discourse and leveling Jewish male privilege, my generation of Jewish feminists will, I hope, extend that trajectory to question the nature of all authority within our tradition, liberating it from its captors.

My Judaism has evolved to the point where I go from peaceful Shabbat dinners uptown to raucous clubs downtown and dance until 4 A.M., feeling neither guilt nor contradiction. I host holiday gatherings for all of my friends, Jewish and non-Jewish, white, black and brown, and welcome everyone as children of Israel. I can say a *shehechianu* blessing when being arrested at a protest, to thank God for delivering me to that moment. My generation of Jewish feminists is creating a Judaism so seamless that the spiritual, political, social and personal are not just related, but are virtually the same thing. We are allowing ourselves to be Jewish in the way that riot grrls taught us to be feminist—explosively, boundlessly, beyond definition and with an almost erotic hunger for transcendence.

We are on our way.

Coatlicue's* Rules: Advice from an Aztec Goddess

❧ Pat Mora ❧

Rule 1: Beware of offers to make you famous.
I, a pious Aztec mother doing my own housework,
am now on a pedestal, "She of the Serpent Skirt,"
hands and hearts dangling from my necklace, a faceless
statue, two snake heads eye-to-eye on my shoulders,
goddess of earth, also, death which leads to

Rule 2: Retain control of your own publicity.
The past is the present. Women are women; balls, balls.

I'm not competitive and motherhood isn't
about numbers, but four hundred sons and a daughter
may be a record even without the baby.
There's something wrong in this world
if a woman isn't safe even when she sweeps
her own house, when any speck can enter even through
the eye, I'll bet, and become a stubborn tenant.

Rule 3: Protect your uterus. Conceptions, immaculate
and otherwise, happen. Women swallow sacred
stones that fill their bellies with elbows and knees.
In Guatemala, a skull dangling from a tree whispers,
"Touch me," to a young girl, and a clear drop
drips on her palm and disappears. The dew
drops in, if you know what I mean. The saliva moved
in her, the girl says. Moved in, I say,
settled into that empty space, and grew. Men know.
They stay full of themselves, keeps occupancy down.

Rule 4: Avoid housework. Remember, I was sweeping,
humming, actually, high on Coatepec, our Serpent

Mountain, humming loud so I wouldn't hear
all those sighs inside. I was sweeping slivers,
gold and jade, picking up after four hundred sons
who think they're gods, and their spoiled sister.

I was sweep-sweeping when feathers fell on me, brushed
my face, the first light touch in years, like in a dream.
At first, I just blew them away, but then I saw it,
the prettiest ball of tiny plumes, glowing green and gold.
Gently, I gathered it. Oh, it was soft as baby hair
and brought back mother shivers when I pressed it
to my skin. I nestled it like I used to nestle them,
here, when they finished nursing. Maybe I even stroked
the roundness. I have since heard that feathers
aren't that unusual at annunciations, but I was innocent.

After I finished sweeping, I looked in vain inside
my clothes, but the soft ball had vanished, well,
descended. I think I showed within the hour,
or so it seemed. They noticed first, of course.

Rule 5: Avoid housework. It bears repeating.
I was too busy washing, cooking corn, beans, squash,
sweeping again, worrying about my daughter,
Painted with Bells, when I began to bump into their frowns
and mutterings. They kept glancing at my stomach,
started pointing. I got so hurt and mad, I started crying.
Why is it they always get to us?

One wrong word or look from any one of them doubles me over,
and I've had four hundred and one without anesthetic.
Near them I'm like a snail with no shell on a sizzling day.
They started yelling, "Wicked, wicked," and my daughter,
right there with them, my wanna-be warrior boy.
And then I heard the whispers.

The yelling was easier than, "Kill. Kill. Kill. Kill."
Kill me? Their mother? One against four hundred and one?
All I'd done was press that softness into me.

Rule 6: Listen to inside voices. You mothers know
about the baby in a family, right? Even if he hadn't talked
to me from deep inside, he would have been special.
Maybe the best. But as my name is Coatlicue, he did.
That unborn child, that started as a ball of feathers all soft
green and gold, heard my woes, and spoke to me.
A thoughtful boy. And formal too. He said, "Do not be afraid,
I know what I must do." So I stopped shaking.

Rule 7: Verify that the inside voice is yours.
I'll spare you the part about the body hacking
and head rolling. But he was provoked, remember.
All this talk of gods and goddesses distorts.

Though this planet wasn't big enough for all of us,
the whole family has done well for itself I think.
I'm the mother of stars. My daughter's white head rolls
the heavens each night, and my sons wink down at me.
What can I say—a family of high visibility.
The baby? Up there also, the sun, the real thing.
Such a god he is, of war unfortunately, and the boy
never stops, always racing across the sky,
every day of the year, a ball of fire since birth.

But I think he has forgotten me. You sense my ambivalence.
I'm blinded by his light.

Rule 8: Insist on personal interviews.
The past is the present, remember. Men carved me,
wrote my story, and Eve's, Malinche's, Guadalupe's,
Llorona's, snakes everywhere, even in our mouths.

Rule 9: Be selective about what you swallow.

Discussion Questions

1. What is your reaction to the experience that provoked Carol Christ's "anger at God"? Could you identify with her feelings? Do you find her anger to be an understandable response to the situation she describes? In your view, is it appropriately directed at God? Do you believe that similar experiences occur or might be likely to occur today?

2. In Daly's view, how did "the symbolic glorification" of women actually harm real women? Does Daly's text suggest "anger at God" such as that expressed by Carol Christ in the previous selection? In light of her critique, does it seem to you that such anger would be justified?

3. What is the link between the artistic tradition that Margaret Miles discusses, on the one hand, and violence against women, on the other? Does she establish this link convincingly, in your view? Do you agree with her argument that American popular culture exhibits evidence of this misogynist inheritance? If you do, can you give any examples of how it does so?

4. Frances Wood argues that the Black church has often been oppressive in its treatment of women. According to her, how have Black women been discouraged from speaking out against this abuse? Do you see common elements between Wood's critique

of the Black church and the analyses made by Christ, Daly, and Miles? In your view, which elements are shared and which are specific to the Black church and the situation of Black women as Woods describes it?

5. According to Jones, what has "learning feminism" involved for her? What is the relationship between the messages Jones received from her family and those she received from her church about the prospects for her future and what was expected of her? How is she helped, in college, to overcome her fear that she will never be able to find a place for herself? As she begins to experience independence and success, how does Jones's approach to her sexuality contrast with the rest of her life? What are the areas of her experience that Jones has to come to terms with as she arrives at a place of "wholeness"? What do you see as the "Tightrope" and the "Bed of Feathers" to which her title refers?

6. In her first piece, "The Issue of Woman–Man Equality in the Islamic Tradition," Riffat Hassan maintains that the Qur'an does not view women as inferior or subordinate. Why then has the Islamic tradition often presented women in that way? What is your reaction to Hassan's personal story? Can you relate to her struggle to remain faithful to Islamic tradition while seeking to reform it?

7. In "Why Women Need the Goddess," Carol Christ makes a systematic case for the psychological and political necessity of the Goddess symbol for women. Name several important ways in which, according to Christ, the Goddess symbol benefits women. Try to put them into your own words. Do you find these arguments convincing? How does Christ's advocacy of Goddess spirituality compare to the stance of thinkers like Kwok Pui-lan and Riffat Hassan, who seek to reform aspects of Christianity and Islam respectively?

8. How does Judith Plaskow's retelling of the story of Adam and Eve in the "The Coming of Lilith" compare to the version with which you may be familiar? How does the presence of Lilith disrupt the dynamic between Eve and Adam, and between the first human beings and God? What is the tone of Plaskow's story? What do you think is the purpose in envisioning a different version of human beginnings from that which is presented in the Bible itself? In an early commentary on her story, Plaskow referred to it as a myth, or creative retelling in a feminist mode, of the Biblical story. From a later perspective, however, she characterized her tale as a form of midrash. What is midrash? What do you think the author means by classifying her tale in this way?

9. What alienated Bleyer from the Judaism of her family and community in her Riot Grrl days? How does Bleyer explain her attraction to the life of the Yeshiva? Can you understand how she is able to view a life of such restrictions as part of her "ever-gnawing quest for freedom"? Bleyer seems to regard the Riot Grrl and Yeshiva ways of life as pointing in a single direction in her life. Can you find any connection between the values she discerned in these apparently opposing worldviews? From her vantage point as both a former Riot Grrl and someone who has seriously considered Orthodoxy, what is her attitude toward mainstream feminism in general and, in particular, the Jewish feminism that her generation inherited? Bleyer reports feeling "a strange mix of scorn and fondness for Orthodoxy." Does her goal for her generation of Jewish feminists, "to question the nature of all authority within our tradition," seem utopian or realistic to you? How would you contrast Bleyer's experience with Ryiah Lilith's spiritual search in a Jewish context, as described in "Challah for the Queen of Heaven"?

10. In Pat Mora's poem, "Coatlicue's Rules: Advice from an Aztec Goddess," who is speaking? What culture or tradition does she represent? What kind of story does she tell? How would you characterize the tone in which she tells it? If this person's story has been told before, what is her purpose in retelling it now? What kind of imagery does the poem

employ? How does the speaker, who is female, feel about her male counterparts? What is her advice to other females? Both this poem by Pat Mora and "The Coming of Lilith" by Judith Plaskow represent creative retellings of a culture's or a tradition's creation myth. How would you compare the two? What is the effect of such creative retellings of foundational cultural stories? Do you feel inspired to create a myth of your own?

Suggested Readings

Adams, Carol J. and Marie M. Fortune, eds. *Violence Against Women and Children: A Christian Theological Sourcebook.* New York: Continuum, 1995.

Adler, Margot. *Drawing Down the Moon: Witches, Druids, Goddess-Worshippers, and Other Pagans in America Today.* New York: Penguin/Arkana, 1997.

Adler, Rachel. *Engendering Judaism: An Inclusive Theology and Ethics.* Philadelphia: Jewish Publication Society, 1998.

Ahmed, Leila. *Women and Gender in Islam: Historical Roots of a Modern Debate.* New Haven, CT: Yale University Press, 1992.

Beauvoir, Simone de. *The Second Sex.* New York: Knopf, 1953.

Cannon, Katie G. *Black Womanist Ethics.* Atlanta: Scholars Press, 1988.

Christ, Carol P. *Diving Deep and Surfacing: Women Writers on Spiritual Quest.* Boston: Beacon, 1980.

———. *Laughter of Aphrodite: Reflections on a Journey to the Goddess.* San Francisco: Harper & Row, 1987.

———. *Odyssey with the Goddess: A Spiritual Quest in Crete.* New York: Continuum, 1995.

———. *Rebirth of the Goddess: Finding Meaning in Feminist Spirituality.* Reading, MA: Addison-Wesley, 1997.

———. "Feminist Theology as Post-Traditional Thealogy." In *The Cambridge Companion to Feminist Theology,* Susan Frank Parsons, ed., Cambridge, UK: Cambridge University Press, 2002, 79–96.

———. *She Who Changes: Re-imagining the Divine in the World.* New York: Palgrave Macmillan, 2003.

Christ, Carol P. and Judith Plaskow, eds. *Womanspirit Rising: A Feminist Reader in Religion.* San Francisco: Harper & Row, 1979.

Daly, Mary. *The Church and the Second Sex.* New York: Harper & Row, 1968.

———. *Beyond God the Father: Toward a Philosophy of Women's Liberation.* Boston: Beacon, 1973.

———. *Gyn/ecology: The Metaethics of Radical Feminism.* Boston: Beacon, 1978.

———. *Pure Lust: Elemental Feminist Philosophy.* Boston: Beacon, 1984.

———. *Outercourse: The Be-dazzling Voyage.* San Francisco: HarperSanFrancisco, 1992.

———. *Quintessence—Realizing the Archaic Future: A Radical Elemental Feminist Manifesto.* Boston: Beacon, 1998.

Daly, Mary and Jane Caputi. *Webster's First New Intergalactic Wickedary of the English Language.* Boston: Beacon, 1987.

Dame, Enid, Lilly Rivlin, and Henny Wenkart, eds. *Which Lilith?: Feminist Writers Re-create the World's First Woman.* Northvale, NJ: Jason Aronson, 1998.

Douglass, Kelly Brown. *Sexuality and the Black Church.* Maryknoll, NY: Orbis, 1999.

Downing, Christine. *The Goddess: Mythological Images of the Feminine.* New York: Continuum, 2000.

Eller, Cynthia. *Living in the Lap of the Goddess: The Feminist Spirituality Movement in America.* New York: Crossroad, 1993.

Fletcher, Karen Baker. *Sisters of Dust, Sisters of Spirit: Womanist Wordings on God and Creation.* Minneapolis, MN: Fortress, 1998.

Fiorenza, Elisabeth Schüssler and M. Shawn Copeland, eds. *Violence Against Women.* Maryknoll, NY: Orbis, 1994.

Goldenberg, Naomi. *The Changing of the Gods: Feminism and the End of Traditional Religions.* Boston: Beacon, 1979.

Hackett, Jo Ann. "In the Days of Jael: Reclaiming the History of Women in Ancient Israel." In *Immaculate and Powerful: The Female in Sacred Image and Social Reality,* Clarissa W. Atkinson et al., eds., Boston: Beacon, 1985, 15–38.

Hoagland, Sarah Lucia and Marilyn Frye, eds. *Feminist Interpretations of Mary Daly.* University Park: Pennsylvania State University Press, 2000.

Howland, Courtney W., ed. *Religious Fundamentalisms and the Human Rights of Women.* New York: Palgrave, 1999.

Journal of Feminist Theology: The Journal of the Britain and Ireland School of Feminist Theology 24 (2000) [devoted to Mary Daly].

Madsen, Catherine. "The Thin Thread of Conversation: An Interview with Mary Daly." *Cross Currents* 50 (2000): 332–348.

Michem, Stephanie. *Introducing Womanist Theology.* Maryknoll, NY: Orbis, 2002.

Miles, Margaret. *Seeing and Believing: Religion and Values in the Movies.* Boston: Beacon, 1996.

Nadell, Pamela. *Women Who Would Be Rabbis: A History of Women's Ordination, 1889–1995.* Boston: Beacon, 1998.

Nason-Clark, Nancy. "Woman Abuse and Faith Communities: Religion, Violence, and the Provision of Social Welfare." In *Religion and Social Policy*, Paula D. Nesbitt, ed., Walnut Creek, CA: AltaMira, 2001, 128–145.

Orion, Loretta. *Never Again the Burning Times: Paganism Revived.* Prospect Heights, IL: Waveland, 1995.

Plaskow, Judith. *Standing Again at Sinai: Judaism from a Feminist Perspective.* San Francisco: HarperSanFrancisco, 1990.

Plaskow, Judith and Carol P. Christ, eds. *Weaving the Visions: New Patterns in Feminist Spirituality.* San Francisco: Harper & Row, 1989.

Rigney, Barbara. *Lilith's Daughters: Women and Religion in Contemporary Fiction.* Madison: University of Wisconsin Press, 1982.

Roald, Anne Sofie. *Women in Islam: The Western Experience.* New York: Routledge, 2001.

Ross, Rosetta E. *Witnessing and Testifying: Black Women, Religion, and Civil Rights.* Minneapolis, MN: Fortress, 2003.

Ruether, Rosemary. "The Western Religious Tradition and Violence Against Women in the Home." In *Christianity, Patriarchy, and Abuse*, Joanne Carlson Brown and Carole R. Bohn, eds., New York: Pilgrim Press, 1989, 31–41.

Russell, Letty, Kwok Pui-lan, Ada Maria Isasi-Diaz, and Katie Cannon, eds. *Inheriting Our Mothers' Gardens: Feminist Theology in Third World Perspective.* Louisville, KY: Westminster, 1988.

Salomonsen, Jone. *Enchanted Feminism: Ritual, Gender and Divinity among the Reclaiming Witches of San Francisco.* New York: Routledge, 2002.

Stanton, Elizabeth Cady. *The Woman's Bible.* Boston: Northeastern University Press, 1993.

Webb, Gisela, ed. *Windows of Faith: Muslim Women Scholar-Activists in North America.* Syracuse, NY: Syracuse University Press, 2000.

Web Sites

Bridges: A Journal for Jewish Feminists and Our Friends, http://bridgesjournal.org/
Center for the Prevention of Sexual and Domestic Violence (now known as Faith Trust
Institute), http://www.cpsdv.org/
Covenant of the Goddess, CoGWeb, http://www.cog.org/
Fanya Gottesfeld Heller Center for the Study of Women in Judaism, Bar-Ilan University,
http://www.biu.ac.il/JS/jwmn/
Hadassah-Brandeis Institute, Brandeis University, http://www.brandeis.edu/hirjw/about.html
Islam for Today, Women in Islam, http://www.islamfortoday.com/women.htm
Jewish Feminist Resources, http://www.jew-feminist-resources.com/index.html
Lilith: The Independent Jewish Women's Magazine, http://www.lilithmag.com/
Maryams.net, Muslim Women and Their Islam, http://www.maryams.net/
Muslim Women's League, http://www.mwlusa.org
RCG San Antonio (The Re-Formed Congregation of the Goddess), http://rcgsa.org/index.html
Resources for and about Muslim Women, http://www.jannah.org/sisters/index.html
SisterSpirit, http://home.teleport.com/~sistersp/
Under Shekhina's Wings, Cross-Cultural Women's Spirituality, http://www.geocities.com/
Athens/1501/
University of California at Santa Barbara, Black Feminism Bibliography, "Womanist Spirituality
and God-talk," http://www.library.ucsb.edu/subjects/blackfeminism/ah_womanisttheol.html
Weisbard, Phyllis Holman. "Annotated Bibliography and Guide to Archival Resources on the
History of Jewish Women in America," University of Wisconsin, http://www.library.wisc
.edu/libraries/WomensStudies/jewwom/jwmain.htm

PART III

EMBODYING OUR HOPE

so they went out
clay and morning star
following the bright back
of the woman

as she walked past
the cherubim
turning their fiery swords
past the winged gate

into the unborn world
chaos fell away
before her like a cloud
and everywhere seemed light

seemed glorious
seemed very eden

—LUCILLE CLIFTON, "the story thus far"

Nelle Morton's "The Goddess as Metaphoric Image," which begins Part III, is an early piece in feminist theology by one of the field's founding mothers. It points the way to several topics that have been more fully elaborated as the field was developed. These include: women's discovery of the power of community, the claiming of the body and affirmation of female sexuality, the search for analogs of our experience in the myths of traditional societies, and the use of goddess imagery as a tool for psychological and emotional healing. Because Morton's approach is eclectic, searching for images in a variety of traditions, this piece can be compared fruitfully with the work by Sandra Cisneros, who elaborates a kind of goddess devotion from within her own Mexican American heritage. Morton's piece may also be compared to the selection by Judith Plaskow, who argues for a basis for sexual affirmation *within* the Jewish tradition. Morton, by way of contrast, writes here that the God of patriarchal religions "has become a dead metaphor."

The essay "Guadalupe the Sex Goddess," by Mexican American writer Sandra Cisneros, illustrates some of the themes of feminist theology as reflected in the work of a creative writer. Cisneros, like the farm worker María Elena Lucas, whose reflections appear in Part I, speaks from within the context of her Latina heritage, seeking to interpret the image of the Virgin of Guadalupe as a model for her own empowerment. But whereas Lucas's language and assumptions remain within a traditional Roman Catholic framework, Cisneros, like Carol Christ, makes a case for why women might "need the goddess." Like Nelle Morton in the preceding selection, she sees in the goddess image a bridge back to her woman-self and her female body. Cisneros' language is direct and compelling, and more sexually charged than in any of the other selections; for her the reclaimed Guadalupe image serves as a mirror in which to view herself as a woman and a sexual being.

Irene Monroe is an African American writer, educator, activist, and, in her own characterization, public theologian. In the interview included here, she envisions a society free of hierarchies of oppression and describes her pastoral and educational work within Black churches to that end.

Monroe critiques the way in which Black churches have simultaneously included and marginalized their homosexual members, as well as the exclusion of the queer voice from womanist discourse. At the same time, she makes clear her own continuing commitment to the Black Church, seeing her connection to it, and to the experience of the people who attend it, as a precondition to her ability to offer such critiques. Monroe's own story, as related here, provides a dramatic example of personal rejection based on sexual orientation. Her refusal to closet herself as a lesbian in order to further her professional goals is linked, theologically, to her sense of the struggle for gay rights and gay inclusion as a prophetic movement.

Monroe's vision is future-oriented, action-oriented, and hopeful, notwithstanding the vicissitudes of her own experience. Of the inclusive paradigm she envisions in the arenas of womanism, Black theology, and the queer movement, she says, "Presently, it's not there. We have to create it ourselves."

In "Toward a New Theology of Sexuality," Judith Plaskow argues that Judaism has turned away from a definition of sexuality that emphasizes mutuality, self-expression, and positive energy, to a perspective that sees sexuality, especially women's sexuality, as something that must be controlled and expressed only within heterosexual marriage. She proposes a new theology based on a feminist definition of sexuality as "part of a continuum of embodied self-expression ... [and] erotic energy that ideally suffuses all activities in our life." Plaskow advocates "living dangerously ... choosing to take responsibility for working through the possible consequences of sexual feeling rather than repressing sexual feeling and thus feeling more generally." For her, "to be alive is to be sexually alive." Sexuality, the erotic, energizes bonds to others and to God and, thus, is deeply connected to spirituality. Ultimately, Plaskow's piece rests on a rejection of mind–body duality and celebrates sexuality as a source of knowledge about the self, the world, and God.

In an excerpt from "The Good Mother: From Gaia to Gilead," Ellen Cronan Rose discusses dangers she sees in the use of the term *mother earth* by some ecofeminists. Identifying woman with nature has been used to exploit and oppress women. Some feminists have tried to reclaim this identity as a way to assert women's positive qualities and their superiority over men. For Rose, however, imagining Earth as "mother" may reinforce a definition of women primarily in terms of their maternal roles, and may also reflect fear of the power of women's reproductive capacities. She notes that these images of women have currency in a culture in which "male views of mothers' value prevail" and women's reproductive freedoms are compromised under the guise of "protecting" them. Rose's article brings together a focus on the connections between ecofeminism and feminist spirituality with a critical examination of the identification of woman with nature raised by Sherry Ortner in her classic essay "Is Female to Male as Nature Is to Culture?" (Ortner 1974).

The last selection in this part is by Rosemary Radford Ruether, a leading figure in feminist theology and one of its most prolific theorists. In linking religious and environmental issues in these excerpts from *Gaia and God: An Ecofeminist Theology of Earth Healing*, she writes that "Western cultural traditions . . . , of which Christianity is a major expression, have justified and sacralized . . . relationships of domination." She also argues that while women have often been victimized within this context, those of us who are the inheritors of the Western tradition, women as well as men, must take responsibility for it and for the destruction which it has wrought. The discussion in this selection focuses on problems that are societal and planetary in scope. In that way it is different from the other selections in this book that, while offering social and cultural critique, tend to take the individual as the primary unit of analysis. Ruether, like many other writers on ecofeminism, extends the reach of a feminist theological analysis to questions concerning the human relationship to Nature, and raises questions about the consequences that our religious traditions and cultural practices may have for it and for us.

References

Clifton, Lucille. 2000. the story thus far. In Lucille Clifton, *Blessing the Boats: New and Selected Poems 1988–2000*. Rochester, NY: BOA Editions, Ltd., 80.

Ortner, Sherry. 1974. Is female to male as nature is to culture? In M. Z. Rosaldo and L. Lamphere, eds., *Woman, Culture, and Society*, 67–87. Stanford, CA: Stanford University Press.

The Goddess as Metaphoric Image*

❖ *Nelle Morton* ❖

When I speak of the Goddess as metaphoric image I am in no way referring to an entity "out there" who appears miraculously as a fairy godmother and turns the pumpkin into a carriage. I am not even referring to a Goddess "back there" as if I participate in resurrecting an ancient religion. In the sense that I am woman I see the Goddess in myself, but I need something tangible, a concrete image or a concrete event, to capture my full attention to the present and draw me into the metaphoric process. . . .

The context in which I experienced the Goddess the first time grew out of a kind of unconscious awareness that, even though conceptually I no longer accepted a God "out there" nor defined a "God within" as male, on the level of imagery the maleness was still alive and functioning in me on most unexpected occasions.

In 1972 at Grailville the second national conference on women exploring theology was held. One morning its sixty-five or so women delegates gathered for worship sitting informally in semicircular fashion on the floor of the oratory. The atmosphere of conditioned meditation—soft lighting, high altar up front, much space—was bypassed by the women perhaps intuitively, perhaps by overt intent of the leaders. A space indicated by cushions on the floor set aside was marked off as sacred. A screen hid the phallic symbol up front. A bouquet of wildflowers on the low table in front of the screen added to the informality. The women faced one another.

Most of us did not understand at the beginning what was taking place. I was aware early, however, that something new and different was happening to me—something far more than the caring I experienced in the presence of an all-woman community. The climax came near the end when the leader said: "Now, SHE is a new creation." It was not something I heard with my ears, or something I reasoned, or something I was being told. Everything seemed to coalesce and I felt hit in the pit of my stomach. It was as if the leader had said, "You are now coming into your full humanity. That which has been programmed out is authentically yours—essentially you." It was as if intimate, infinite, and transcending power had enfolded me, as if great wings had spread themselves around the seated women and gathered us into a oneness. There were no ifs or buts. I was not hearing a masculine word from a male priest, a male rabbi, or a male minister. I was sensing something direct and powerful—not filtered by the necessity to transfer or translate from male experience and mentality into a female experience and then apply to myself. The words used in the service were exclusively female words.

Suddenly I came to, my hand on my stomach, my mouth open. I was almost sure I had said aloud, "Oh!" I wondered if I had made a fool of myself! When I looked about me, it seemed many other women were responding as I had. The leader paused. Then one of the women lifted her fist into the air and shouted "Yeah! Yeah!" All the women followed as the oratory rang with "Yeah! YEAH! YEAH!"

That is the first time I *experienced* a female deity. I had conceptualized one before, but I had not experienced one directly. It was also the first time I realized how deeply I had internalized the maleness of the patriarchal god and that in so doing I had evoked cosmic support of male rulership of the earth and had reneged on my own woman identity. Not until that moment did I realize that women had no cosmic advocate in any of the five major patriarchal religions of the world. I knew that I had much unfinished business, which I have been working on now for ten years.

My second experience of the Goddess occurred in 1976. I had already moved to a retirement community in California. In August, en route to Dublin to address the World Federation of Methodist Women, I had stopped at Grailville as resource leader to the Seminary Quarter for Women. Soon after my flight to New York had left the Cincinnati airport, the sky turned dark and we were caught in extremely turbulent weather. All my life I had been frightened of heights. I couldn't remember a time when I was at ease in the air—even in smooth skies. I must have had some traumatic experience with heights when a child, since each time I boarded a plane I reverted to a most irrational state, far from the mature faith I considered I now had. Usually I clasped my hands together and called on the powerful male deity in the sky for protection. I must have reverted to the faith I had when the phobia first latched itself in my unconscious; the phobia and the child faith images surfaced simultaneously. I usually asked the God Father to keep the plane safe. I even made promises and confessed my wrongdoing. I always asked safety for others in the plane and for all the planes flying as "He had the whole world in His hands." Once seized by such fear I had to keep up the pleas for safety throughout the journey. Then at the end of the journey, there was always much thanking to do.

In this particular storm en route to New York I decided it was past time to let my mature intelligent self take over. The thought came—what would happen if I invoked the Goddess! How does one call on the Goddess anyway? And which Goddess? I no sooner had such a thought than I leaned back in my seat and closed my eyes. Suddenly, it was as if someone had cased into the vacant seat next to me and placed her hand on my arm. "Relax," she said. "Let go of all your tightness. Feel your weight heavy against the seat and your feet heavy on the floor. The air has waves as does the ocean. You can't see them, but if you let yourself be carried by them you can feel their rhythm—even in turbulence. The pilot has been here before. He knows what he is doing. Even in the worst weather. Ever so faintly . . . now . . . can you feel the currents, the ordinary currents of the air? Now breathe, breathe deeply. Ride the waves. Let yourself become a part of the rhythm."

I did as she directed. Fear left my muscles. I did indeed feel the rhythm. Soon, I was enjoying the ride. Then came the question, How does one thank the Goddess? I opened my eyes. The seat was vacant. She had gone. I began to feel such power within, as if she had given me myself. She had called up my own energy. I was unafraid. Nor have I been afraid in a plane since that day. A new thing I recognized immediately: the Goddess works herself out of business. She doesn't hang around to receive thanks. It appears to be thanks enough for her that another woman has come into her own. I did not feel guilty. . . .

It was midafternoon some years later. I sat in my living room in a large armchair with my feet on a hassock, facing windows that opened onto the street. I could not throw off a blueness that had nagged me off and on all day. As I relaxed, I decided to give myself to it wholly, go to the root of it, release its energy and learn at least why it had not let go of me. As I began following it down, ready to face most anything to be rid of it, I thought of the Goddess and how she had come to my rescue on the plane, and nurtured me in other situations. As I let go and opened myself to her, in she swept suddenly through the left side of the windows in front of me. As she reached my chair she stepped aside, bowed my mother into the room, then disappeared. My mother floated in on a river of blood. It seemed all the blood in front of her was blood she had shed in her lifetime, and behind her, all the blood I had shed. She came directly to my chair, bent over me, and began speaking: "Nelle, I have made a great mistake with you children. I have allowed you to think—no, I have *taught* you—that menstruation is an illness. You were the oldest and I did learn something from you, but you suffered more than your two sisters. Never did I let you go swimming, play tennis, or hike during your periods. I didn't even let you do dishes, or take your turn with the chores about the house. It seemed the more I cared for you, the more pain your period brought. Huge clots of blood could not be absorbed by any napkin. Often the first day you had to miss school. Many times we had to have a doctor give you a shot, the pain was so intense. He kept promising that having a baby would be your only cure. Not only did you learn from me that menstruation was an illness but also that it was something to be ashamed of.

"I began sensing my mistake when you reached menopause and your doctor suggested that your dread of menopausal distress might be due to internalized negative attitudes toward blood and the body. He then proposed you purchase bath oils, bubble bath soap, bath powders, and luxuriate in your body, revel in its sensuousness. You did and have never to this day had a hot flash. Now I have learned that many of these conditions derived from patriarchal attitudes toward women and the mysterious power women possess. While I had these negative attitudes and passed them on to you girls, you, Nelle, internalized them—so deeply that they are now in your very bone marrow and too deep to be exorcised.

"Remember years ago your doctor prescribed sperm to start a baby. Now another doctor has fed you male hormones for six years. Both referred you to a male for a cure of patriarchal attitudes. Ha! Forget it! And forget all this visualizing of whole red blood cells which you will never have. Remember the hematologist who described your cells as shown under a microscope—'wild and bizarre.' Be thankful for your 'wild and bizarre' blood cells. They are keeping you alive. They are now normal for you."

My depression lifted immediately as I received this beautiful gift from my mother. I jumped from my chair and kissed her on the mouth, which she had never allowed us to do because of a lung disease she feared she might transmit to us. But in that kiss I had all the loving hugs she had ever given me. Then she disappeared.

Immediately on the right side of the window appeared an enormous spider with a gray body and large orange legs. She lifted one leg high above the other as she walked toward me on the darkness. I was not afraid, somehow. As the spider reached me she held out her two front legs on which hung some woven material. All she said was, "Your mother spun this for you." As I took the material the spider dissolved into me, as did the Goddess and then my mother. I opened my eyes. It was dark outside. My entire attitude toward my illness had changed. But I remained puzzled by the spun cloth, which was neither practical nor by my standards particularly beautiful.

In not one of the above incidents was the Goddess actually summoned or invoked. Therefore, her coming, and the way she came in each case, was a surprise. . . . My greatest surprise and shock came perhaps in the last experience—the surprise of relating my internalized male attitudes toward women's blood to my present very serious blood difficulty—"too deep to exorcise." I am able now to receive the "bizarre and wild cells" as a special gift. In that sense the Goddess gave me back my life and called me to live fully with what I have, adjusting my activities to what energy I can summon and use creatively. Since then I have resumed my writing. I participate in social and political issues as I am able. It is as if the Goddess restored that part of myself that was wasted with fear from false images in my unconscious.

I began to see more clearly how we act out of images rather than concepts, especially in crisis situations; how the fear of heights automatically summoned up the God-image I had as a child when the phobia first planted itself as image deep in my unconscious. The Goddess caused the old image to surface and shatter so I could experience the flight from a more mature perspective which in many ways was mine already, but unused. I began to see more clearly how the God of patriarchal religions could have been a living metaphor at one time. But over the centuries the word has been filled with such male, power-over, and status quo images it has become a dead metaphor.

The Goddess ushered in a reality that respects the sacredness of my existence, that gives me self-esteem so I can perceive the universe and its people through my woman-self and not depend on the perception conditioned by patriarchal culture and patriarchal religion. I do not have to receive my identity or renew it through another gender, be the representative of that gender a minister, father, boss, professor, colleague, husband, or male lover. As I see the gift of myself aborted by social and political structures I renew my responsibility to the world—to help break the patriarchy that creates discriminations, oppressions, poverty, and wars. These for me have become woman issues and never again "causes." I perceive the world and its people from the perspective of where women have been put as women in the hierarchy.

The Goddess introduced me to a profound sense of community I had never before experienced. The bonding of women—from that small group at Grailville in 1972 to the small ritual, working, and action groups to which I now belong and the celebrating groups and the networks of women across the country and even around the world—continuously energizes and supports me. Beyond these groups, or because of them, rises the vision of what women can be and will become as we receive our full humanity and achieve political power. The vision enlarges to include those women still blinded by the patriarchal fog, and imprisoned in a seemingly unbreakable vise. There is something of the past the vision resurrects (as Virginia Woolf urges us to resurrect Shakespeare's sister). Our research in history, literature, theology, and other fields is beginning to break open the tombs of our foresisters and enable them to walk the earth again, to claim the earth as sacred and for the good, health, and justice of all people.

The Goddess has cleared away much of the theological mystification to which I had subjected myself—which kept me from seeing and enjoying the sheer humanness of another as we came into physical proximity. Human beings did not come from another world nor are we headed for one. Nor did we descend from the sky but out of the womb of our mother, our mother's mother, and our mother's mother's mother. Recognizing our origin, we experience *presence*. . . . This kind of physical experience that is nourishing and loving and in touch with cosmic energy rises out of our common bonding and vision and our rootedness in the earth. Julia Kristeva pointed out that such an experience is answerable to a logic other than scientific," that it is experience dedicated to the search for "a little more truth" and for power shared and power from within rather than power-over.

Since the Goddess works herself out of the picture, we are better able to come into our full and whole inheritance that would make us one in our bodies, minds, and spirits. We can claim our sexuality as pervasive and as ourselves. We can claim our bodies as ours and as ourselves and our minds as our own and ourselves. This sense of oneness within and with one another has brought us into more erotic relationship with one another as women. For once a woman comes to see beauty in another woman's mind and in her own mind and to love with the mind, she discovers another dimension of power that is self-fulfilling.

The Goddess shattered the image of myself as a dependent person and cleared my brain so I could come into the power that was mine, that was me all along, but that could never have been appropriated until the old limiting image was exorcised or shattered.

The last experience with the Goddess ushering in my mother has proved most profound of all—the gift of my mother herself. Since blood is a powerful symbol of life, I see her blood as saying she has rebirthed me, and my blood as saying I have given birth to my mother. The kiss, still vivid, remains the seal of that blood covenant.

The spider! Surprise again! Who could have imagined a spider in this sequence! Especially one so large (about my size), orange and gray with elegant long legs stepping so lightly on the dark, and one which did not evoke fear!

I have not been able to identify the spider scientifically. The spider that comes closest to her color and shape is a tiny American House Spider—the *Sisyphoides*—a cobweb weaver. But since the Goddess does not allow herself to be limited to patriarchal time or space, the myth of the spider should be much more fruitful than the scientific identification or study of it.

Several tribes of the early American Indians, especially the Hopi, reverenced the Spider Woman as Creator of the earth and all underneath the earth. Making her home underneath the earth, she was known as the Earth Mother, "as old as time . . . as young as eternity." She was said to croon, "I receive Light and nourish Life. I am the Mother of all that shall ever come." Yet the Spider Woman resided in the Underground.

The Mexicans saw the spider in a great hole in the west where the sun went down and perceived her as an archetypal womb sucking into death all who have ever been born. The Aztecs called her the "place of the Women" from which all humankind once crawled. The spider as this womb represented life and "time before time . . . before the birth of the sun."

As Goddess of life and death the spider was also the Great Mother, a spinner of destiny. The new child is the fabric of her body or, to turn that about, the fabric of her body is the new child. Finally, the Spider Goddess appears as a "journey or a way, always as walked or danced archetype," as labyrinth or spiral.

Relating myth to my experience, I see that the spider's prominent legs "walking on the darkness" affirm my journey; the spun cloth—fabric of my mother's body—affirms my own new birth. Yet the cloth being not usable in patriarchal time and space, and the Goddess not limited to time or space, the cloth could have a double meaning—death as well as birth. Since I possess no tangible evidence of the cloth, it must have disappeared in me along with the Goddess, my mother, and the spider. So *I am the new child.*

The afternoon's journey brought the relationship with my mother into sharp consciousness. "The true mystery," declared Erich Neumann, "through which the primordial situation is restored on a new plane is this: the daughter becomes identical with the mother [and she is] transformed in every respect. This unity . . . is the central content of the Eleusinian mysteries."

The triple appearance of the Goddess—as herself, as my mother, as the spider— and ME! Blessed thrice! . . .

The appearance of the Goddess in the present wave of the woman movement looms as an important phenomenon and promises to become more so as the people of the world turn to our own inner power and integrity. . . . The Goddess has begun to expose the artificiality in the elaborate hierarchical system of a male-oriented deity. But perhaps the most important function of the Goddess is the transformation of women ourselves. . . . The reappearance of the Goddess at this time in history takes on profound metaphorical significance and global proportions. Women are no longer minus a cosmic advocate, rooted in creation itself, to provide legitimation for and to affirm our experiences.

Guadalupe the Sex Goddess

❖ *Sandra Cisneros* ❖

In high school I marveled at how white women strutted around the locker room, nude as pearls, as unashamed of their brilliant bodies as the Nike of Samothrace. Maybe they were hiding terrible secrets like bulimia or anorexia, but to my naive eye then, I thought of them as women comfortable in their skin.

You could always tell us Latinas. We hid when we undressed, modestly facing a wall, or, in my case, dressing in a bathroom stall. We were the ones who still used bulky sanitary pads instead of tampons, thinking ourselves morally superior to our white classmates. *My mama said you can't use tampons till after you're married.* All Latina mamas said this, yet how come none of us thought to ask our mothers why they didn't use tampons *after* getting married?

Womanhood was full of mysteries. I was as ignorant about my own body as any female ancestor who hid behind a sheet with a hole in the center when husband or doctor called. Religion and our culture, our culture and religion, helped to create that blur, a vagueness about what went on "down there." (So ashamed was I about my own "down there" that until I was an adult I had no idea I had another orifice called the vagina; I thought my period would arrive via the urethra or perhaps through the walls of my skin.)

No wonder, then, it was too terrible to think about a doctor—a man—looking at you down there when you could never bring yourself to look yourself. *¡Ay, nunca!* How could I acknowledge my sexuality, let alone enjoy sex, with so much guilt? In the guise of modesty my culture locked me in a double chastity belt of ignorance and *vergüenza*, shame.

I had never seen my mother nude. I had never taken a good look at myself either. Privacy for self-exploration belonged to the wealthy. In my home a private space was practically impossible; aside from the doors that opened to the street, the only room with a lock was the bathroom, and how could anyone who shared a bathroom with eight other people stay in there for more than a few minutes? Before college, no one in my family had a room of their own except me, a narrow closet just big enough for my twin bed and an oversized blond dresser we'd bought in the bargain basement of *el Sears*. The dresser was as long as a coffin and blocked the door from shutting completely. I had my own room, but I never had the luxury of shutting the door.

I didn't even see my own sex until a nurse at an Emma Goldman Clinic showed it to me—*Would you like to see your cervix? Your os is dilating. You must be ovulating. Here's a mirror, take a look.* When had anyone ever suggested I take a look or allowed me a speculum to take home and investigate myself at leisure!

I'd only been to one other birth control facility prior to the Emma Goldman Clinic, the university medical center in grad school. I was twenty-one, in a strange town far from home for the first time. I was afraid and I was ashamed to seek out a gynecologist, but I was more afraid of becoming pregnant. Still, I agonized about going for weeks. Perhaps the anonymity and distance from my family allowed me finally to take control of my life. I remember wanting to be fearless like the other women around me, to be able to have sex when I wanted, but I was too afraid to explain to a would-be lover how I'd only had one other man in my life and we'd practiced withdrawal. Would he laugh at me? How could I look anyone in the face and explain why I couldn't go see a gynecologist?

One night a classmate I liked too much took me home with him. I meant all along to say something about how I wasn't on anything, but I never quite found my voice, never the right moment to cry out—*Stop, this is dangerous to my brilliant career!* Too afraid to sound stupid, afraid to ask him to take responsibility too, I said nothing, and I let him take me like that with nothing protecting me from motherhood but luck. The days that followed were torture, but fortunately on Mother's Day my period arrived, and I celebrated my nonmaternity by making an appointment with the family-planning center.

When I see pregnant teens, I can't help but think that could've been me. In high school I would've thrown myself into love the way some warriors throw themselves into fighting. I was ready to sacrifice everything in the name of love, to do anything, even risk my own life, but thankfully there were no takers. I was enrolled at an all-girls' school. I think if I had met a boy who would have me, I would've had sex in a minute, convinced this was love. I have always had enough imagination to fall in love all by myself, then and now.

I tell you this story because I am overwhelmed by the silence regarding Latinas and our bodies. If I, as a graduate student, was shy about talking to anyone about my body and sex, imagine how difficult it must be for a young girl in middle school or high school living in a home with no lock on the bedroom door, perhaps with no door, or maybe with no bedroom, no information other than misinformation from the girlfriends and the boyfriend. So much guilt, so much silence, and such a yearning to be loved; no wonder young women find themselves having sex while they are still children, having sex without sexual protection, too ashamed to confide their feelings and fears to anyone.

What a culture of denial. Don't get pregnant! But no one tells you how not to. This is why I was angry for so many years every time I saw *la Virgen de Guadalupe*, my culture's role model for brown women like me. She was damn dangerous, an ideal so lofty and unrealistic it was laughable. Did boys have to aspire to be Jesus? I never saw any evidence of it. They were fornicating like rabbits while the Church ignored them and pointed us women toward our destiny—marriage and motherhood. The other alternative was *puta*hood.

In my neighborhood I knew only real women, neither saints nor whores, naive and vulnerable *buerquitas* like me who wanted desperately to fall in love, with the heart and soul. And yes, with the *panocha*, too.

As far as I could see, *la Lupe* was nothing but a goody two shoes meant to doom me to a life of unhappiness. Thanks but no thanks. Motherhood and/or marriage were anathema to my career. But being a bad girl, that was something I could use as a writer, a Molotov to toss at my papa and *el Papa* who had their own plans for me.

Discovering sex was like discovering writing. It was powerful in a way I couldn't explain. Like writing, you had to go beyond the guilt and shame to get to anything good. Like writing, it could take you to deep and mysterious subterranean levels. With each new depth I found out things about myself I didn't know I knew. And, like writing, for a slip of a moment it could be spiritual, the cosmos pivoting on a pin, could empty and fill you all at once like a Ganges, a Piazzolla tango, a tulip bending in the wind. I was no one, I was nothing, and I was everything in the universe little and large—twig, cloud, sky. How had this incredible energy been denied me!

When I look at *la Virgen de Guadalupe* now, she is not the Lupe of my childhood, no longer the one in my grandparents' house in Tepeyac, nor is she the one of the Roman Catholic Church, the one I bolted the door against in my teens and twenties. Like every woman who matters to me, I have had to search for her in the rubble of history. And I have found her. She is Guadalupe the sex goddess, a goddess who makes me feel good about my sexual power, my sexual energy, who reminds me I must, as Clarissa Pinkola Estés so aptly put it, "[speak] from the vulva . . . speak the most basic, honest truth," and write from my *panocha.*

In my research of Guadalupe's pre-Columbian antecedents, the she before the Church desexed her, I found Tonantzin, and inside Tonantzin a pantheon of other mother goddesses. I discovered Tlazolteotl, the goddess of fertility and sex, also referred to as Totzin, Our Beginnings, or Tzinteotl, goddess of the rump. *Putas*, nymphos, and other loose women were known as "women of the sex goddess." Tlazolteotl was the patron of sexual passion, and though she had the power to stir you to sin, she could also forgive you and cleanse you of your sexual transgressions via her priests who heard confession. In this aspect of confessor Tlazolteotl was known as Tlaelcuani, the filth eater. Maybe you've seen her; she's the one sold in the tourist markets even now, a statue of a woman squatting in childbirth, her face grimacing in pain. Tlazolteotl, then, is a duality of maternity *and* sexuality. In other words, she is a sexy mama.

To me *la Virgen de Guadalupe* is also Coatlicue, the creative/destructive goddess. When I think of the Coatlicue statue in the National Museum in Mexico City, so terrible it was unearthed and then reburied because it was too frightening to look at, I think of a woman enraged, a woman as tempest, a woman *bien berrinchuda*, and I like that. *La Lupe* as *cabrona.* Not silent and passive, but silently gathering force.

Most days I, too, feel like the creative/destructive goddess Coatlicue, especially the days I'm writing, capable of fabricating pretty tales with pretty words, as well as doing demolition work with a volley of *palabrotas* if I want to. I am the Coatlicue-Lupe whose square column of a body I see in so many Indian women, in my mother, and in myself each time I check out my thick-waisted, flat-assed torso in the mirror.

Coatlicue, Tlazolteotl, Tonantzin, *la Virgen de Guadalupe.* They are each telescoped one into the other, into who I am. And this is where *la Lupe* intrigues me—not the Lupe of 1531 who appeared to Juan Diego, but the one of the 1990s who has shaped who we are as Chicanas/*mexicanas* today, the one inside each Chicana and *mexicana.* Perhaps it's the Tlazolteotl-Lupe in me whose *malcriada* spirit inspires me to leap into the swimming pool naked or dance on a table with a skirt on my head. Maybe it's my Coatlicue-Lupe attitude that makes it possible for my mother to tell me, *No wonder men can't stand you.* Who knows? What I do know is this; I am obsessed with becoming a woman comfortable in her skin.

I can't attribute my religious conversion to a flash of lightning on the road to Laredo or anything like that. Instead, there have been several lessons learned subtly over a period of time. A grave depression and near suicide in my thirty-third year and its subsequent retrospection. Vietnamese Buddhist monk Thich Nhat Hanh's writing that has brought out the Buddha-Lupe in me. My weekly peace vigil for my friend Jasna in Sarajevo. The writings of Gloria Anzaldúa. A crucial trip back to Tepeyac in 1985 with Cherríe Moraga and Norma Alarcón. Drives across Texas talking with other Chicanas. And research for stories that would force me back inside the Church from which I'd fled.

My *Virgen de Guadalupe* is not the mother of God. She is God. She is a face for a god without a face, an *indígena* for a god without ethnicity, a female deity for a god who is genderless, but I also understand that for her to approach me, for me to finally open the door and accept her, she had to be a woman like me.

Once, watching a porn film, I saw a sight that terrified me. It was the film star's *panocha*—a tidy, elliptical opening, pink and shiny like a rabbit's ear. To make matters worse, it was shaved and looked especially childlike and unsexual. I think what startled me most was the realization that my own sex has no resemblance to this woman's. My sex, dark as an orchid, rubbery and blue purple as *pulpo*, an octopus, does not look nice and tidy, but otherworldly. I do not have little rosette nipples. My nipples are big and brown, like the Mexican coins of my childhood.

When I see *la Virgen de Guadalupe* I want to lift her dress as I did my dolls' and look to see if she comes with *chones*, and does her *panocha* look like mine, and does she have dark nipples too? Yes, I am certain she does. She is not neuter like Barbie. She gave birth. She has a womb. *Blessed art thou and blessed is the fruit of thy womb . . .* Blessed art thou, Lupe, and, therefore, blessed am I.

Rev. Irene Monroe

❧ *Gary David Comstock* ❧

Irene Monroe is a Ph.D. candidate in the Religion, Gender, and Culture Program at Harvard Divinity School. Her community activities in the Boston area have included Christian education ministry with Old Cambridge Baptist Church's high-school-age parishioners, assistant pastoring at United Baptist Church in Jamaica Plain, and serving on the advisory board of the Women's Theological Center. In 1997, *Boston Magazine* presented her as one of "The 50 Most Intriguing Women in Boston"; in 1998, she was selected to be a Grand Marshall of the Boston Gay Pride parade; in 1999, *OUT Magazine* named her as one of the 100 queer "People Who Rocked 1998" and PBS featured her in its gay newsmagazine *In the Life*.

Several newspapers have covered her life and work. The *Boston Globe* described her infancy as follows:

> Irene Monroe does not have a birth certificate because . . . when she was probably 6 months old, someone "discarded" her—that is the word she uses, quite sadly—in a trash can in a park in Brooklyn.
>
> She was found—by chance, because that side of the park was not scheduled for cleanup that day—by city garbage men.

After being rescued from the trash can, Monroe was taken to the New York Foundling Hospital, where she was put in the care of the woman who gave her a very personal name: Sister Irene, a fan of Marilyn Monroe. "It's a wonderful name," she says, "and I'd never change it as a lot of blacks have changed their white names, because by giving me a name, she made me who I am."

She endured foster care settings with abusive, functionally illiterate foster parents and went on to graduate from Wellesley College and Union Theological Seminary.

Rev Monroe writes a column, "The Religion Thang," for the New England gay newspaper *In Newsweekly*, and has also contributed articles to several journals, newspapers, and collections. Her essay, "Louis Farrakhan's Ministry of Misogyny and Homophobia," is anthologized in *The Farrakhan Factor: African American Writers on Leadership, Nationhood, and Minister Louis Farrakhan*; she was guest editor of the *Journal of Women and Religion*'s special issue on "The Intersection of Racism and Sexism"; and she is included in *African American Quotations*. She has conducted workshops and given addresses in schools and churches throughout the country and for such organizations as the National Conference of Christians and Jews, National Association of Social Workers, and National Black Gay and Lesbian Leadership Forum.

Say something about the recognition you've received in the news media.

Like the *Boston Magazine* article, right. Fifty of the "most intriguing" women . . . they should have said "bizarre" (*laughs*). That was because of a number of things, among them my being the first African American woman marshall for Boston Pride. I see my role, particularly as an out lesbian, as a public theologian. I feel that to acquire this kind of education and not to put it into practice is just talking among my elite colleagues. So, that's why I do a more public kind of ministry now, like writing the column and giving a lot of talks, to make things more accessible to a group of people who are desperately in need of information and affirmation.

You went right from getting your M. Div. at Union to the program at Harvard?

Yes, I'm an old, colored woman, so I don't have too much time (*laughs*).

How old are you?

Forty-four. I chose this particular doctoral program at Harvard because it's new and would allow me to study the relationship between gender identity and sexual orientation in a way that other doctoral programs wouldn't.

Somewhere along the line you got to pastor Presbyterian churches?

Yes, while at Union, but let me explain the glitch, because I don't want to in any way promote the Presbyterian Church as gay friendly. Race played a major factor in my getting to the Presbyterian Church. Urban Black Presbyterian churches are dying for the most part. Nobody—Black or white—wants to pastor them. The few Black men who get through the Presbyterian ordination process have the pick of the litter, and they're not going to go to these struggling, dying Presbyterian Churches. The thing about being a pastor in the Presbyterian church is you have to be schooled, unlike if you're Baptist, Methodist, or Pentecostal in the Black tradition; and Presbyterian really is a white denomination unlike what we call the Black denominations. So, the point of my getting to pastor is not that they're pro-queer at any level; it's because those churches were and still are dying. They need to fill them with Black clergy, because a lot of them don't want white ministers. They want a Black feel, Black ownership, a Black worship service. And that's why I got those positions. Clearly I'm out—if you saw me or knew me, it's impossible for me not to be—but that's not what they're dealing with. They need to salvage as many of these dying Black churches as they can. So, I usually tell people I don't even talk about it, because under no circumstances do I want folks to think that the Presbyterian Church is queer friendly.

I also don't identify Presbyterian. I didn't grow up Presbyterian. I grew up at best as what you would call "Baptecostal." I come out of a tradition of storefront churches, which is what many African Americans come out of. A lot of these storefront Black churches call themselves Baptist, but they're really Pentecostal; and they're not part of what you'd call the mainline Black denominational churches, like AME [African Methodist Episcopal]. You can't be storefront and be AME, but you can be storefront and say you're Baptist. Saying you're Baptist as opposed to saying you're Pentecostal is a bit of class pretension. I really identify as a conglomerate of both of them, Baptist and Pentecostal.

When did you make the move out of the Pentecostal storefront tradition?

I would say that I never have, even when I was pastor at Bethany Presbyterian and at Soundview Presbyterian. One of the things I found as I was studying the Book of Order, Presbyterian policy, and hating it, was that I go to pastor these local churches and see that what you've really got is Black church housed in a Presbyterian edifice. It's Presbyterian by name, but it really is Black church. And the class distinction is very interesting. Soundview is in a more economically distressed area in the Bronx, where people don't own their homes, they live in housing projects and apartment buildings. They're renters. There you see what I call Baptecostal tradition, very vibrant. But then when I was at Bethany Presbyterian in a Black middle-class area in Englewood, New Jersey, you don't see as much of that, but even Bethany doesn't get away from what we call Black religious tradition.

What's your view of queer Black people within organized religion?

I think for the most part those of us in the Black church are in at a tremendous cost, because most of us are in various ways cloaking our true identity. For example, if you are a gay male, there is a place for you in the Black church—in the choir or as choir masters. Really, we call gay males the choir queens. And that's sort of your entertainment aspect in the Black church. Music is very essential to Black church worship. King even said that you can't get good music unless you've got some gay boys up there in the choir. But even that visible role within the Black church—and everybody knows that the choir master or many of the boys in the choir are gay—is acknowledged by bifurcating their identity, like we forgive and love the sinner, we forgive the sin and thank God the sinner knows enough to come to church and serve God. Also, these positions are provisional or marginal within the church, because they have nothing to do with altering its administrative hierarchy, which is very gender specific and very patriarchal. These roles are essential and visible. They have prestige but no power to cause any kind of what I call a paradigm shift or systemic change within the body of the entire church. They will not improve or increase awareness about homophobia or about this group of people being oppressed.

Now for Black lesbians. I think when all of us who are queer go to Black church, we're all going in some form of drag; and the boys love it because they love the robes anyway (*laughs*). But part of the Black church is that the dress code is rigid, and you don't even have to voice it because it's instilled in the practice of each person who goes to church. It's passed on generationally that we have this rigid dress code. So, when I say we cloak our identity, the code says you can be lesbian but you make sure that you wear your dress. You wear dresses to Black churches, if you're female. Even if you are a butch woman who can't wear dresses as well as a real drag queen, the point is that you give the external surface of what is called proper clothing, proper decorum, which is heterosexual, of course. That's explicit as well as implicit. So, in that sense the doors of the church are open to you, but not for you to give voice, whether as a gay man or a lesbian woman or, God forbid, we won't even dare mention transgender. If you are gay or lesbian in the Black church, you don't have any key role in the church because if, God forbid, you should be superintendent of Sunday School, you'll give a wrong message to the children.

Also, there's a tremendous belief that we are an abomination to God because the Bible says it. I just want to say a little bit about our selective use of Biblical scripture. In the Genesis text we have the curse of Ham that legitimates slavery and then we have the Ephesians text where Apostle Paul says that slaves ought to be obedient to their slave masters. What we did with those damaging and damning texts was that we ignored them and took a Bible that was used to enslave us—not to make us better Christians, but to make us better slaves—and turned it around into a tool of liberation. It's always rather disheartening to know how we can be selective in developing a canon within a canon that gives us a sense of affirmation about who we are, but we can't understand or do that when it comes to women, as well as when it comes to lesbian/gay/bisexual/transgendered people. So, we're very literalist when it comes to other minorities, but certainly not when it comes to those damning and damaging passages about Black people.

Part of that has a lot to do with the way in which we construct Black identity and understand racism. The dominant belief in the African American community that racism is the only and ultimate oppression we face as Black people not only ignores the oppression of other groups of people, but it also ignores the oppression of sexism and homophobia within our community. It sets up what I call a hierarchy of oppressions which make people fight among themselves and believe that one oppression—only their oppression—is greater than any other oppression. So, for instance, if it is the belief that racism is far greater than sexism or homophobia or anti-Semitism, and you try to introduce and recognize any other forms of oppression that exist within your community, you are seen as threatening and trying to dilute the whole notion of solidarity toward liberation. Even though there are women and men, gay and straight, within the community, people are dismissive of how other groups within your community are oppressed. If racism is the ultimate oppression, it allows you to be dismissive of sexism; and if you're dismissive of sexism, then that allows you to be dismissive of women, straight or gay. It also allows you to be dismissive of homophobia and therefore of gay people within the community. So, what it leaves you with is straight Black men as the ones whose oppression counts.

The nonsense of this is that you really can't talk about a liberation movement or constructing a theology, ideology, or a politic that is inclusive because three quarters of your population is gone—dismissed—in this hierarchy of oppressions. In its simplest form, I call it Black patriarchy. When I give talks at Black churches or to Black groups, I do a graph so that people can visually get it. But even showing people, as we say, the light doesn't mean that they change, because there's something in place that benefits them to keep that kind of inequity in place: familiarity, comfort, simplicity, maybe even the security of knowing one's place or thinking that other people don't count as much.

I say we've got to move from a hierarchy of oppressions, which I show on rungs in a pyramid shape. At the top is racism and under it are various other rungs with different oppressions. We need to move toward what I call a wheel of oppressions on which each spoke represents a different kind of oppression and has equal weight. It allows everybody to speak from their particular oppression and is meant to open a dialogue in which everybody has a right to be heard. In the hierarchy of oppression with racism as the ultimate oppression, only two races—Blacks and whites—control the dialogue. Even though we don't like what we're saying to each other, those two groups control the dialogue, exclude Asians, Latinos, and other minorities, and don't try to understand in a more comprehensive way what racism is, particularly in the American context. Many people feel that lesbian, gay, bisexual, and transgender people can hide their oppressions, that the pain we feel for who we are we bring on ourselves. While many African Americans do not see a connection between the suffering of queers and themselves, because queerness is a "white disease," many white queers do not see their connection to the suffering of Blacks. But I try to point out that the struggle against racism is legitimate if we are also fighting anti-Semitism, sexism, classism, etc. All of these isms are merely tools of oppression that will continue to keep us fractured instead of united toward a common goal, a multicultural democracy. As Martin Luther King Jr. said, "It is not possible to be in favor of justice for some people and not be in favor of justice for all people. Justice cannot be divided."

As one of a few openly queer Black clergy, where do you draw your strength from?

From a number of places and people, but I have to tell you what was my transforming moment. I wanted to go to ITC, which is the Interdenominational Theological Center down in Atlanta, or to Howard University Theological School in Washington, D.C. And I'll tell you why: because I come out of the Black church, and my feeling was, "Who better to train me for ministry in the Black church than a Black seminary?" It just seemed to make sense to me. I'd gone to Wellesley and knew about elite white schools in the Northeast, and that was fine, but I said to myself, "If I'm going to be a Black Baptist minister, I'll go down to either D.C. or Atlanta and learn from professors who are schooling folks for the Black church."

I applied to both institutions and I got rejected because I am queer. And they openly told me that. I'll tell you briefly the story in Atlanta. The admissions woman called me and said, "I want to talk with you about your application and I'm worried." She said, "Academically you're strong," and she went on to give me some accolades about how strong I was compared to the rest of the applicant pool. And I'm thinking, "This is excellent. This probably means I'll get a lot of financial aid." "But," she said, "your faith statement is very problematic," and she referred to where I had talked about being a born-again Black lesbian Christian. I honestly had written about having been closeted and fearful of being Black and lesbian and also Christian, about letting go of that fear, about how I felt I embraced the wonder of God. She went on to say that the committee had tremendous trouble with that part of my application, and she told me I had two options: Right then as we were talking I was provisional, but that status could change if I would agree to be closeted in the program. If I wouldn't agree to be closeted, I would be rejected. I went on to explain that I couldn't believe that I would be the only lesbian there, and she just said, "Listen, what you need to under-stand is that you would have no support from the student body or faculty and that there wouldn't be a church in Atlanta that would take you for the field placement required of all students in the M.Div. program." I said, "What about King's church, what about Ebenezer Baptist Church?" She gave me this response like, "Girl, please!"

We talked some, and I was clearly upset. I said that I was very shocked that she even felt comfortable making this call, because wasn't Richard Allen and his folks not being able to worship in a white church what gave birth to the Black church? That had to be a first. And there was a time when Black women couldn't enter seminary, so there had to be a first. And I even joked that I wouldn't mind being their "demo dyke" and assured her that being down there I'd find others in the school. She didn't find that humorous at all. But I had to make a decision, and I said to her that I really felt called to be who I really am, that this was one of those times when I didn't want to leave my identity at the threshold of the church. I wanted to bring it fully in. So she thanked me, and three days later I got my rejection letter. I cried for many months, feeling a whole bunch of stuff about the Black church and the call to justice it is not taking.

So, I went to Union two years later, not because it was my first choice, but my only choice. I had to look at Union as the opportunity to go where there was an open door, and that's how I got to the Presbyterian Church, because of Union's ties with it. It's not that I have any love for the Presbyterian Church or Black Presbyterians for that matter; it's because there was an open door. So, my charge to ministry came from some place not anticipated. I feel as though I've been on a journey without a road map, but I have managed to move forward. I really do think there's a door open somewhere and it will be revealed to me. It will not come in a way that I envision it, but it will come.

And one of my best educational experiences, I have to tell you, was Union Theological Seminary. I am who I am today because it placed its stamp on me and formed me. It gave me my voice, and I took it and ran with it. I feel blessed to have gone to Union. It's an ideological battlefield, as you well know. And you know what chapel is like at noon from Monday through Thursday. I used to call it "Showtime at the St. James," because of the various worshiping traditions students brought to Union. But it was a tremendous learning experience for me, and it really transformed me in some very wonderful ways. There's a queer student body as well as faculty, which are wonderful. Ethics professor Bev Harrison was my advisor and sort of mentored me through the M.Div. program, because as a queer Black Christian I was having enormous difficulty with both the Black faculty and Black student body there. One Black professor blocked my getting a field placement at one of the prodigious Black churches in Brooklyn because I was lesbian.

Coming up here to Harvard was a change because it's conservative. We have no queer faculty. I am Professor Gomes's head teaching fellow and have been with him for five years. The kind of affirmation and prophetic edge I got at Union calls me at this point to go out and take what I've learned to the community. So, where Harvard has not been for me the most supportive place, the queer community of Boston has been, Blacks as well as whites.

In the 1960s, African Americans pushed the doors open around integration and brought forth the prophetic call about race. We bring the prophetic call about sexual orientation. The struggle is very similar. Do you see the connection? They were the prophetic voice of the '50s and '60s, and now we are the prophetic voice. Our struggle is a lot harder, because we have been spiritually abused by our faith tradition. What we have done is gone away from the church, and now we must push back into the church and transform it—at least those of us who can do it. We should not castigate those folks who can't come out, but we want to provide a way that should they come out they know it's okay. Those of us who can transform the church, whether inside or out, ought to do it. I'm doing it in my way now, as I said earlier, by moving from parish ministry to being a public theologian. I believe—and I know I sound crazy—that I along with you and others can change the world. I think we do it in our different ministries.

Somehow you're able to stand up and take the risk, while others aren't. Why do you think you're one who can be the prophetic voice?

I am one of many prophetic voices who stand up. I believe that no lie lives forever and that lies left unchallenged get more power. There's a time when we all were closeted. We remember that being in that closet had too much power over us. We missed some blessed opportunities by being in the closet and by not fully embracing who we are and, if called to ministry, who God calls us to be. I know it sounds kind of hokey, but I really do believe that.

But what gave you the strength and hope to see through the lie?

I was in the Stonewall riots in 1969. I was fourteen years old. It's a real hoot in terms of how many of the Black gangs got down there that first night. It had everything to do with, if you remember anything about the '60s, it being a very rebellious period in our history. Back then race relationships were very tense. We were spinning off the Black Power movement, and back then we called cops "pigs." In Brooklyn on one of those hot, lazy kind of nights when people are just hanging from fire escapes and sitting on stoops, we get this message—and messages travel in various ways in these Black enclaves and street gangs—that the pigs are beating up on our fags down in the Village. Now, mind you as with most folks—but especially if you live in your Brooklyn enclave—you're very tribal, you don't really travel out of your enclave that much, and folks haven't heard of the Village, myself included. We're fourteen, fifteen, sixteen; we're rebellious anyway, and suddenly we had a reason to rebel, a context for rebellion. So folks got on the train, and of course we didn't pay, we just jumped the turnstile. And really to be honest with you, we're saying, "We gonna whip some cop's ass tonight. There's gonna be a fight tonight."

And we get down there, and it was a transforming moment for me, because I had some inklings that I was queer but I didn't have a name for it. The only face I had for it was what I call your diva queens who we would see in the neighborhood and who people jeered at. But I hadn't seen other forms of queerness, so that night was transformative. It was so moving just to fight anywhere, but here to fight for a cause was incredible—to really understand what this was all about and that these people had a right to be who they were. I understood it because of being Black and feeling I had a right to be who I was. In those days, we were saying, "Say it loud, I'm Black and I'm proud," and we were donning these big Angela Davis Afros. I swear to you I understood that moment. And I understood it not because I saw it in whiteface, but because I saw it in Blackface. I really got it that these human rights struggles tie us all to one another in a profound way. Those are the sort of things that keep me hopeful.

In your work, do you draw more from resources inside or outside of organized religion?

I do a balance of both. I don't want to lose the pulse of what's going on in the Black church. I'll keep going to a Black church, because I think my attempts to critique the Black church would be rather disingenuous if I didn't stay connected to it, as problematic and assaulting as it is when you hear the minister railing and ranting about homosexuality and a whole bunch of stuff and you say, "Jesus, help me through this." But I sit there because there's something, first of all, about his feeling called, and there's something that these people are hearing in a way that they find liberating and salvific. Even if it is through years of indoctrination, something else is going on for these people other than a moment of spewing bigotry.

So, you have stayed connected?

Yes, I have to. I also stay connected with the queer community, because I can't talk about this stuff and not be out on the street. Then I find ways to mix both. My column is one way. But I also hit more popular types of journals, as well as books— like the *Farrakhan Factor* is a commercial book as opposed to an academic book. I'm not only interested in talking to my colleagues. We're not really affecting change just by talking among ourselves. We may think we are in our head, but I'm talking about really affecting the lives of people. I think that only comes if you have pastored. Maybe if I hadn't pastored, I wouldn't know what changing lives and situations really involves. When you're down there in the trenches, you know. So, you've got to get out there.

African American lesbians and gay men talk about feeling cut off from their people when they can't go to their church as open queer folks. Can you say something about that?

Yes. The Black church has really been a spiritual and social institution within our community. E. Franklin Frazier describes the Black church as a "nation within a nation." The Black church had a multiplicity of roles: social, educational, as well as spiritual. Even more when we were living more evidently in segregated America, everything centered around the Black church. That's where you went when you wanted to know what was going on in the world, what you should do to do right, as well as how you could move forward educationally or professionally. You got all that information from the Black church. It also cushioned you and was your refuge against racism. If you couldn't be anybody in the white world, in the Black church you were somebody. So, to be cut off from the Black church is really being cut off from the Black community, the Black family, because "ain't no place else" can you just by virtue of being Black be somebody. You're a child of God, you're someone with dignity, you're someone who holds the promise of a new world, of God's kingdom will be done. To be cut off from the Black church is to be cut off from your lifeline. It was the main organ that shaped the entire Black community. And it still does that. Not as much now though, since we moved into a period of integration, but it still—and somewhat in an anemic way, I must say—has a main function in the Black community.

Do you know of any out African American gay men or lesbians who remain in the church and still feel that connection?

No. What we've done—and I'm terribly troubled by it in some ways, because I understand it as a reactionary response to a void—is create Unity Fellowship Church, a Black queer denomination that has many local churches now throughout the country. And Bishop Carl Bean of Unity says he is providing an alternative for Black queers. They can come on Sunday morning and practice the religion that is such an important aspect of forming Black identity and sense of self. He's created— some would say "resurrected"—these Black churches, but the denominational structure and liturgy have not changed at all. So, in place of what I call the Black church's usual heterosexual patriarchy, you now have what I call homosexual patriarchy. You still have Black men in power, so nothing has changed and nothing really is salvific or liberating about those churches other than the fact that they provide an open door, but at a tremendous expense for women and transgendered people, depending on how you're transgendered.

What do you tell gay men or lesbians who are looking for a spiritual home or spiritual connection? What's the alternative?

I tell them two things: One is to get with like people, and two is that any journey you take is an arduous one because it's just not laid out there before you. The task is for forerunners—foresisters and forebrothers—to create the path rather than simply to find it laid out for you, because it isn't there—yet. The call, believe it or not, is for you to fill the void. A lot of people don't want to do that, but that's how I see it. There's a void. We all see it, speak about it, and want it to be filled, but that won't be done until we step up to the task and realize that we have to put it in place. That's what my ancestors did when they wanted freedom. They envisioned it. Harriet Tubman had a dream. She said, "I'm going to conduct a railroad out of here." People had different visions of it. But the point is that not to do anything does not cause any type of change. You have to do something. It does not exist unless we do it.

It reminds me of womanist theology, which I'm so annoyed with because it doesn't address issues of sexual orientation, even though some of the women constructing and shaping womanist theology are queer. They also don't address class issues. And I keep saying, "You know, I'm sick of it," but the point is that they're not going to change it. It's up to me and others like me to do it, and so I address the issue of sexual orientation and don't call myself "womanist." I've got to create something different so that those of us who feel alienated by the womanist discourse now have a place to begin to talk about how our voice ought to be incorporated into the feminist and Black theological discourses. Presently, it's not there. We have to create it ourselves. That's what the queer movement is about. It wasn't always a movement, not until at some point we had to say, "Look, we're sick of getting our ass whipped! We got to do something."

The article I'm writing now talks about the class and race division in the queer community. We have to educate white queer folks to the fact that, "Yes, you are oppressed because of your sexual orientation, but you have white-skin privilege. You have to put that in check in order to be able to talk to people of color." But then when I talk to people of color, I have to say to them, "We don't have a patent on oppression because we're Black." We all have to understand that when you have an attitude that impedes the possibility for discourse, you need to go about the business of changing things. I give two different types of talks to the different communities, but the point is that it's essential that we all find a way to work together.

You know what I like about the queer movement, although I see that we're light years away, is that it really is a profoundly prophetic movement, and you want to know why? Because it's global. Anywhere in the world you're going to find somebody queer. So, unlike the Civil Rights movement, which was particular to here, Black, and in some sense homogenous, the queer movement crosses race, class, ethnicity, all of those social barriers. And it's everywhere in the world.

Toward a New Theology of Sexuality

❧ *Judith Plaskow* ❧

Feminist reconceptualization of the energy/control model of sexuality and affirmation of the profound connection between sexuality and spirituality provide directions for rethinking the ambivalent attitudes toward sexuality within Judaism. Acceptance and avowal of a link between sex and spirit is, as I argued earlier, by no means foreign to Jewish experience. In the mysteries of the marriage bed on Sabbath night; in the sanctity of the Song of Songs; for mysticism, in the very nature and dynamics of the Godhead, sexual expression is an image of and path to the holy.[1] Yet again and again in theology and practice, Judaism turns away from and undermines this acknowledged connection by defining sexuality in terms of patriarchal possession and control. Where women's sexuality is seen as an object to be possessed, and sexuality itself is perceived as an impulse that can take possession of the self, the central issues surrounding sexuality will necessarily be issues of control: Who has the right to control a particular woman's sexuality in what situation? How can a man control his own sexual impulses, given the constant bombardment of female temptation? How can the law control women and the relations between men and women so that the danger of illicit sexual relations (relations with a woman whose sexuality is owned by some other man) is minimized? All these questions make perfect sense as related aspects of a patriarchal system, but they are inimical to the mutuality, openness, and vulnerability in sexual relations that tie sexuality to the sacred.

Recognizing then that the role of women's sexuality in the institution of the family, the rules surrounding the relations of the sexes, and the energy/control paradigm of sexuality are all connected pieces of a patriarchal understanding of sexuality, the question becomes: What would it mean to develop a model of sexuality that is freed from this framework? How can we think about sexuality in a way that springs from and honors the experience of women? How can we develop a positive feminist discourse about sexuality in a Jewish context?

In line with the fundamental feminist insight that sexuality is socially constructed, a Jewish feminist understanding of sexuality begins with the insistence that what goes on in the bedroom can never be isolated from the wider cultural context of which the bedroom is part.[2] The inequalities of the family are prepared for by, and render plausible, larger social inequalities, and the task of eradicating sexual inequality is part of the wider feminist project of ending hierarchical separation as a model for communal life.[3] Thus a Jewish feminist approach to sexuality must take sexual mutuality as a task for the whole of life and not just for Friday evening, fitting its commitment to sexual equality into its broader vision of a society based on mutuality and respect for difference.

It is striking that one of the profoundest images of freedom and mutuality in sexual relations that the Jewish tradition has to offer is at the same time its central image of the connection between sexuality and spirituality. Unlike the Garden of Eden, where Eve and Adam are ashamed of their nakedness and women's subordination is the punishment for sin, the Garden of the Song of Songs is a place of sensual delight and sexual equality. Unabashed by their desire, the man and woman of these poems delight in their own embodiment and the beauty surrounding them, each seeking the other out to inaugurate their meetings, each rejoicing in the love without dominion that is also the love of God.[4] Since this book offers a vision of delight that is easier to achieve in a sacred garden than in the midst of the demands of daily living, it is perhaps no criticism of the institution of marriage that the couple in the Song of Songs is not married. Yet the picture of mutuality, and the sacredness of mutuality, offered by this book stand in fundamental tension with the structures of marriage as Judaism defines them. When the central rituals of marriage and divorce celebrate or enact the male acquisition and relinquishment of female sexuality, what are the supports and resources for the true reciprocity of intimate exchange that marks the holiness of *Shir Hashirim* (Song of Songs)? Despite the efforts of the tradition to legislate concern for women's sexual needs, the achievement of mutuality in the marriage bed is extremely difficult in the absence of justice for women in those institutions that legitimate and surround it.

A central task, then, of the feminist reconstruction of Jewish attitudes toward sexuality is the radical transformation of the institutional, legal framework within which sexual relations are supposed to take place. Insofar as Judaism maintains its interest in the establishment of enduring relationships both as a source of adult companionship and development and as a context for raising and educating children, these relationships will be entered into and dissolved by mutual initiative and consent. "Marriage" will not be about the transfer of women or the sanctification of potential disorder through the firm establishment of women in the patriarchal family, but the decision of two adults—any two adults—to make their lives together, lives that include the sharing of sexuality. Although, in the modern West, it is generally assumed that such a commitment is a central meaning of marriage, this assumption is contradicted by a religious (and secular) legal system that outlaws homosexual marriage and institutionalizes inequality in its basic definitions of marriage and divorce.

This redefinition of the legal framework of marriage, which accords with the feminist refusal to sanctify any hierarchical relationship, is also based on the important principle that sexuality is not something we can acquire or possess in another. We are each the possessor of our own sexuality—in Adrienne Rich's phrase, the "presiding genius" of our own bodies. The sharing of sexuality with another is something that should happen only by mutual consent, a consent that is not a blanket permission, but that is continually renewed in the actual rhythms of particular relationships. This principle, simple as it seems, challenges both the fundamental assumptions of Jewish marriage law and the Jewish understanding of what women's sexuality is "about." It defines as immoral legal regulations concerning the possession, control, and exchange of women's sexuality, and disputes the perspective that a woman's sexuality is her contribution to the family rather than the expression of her own embodiment.

But if one firm principle for feminist thinking about sexuality is that no one can possess the sexuality of another, it is equally the case that from a feminist perspective, sexuality is not something that pertains only or primarily to the self. Indeed, our sexuality is fundamentally about moving out beyond ourselves. As ethicist James Nelson puts it,

> The mystery of sexuality is the mystery of the human need to reach out for the physical and spiritual embrace of others. Sexuality thus expresses God's intention that people find authentic humanness not in isolation but in relationship.[5]

Our capacity for intimacy, for sharing, for touch is rooted in our early relations with others; and throughout our lives, we seek genuine connection, longing for at least some relationship(s) that can touch the core of our being. The connecting, communicative nature of sexuality is not something we can experience or look for only in sexual encounters narrowly defined, but in all real relationships in our lives. We live in the world as sexual beings. As Audre Lorde argues, our sexuality is a current that flows through all activities that are important to us, in which we invest our selves. True intellectual exchange, common work, shared experience are laced with sexual energy that animates and enlivens them. The bonds of community are erotic bonds. The power that is generated by real community, that gives us access to a greater power that grounds and embraces us, is in part the power of our own sexual, life energy that flows through community and enlarges and seals it. We are all, women and men, embodied, sexual persons who respond sexually to the women and men among whom we live.

This erotic nature of community is by no means lost on Judaism; indeed, it is the subject of profound ambivalence in both the midrash and law. The story I described earlier in which the rabbis blind rather than kill the imprisoned *yetzer harad** concedes the vital role of the sexual impulse in the creation and maintenance of the world. A similar ambivalence underlies the extensive rabbinic legislation enforcing the separation of the sexes, legislation that tries to protect against the feelings it recognizes, even as it acknowledges the sexual power of community and the continuity of sexuality with other feelings. If the energy of community is erotic, there are no guarantees that eroticism will stay within prescribed legal boundaries rather than breaking out and disrupting communal sanctity. The strict "fence around the law" felt necessary when it comes to sexual behavior is itself testimony to the power of sexuality.

It is tempting for a feminist account of sexuality to deny the disruptive power of the erotic, and to depict the fear of it in rabbinic thought as simply misplaced. But it is truer to experience to acknowledge the power of sexuality to overturn rules

---

*The evil inclination, sometimes identified with sexual impulses.

and threaten boundaries. Then feminists can embrace this power as a significant ally. There is no question that the empowerment that comes from owning the erotic in our lives can disturb community and undermine familiar structures. On the level of sexual behavior, if we allow ourselves to perceive and acknowledge sexual feelings, there is always the danger we may act on them, and they may not correspond to group consensus about whom we may desire and when. The potentially disruptive effects of sexual feelings exist for communities with stringent sexual ethics that carefully restrict permitted behavior, but also for those with more open boundaries. Starhawk, in discussing the dynamics of political action and other small resistance and countercultural groups, formulates three pessimistic laws of group dynamics: (1) Sexual involvement in small groups is bound to cause problems. (2) "In any small group in which people are involved, sooner or later they will be involved sexually. (3) Small groups tend to break up."[6] Not only the values of a group can be trampled upon by unlooked-for sexual connections but—given the feelings of fear, vulnerability, pain, and anger that can accompany the birth and demise of relationships—sexual liaisons can threaten a group's ability to function cohesively as a community.

When the erotic is understood not simply as sexual feeling in the narrow sense but as our fundamental life energy, the owning of this power in our lives is even more threatening to established structures. In Audre Lorde's terms, if we allow the erotic to become a lens through which we evaluate all aspects of our existence, we can no longer "settle for the convenient, the shoddy, the conventionally expected, nor the merely safe."[7] Having glimpsed the possibility of genuine satisfaction in work well done, we are less likely to settle for work that is alienating and meaningless. Having experienced the power and legitimacy of our own sexual desire, we are less likely to subscribe to a system that closely and absolutely prescribes and proscribes the channels of that desire. Having experienced our capacity for creative and joyful action, we are less likely to accept hierarchical power relationships that deny or restrict our ability to bring that creativity and joy to more and more aspects of our lives. It may be that the ability of women to live within the patriarchal family and the larger patriarchal structures that govern Jewish life depends on our suppression of the erotic, on our numbing ourselves to the sources of vision and power that fuel meaningful resistance. It may also be that the ability of Jews to live unobtrusively as a minority in a hostile culture has depended on blocking sources of personal power that might lead to resistance that feels foolish or frightening. Obviously, from a patriarchal perspective, then—or the perspective of any hierarchical system—erotic empowerment is dangerous. That is why, in Lorde's words, "We are taught to separate the erotic demand from most vital areas of our lives other than sex,"[8] and that is why we are also taught to restrain our sexuality, so that it too fits the parameters of hierarchical control that govern the rest of our lives.

From a feminist perspective, however, the power and danger of the erotic are not reasons to fear and suppress it but to nurture it as a profound personal and communal resource in the struggle for change. When "we begin to demand from ourselves and from our life-pursuits that they feel in accordance with that joy which we know ourselves to be capable of," we carry with us an inner knowledge of the kind of world we are seeking to create.[9] If we repress this knowledge because it also makes us sexually alive, then we repress the clarity and creative energy that is the basis of our capacity to envision and work toward a more just social order.

It is in relation to this understanding of the power of the erotic that feminist insistence on seeing sexuality as part of a continuum of body/life energy is a particularly crucial corrective to rabbinic attitudes toward sexual control. As I have argued, the rabbis recognized the connection between the sexual impulse and human creativity. "The bigger the man, the bigger the *yetzer*," they said, and advised, "Hold him [the *yetzer hara*] off with the left hand and draw him nigh with the right."[10] Yet at the same time they acknowledged the role of sexuality as an ingredient in all activity, they apparently believed one could learn the fear of a woman's little finger without damaging the larger capacity to act and to feel. To love God with all the heart meant to love God with the good *and evil* impulses, and yet it was imagined one could rein in the so-called evil impulse without diminishing the love of God.[11] If we take sexuality seriously, however, as an expression of our embodiment that cannot be disconnected from our wider ability to interact feelingly with the world, then to learn fear and shame of our own bodies and those of others—even when these feelings are intermixed with other conflicting attitudes—is to learn suspicion of feeling as a basic way of knowing and valuing the world. We should not expect, then, to be able to block out our sexual feelings without blocking out the longing for social relations rooted in mutuality rather than hierarchy, without blocking out the anger that warns us that something is amiss in our present social arrangements, without blocking and distorting the fullness of our love for God.[12]

I am not arguing here for free sex or for more sexual expression, quantitatively speaking. I am arguing for living dangerously, for choosing to take responsibility for working through the possible consequences of sexual feelings rather than repressing sexual feeling and thus feeling more generally. I am arguing that our capacity to transform Judaism and the world is rooted in our capacity to be alive to the pain and anger that is caused by relationships of domination, and to the joy that awaits us on the other side. I am arguing that to be alive is to be sexually alive, and that in suppressing one sort of vitality, we suppress the other.

I mentioned above Starhawk's three laws of group dynamics that acknowledge the potential disruptiveness of sex to the creation of community. On the basis of more experience, she adds a fourth: A group that has survived one breakup between members is more likely to survive subsequent ones, and may experience a deepened sense of trust and safety because of what it has been through.[13] This fourth law points to the possibility that even the disruptions caused by sexuality can be a source of power if we refuse to look away from the feelings they evoke in us, maintaining our commitment to the building of community in full cognizance of its erotic bonds.

The question becomes, then: Can we affirm our sexuality as the gift it is, making it sacred not by cordoning off pieces of it, but by increasing our awareness of the ways in which it connects us to all things? Can we stop evicting our sexuality from the synagogue, hiding it behind a *mechitzah*** or praying with our heads, and instead bring it in, offering it to God in the experience of full spiritual/physical connection?[14] Dare we trust our capacity for joy—knowing it is related to our sexuality—to point the direction toward new and different ways of structuring communal life?

While I am suggesting that the implications of a changed conception of sexuality go well beyond the sexual sphere, it is also the case that they shape that sphere. The ability to feel deeply in the whole of our lives affects what we want and are willing to accept in the bedroom, just as what we experience in the bedroom prepares us for mutuality or domination in the rest of our lives. A new understanding of sexuality and a transformed institutional context for sexual relationships will have significant impact on personal sexual norms. If the traditional models and categories for understanding sexuality are no longer morally acceptable from a feminist perspective, but sexuality is fundamentally about relationships with others, what values might govern sexual behavior for modern Jews?

It should be clear from all I have said thus far that rejection of the traditional energy/control model of sexuality and of ownership as a category for understanding sexual exchange is by no means synonymous with a sexual ethic of "anything goes." On the contrary. I would argue—and the current move back toward sexual repression supports this—that the obsession with sexuality in US culture for the last twenty years, the pressures toward early sexual activity for women and men, the expectation that sex could compensate for dissatisfactions in every other area of life, all reflect a reversal of traditional paradigms that does not succeed in moving beyond them. If the Jewish tradition says sex is a powerful impulse that needs to be controlled, certain strains in modern culture say it is healthier to act out our impulses. If the tradition says men may have affairs but women may not, certain strains in modern culture give women "permission" to be promiscuous on male terms. If the tradition says sex has a place in life, but it must not be allowed to take over, modern culture offers sex as a panacea for all that ails us. But when sex is understood as a particular impulse that we act out instead of control, the result is an alienated sexuality that can never rescue us from the alienation in the rest of our lives. If greater genital expression were really the solution to our social miseries, says Beverly Harrison, we would expect ours to be the happiest society around. In fact, however, since, in Audre Lorde's terms, our "erotic comings-together . . . are almost always characterized by a simultaneous looking away," sexual encounters often leave us feeling used and abused rather than renewed and connected.[15]

To see sexuality as an aspect of our life energy, as part of a continuum with other ways of relating to the world and other people, is to insist that the norms of mutuality, respect for difference, and joint empowerment that characterize the larger feminist vision of community apply also—indeed especially—to the area of sexuality. If, in our general communal life, we seek to be present with each other in such a way that we can touch the greater power of being in which all communities dwell, how much more should this be true in those relationships which are potentially the

---

*"The partition separating women and men in traditional synagogues.

most open, intimate, and vulnerable in our lives? The Song of Songs, because it unifies sensuality, spirituality, and profound mutuality, may offer us the finest Jewish vision of what our sexual relationships can be, a vision that at the same time points to the transformation of our common life. Beverly Harrison places the unification of these elements in a feminist framework:

> A feminist moral theology requires that we ground our new ethics of sexuality in a "spirituality of sensuality." . . . Sexuality is indispensable to our spirituality because it is a power of communication, most especially a power to give and receive powerful meaning—love and respect or contempt and disdain. . . . The moral norm for sexual communication in a feminist ethic is radical mutuality— the simultaneous acknowledgment of vulnerability to the need of the other, the recognition of one's own power to give and receive pleasure and to call forth another's power of relation and to express one's own.[16]

It is important to note that this "spirituality of sensuality" and mutuality specifies and intensifies for sexual ethics what are also broader norms for interaction with the world.

The unification of sexuality and spirituality is a sometime gift, a measure of the possible, rather than the reality of everyday. What keeps this unification alive as a recurring possibility is the exercise of respect, responsibility, and honesty— commensurate with the nature and depth of the particular relationship—as basic values in any sexual relationship. In terms of concrete life choices, I believe that radical mutuality is most fully possible in the context of an ongoing, committed relationship in which sexual expression is one dimension of a shared life. Traditional insistence that sex be limited to heterosexual marriage might find its echo in support for and celebration of long-term partnerships as the richest setting for negotiating and living out the meanings of mutuality, responsibility, and honesty amidst the distractions, problems, and pleasures of daily life. Such partnerships are not, however, a choice for all adults who want them, and not all adults would choose them, given the possibility. To respond within a feminist framework to the realities of different life decisions and at the same time affirm the value of sexual well-being as an aspect of our total wellbeing, we need to apply certain fundamental values to a range of sexual choices and styles. While honesty, responsibility, and respect are goods that pertain to any relationship, the concrete meaning of these values will vary considerably depending on the duration and significance of the connection involved. In one relationship, honesty may mean complete and open sharing of feelings and experiences; in another, clarity about intent for that encounter. In the context of a committed partnership, responsibility may signify lifelong presence, trust, and exchange; in a brief encounter, discussion of birth control, AIDS, and safe sex. At its fullest, respect may mean regard for another as a total person; at a minimum, absence of pressure or coercion, and a commitment, in Lorde's terms, not to "look away" as we come together. If we need to look away, then we should walk away: The same choices about whether and how to act on our feelings that pertain to any area of moral decision making are open to us in relation to our sexuality.

The same norms that apply to heterosexual relationships also apply to gay and lesbian relationships.[17] Indeed, I have formulated them with both in mind. There are many issues that might be considered in reevaluating traditional Jewish rejection of homosexuality.[18] But the central issue in the context of a feminist reconceptualization of sexuality is the relationship between homosexual choice and the continuity between sexual energy and embodied life energy. If we see sexuality as part of what enables us to reach out beyond ourselves, and thus as a fundamental ingredient in our spirituality, then the issue of homosexuality must be placed in a somewhat different framework from those in which it is most often discussed. The question of the morality of homosexuality becomes one not of halakhah or the right to privacy or freedom of choice, but the affirmation of the value to the individual and society of each of us being able to find that place within ourselves where sexuality and spirituality come together.[19] It is possible that some or many of us for whom the connections between sexuality and deeper sources of personal and spiritual power emerge most richly, or only, with those of the same sex could choose to lead heterosexual lives for the sake of conformity to halakhah or wider social pressures and values. But this choice would then violate the deeper vision offered by the Jewish tradition that sexuality can be a medium for the experience and reunification of God.[20] Historically, this vision has been expressed entirely in heterosexual terms. The reality is that for some Jews, however, it is realized only in relationships between two men or two women. Thus what calls itself the Jewish path to holiness in sexual relations is for some a cutting off of holiness—a sacrifice that comes at high cost for both the individual and community. Homosexuality, then, does not necessarily represent a rejection of Jewish values but the choice of certain Jewish values over others—where these conflict with each other, the choice of the possibility of holiness over control and law.

Potential acceptance of gays and lesbians by the Jewish community raises the issue of children—for Judaism a primary warrant for sexual relations, and the facade that prejudice often hides behind in rejecting homosexuality as a Jewish choice. Again to place this issue in the context of a feminist paradigm for understanding sexuality, procreation is a dimension of our sexuality, just as sexuality itself is a dimension of our embodied personhood. If sexuality allows us to reach out to others, having children is a way of reaching out beyond our own generation, affirming the biological continuity of life and the continuity of Jewish community and communal values. Insofar as Jewish communities have an important stake in the rearing of Jewish children, it is in their interest to structure communal institutions to support in concrete ways all Jews who choose to have children, including increasing numbers of lesbians and gay men.[21] But, just as Judaism has always recognized that procreation does not exhaust the meaning of sexuality, so having children does not exhaust the ways in which Jews can contribute to future generations.[22] Recognizing the continuities between sexuality and personal empowerment strengthens the conviction of the inherent value of sexuality as an expression of our personhood and of our connection with and love for others. The sense of integrity and self-worth that a loving sexual relationship can foster enhances the capacity to make commitments to the future, whether this takes the form of bearing and raising children or nurturing communal continuity in other ways.

Lastly, but underlying all that I have said, sexuality as an aspect of our life energy and power connects us with God as the sustaining source of energy and power in the universe. In reaching out to another sexually with the total self, the boundaries between self and other can dissolve and we may feel ourselves united with larger currents of energy and sustenance. It is also the case, however, that even in ordinary, daily reachings out to others, we reach toward the God who is present in connection, in the web of relation with a wider world. On the one hand, the wholeness, the "all-embracing quality of sexual expression" that includes body, mind, and feeling, is for many people the closest we can come in this life to experiencing the embracing wholeness of God.[23] On the other hand, the everyday bonds of community are also erotic bonds through which we touch the God of community, creating a place where the divine presence can rest. Feminist metaphors that name God not simply as female but sexual female—beautiful, filled with vitality, womb, birthgiver—seek to give imagistic expression to the continuity between our own sexual energy and the greater currents that nourish and renew it. Feminist images name female sexuality as powerful and legitimate and name sexuality as part of the image of God. They tell us that sexuality is not primarily a moral danger (though, of course, it can be that), but a source of energy and power that, schooled in the values of respect and mutuality, can lead us to the related, and therefore sexual, God.

Notes

1. Arthur Green, "A Contemporary Approach to Jewish Sexuality," *The Second Jewish Catalog*, edited by Sharon Strassfeld and Michael Strassfeld (Philadelphia: The Jewish Publication Society, 1976), 98.
2. Beverly Wildung Harrison, "Sexuality and Social Policy," in *Making the Connections: Essays in Feminist Social Ethics* (Boston: Beacon Press, 1985), 83–114; Ruby Rich, "Feminism and Sexuality in the 1980s," *Feminist Studies* 12 (Fall 1986): 549–58.
3. See Mariana Valverde's insistence that the eroticization of equality is a central task of feminism, *Sex, Power, and Pleasure* (Toronto: The Women's Press, 1985), 43.
4. James Nelson, *Between Two Gardens: Reflections on Sexuality and Religious Experience* (New York: Pilgrim Press, 1983), 7; Phyllis Trible, *God and the Rhetoric of Sexuality* (Philadelphia: Fortress Press, 1978), chapter 5; Arthur Waskow, *Godwrestling* (New York: Schocken Books, 1978), chapter 6.
5. Nelson, *Between Two Gardens*, 6.
6. Starhawk, *Truth or Dare: Encounters with Power, Authority, and Mystery* (San Francisco: Harper & Row, 1987), 153.
7. Audre Lorde, "Uses of the Erotic: The Erotic as Power," in *Sister Outsider* (Trumansburg, NY: The Crossing Press, 1984), 57.
8. Ibid., 55. Compare Starhawk, *Dreaming the Dark: Magic, Sex, and Politics* (Boston: Beacon Press, 1982), 141.
9. Lorde, "Uses of the Erotic," 57; compare Starhawk, *Dreaming the Dark*, 141.
10. Louis Epstein, *Sex Laws and Customs in Judaism* (New York: KTAV Publishing House, 1967), 14.
11. Robert Gordis, *Love and Sex: A Modern Jewish Perspective* (New York: Farrar Strauss & Giroux, 1978), 106.

12. Beverly Wildung Harrison, "The Power of Anger," *Making the Connections*, 13–14; Lillian Smith, *Killers of the Dream* (New York and London: W.W. Norton, The Norton Library, 1978), 81–85.

13. Starhawk, *Truth or Dare*, 153.

14. See, for example, Waskow, *Godwrestling*, 59; Norton, *Between Two Gardens*, 3–4.

15. Harrison, "Sexuality and Social Policy," 85; Lorde, "Uses of the Erotic," 59.

16. Harrison, "Misogyny and Homophobia: The Unexplored Connections," *Making the Connections*, 149–50.

17. For a clear statement of this principle, see James Nelson, *Embodiment: An Approach to Sexuality and Christian Theology* (Minneapolis, MN: Augsburg Publishing House, 1978), 126 and chapter 8; and Bradley Artson, "Judaism and Homosexuality," *Tikkun* 3 (March/April 1988), 92–93.

18. The best consideration of this issue in a Jewish context that I am aware of is Artson, "Judaism and Homosexuality," 52–54, 92–93. See also Hershel Matt, "Sin, Crime, Sickness or Alternative Life Style? A Jewish Approach to Homosexuality," *Judaism* 27 (Winter 1978): 13–24 and Arthur Waskow, "Down-to-Earth Judaism: Sexuality," *Tikkun* 3 (March/April 1988), 48–49, 88–89. *Twice Blessed: On Being Lesbian, Gay, and Jewish*, Christie Balka and Andy Rose, eds. (Boston: Beacon Press, 1989) appeared too late to be considered here.

19. I am grateful to Denni Liebowitz for putting the issue in this way; conversation, fall 1983.

20. Compare Waskow, "Down-to-Earth Judaism," 88.

21. Martha Ackelsberg, "Families and the Jewish Community: A Feminist Perspective," *Response* 14 (Spring 1985): 15–16.

22. David M. Feldman, *Marital Relations, Birth Control, and Abortion in Jewish Law* (New York: Schocken Books, 1974), chapters 2, 4, 5; Martha Ackelsberg, "Family or Community?" *Sh'ma* 17/330 (March 20, 1987): 76–78.

23. Green, "A Contemporary Approach," 98.

The Good Mother: From Gaia to Gilead

❧ *Ellen Cronan Rose* ❧

What would be the consequences, for earth and for women, of a wholesale acceptance of mother earth rhetoric?[1] (I will leave to the ecologists detailed consideration of the consequences to the planet of promulgating the notion of mother earth, although I will mention in passing that rage and resentment, as well as love and gratitude, are standard filial emotions and that space exploration offers one way of leaving mother and childhood behind.) In a culture that, despite the women's movement, is still fundamentally

"The Good Mother: From Gaia to Gilead" from *Frontiers: A Journal of Women's Studies* XII (1). © Frontiers Editorial Collective. Reprinted by permission of University of Nebraska Press.

patriarchal, for feminists to construct (or at least construe) nature as mother and goddess virtually *invites* the at best ambivalent, at worst misogynist rhetoric manifested in a book like *Voice of the Planet*. It also invites the condescension and barely disguised glee of Philip S. Lansky, M.D., who wrote in his column in a New Age magazine: "The Earth is currently terrified. Now, that's a shocker, isn't it? Great big Earth Goddess. Ol' cosmic Mama herself. The Big Lady quaking in her well worn earth boots. Mama Terra needs some real TLC. Just throwing her into a recyclin' center ain't enough. She's scared. She needs some powerful comfortin'."[2]

Lansky suggests we "read her stories and play her music, like Paul Winter does."[3] In a culture that serializes *Voice of the Planet* on cable television on a channel that calls itself "the environmental network of the '90s"[4] and circulates the New Age magazine that carries Philip Lansky's column in organic food stores, one does not help women by emphasizing their maternal status, actual or potential.[5] In such a culture, male views of mothers' value prevail, to the benefit of men and children (especially sons) and at the cost of women's nonreproductive freedoms. Fetal protection policies in the workplace, fetal rights legislation, erosion of abortion rights, and discussion of the contractual obligations of surrogate mothers suggest that the idea of maternal solicitude can all-too-easily segue to the more sinister conception of a (potential) mother as a fetal container. Additionally, in a culture that is increasingly capitalistic, emphasizing women's procreative capacities can encourage viewing them as a "reproductive environment,"[6] congenial to exploitation by pharmaceutical interests and the medical establishment.

In a particularly searching article on "The Place of Women in Polluted Places," Lin Nelson warns women to "be vigilant and determined in the face of those protectors—in education, science, medicine and public health, and economic development—who would use gender and reproductive status (and race, class, susceptibility, and other identifiers) to accommodate us all to an industrial complex . . . in a political atmosphere of increasing authoritarianism."[7] She continues, "If women are deemed to be especially vulnerable [to toxic hazards], we may be offered special protections and restrictions and we may be held specially liable for our conduct and whereabouts in a toxic world. Instead of controlling pollution and polluters, we may be subject to more social control."[8]

In Margaret Atwood's novel, *The Handmaid's Tale*, a reproductive crisis is brought about by an environmental crisis (toxicity in the environment has rendered most women—and probably men, too—sterile). The Gileadeans' "solution" to this crisis is to attack not environmental pollution but women, exalting and expropriating the reproductive capabilities of some women for the benefit of the state. Continuing capitalist exploitation of natural resources, coupled with regressive social policies and popular culture propaganda shackling women to their (biological) reproductive functions, threatens to make this dystopian fiction all too real. Already we are seeing environmental hazards to reproduction similar to those that brought about fictional Gilead's crisis in fertility.[9] In Atwood's words, "The air got too full, once, of chemicals, rays, radiation, the water swarmed with toxic molecules, all of that takes years to clean up, and meanwhile they creep into your body, camp out in your fatty cells. Who knows, your very flesh may be polluted, dirty as an oily beach, sure death to shore birds and unborn babies."[10]

Already there are those, like the Gileadean "aunts" who indoctrinate "hand-maids" into reproductive service to the state, who characterize pro-choice feminists as "unwomen" and "godless."[11] Is it implausible to fear that, like the fictional hand-maids, real women may come to be seen as "two legged wombs . . . sacred vessels, ambulatory chalices"?[12]

. . . As Karen Warren points out, "It mystifies women's experiences to locate women closer to nature than men, just as it underplays important aspects of the oppression of women to deny the connection of women with nature, for the truth is that women, like men, are both connected to nature and separate from it, natural and cultural beings."[13] As cultural actors, white, middle-class, Western women as well as men have polluted earth, air, and water; they have damaged the ozone layer with their spray deodorants, refrigerators, and air conditioners; they have taken the kids to McDonald's to eat hamburgers made from beef grown where once there was rain for-est; they have diapered their babies with nonbiodegradable Pampers. Claiming that we (women) "know" Gaia because of features "she" and "we" share (her "womblike caves," the "moon-rhythm blood of [our] menses")[14] may indicate an effort to avoid environmental guilt. But I think there is more to it than that. . . .

. . . Confronted by hazards to, loss of control over, and potential usurpation of their reproductive capacities and choices, women might well feel anxiety, which some may attempt to solace with imagery that affirms women's power, agency, and boundless fecundity.

Even women who do not perceive developments in reproductive technology as a sinister patriarchal plot to render them obsolete may share with (some) men the fear that technology is running amok, that—as in Michael Tobias's futuristic nightmare of a genetically engineered biosphere maintained by heartless, antihuman robots—life in the twenty-first century may be unlivable. Jalna Hanmer quotes an "inclusive definition" of technological reproduction from the *Journal of the American Medical Association* that was adopted by a congressional subcommittee on science, research, and development. Its offhand remark that "manufacture" is "better" than (re)production is chilling:

> [Technological reproduction is] anything to do with the manipulation of the gametes [eggs or sperm] or the fetus, for whatever purpose, from conception other than by sexual union, to treatment of disease in utero, to the ultimate manufacture of a human being to exact specifications. . . . Thus the earliest procedure . . . is artifi-cial insemination; next . . . artificial fertilization . . . next artificial implantation . . . in the future total extra corporeal gestation . . . and finally, what is popularly meant by [reproductive] engineering, the production—or better, the biological manufac-ture—of a human being to desired specification.[15]

The thought that it is we who have damaged the planet so seriously that the harm may be irreparable and we who have elevated technology to godhood can only intensify our terror. And so, women as well as men, we cry for mommy.

Carroll Smith-Rosenberg says that during times of social upheaval, people "seek though imagery and myth to mitigate their feelings of helplessness." The more extreme and pervasive the social crisis, she asserts, the more likely it is that "bodily and familial imagery will assume ascendancy." Under great stress, "individuals will revert to their most primitive experience of human interaction and social ordering."[16] The closing decades of the twentieth century have been jarred by a series of political, economic, and existential shocks—among them, the decline of Western hegemony and the consequent realignment of power; the arguable failures of both capitalism and state socialism; and the post-Hiroshima acknowlegment of technology's amorality. A number of commentators have drawn a connection between this set of historic upheavals and the recent upsurge in neoconservative profamily rhetoric, but if Smith-Rosenberg is right, the retreat to the family will be apparent at the level of myth and image, as well as of regressive legislation.

The revival of mother earth imagery suggests that, at a time when an ecological and technological crisis of global proportions summons responsible adults to devise creative solutions, there has occurred instead a wholesale regression to infancy, when mother seemed omnipotent. As we have seen, this evokes masculine anxiety, hostility, and consoling fantasies of leaving (mother) earth behind for the brave new world of Biosphere II. Mother earth rhetoric also reveals feminine nostalgia for pre-Oedipal, precultural fusion with a benevolent, all-powerful (imaginary) mother. Although neither the masculine nor the feminine fantasy is likely to produce practical solutions to environmental problems, in the current political climate, mother earth mythology may have all too tangible and negative consequences for women.

If reviving mother earth imagery is going to bring out the child in us, then we would be well advised to find a nongendered, non-anthropomorphic way to represent nature. Can we not think of nature as "dynamic and alive," even if "nonhuman"?[17] Can we not care about the earth without personifying it?

Feminist theologian Carol P. Christ suggests that we can, although she herself finds the idea of "an intelligence" or "Great Spirit" of the universe personally meaningful. "There is a human tendency," she believes, "to name this unnameable with personal language, to believe that it cares as we care": "Sometimes I feel that I hear the universe weeping or laughing, speaking to me. But I do not know. What I do know is that whether the universe has a center of consciousness or not, the sight of a field of flowers in the color purple, the rainbow, must be enough to stop us from destroying all that is."[18]

Notes

1. Yaakov Jerome Garb concludes that the ubiquity of the whole earth image—which adorns the cover of [Michael Tobias's] *Voice of the Planet* (New York: Bantam, 1990), for instance, as well as Greenpeace posters and bumper stickers—tells us some very disquieting things about "the fundamental ways in which contemporary culture construes its relationship to nature." See his "Perspective or Escape? Ecofeminist Musings on Contemporary Earth Imagery," in [Irene] Diamond and [Gloria Feman] Orenstein, eds. *Reweaving the World: The Emergence of Ecofeminism* (San Francisco: Sierra Club, 1990), p. 265. Garb considers the advisability of replacing that image, as some ecofeminists urge, with the image of earth as a goddess, and he concludes that "we should check carefully whether we really want to view our relationship with the Earth through genderized lenses": "What

baggage will carry over from one domain to another (especially in a culture whose relation to both women and mothers is as misogynous as ours is)? What are the consequences—for both Earth and women—of reinforcing this age-old alignment between them?" See Garb, "Perspective or Escape?" p. 277. Surprisingly, given his concern, Garb does not consider certain posters and bumper stickers on which the injunction "Love Your Mother" is attached to the whole earth image.

2. Philip S. Lansky, "Health Today," *New Frontiers,* June 1990, p. 21.

3. Ibid.

4. An ad in *TV Guide* in August 1990 read as follows: "First there was Sports TV, then there was Music TV, now there is Eco TV: Network Earth. Network Earth. The first-ever video magazine on the environment. Upbeat and aware. Ecologically in tune. Your connection to the state of the earth. And your chance to become involved. Premiering Sunday, 11 P.M. on TBS. The environmental network of the '90s." See *TV Guide*, advertisement for TBS cable television network, August 11–17, 1990, p. 83.

5. Jeffner Allen says that "motherhood is dangerous to women. If woman, in patriarchy, is she who exists as the womb and wife of man, every woman is by definition a mother: she who produces for the sake of men. A mother is she whose body is used as a resource to reproduce men and the world of men, understood both as the biological children of patriarchy and as the ideas and material goods of patriarchal culture. Motherhood is dangerous to women because it continues the structure within which females must be women and mothers and, conversely, because it denies to females the creation of a subjectivity and world that is open and free." See Jeffner Allen, "Motherhood: The Annihilation of Women," in [Joyce] Trebilcot, ed., *Mothering: Essays in Feminist Theory*, p. 315.

6. Lin Nelson, "The Place of Women in Polluted Places," in Diamond and Orenstein, eds., *Reweaving the World*, pp. 173–188.

7. Ibid., p. 175.

8. Ibid., p. 186.

9. Reproductive anxiety surfaces even in the programmatic booklet put out by a California environmental group to commemorate Earth Day 1990. This publication, *50 Simple Things You Can Do to Save the Earth,* is dedicated "to the not-yet-born." See Earth Works Group, *50 Simple Things You Can Do to Save the Earth* (Berkeley, Calif.: Earth Works Press, 1989).

10. Margaret Atwood, *The Handmaid's Tale* (New York: Fawcett, 1985), p. 143.

11. Ibid., pp. 152–153.

12. Ibid., p. 176.

13. Karen J. Warren, "Feminism and Ecology: Making Connections," *Environmental Ethics* 9 (Spring 1987): 3–21.

14. Charlene Spretnak, "Ecofeminism: Our Roots and Flowering," in Diamond and Orenstein, eds., *Reweaving the World*, p. 5.

15. Quoted in Jalna Hanmer, "Reproductive Technology: The Future for Women?" in *Machina Ex Dea: Feminist Perspectives on Technology,* ed. Joan Rothschild (New York: Pergamon, 1983), p. 183 (ellipses in Hanmer).

16. Carroll Smith-Rosenberg, *Disorderly Conduct: Visions of Gender in Victorian America* (New York: Oxford University Press, 1985), p. 90.

17. Carolyn Merchant, "Ecofeminism and Feminist Theory," in Diamond and Orenstein, eds. *Reweaving the World*, p. 105.

18. Carol Christ, *Laughter of Aphrodite: Reflections on a Journey to the Goddess* (San Francisco: Harper, 1987).

Gaia and God:

An Ecofeminist Theology of Earth Healing*

❧ *Rosemary Radford Ruether* ❧

Gaia and God, ecofeminism, and earth healing: these vast concepts point to the wide-ranging agenda that I seek to explore in this book. Are Gaia, the living and sacred earth, and God, the monotheistic deity of the biblical traditions, on speaking terms with each other? Ecology and feminism, brought together in the unified perspective of ecofeminism, provide the critical perspective from which I seek to evaluate the heritage of Western Christian culture. The goal of this quest is earth healing, a healed relationship between men and women, between classes and nations, and between humans and the earth. Such healing is possible only through recognition and transformation of the way in which Western culture, enshrined in part in Christianity, has justified such domination. . . .

If dominating and destructive relations to the earth are interrelated with gender, class, and racial domination, then a healed relation to the earth cannot come about simply through technological "fixes." It demands a social reordering to bring about just and loving interrelationship between men and women, between races and nations, between groups presently stratified into social classes, manifest in great disparities of access to the means of life. In short, it demands that we must speak of eco-justice, and not simply of domination of the earth as though that happened unrelated to social domination.

Classical Western cultural traditions, which were codified between 500 B.C.E. and 800 C.E., and of which Christianity is a major expression, have justified and sacralized these relationships of domination. Thus we inherit not only a legacy of systems of domination, but also cultures that teach us to see such relations as the "natural order" and as the will of God.

In particular, the way these cultures have construed the idea of the male monotheistic God, and the relation of this God to the cosmos as its Creator, have reinforced symbolically the relations of domination of men over women, masters over slaves, and (male ruling-class) humans over animals and over the earth. Domination of women has provided a key link, both socially and symbolically, to the domination of earth, hence the tendency in patriarchal cultures to link women with earth, matter, and nature, while identifying males with sky, intellect, and transcendent spirit.

But these classical traditions did not only sacralize patriarchal hierarchy over women, workers, and the earth. They also struggled with what they perceived to be injustice and sin and sought to create just and loving relations between people in their relation to the earth and to the divine. Some of this effort to name evil and struggle against it reinforced relations of domination and created victim-blaming spiritualities and ethics. But there are also glimpses in this heritage of transformative, biophilic relationships.

These glimpses are a precious legacy that needs to be separated from the toxic waste of sacralized domination. We do not need to and should not totalize negative judgment against past biblical and Christian cultures. It would be surprising indeed if there were no positive insights that could be reclaimed from three thousand years of collective human struggle about the meaning of life and the way to live justly and well. Ecofeminist critics of classical culture are surely not the first humans to have positive sensibilities.

A healed relation to each other and to the earth then calls for a new consciousness, a new symbolic culture and spirituality. We need to transform our inner psyches and the way we symbolize the interrelations of men and women, humans and earth, humans and the divine, the divine and the earth. Ecological healing is a theological and psychic-spiritual process. Needless to say, spirituality or new consciousness will not transform deeply materialized relations of domination by themselves. We must be wary of new forms of privatized intrapsychic activity, divorced from social systems of power. Rather we must see the work of eco-justice and the work of spirituality as interrelated, the inner and outer aspects of one process of conversion and transformation.

I juxtapose the terms *Gaia* and *God* in the title of this book because all the issues that I wish to explore finally pose the question of the relationship between the living planet, earth, and the concept of God as it has been shaped in the Western religious traditions. *Gaia* is the word for the Greek Earth Goddess, and it is also a term adopted by a group of planetary biologists, such as James Lovelock and Lynn Margulis, to refer to their thesis that the entire planet is a living system, behaving as a unified organism.

The term *Gaia* has caught on among those seeking a new ecological spirituality as a religious vision. Gaia is seen as a personified being, an immanent divinity. Some see the Jewish and Christian male monotheistic God as a hostile concept that rationalizes alienation from and neglect of the earth. Gaia should replace God as our focus of worship. I agree with much of this critique, yet I believe that merely replacing a male transcendent deity with an immanent female one is an insufficient answer to the "god-problem."

We need a vision of a source of life that is "yet more" than what presently exists, continually bringing forth both new life and new visions of how life should be more just and more caring. The human capacity for ethical reason is not rootless in the universe, but expresses this deeper source of life "beyond" the biological. Consciousness and altruistic care are qualities that have some reflection in other animals, and indeed are often too poorly developed in our own species. To believe in divine being means to believe that those qualities in ourselves are rooted in and respond to the life power from which the universe itself arises. . . .

I have been influenced throughout my life by what creation theologian Matthew Fox calls "deep ecumenism." Growing up in a combined Protestant and

Roman Catholic family, with extended family that included Jews, Mexicans, Unitarians, Quakers, and Russian Orthodox, a multiplicity of perspectives living together has always seemed normal. Early in my education I entered into a dialogue with preclassical religions and cultures that lie behind the Hebrew world of the Ancient Near East, and also with the classical Greek world, acknowledging these "pagan" cultures as genuine theophanies or encounters with the divine. I decided that the three monotheistic faiths of Judaism, Christianity, and Islam were incorrect in rejecting polytheistic "nature" religions as simply false and evil.

This attraction to and positive evaluation of the ancient non-biblical religions of the Near Eastern and Greek worlds has also disposed me to a similar openness to the non-biblical religions and cultures of other areas of the world: the Mayan, Incan, and Mexican cultures that underlie colonized and Christianized Latin America. In other parts of the world I have visited, such as South Africa, the Philippines, Korea, and India, there also are the heritages of indigenous, non-Christian cultures. Those creating feminist, ecological, and liberation spiritualities today seek to synthesize these heritages: Western, Eastern, and indigenous. I have also been involved in dialogues between "classical" religions: between Christianity and Judaism, Islam, and Buddhism.

However, I have not sought to write this book as a "world religions" ecofeminist theology. I believe that a plurality of ecofeminist perspectives must arise from many cultural backgrounds and enter into dialogue with each other. No one person can do it all. My primary task is to speak from that broad configuration of culture that has shaped me and my context. This is a Western Christianity, which looks back to the ancient Near Eastern, Hebrew, and Greek worlds and stands in the post-Christian world of secularity. This is the context for which I feel called to take responsibility, without making any privileged truth or value claims for this culture.

I believe, with Jeremy Rifkin, that there is something like a new global consciousness arising from the union of these concerns and movements for a new society and spirituality. But we need to allow "every voice to be lifted," to gather together in mutual interaction and transformation the many cultural heritages of humanity, some that have been unjustly dominant and yet do not lack precious resources, and others that have been deeply silenced and rightly claim space to flower again.

I wish to play my part in that new consciousness and social vision in this book, but not to preempt a conversation that is still very far from fruition. Deep repentance needs to happen among the powerful of the earth, to whose community I mostly belong. We need to bring the mad bombers out of the sky and make them stand before the rubble, the charred bodies of the dead, the sufferings of the living, and call them to account. We who belong to this community, however, also have to take responsibility for these mad bombers as our brothers (and sometimes sisters!).

We also need to bring from our heritage the language to critique violence to other people and to the earth and to envision an alternative world of healing and wholeness. In this book I hope to make a contribution to this process of calling the Western, Christian, and American worlds to account for their profligate violence. I also hope to contribute something to generating hope for a saner world, as the ground of resistance to this violence.

The Covenantal Tradition: Hebraic Roots

The Bible has been made to appear to Western Christians to be much more antinature than it is by a particular line of biblical interpretation, shaped in nineteenth-century western European Protestantism, that thought in terms of a sharp dualism between history and nature. History was seen as the true realm of the human, ascendant over "nature," and, for that reason, the authentic sphere of the presence of the true "God" of the Bible. "Nature" was understood as subhuman, as the sphere of necessity, and the realm to be negated in order to ascend into humanness and freedom. Divinities revealed in and though nature were, by definition, false gods. . . .

Much of the ecological critique of the Bible has focused on the concept of "dominion" over nature granted to "man" by God. However, despite some hyperbolic claims to have given "man" power over "all" of nature, the biblical picture is one of keen awareness of the limits of human power. One such limit is human transience. In the words of Ecclesiasticus (17:1–2): "The Lord created man out of the earth and turned him back to it again. He gave to men few days, a limited time, but granted them authority over the things upon the earth."

Moreover, as biblical scholars have been quick to reply, human authority over nature remains always delegated authority. Nature is not private property to be done with as one wishes, but stewardship over an earth that remains ultimately God's. To abuse this trust in destructive relations to nature is to bring divine wrath upon one's head. God, not "men," is in control of nature. Neither nature's blessings nor nature's destructive power is handed over into autonomous human hands.

Humans can hope for blessings if they are faithful to God and just toward one another, and can expect devastating wreckage when they are not. But even "good works" are not assurance of blessing, for sometimes God makes the righteous suffer, while the wicked thrive. When disaster strikes the righteous man, nature itself teaches him that in this too lies the work of God:

> But ask the animals, and they will teach you; the birds of the air, and they will tell you; ask the plants of the earth, and they will teach you; and the fish of the sea will declare to you. Who among all these does not know that the hand of the Lord has done this? In his hand is the life of every living thing and the breath of every human being. (Job 12:7–10)

Hebrew thought knit the covenantal relation of God to Israel in a close relation to the gift of the "land." . . . But the other side of this same perspective is the understanding that Israel's own tenure in the land is contingent on its righteousness. The gift of the land is not a possession that can be held apart from relation to God. If Israel "pollutes" the land with iniquity, "the land will vomit you out for defiling it, as it vomited out the nation that was before you" (Leviticus 18:28). . . .

A covenantal vision of the relation of humans to other life forms acknowledges the special place of humans in this relationship as caretakers, caretakers who did not create and do not absolutely own the rest of life, but who are ultimately accountable for its welfare to the true source of life, God. This covenantal vision recognizes that humans and other life forms are part of one family, sisters and brothers in one community of interdependence. Although we have limited rights of use of other life forms, and also responsibilities of care and protection toward them, there is an ultimate thouness at the heart of every other living being, whether it be a great mountain lion or swaying bacteria, that declares its otherness from us.

The covenantal relation between humans and all other-life forms, as one family united by one source of life, forbids this otherness from being translated into destructive hostility. We have no right to wipe out any other life form because it is different from us. But rather, we encounter each other being simultaneously as "other" and as kin, as indeed we encounter each human person. The plant stretching toward the sun, the animal whose eyes warily encounter ours as it pauses in its tasks, reveal their own being in and for themselves.

This means that the other life forms finally cannot simply pass into our power as property, as "things" without their own life and being. Each has its own distinct relation to God as source of life, and not necessarily for our purposes, a vision eloquently revealed in the voice of God to Job from the whirlwind. Thus, even in order to make use of animals and plants for food and clothing and other needs, there must remain an ultimate *caveat* against reducing animals or plants, soils, or mountains to the status of "things" under our power.

Each life form has its own purpose, its own right to exist, its own independent relation to God and to other beings. Encompassing our relation to nature as usable things there must remain the larger sensibility, rooted in the encounter with nature as "thou," as fellow beings each with its own integrity. It is not idle sentiment to thank the animals and plants that provide the sources of our life before we make use of any material thing. The prayer of thanksgiving before every meal is required if we are to begin to be in right relation to our fellow beings in the covenant of creation.

Toward an Ecofeminist Theocosmology

Ecofeminist theology and spirituality has tended to assume that the "Goddess" we need for ecological well-being is the reverse of the God we have had in the Semitic monotheistic traditions; immanent rather than transcendent, female rather than male identified, relational and interactive rather than dominating, pluriform and multicentered rather than uniform and monocentered. But perhaps we need a more imaginative solution to these traditional oppositions than simply their reversal, something more like Nicholas of Cusa's paradoxical "coincidence of opposites," in which the "absolute maximum" and the "absolute minimum" are the same. . . .

How do we connect ourselves and the meaning of our lives to these worlds of the very small and the very big, standing in between the dancing void of energy that underlies the atomic structure of our bodies and the universe, whose galaxies, stretching over vast space and time, dwarf our histories? Even our bodies, despite the appearance of continuity over time, are continually dying and being reborn in every second. Over a period of seven years, every molecule of our body has been replaced.

In this universe of the very small and the very big, can the human only appear lost, crying out with Pascal, "The eternal silence of those infinite spaces terrifies me!"? Or is it a universe in which it makes sense to speak of values, of life and death, good and evil, as meaningful distinctions within which we can hope for a "better world"? Is it a universe with which we can commune, as heart to heart, thought to thought, as I and Thou?

As humans stand peering down through their instruments into the subatomic realm and outward into the galaxies, it cannot but be evident that, for us, the human remains the "mean" or mediator between the worlds. This is so because what we perceive can only be known and evaluated from the context of our own standpoints. But also because we are faced with the recognition that humans alone, amid all the earth creatures and on all the planets of these vast galaxies, are capable of reflective consciousness. We are, in that sense, the "mind" of the universe, the place where the universe becomes conscious of itself.

Reflective consciousness is both our privilege and our danger. At least for the last several thousand years of cultural history, male ruling-class humans have used this privilege of mind to set themselves apart from nature and over dominated women and men. Thereby they denied the web of relationships that bind us all together, and within which these males themselves are an utterly dependent part. The urgent task of ecological culture is to convert human consciousness to the earth, so that we can use our minds to understand the web of life and to live in that web of life as sustainers, rather than destroyers, of it.

But also, as Teilhardian and Process thought have argued, reflective consciousness, while it distinguishes the human from animals, plants, cellular bacteria and nonbiotic aggregates of molecules, it does so only relatively, not absolutely. The capacity to be conscious is itself the experience of the interiority of our organism, made possible by the highly organized living cells of our brains and nervous systems that constitute the material "base" of our experience of awareness.

Consciousness is one type of highly intense experience of life, but there are other forms present in other species, sometimes with capacities that humans lack, as in fish that can hear ranges of sound or animals that can see ranges of light not possible to our ears and eyes. Nor can we simply draw a line between us, together with large-brained mammals, and other beings, as a distinction of "living persons" and "dead bodies." For plants too are living organic beings that respond to heat, light, water, and sound as organisms, and even chemical aggregates are dancing centers of energy.

Human consciousness, then, should not be what utterly separates us from the rest of "nature." Rather, consciousness is where this dance of energy organizes itself in increasingly unified ways, until it reflects back on itself in self-awareness. Consciousness is and must be where we recognize our kinship with all other beings. The dancing void from which the tiniest energy events of atomic structures flicker in and out of existence and self-aware thought are kin along a continuum of organized life-energy.

Our capacity for consciousness, which allows us to roam through space and time, remembering past ages, exploring the inner workings of all other existing beings on earth or on distant planets, also makes us aware of the ephemeral nature of our "self." Our capacity for consciousness is sustained by a complex but fragile organism. Cut that organism at its vital centers, in the brain or in the heart, and the light of consciousness goes out, and with it our "self."

It is this juxtaposition of the capacity of consciousness to roam through space and time, and its utter transience in its dependence on our mortal organisms, that has generated much of the energy of what has been called "religion" in the past. Much of this religious quest has sought to resolve this contradiction by denying it, imagining that consciousness was not really dependent on the mortal organism. The mental self could survive, and even be "purified" and strengthened, by the demise of the body. This concept of the "immortal self," survivable apart from our particular transient organism, must be recognized, not only as untenable, but as the source of much destructive behavior toward the earth and other humans.

An ecological spirituality needs to be built on three premises: the transience of selves, the living interdependency of all things, and the value of the personal in communion. Many spiritual traditions have emphasized the need to "let go of the ego," but in ways that diminished the value of the person, undercutting particularly those, like women, who scarcely have been allowed individuated personhood at all. We need to "let go of the ego" in a different sense. We are called to affirm the integrity of our personal center of being, in mutuality with the personal centers of all other beings across species and, at the same time, accept the transience of these personal selves.

As we accept both the value and the transience of the self, we can also be awakened to a new sense of kinship with all other organisms. Like humans, the animals and the plants are living centers of organic life who exist for a season. Then each of our roots shrivels, the organic structures that sustain our life fail, and we die. The cutting of the life center also means that our bodies disintegrate into organic matter, to enter the cycle of decomposition and recomposition as other entities.

The material substances of our bodies live on in plants and animals, just as our own bodies are composed from minute to minute of substances that once were parts of other animals and plants, stretching back through time to prehistoric ferns and reptiles, to ancient biota that floated in the primal seas of earth. Our kinship with all earth creatures is global, linking us to the whole living Gaia today. It also spans the ages, linking our material substance with all the beings that have gone before us on earth and even to the dust of exploding stars. We need new psalms and meditations to make this kinship vivid in our communal and personal devotions.

But, even as we take into our spirituality and ethical practice the transience of selves, relinquishing the illusion of permanence, and accepting the dissolution of our physical substance into primal energy, to become matter for new organisms, we also come to value again the personal center of each being. My eye catches the eye of a bird as it turns its head toward me on the side of the tree, and then continues its tasks. Brendan spies me coming up the path, and with flashing red fur is at the door, leaping in circles with unfeigned delight. My body, stretching in the sun, notices a tiny flower pushing up through the soil to greet the same sun. And we know our kinship as I and Thou, saluting one another as fellow persons.

Compassion for all living things fills our spirits, breaking down the illusion of otherness. At this moment we can encounter the matrix of energy of the universe that sustains the dissolution and recomposition of matter as also a heart that knows us even as we are known. Is there also a consciousness that remembers and envisions and reconciles all things, as the Process theologians believe? Surely, if we are kin to all things and offspring of the universe, then what has flowered in us as consciousness must also be reflected in that universe as well, in the ongoing creative Matrix of the whole.

As we gaze into the void of our future extinguished self and dissolving substance, we encounter there the wellspring of life and creativity from which all things have sprung and into which they return, only to well up again in new forms. But we also know this as the great Thou, the personal center of the universal process, with which all the small centers of personal being dialogue in the conversation that continually creates and recreates the world. The small selves and the Great Self are finally one, for as She bodies forth in us, all the beings respond in the bodying forth of their diverse creative work that makes the world.

The dialogue can become truncated. We can seek to grasp our ego centers of being in negation of others, proliferating our existence by diminishing that of others, and finally poisoning the wellspring of the life process itself. Or we can dance gracefully with our fellow beings, spinning out our creative work in such a way as to affirm theirs and they ours as well.

Then, like bread tossed on the water, we can be confident that our creative work will be nourishing to the community of life, even as we relinquish our small self back into the great Self. Our final gesture, as we surrender ourself into the Matrix of life, then can become a prayer of ultimate trust: "Mother, into your hands I commend my spirit. Use me as you will in your infinite creativity." . . .

We need a foundation for ethical theory that is not based on a dualistic negation of the "other," whether woman or animal or body, pagans, gentiles, or barbarians (or the countercultural reversals of these projections) as the bearers of our "shadow." This does not mean that there is no such thing as evil, or that ethical distinctions as such should be repudiated for an acceptance of all that is as good or, at least, necessary. The difference between starving a child or torturing a prisoner, and nurturing their lives, is real, and reflect decisions made by actual people.

But the reality of evil does not lie is some "thing" out there. It cannot be escaped, and indeed is exacerbated by efforts to avoid it by cutting ourselves off from that "thing." Rather, evil lies in "wrong relationship." All beings live in community, both with members of their own species and with others for which they depend for food, breath, materials for construction, and affective feedback. Yet there is a tendency in the life drive itself in each species to maximize its own existence and hence to proliferate in a cancerous way that destroys its own biotic support.

This is not just a human tendency. As Lynn Margulis has pointed out, even ancient bacteria tended toward this proliferating growth, in which the consuming of others finally threatens to destroy both the environment and the species. The life force itself is not unequivocally good, but becomes "evil" when it is maximized at the expense of others. In this sense "good" lies in limits, a balancing of our own drive for life with the life drives of all the others in which we are in community, so that the whole remains in life-sustaining harmony. The wisdom of nature lies in the development of built-in limits through a diversity of beings in interrelation, so that none outruns its own "niche."

Humans, particularly since the development of agriculture, have been able to develop the food base to escape the built-in limits of other species, and even of their own species in the hunter-gatherer mode. They have been able to grow their own food base and thus maximize their own lives, using land, plants, and animals as objects of control and manipulation. In the process some humans (dominant males) also have learned to maximize their own lives, both for leisure and consumption, over against other humans. The human community itself was fissured into controlling "subjects" and exploited "objects."

It is more misleading than helpful to speak about this development of systems of domination as a "fall." It might be called a "loss of innocence" and the beginning of deceit. But we need to be clear that all was not idyllic before, nor did there enter into history at that time a totally new capacity for evil not present before. Rather, a possibility in nature, the maximizing of some against others, was appropriated in a new way, organized in such a way that self-correcting limits could be avoided by those who profited. The price of exploitation was borne by the exploited.

Only as the system of exploitation reaches its maximal stage does it begin to undermine the quality of life of those at the "top," and thus force them to recognize that the whole house of cards is about to topple. Their first instinct is to stave off this demise by accelerating the exploitation of those they dominate, while seeking to maintain their own comfortable life-style with the dwindling resources of the whole. The rich try to stay rich while the poor get poorer, and the destruction of the environment increases.

Eventually the whole system collapses. This has happened before, as in the disappearance of "lost civilizations," and in a more extensive way, in the "fall" of Rome. The difference today is that the system of exploitation is global, and the possibility of destruction correspondingly global. There are not the same spaces to retreat from the collapse. Thus we face a cancerous proliferation of our species that could not only bring it to extinction, but pull much of the planetary life system down with it.

However, civilizations have not only created domination and cultures of deceit that justified domination. They have also created critical cultures designed to unmask deceit and spiritualities that awakened compassion for others, thus rebuilding culturally the balances of self-limitation and respect for the lives of others that make for good community. We inherit in our Christian tradition (as do others in their traditions) both cultures of domination and deceit and cultures of critique and compassion. We need to build on and develop the second culture to unmask and check the power of the first culture.

Envisioning a Good Society

Let us begin by envisioning something of the goal that we seek, not in the sense of a static "once-for-all" future perfection, but in the sense of healthy societies that can be sustained from season to season, which are no longer building up toxicities of destruction. This vision must start with a principle of equity: equity between men and women; between human groups living within regions; equity across human communities globally; equity between the human species and all other members to the biotic community of which we are a part; and finally equity between generations of living things, between the needs of those alive now and those who are to come.

Rebuilding human society for a sustainable earth will require far more than a plethora of technological "fixes" within the present paradigm of relations of domination. It will demand a fundamental restructuring of all these relations from systems of domination/exploitation to ones of biophilic mutuality. New technologies may well have their place, although there may also be a need to rediscover old techniques of agriculture, architecture, artisanry, and community-building as well. But technique cannot be divorced from its social and psychic contexts. A new technique or a recovery of an old one will not "take" without transformed political relations and cultural consciousness.

A healed earth is one in which all the patterns of destruction . . . have been deeply transformed, the patterns that are resulting in proliferating population, deepening poverty, famine, soil erosion, deforestation, the extinction of species, air and water pollution, energy crises, and militarism. Just as the patterns that are producing this vast reign of death are interrelated, so a new life-sustaining community of humans as part of the biosphere of Gaia are interrelated. This does not mean that there are not many incremental steps toward this new pattern, but these incremental steps have to be guided by a holistic vision. . . .

Although greatly reducing the environmental impact of human production, transportation, consumption, and waste is critical for a sustainable society, and must demand the greatest changes from the most affluent societies, a significant curbing and eventual reduction of human population itself is also necessary. If human population is allowed to double once again in forty years or less, and hits 8 billion to 10 billion in the first third of the twenty-first century, all the [other] measures . . . will go for naught. Humanity has no real alternative to population control. The question is, do we want population control to happen voluntarily, before conception, or violently by war, famine, and disease?

The promotion of effective birth control on a widespread basis sufficient to halt and reduce the world population explosion is only secondarily a matter of developing and distributing technologies, although this is not unimportant. It is, above all, a matter of how women and their bodies are socially and culturally appropriated. Many cultural, social, and economic forces impede the empowerment of women as moral agents of their own reproductive powers: poverty, demographic war, and the whole complex of attitudes that spring from patriarchy. . . .

The empowerment of women as moral agents of their own sexuality and reproduction is thus an integral part of any authentic population policy. The female child needs to be valued equally with the male. This is only possible if the adult female is also seen as an autonomous person who will be an active cultural and economic agent in her own right, and not just an adjunct to a male-centered society. Only when women can no longer be beaten by men, raped by men, and traded between men as commodities, can they cease to be treated or to see themselves as passive bodies to be acted upon by men.

Women need a sense of their own integrity and to have that integrity affirmed by males. They need to have a full range of life opportunities for their many creative roles, of which reproduction is only one. They need to have the knowledge and technology of birth control and the right to enforce these in sexual relations with men. They need to have a sense that their daughters, as much as their sons, will have these many options and will be given education for them. Finally they need to see themselves as responsible agents for a just and sustainable society in their communities. . . .

It is the male rather than the female life-style that needs, however, the deeper transformation. Males need to overcome the illusion of autonomous individualism, with its extension into egocentric power over others, starting with the women with whom they relate. Men need to integrate themselves into life-sustaining relations with women as lovers, parents, and coworkers. They need to do regularly what they have hardly ever done, even in preagricultural societies: feed, clothe, wash, and hug children from infancy, cook food, and clean up wastes.

Only when men are fully integrated into the culture of daily sustenance of life can men and women together begin to reshape the larger systems of economic, social, and political life. They can begin to envision new cultural consciousness and organizational structures that would connect these larger systems to their roots in the earth and to sustaining the earth from day to day and from generation to generation. . . .

The time is short for major changes, if we are to save much of the biotic system of the earth that is in danger. The Worldwatch Institute estimates that we have about forty years for major global shifts to be carried out voluntarily (until 2030). After that time major disasters of famine and collapse of life systems, under the pressures of exploitative use, will take place, and there could well be very dangerous militarist and totalitarian responses from threatened elites, as indeed is already happening.

In speaking about the urgency of the situation before audiences, I am often asked if I am "optimistic" about the possibilities for change. The assumption behind this question seems to be that we have two ideational stances toward these crises: optimism or pessimism. But I am inclined to think that both these stances get us off the hook. If we are "optimistic," it suggests that change is inevitable and will happen in the "natural" course of things, and so we need not make much effort ourselves. Someone else will take care of it. If we are "pessimistic," change is impossible, and therefore it is useless to try. In either case we have the luxury, as critical but comfortable elites in the United States, to question the present system without being responsible for it.

What we need is neither optimism nor pessimism, in these terms, but committed love. This means that we remain committed to a vision and to concrete communities of life no matter what the "trends" may be. Whether we are immediately "winning" or "losing" cannot shake our rooted understandings of what biophilic life is and should be, although we need to adapt our strategies to the changing fortunes of the struggle. We also remain clear that life is not made whole "once and for all," in some static millennium of the future. It is made whole again and again, in the renewed day born from night and in the new spring that rises from each winter.

Being rooted in love for our real communities of life and for our common mother, Gaia, can teach us patient passion, a passion that is not burnt out in a season, but can be renewed season after season. Our revolution is not just for us, but for our children, for the generations of living beings to come. What we can do is to plant a seed, nurture a seed-bearing plant here and there, and hope for a harvest that goes beyond the limits of our powers and the span of our lives.

Discussion Questions

1. In what types of situations did Nelle Morton experience the presence of the Goddess, which she describes in "The Goddess as Metaphoric Image"? What aspect of herself does the Goddess help Morton to make peace with? How do you interpret the Goddess that Morton describes; what kind of entity is she? Do you see any connection between this piece and the following one, Cisneros's "Guadalupe the Sex Goddess"?

2. According to Sandra Cisneros, why did she as a young woman reject the figure of the Virgin of Guadalupe? What hidden aspects of Guadalupe did her research lead her to? In her essay, Cisneros uses quite explicitly sexual imagery. Why do you think she chooses to speak in this way? Does it seem to you that there are similarities between the Goddess described by Nelle Morton in the previous selection and the Virgin of Guadalupe as Cisneros reimagines her? The Virgin of Guadalupe has been a powerful religious symbol in Latin America and in U.S. Hispanic communities for centuries. Does it seem to you that Cisneros is leaving behind her Latino Catholic heritage by reenvisioning the Guadalupe image in this way?

3. How would you explain the point that Irene Monroe makes (in the interview by Comstock) about the selective use of Biblical texts within Black churches that denounce homosexuality? What is the connection between Monroe's work in Black churches and her vision of a multicultural democracy, as she describes it? Given the rejection she has suffered, what is Monroe's attitude toward participating in the Black church? What do you understand Monroe to mean by a "prophetic voice" and why does she say that the queer movement is prophetic?

4. As with other essays in this collection, Judith Plaskow's essay pushes against the boundaries of the tradition she represents—in Plaskow's case, Judaism—with respect to its traditionally held views of sexuality and sexual ethics. What is the role of sexuality in the ethical vision that Plaskow elaborates here?

5. Advocates of ecofeminism have often claimed and stressed a close relationship between women and nature as a way of asserting women's positive and "special" attributes. Why does Ellen Cronan Rose warn feminists against this line of argument? What danger does she see in the "mother earth" metaphor, or in environmental

advocacy that relies on imaging the earth as "mother"? Does her argument make sense to you in view of the prevailing cultural images of mothers and motherhood with which you are familiar?

6. Explain how, in Rosemary Ruether's analysis, the Western religious tradition is connected to the environmental crises of the era in which we live. Is Ruether's assertion of this connection convincing to you? Where does Ruether see women, in the context of this connection? Where does responsibility for this state of affairs lie? In view of this analysis, how does Ruether seem to suggest people should relate to their religious traditions? Does this analysis suggest that religious people should adopt a particular stance with respect to environmental issues? What is the stance that Ruether, in this piece, appears to advocate?

Suggested Readings

Adams, Carol J., ed. *Ecofeminism and the Sacred.* New York: Continuum, 1993.

Christ, Carol P. "Rethinking Theology and Nature." In *Weaving the Visions: New Patterns in Feminist Spirituality*, Judith Plaskow and Carol P. Christ, eds. San Francisco: Harper & Row, 1989.

Davies, Susan E. and Eleanor H. Haney, eds. *Redefining Sexual Ethics.* Cleveland, OH: Pilgrim, 1991.

Deane-Drummond, Celia. "Creation." In *The Cambridge Companion to Feminist Theology*, Susan Frank Parsons, ed., Cambridge, UK: Cambridge University Press, 2002, 190–205.

Fletcher, Karen Baker. *Sisters of Dust, Sisters of Spirit: Womanist Wordings on God and Creation.* Minneapolis, MN: Fortress, 1998.

Fuss, D. *Essentially Speaking: Feminism, Nature and Difference.* New York: Routledge, 1989.

Gebara, Ivone. *Longing for Running Water: Ecofeminism and Liberation.* Translated by David Molineaux. Minneapolis, MN: Fortress, 1999.

Griffin, Susan. *Women and Nature: The Roaring Inside Her.* New York: Harper & Row, 1978.

Heyward, Carter. *Touching Our Strength: The Erotic as Power and the Love of God.* San Francisco: HarperSanFrancisco, 1989.

McFague, Sallie. *Models of God: Theology for an Ecological, Nuclear Age.* Philadelphia: Fortress, 1987.

Merchant, Carolyn. *The Death of Nature: Women, Ecology and the Scientific Revolution.* New York: HarperCollins, 1980.

———. *Earthcare: Women and the Environment.* New York: Routledge, 1996.

Ortner, Sherry. "Is Female to Male as Nature Is to Culture?" In *Woman, Culture, and Society*, Michelle Zimbalist Rosaldo and Louise Lamphere, eds., Stanford, CA: Stanford University Press, 1974, 67–88.

Plant, Judith, ed. *Healing the Wounds: The Promise of Ecofeminism.* Philadelphia, PA: New Society, 1989.

Ranke-Heinemann, Uta. *Eunuchs for the Kingdom of Heaven: Women, Sexuality and the Catholic Church.* New York: Doubleday, 1990.

Ruether, Rosemary Radford. *Women Healing Earth: Third World Women on Ecology, Feminism, and Religion.* Maryknoll, NY: Orbis, 1996.

———. "Ecofeminism: Symbolic and Social Connections of the Oppression of Women and the Domination of Nature." In *This Sacred Earth: Religion, Nature, Environment*, R. S. Gottlieb, ed., New York: Routledge, 1996, 322–333.

Spretnak, Charlene. "Toward an Eco-Feminist Spirituality." In *Healing the Wounds: The Promise of Ecofeminism,* J. Plant, ed., Philadephia, PA: New Society, 1989, 127–132.

Warren, Karen, *Ecological Feminism.* Bloomington: Indiana University Press, 1991.

———. *Ecological Feminist Philosophies.* Bloomington: Indiana University Press, 1996.

Warren, Karen and Barbara Wells-Howe, eds. *Ecological Feminism.* New York: Routledge, 1994.

Warren, Karen and Nisvan Erkal, eds. *Ecofeminism: Women, Culture, Nature.* Bloomington: Indiana University Press, 1997.

Web Sites

ChristianLesbians.com, http://www.christianlesbians.com/

Conference for Catholic Lesbians, Inc., http://www.catholiclesbians.org/

Ecofeminism List, http://groups.yahoo.com/group/EcoFeminism/

Ecofeminism.net, http://www.ecofeminism.net/

Ecofeminism Web Ring, http://www.ecofem.org/

Eve Online, Ecofeminist Visions Emerging, http://eve.enviroweb.org/

Green Information, http://www.greeninformation.com

Lesbian.com, "Jewish Lesbians." http://www.lesbian.com/jewish/jewish_intro.html

Orenstein, Gloria. "Ecofeminism." Web site created by students in Orenstein's Ecofeminism class. http://www-rcf.usc.edu/~orenstei/ecofem/

SAFRA Project, http://www.safraproject.org

Scovill, Nelia Beth. "The Liberation of Women in Religious Sources." *The Religious Consultation on Population, Reproductive Health & Ethics.* http://www.religiousconsultation.org/liberation.htm

The Witness, http://thewitness.org

Under Shekhina's Wings, Cross-Cultural Women's Spirituality, http://www.geocities.com/Athens/1501/

WAF (Women Against Fundamentalisms), http://waf.gnapc.org

Wisdom University, http://www.creationspirituality.org/

INDEX